*The Fall
of the
Packard
Motor Car
Company*

The Fall
of the

Motor Car
Company

JAMES A. WARD

Stanford University Press
Stanford, California

Stanford University Press
Stanford, California
© 1995 by the Board of Trustees of the
Leland Stanford Junior University

Printed in the United States of America
CIP data are at the end of the book

For H. L. Ingle, Friend

Acknowledgments

Seven years is a long time to work on a project, and over that span I incurred numerous debts to many people who encouraged this book. It would be much easier to issue a blanket thanks and avoid inadvertently omitting a deserving few, but I would rather live dangerously and try to recognize them all. Close to home, I would like to thank the University of Tennessee at Chattanooga's Faculty Research Committee for two research grants that funded a goodly portion of three trips to South Bend and a westward swing to Independence, Missouri, and Abilene, Kansas. Paul Gaston, former Dean of Arts & Sciences at UTC, was kind enough to award me a sabbatical in 1992 that enabled me to write the last half of the manuscript. Neal Coulter, UTC reference librarian, a man who can find books we do not have, tracked down endless tomes, articles, and manuscript collections, and even hauled materials from other libraries back for my use. He grumbled all the time and was not the least bit interested in Packard, but I think it would not be too much to say that, without him, this volume would still be unfinished.

Librarians and archivists rarely receive the gratitude they deserve. The whole staff at the Studebaker National Museum in South Bend, which houses the largest collection of Packard records, was great. Director Tom Brubaker went far beyond the usual courtesies afforded a visiting scholar; he allowed me to microfilm Packard's board minutes, photocopy thousands of documents, and browse through his entire collection. During the hot summer weeks I worked in South Bend he had files brought to his air-conditioned museum headquarters, where it was much more comfortable to work. He even took me to lunch at Notre

Dame's faculty club. His secretary, Edna Kappler, afforded me every convenience and, despite my constant interruptions of her normal work, always retained her sense of humor. My first summer there, Jeanne Denham, the archivist, introduced me to the 70 tons of Packard materials. The following year, Bill Brockman, operations manager for the museum, located boxes of correspondence and brought them over to the museum for me. Tom Downey, curator of collections, has been a great help in running down information and providing advice.

Just north of South Bend, Ed Mark, owner and president of Packard Industries, a firm that owns the Packard name and manufactures modular office furniture, gave me a tour of his extensive Packard automobile collection, now a museum, and let me use his complete runs of the *Packard Cormorant* and *Packards International Magazine*. Moreover, many of his photographs grace this volume.

James Pearsall, who lives in Zarephath, New Jersey, a town left out of every atlas of my acquaintance, is a Packard expert and is generous with his time and expertise. Jim is also noted for his candor and I thank him for his suggestions and all the photographs he contributed for this volume; his help has made this a much better book.

Richard Langworth, editor of the *Packard Cormorant*, has also been most helpful in the preparation of this volume. Not only does he publish a first-rate automotive magazine, from which I have learned a great deal, but he allowed me to copy several photographs from it for use here.

I have never been a fan of the idea that presidential libraries should be located in out-of-the-way towns, but the staffs at Truman's and Eisenhower's libraries could not have been more helpful. I especially wish to express my gratitude to Phillip Lagerquist, Benedict Zobrist, and Dennis Bilger at the Truman Library for making my stay there so pleasant. Likewise, Martin Teasley and David Haight at the Eisenhower Library pointed out documents that I might have otherwise overlooked and provided me with comfortable and efficient working space.

Several former Packard hands added much to this book. Lyman Slack, the last surviving Packard director, responded to my numerous queries with long, thoughtful epistles that filled numerous gaps in my knowledge. Richard H. Stout, who has published his own automobile history, *Make 'Em Shout Hooray!* (New York, 1988), gave me an inside view, from the middle-management perspective, of Packard's last days. Michael Kollins, a volunteer in the Detroit Public Library's Automotive History Collection, granted me an interview in which he spoke his mind openly about his long tenure at Packard and what he thought had gone haywire at the East Grand headquarters. Margery Gilman, Max Gilman's daughter-in-law, gave me an intimate glimpse into Gilman's personality and lifestyle I could not have found elsewhere. Sinclair Weeks, Jr., whom I met at breakfast in Abilene and whose father was active in attempts to bail out Studebaker-Packard in 1956, provided me with leads on the whereabouts of his father's papers.

I followed his suggestions and others and thereby incurred debts to archivists of numerous collections. I wish to thank Philip Cronenwett, Curator of Manuscripts, Dartmouth College Library, for his help; John Gibson and Ron Grantz at the Detroit Public Library, for tracking down Packard materials; and Kermit Pike, Director of the Library, Western Reserve Historical Society, who gathered George M. Humphrey's papers for me, including those that had just emerged from a time lock.

Several historians generously offered the results of their own research. Robert Ebert, Buckhorn Professor of Economics at Baldwin-Wallace College in Berea, Ohio, sent me a copy of his unpublished manuscript, "Ask the Man Who Owns One: The Story of Packard," a pathbreaking study of the company. He also included his notes from his interview with James J. Nance in 1961. Menno Duerksen, a well-known automotive writer and historian, generously mailed me copies of his Owen Goodrich material. A career Packard employee, Goodrich started several histories of Packard, and his fragments were replete with keen observations and insights. Loren Pennington, recently retired from Emporia State University, gave me a copy of his unpublished article, "Prelude to Chrysler: The Eisenhower Administration Bails Out Studebaker-Packard," and talked to me at length in Emporia about his progress on his own history of Studebaker. And lastly, H. L. Ingle, my valued colleague, who knows nothing about Packard and cares less, and who had his head planted firmly in the seventeenth century writing his biography of George Fox, the Quaker, while I worked on Packard, nevertheless did at innumerable Chattanooga Lookouts baseball games listen to my interminable rantings about Packard's troubles, and he merits my public thanks and deserves his own page in this volume.

This book would have never made it to the publisher without the unflagging help of the UTC history department's secretaries, Elke Lawson and Michaele Kennedy, who know how to make computers work. As the last breathing historian on this planet who had not yet entered the world of bytes and floppy disks, I depended entirely upon them to keep track of three or four revisions on little plastic squares that they magically manipulated to reveal words.

After they forced me to learn to use the machine, however, daughter Anne Elizabeth, in training to become a historian, taught me many useful tricks. She also wanted me to mention that she too endured the research trips to South Bend and my endless discourses on Packard. And for all that, I thank her.

This book would have never made it out of typescript without the friendly help of Barbara Phillips, the copy editor, who went through my bushy manuscript with an unyielding eye for stupidities large and small. Lynn Stewart, the associate editor, proved an editorial trail boss with a sense of humor who jostled the book-building process along on time. Eleanor Mennick took a cue from Packard and designed a volume in harmony with Packard's classic styling traditions. Finally, Norris Pope, Director of Stanford University Press, demonstrated the proper appreciation for things Packard and for this book.

And to my wife, Roberta Shannon Ward, I extend my profound thanks for enduring all the research trips, humoring me in my enthusiasm for everything Packard, and reading every word of the manuscript. More importantly, she honestly told me when it was poorly written, made no sense, was grammatically incorrect, or had just wandered into the wrong lane. She deserves a medal for putting up with Packard and the perpetual mess in my office. I cannot give her one, but I can publicly thank her for making me happy.

J. A. W.
December 12, 1994

Contents

Introduction: Why Packard?   1

1   Ascent of the Marque   9

2   Episcopalian Cars for Methodists   25

3   The Dogs of War   43

4   A Troubled Packard   53

5   The Ferry Years   67

6   "Hail to the Chief"   83

7   "God Save the King–and Packard!"   107

8   "Rapidly Approaching Bankruptcy"   131

9   "The Shotgun Wedding"   141

10   Slow Off the Line   161

11   "Life or Death for Packard in 1955"   183

12   The "Sitting Duck"   197

13   Seeking a "Safe Harbor"   211

14   "Love Without Marriage"   229

15   "Ask the Man Who Owned One"   249

Epilogue: The Autopsy   259

Notes   271

Bibliography   297

Index   303

*The Fall
of the
Packard
Motor Car
Company*

Introduction

Why
Packard?

One has to ask why another book on Packard, when eight have appeared in the past thirty years and when at least one of these, Beverly Rae Kimes's *Packard*, is a first-rate piece of work. The answer is that I think I have something to say that places a different light on Packard's decline and fall. Moreover, I approach this whole subject as a historian who just happens to be an automobile aficionado rather than as a car enthusiast who wants to try his hand at history. I view the automobile industry in a broader perspective and attempt to portray the company's affairs against larger social, economic, and political backgrounds.

My personal interest in Packard was piqued when I learned that the company was founded by James Ward Packard. Although he was not a relative of mine, that mote stayed with me. At first I thought I might write a biography of him, but I soon became more fascinated by his car company. After reading the Packard histories, I realized that I had little to add to the company's early history and nothing of substance about the cars themselves, but many questions remained about the company's death. And with a long-standing scholarly interest in the railroad business, I was curious about the interplay of institutions and personalities at Packard. At a more basic level, I relished the opportunity to work with typewritten corporate records. Twenty years of deciphering crabbed hands in faded letterbook impressions left by harried nineteenth-century railway entrepreneurs have taken their toll.

Lest all of the above presage a dull, typically pedantic corporate history, I hasten to add that many more interesting aspects of Packard's long history and rapid demise beguiled me. The incongruity of an avowedly aristocratic automobile's success in a nation that considers itself a bastion of middlebrow democratic tastes was intriguing. So were the elements of a Horatio Alger story in the Packard tale. Alger promised that attention to morality and hard work, along with a dollop of luck, would bring success to any underdog. And Packard was a decided underdog in the postwar automobile world—all the so-called Independents were. But all the company's employees, from the 40- and 50-year veterans of the assembly line to executives in their stodgy East Grand Boulevard offices, bent every effort to compete with the Big Three. Many writers, in the best Alger tradition, have searched for the fatal corporate flaw that doomed the revered manufacturer. They have blamed faulty organization, lazy workers, greedy politicians, incompetent executives, and the futility of competing with the giants in the business. Some Packard observers obviously hail from the school that believes that the good guys always win, a truism Gary Cooper, Tom Mix, Hopalong Cassidy, and the Lone Ranger instilled in the public's mind, and look for corporate villains in this morality play. Heroes and villains make compelling history, and Packard was favored with a colorful cast of characters in its declining years.

Aristotle is the oft-quoted master of the reverse of Alger's themes. Although I have never seen his name linked with Packard's, his notion of the tragic hero, the man who falls from great heights for reasons outside his own control, applied to Packard; it says legions about personal and corporate self-delusions. The sense of Packard's tragedy was in many respects an illusion, but that made it no less powerful. Had the company collapsed in 1934 when it was producing its classic, beautifully hand-crafted Twin Sixes, its death would have been without doubt tragic, but more easily understood. The irony, however, was that Packard disappeared in the greatest car-buying spree America had ever seen. Everybody was buying new cars in 1955 and 1956, but not many were driving Packards home from the showrooms. Two decades earlier, when the other two famous P's, Peerless and Pierce Arrow, went out of business along with such famous names as Locomobile, Hupmobile, Franklin, Auburn, Cord, Duesenberg, and Marmon in the depths of a faltering national economy, Packard successfully adapted, brought out new, cheaper cars, changed its manufacturing techniques, pitched its advertising to a different clientele, shed its aristocratic identity, and prospered. The company's strength and resiliency surprised even its own architects. Yet when the firm tried to repeat that strategy, only in reverse (that is, by going up in price and prestige), in the 1950's, it died. Out of the rubble of its abandoned Detroit plants emerged a dedicated corps of fans devoted to keeping Packard's memory alive and its cars on the road. Their loyalty to the marque has taken on many of the aspects of a lost cause, in part because Packard's death throes were shielded from the public's gaze. The company died in private, well-upholstered, paneled meeting rooms in New York, Washington, D.C., Detroit, and South Bend.

Packard was a company where people mattered. The firm always had a distinct personality, an image fashioned by the men who guided its destinies. Over the automaker's 59-year life span, seven men ruled the corporate fiefdom on East Grand in a highly benevolent and paternalistic manner. With a compliant board of directors, Packard's presidents were free to liberally dispense rewards and punishments. They were regarded by their employees with awe. Owen Goodrich, who spent most of his adult life at Packard, never tired of retelling a story of how president Alvan Macauley once stopped and held a door for him. As minor as that incident might seem, Goodrich viewed it as a sign of the humbleness of the mighty.

On a grander scale, Packard's paternalistic leadership focused decision-making responsibilities. Unlike General Motors after Alfred Sloan's reorganization created layers of committees that laboriously shaped policies and cars, and unlike Ford after Henry became distracted by age and other interests in the 1930's and left his company without any recognizable managerial structure (until Henry Ford II and his whiz kids reformed the family firm after World War II), Packard had crisp, well-defined lines of authority—all of which led directly to the president's suite. Such paternalism delights historians who love to deal with personalities, but it also makes thematic analysis more difficult. Personalized companies are more prone to policy zigs formulated at their leaders' whims. The ultimate result, however, is exciting history.

Perhaps Packard's most whimsical change of corporate policy, at least in the public's eye, was its 1954 merger with Studebaker. Its own president admitted that it was a "shotgun wedding." In the real world, however, the bride and groom usually know what they are getting; in the Packard version, neither company did. Because the merger was not underwritten by outside investment houses and was "friendly," there was no in-depth investigation. Each knew the other was in serious trouble, but Packard officials did not know just how weak their marriage partner was until after the rites were concluded.

The merger also posed critical philosophical questions. It was predicated upon the supposition that, to survive, Studebaker-Packard had to offer autos across the price scale. Touting itself as the "4th full line manufacturer," Studebaker-Packard, the 75th-largest company based on sales, competed head to head with the industry's behemoths. Other Independents, by contrast, sought market niches–Nash and Hudson found theirs at the lowest end, undercutting Ford, Chevrolet, and Plymouth with their new Rambler, and American Motors survived another 34 years. It was Studebaker-Packard managers who dreamed the larger dreams and created a more difficult and dangerous task for themselves.

In the final analysis, the chance to look at Packard as a microcosm of larger twentieth-century business practices proved most alluring. The great irony here was that James J. Nance, the company's last president, often chided as the naive outsider from the electrical-appliance industry brought to heel by Detroit's auto moguls, did not set out to make Packard over in some pale reflection of Hotpoint; he tried to make it more like the Big Three. He was brought in to drag the company into the mid-twentieth century. Packard did not die of outmoded administrative organization and skills. Rather, it gagged on the sudden infusion of management techniques already in place at the other automobile companies. Nance was as conventional as "Engine Charlie" Wilson over at General Motors, or the true autocrat of the industry, Henry Ford II, or the blustery "Tex" Colbert at Chrysler. Armed with volumes of an outside consultant's plans for the company, he followed their recommendations to the letter with one addition. Coming from a strong marketing background and graced with an ebullient personality, he made himself a symbol for the "new" Packard. The reams of publicity he garnered made it a foregone conclusion that he would shoulder the praise or the blame for his company's fortunes.

Nowhere was Nance's management style more conventional than in his relations with the government. His approach to federal officials in 1956 was so strikingly similar to Lee Iacocca's 25 years later that it deserves a detailed critical reexamination. Packard and Studebaker based their future automotive plans on the revenues they could expect from their contracts for jet engines and military trucks. When these were cut off after the Korean War, both companies faced liquidity problems in a surprisingly buoyant buyer's market. If there is a tragic aspect to Packard's fall, it is that otherwise talented and able managers had little control over their vital business relations with the federal government. For a company with Studebaker-Packard's anemic cash flow, that was a flaw of tragic proportions.

Packard's demise also reflected postwar America's demographic changes. For eleven years the auto builder was insulated from them by two wars and a prolonged seller's market in which Americans would buy anything on wheels. The company did little to respond to new markets. General Motors executives, however, recognized the changes and moved to satisfy them as early as 1948. The public's fancy for larger, luxurious, and more powerful automobiles should have meant that Packard, long a maker of big powerful cars, was in the thick of the fray. It was not, though. As an Independent, and under a financial cloud, it had to woo the public away from the security of the Big Three's offerings, and it lacked the financial resources to do so.

The lessons to be learned from Packard's experiences are not only how to avoid corporate disaster but also the painful truth that well-meaning men often make intelligent, informed decisions and still fail miserably, for reasons outside their control. As late as 1953, Packard was still profitable and free of debt, the possessor of the tattered remnants of a once-proud reputation, and a producer of automobiles of acceptable quality. Its managers mustered the resources and the will to dramatically alter the company in a desperate last bid to remain solvent and compete with its much larger neighbors. In the final four years of the company's Detroit existence, they made many decisions that remain correct even in hindsight, but unforeseeable and uncontrollable events regularly jinxed them.

Packard's executives, for example, retooled for the 1951 model year just in time for the Korean War. They borrowed and spent heavily to build an up-to-date, fully automated, V-8 engine plant that went into production just after their merger brought them another set of V-8 facilities. Packard's body supplier, Briggs, suddenly went out of business on the eve of bringing out a redesigned 1955 model with the new V-8 and a novel torsion-bar suspension system. This forced Packard to spend millions of dollars for its own body plant, which was fraught with start-up problems. And then after Packard's engineers designed a complex system of interchangeable parts for the 1957 Studebakers and Packards, which would have saved the company millions of dollars, the company's consortium of creditor insurance companies and banks refused to fund the tooling that would have enabled the company to realize its merger economies.

Packard suffered yet another stroke of bad luck when George Mason, president of American Motors, died in October 1954. His death ended any hope for a grand merger of Hudson, Nash, Packard, and Studebaker, which together might have had a better chance of survival. The

American Motors merger on May 1, 1954, and the Studebaker-Packard merger five months later were the prelude to a planned American Motors–Studebaker-Packard deal. Mason's death elevated George Romney, who was much less enthralled with the idea of a grand union, to the vacant presidency. Moreover, Nance and Romney, who were too much alike, disliked each other; Mason's death left the two Independents to go it alone.

In spite of Packard's revitalization program, which gave it the physical capacity to produce quality autos in volume, raised company morale, redefined its corporate image and goals, and brought more changes and advances than at any time since the firm's birth, Packard foundered. National and international events and political developments in Washington, D.C., combined with changes in the domestic car markets and Packard's inherent weaknesses to frustrate its half a dozen years of hard-won improvements. It almost seemed as if Aristotle's tragic process was at work with a vengeance in the twentieth century. But that is what makes Packard such a gripping story. In the 1950's, its leaders recognized their firm's past mistakes, gambled all their modest resources to make their facilities competitive, sold the nation's leading financial institutions on their plans, won support from President Dwight Eisenhower and his administration, captured the public's attention—and almost achieved a comeback. But, in losing, they lost it all.

Chapter 1

Model A, 1899

Ascent of
the Marque

April 10, 1947, dawned overcast in Detroit, cool with intermittent drizzle. By mid-morning, a long procession of custom-built Lincoln limousines formed around St. Paul's Episcopal Cathedral on Woodward Avenue among a damp, unusually quiet horde of onlookers gathered to pay their last respects to Henry Ford. He had put America on wheels; his Model T, designed with ground clearances that enabled farmers to drive over stumps and small calves, had freed millions of farmers from their isolation and changed the nation's culture and morals. Now Detroiters turned out to say good-bye and to watch the funeral procession make its way slowly to the west side of the city, past the General Motors headquarters, out to the family cemetery next to St. Martha's Episcopal Church. Ironically, the man who had built millions of Fords, Mercurys, and Lincolns rode to his final resting place in a 1942 Packard.[1]

Packard still enjoyed that luxury cachet in the early postwar years. It was known as a quality automobile built by men who understood cars and driven by people who appreciated its conservative styling, the rich smell and texture of fine leathers and wools, the sheen of a burled-elm dashboard, and the quiet, powerful performance of Packard's reliable engines and running gear. The big Packards bespoke elegance, comfort, success. For years, practically everybody who was anyone advertised his worldly success with a Packard. Their names were a veritable roll call of world figures: emperors, tsars, and kings. Nicholas II of Russia had his Packard fitted with treads and skis for winter driving; King Alexander of Yugoslavia held a royal record of some sort with his 48 Packards; the Queen of Spain, the Emperor of Japan, the Shah of Iran, the Aga Khan, and the Maharani of Porbander all enjoyed the world's finest motorcar. Lesser personages of Franklin Roosevelt's and Joseph Stalin's ilk preferred cars with the cloisonné red hexagons on the hubcaps, and preferred them armored as well. Harry Truman was often photographed in a White House Packard but his general, Douglas MacArthur, had to pay for his. William Howard Taft needed a car as large as a Packard for comfort, though Nicholas Longworth, House Speaker in 1930, may have bought his to keep his wife, Teddy Roosevelt's irrepressible Alice, pacified. Movie stars by the gaggle, such as Gary Cooper, Clark Gable, Bob Hope, Wallace Beery, and my childhood hero, Tom Mix, flaunted their Packards, many of which had expensive, custom bodies.

Packard did not earn its international prestige by forfeit; its price range was crowded with competitors that produced quality machines. The other two renowned P's, Peerless and Pierce Arrow, were prime competitors until the depression forced them to close down. Cadillac, although an upper-middle-class auto in the 1920's, drew on the resources of General Motors to rival Packard in the following decades. Other firms occasionally challenged Packard as well, but Packard outdistanced them all, if not always in speed and number of cylinders, at least in classic styling, sumptuous comfort, hand-crafted precision, and meticulous attention to detail.[2]

The taste and style that characterized Packard for years were products of the corporation's origins. The brothers Packard, James Ward and William Doud, were men with the financial resources and physical facilities to design and construct their motorcars with a high degree of finish and better than average reliability. And, as later became the norm for presidents of the Packard Motor Car Company, the brothers' proclivities, personalities, and interests profoundly influenced the automobiles they manufactured and sold.[3]

William Doud was the businessman of the two; he had a natural affinity for numbers and money. His brother was the mechanical genius. Their initial car, a single-cylinder machine that boasted between 7 and 9 horsepower, was tested on the streets of Warren, Ohio, on November 7, 1899. It was technically unremarkable but performed well enough that James Ward decided to produce four more. The car became known as the Model A.[4]

When the *Horseless Age* wrote up the car on May 16, 1900, it established several themes that would long distinguish the company. The editor's hyperbole aside, his observation that the car "is solidly built to endure high speeds on rough roads, and workmanship is thorough and first class" could equally well have applied to the 12-cylinder Dietrich-bodied Packard phaetons of the 1930's or the company's 1956 Caribbeans. The editor also noted the Packards' penchant for thoroughly testing their product, a trait that would endure until the late 1930's.[5]

The Packards' new Model B, introduced in 1900, sported the first of many mechanical changes that earned the company its reputation for thorough engineering, which distinguished Packard until it shut down in 1956. The Model B boasted the first steering wheel, the first gas pedal, and the first automatic spark advance. It also offered a central lubrication system, two sets of batteries, and a flexible frame designed for high speeds on rough roads. Although Packard accounted for only a little more than 1 percent of the estimated 4,000 automobiles produced by perhaps 40 or 50 firms in 1900, the company by the autumn of the year was clearly preparing to increase its share of the growing national market.[6] On September 26, the brothers chartered the Ohio Automobile Company with a capital stock of $100,000 and five stockholders.[7]

The auto companies that survived and matured were those that increased their output to perhaps 1,000 cars a year, advertised nationally, and created a widespread network of dealers with the financial resources to supply and repair the machines. Most companies floundered at this barrier and disappeared. Packard, through a series of fortunate coincidences, attracted the attention of wealthy outsiders, the so-called Princes of Griswold Street in Detroit, who invested their money and their talents to completely transform the little Warren auto producer.

The first among the princes was Henry Bourne Joy, son of millionaire railroad man James F. Joy. Henry inherited many of his father's talents, and he had a strong mechanical bent and an outgoing personality as well. Around 1900, he took his brother-in-law, Truman Newberry, son of John Newberry, who had extensive lumber and manufacturing interests in and around Detroit, to New York City to buy a reliable steam engine. As they were walking down the street they fell into conversation with two automobile drivers who were standing at the curb. When a fire engine approached, both drivers spun their Packards' cranks, hopped aboard, and took off after the fire apparatus. Joy and Newberry were thunderstruck at the cars' reliability. Within the hour Joy purchased a new Packard.[8]

Soon after, Newberry followed suit, and the two became Packard devotees. Joy also assumed a personal stake in the company's future when he bought 250 shares of its stock for $25,000. The pulse of the little company suddenly quickened. The Packards upped their capacity to one car per day, and James Ward took to the road to recruit dealers in the larger cities, which were home to the people who could afford his cars. By September 1902, he had signed up seven. At the same time, someone, perhaps Joy, convinced James Ward that a proper motorcar in Packard's price range should have more than one cylinder.[9]

The Packards and Joy were certain that they had a great car to offer the public, but their limited production capacity and out-of-the-way location hindered them. The auto industry was rapidly concentrating in Detroit, where numerous independent machine shops and easy access to wood allowed operating economies. In the early fall of 1902, the Packard brothers and Joy worked out financial arrangements to enable the new company to increase its production and to relocate. On October 13, William Doud proposed to his board that the firm be renamed the Packard Motor Car Company, to remove any geographical attachment, and that its capital stock be increased to $500,000. Both motions passed, and the new stock offering was quickly taken up by Joy and his Detroit friends.[10]

The new investors were all from Joy's and Newberry's Detroit social stratum. Russell A. Alger, son of the former Michigan governor and the secretary of war under President William McKinley, took a $50,000 interest. Another Alger, Fred, who would later sit on Packard's board of directors, bought in for $25,000. Joy took another $25,000 for himself and $10,000 for his brother, Richard. Truman and John Newberry, who owned interests in banks, iron companies, telephone companies, railway manufacturing plants, and the Republican party, each invested $25,000. Among the new Detroit investors, Joseph H. Boyer, who would be instrumental in attracting the next generation of Packard leaders, risked $25,000, and Phillip H. McMillan, shipowner, newspaper publisher, and banker, whose interests would be represented on the company's board until almost the very end, advanced $50,000. The Princes of Griswold Street now controlled Packard, with the Packard brothers' full approbation. The Packards stayed in Warren and managed the plant's day-to-day activities while the princes dominated the board of directors and plotted long-term strategy.[11]

They soon decided to move the factory to Detroit, and Joy, as fastidious as the Packards about doing things correctly, hired the German architect Albert Kahn to draw up plans for the new factory. Kahn, one of the nation's leading industrial architects, designed a two-story factory for Joy's 66.4 acres of land on what was then called Grand Boulevard, a most suitable address for the class of automobiles the company would be producing. The firm took possession of the finished buildings on September 22, 1903, only 90 days after construction began. The following month, the machinery from Warren arrived and the new plant, Packard's home until the spring of 1956, went into production.[12]

Even with its new factory, solid financial backing, and production levels of almost two cars per day, Packard was still a bit player on the automotive stage. From 1899 through 1906, the company sold a grand total of only 1,691 cars—of the 113,507 estimated to have been built and sold in the United States during those years. Despite its small output, however, the firm had garnered a priceless reputation for turning out large, comfortable, reliable, and mechanically sophisticated automobiles for America's upper crust, whose members longed to display their success. More important, Joy turned a loss of $200,000 (in 1904) into a profit of $216,000 the following year. His company would enjoy an unbroken string of earnings until the 1921 depression.[13]

Packard built its reputation on its close attention to innovations and refinements in engineering. As late as 1954 it was still trading on that sterling reputation. That year the firm's public relations people put together a list of Packard's technical "firsts" in the industry, and it was an impressive one: the H-slot gearshift, thermostatic control of water circulation, wheels interchangeable at their hubs, tubed radiators with top and bottom reservoirs, diamond-tipped machines to bore connecting rod ends, rifle bore of oil passages in connecting rods for piston pin lubrication, torsional vibration dampers, spiraled bevel gears, and, probably most important for customers, the first factory training school for dealers, employees, and customers.[14]

Joy's lasting contribution to Packard was his incessant pressure to transform it from a company that produced fine hand-crafted vehicles to one that adopted mass-production techniques yet retained its high quality. When his designers presented their newest creation in 1906, the Model 30, Joy knew he had a sales winner. In the seven production years leading up to the 30's introduction, Packard had manufactured an average of 241 cars per year. The 30 was mounted on a 122-inch wheelbase, powered by a T-head 432-cubic-inch 4-cylinder motor, and graced with a beautiful aluminum body built on a wood frame. It was priced between $4,200 and $5,600 and over the next six years sold 9,540 units. The increased output catapulted the firm by 1907 into the top ranks of auto producers. The seven companies that enjoyed higher sales, Ford, Buick, Reo, Maxwell, Rambler, Cadillac, and Franklin, sold their cars for a fraction of a Packard's cost. Even more startling, Packard manufactured 11,818 vehicles from 1907 to 1912–an average of 1,970 per year.[15]

Joy could take further satisfaction from his bottom-line figures: his profits during the six years of Packard's increased production ranged from $1.3 million to $2.8 million. Ever prudent, he reinvested the bulk of his earnings in physical plant rather than pay them out as dividends, a policy Packard adhered to until its last days. Packard's East Grand Boulevard facilities grew exponentially: by 1911, the plant boasted 1,642,212 square feet.[16]

Even as Joy celebrated his company's successful transition from a small producer to a major corporation, its healthy financial base, and its increasing sales and profits, Packard stood on the brink of yet another major transition. This would mark it as *the* major manufacturer of fine automobiles. The next generation of Packard leaders was ready to take the stage, the generation that would lead the company until World War II. James Ward cleared the way for the managerial turnover when he resigned from the presidency in 1909. Relations with Joy and his fellow princes had been strained since 1903, and James Ward's geographical isolation in Warren had lessened his influence in company councils. Joy, who had been general manager, assumed the vacated presidency and hired a new general manager. This man would lead Packard through its golden age and leave his personal mark on the company to its very end– James Alvan Macauley.

Although not present at the founding, Macauley, for most of the 38 years he gave the company, represented everything Packard cars came to stand for to the public, the press, the automobile industry, and the firm's dealers. By dint of his strong individuality and the company's relatively small size, he imprinted Packard with his personality, quirks and all.

On the face of it, Macauley was something of an oddity in the automobile world. Neither a tinkerer nor a financial wizard, he came to Packard through the legal profession and coincidence. Born in Wheeling, West Virginia, in 1872 to James Macauley, an Irish immigrant who in the Civil War not only had lost an arm but had spent nine months in a Confederate prison, young Alvan grew up in a home where the value of education and hard work was constantly emphasized.[17] He attended James Ward's alma mater, Lehigh University, for two years and earned a law degree at George Washington University. After graduation he worked as a patent attorney with the National Cash Register Company in Dayton, Ohio, a firm that sent Packard a number of its leaders and management ideas until 1956. After four years in Dayton, Macauley took a job with the

American Arithmometer Company, the forerunner of the Burroughs Corporation. The company had close ties to Packard in the person of its president, Joseph H. Boyer, who had been one of the investors who helped Joy take over Packard in 1903. It must have been Boyer who pointed out Macauley's talents to Joy; when Joy assumed Packard's presidency in 1910, he immediately tapped Macauley to take his old job of general manager.[18]

Packard's new officer stood perhaps five feet nine or ten inches tall, sported a clean-shaven square jaw, and had a rather friendly visage, given his reputation for being something of a cold fish. He was a man of innumerable private passions and quirks, but he had only one public passion after 1910 – Packard. For some reason, he hated people who had gold fillings or caps on their teeth, could not stand to have anyone jingle pocket change when he was nearby, and detested all long names. On more than one occasion, Packard's president "persuaded" some of his associates and employees to change their offensive names. After all, *he* had dropped his unwanted first name, James.[19]

Macauley's great strength was that he always seemed to be looking five years down the road with a pretty clear idea of where he wanted Packard to be and with what kind of product. In doing so he relied upon his own intuition; in that respect he was more the automotive artist than the corporate manager. Part of his artistry was his uncanny ability to surround himself with loyal and talented men, subordinates who worshiped him. Yet he allowed them enough freedom to exercise their own creative talents. This rare blend of corporate purpose and freedom helped propel Packard into the upper reaches of the automotive world.

One of his earliest hires, Jesse G. Vincent, was the man most responsible for giving Packard engineers a worldwide reputation for sophistication and excellence. Vincent was a technical genius, a man who combined a passion for automotive mechanics with an aristocratic temperament. His list of Packard's technological firsts reads like a history of the automobile: the V-12 engine, the diesel aircraft engine, the World War I Liberty aircraft motor, four-wheel brakes, auto air-conditioning, power booster brakes, and hypoid gears. And although he was not the father of the automatic transmission, his early work on such devices enabled Packard to become the only Independent to manufacture its own, the Ultramatic.[20]

Born the son of an Arkansas farmer in 1880, Vincent quit school in the eighth grade. He later completed a mechanical engineering course of study through the International Correspondence School in Scranton, Pennsylvania, and in 1903 he moved to Detroit, where he joined

Macauley and Boyer at Burroughs. Soon after, Macauley left for Packard and Vincent went to Hudson as its chief engineer. Macauley lured him away in July 1912 and brought him into Packard as chief engineer. He never left.

Vincent, who loved to get his hands dirty, was a surprisingly genteel man who moved easily through the upper reaches of the clubby auto executives' world. His physical appearance betrayed his affable manner. His rather oval head, just a tad larger than what one would normally expect, displayed an overly broad nose and an exceedingly wide mouth that broke into easy smiles. His one obvious idiosyncrasy was that he was enamored of titles. During World War I he was commissioned a lieutenant colonel; ever after he signed his correspondence, even letters to his family, simply "Colonel." [21]

Macauley and Vincent arrived on the Packard scene at the very moment when the company's product line was again in flux. Despite its success with the Model 30, Packard had lagged badly in technical design when compared to its two closest competitors, Peerless and Pierce Arrow. Both cars advertised their powerful 6-cylinder engines, and Macauley was anxious to catch up. By 1910, Packard's engineers had designed a model that promised performance and reliability, but in characteristic conservative fashion, they road tested it for more than a year before they offered it to the public in 1912. It was a monster—its 525 cubic inches and 74 horsepower could accelerate a two-ton Packard from 0 to 60 miles per hour in 30 seconds. It quickly became the favorite car of unsavory characters in need of speed. [22]

The relatively popular, beautiful, and durable new Model 48 maintained Packard's growing reputation for fine cars but added little luster to it. Jesse Vincent did that. Soon after he arrived at Packard, he set forth the standards a great motorcar had to meet, including "more range of ability, greater smoothness and less noise." In pursuit of such perfection Vincent thought that all he had to do was to mate a pair of well-balanced 6-cylinder engines into a "Twin Six," or a 12-cylinder motor. He began work on the design, probably as early as 1913, and two years later he was testing a prototype. Vincent managed to coax 85 horsepower out of the motor's 424 cubic inches, and it was so quiet, he observed, that "the only thing I can liken it to is the action of steam." [23]

Packard's public introduction of its Twin Six in May 1915 caused an instant public stir. The firm offered something revolutionary that far surpassed anything its competition sold. What really turned Americans' heads was Packard's advertising the Twin Six at $2,000 *less* than the Model 48. The car-buying public responded enthusiastically to the new

Packard, and over the nine years of its production, the factory built 35,102 of Vincent's triumphs. Profits soared as well, from $3.1 million in 1915 to $7 million in 1923.[24]

Vincent's brilliant engineering feat did more for Packard's reputation as a builder of fine cars than all the company's prior efforts combined. His new Packard offered more–more cylinders, more torque, more quietness, and more sheer power–for less money. The public quickly adopted these refinements as the basic definition of a luxury car and came to measure all other autos against them.

Packard's success with its Twin Six exposed a vital flaw in its corporate strategy that would bedevil the company until World War II. Sticking to the luxury-car market, perhaps at best only 10 to 15 percent of all cars sold, guaranteed that the company would manufacture and sell relatively few cars per year. Moreover, the upper ranges of that market were already crowded, and Macauley knew he needed a broader sales base to ensure Packard's financial security. This need dictated production of a less expensive car on which he could realize the savings inherent in mass production without tarnishing his company's image with the lap-robe trade.[25]

Macauley spent his entire career at Packard trying to push the company into the more moderately priced fields. To achieve his goal, he wanted a car almost as good as a Twin Six that would retain the Packard luster but would cost less to manufacture and with a lower price attract a wider audience. He set Vincent to work on such a vehicle. But Vincent overengineered it, and when the new 6-cylinder Model 116 was introduced in September 1920, its price ranged from $3,600 to $4,800, more than some of the Twin Six models.[26] Moreover, the 116's introduction virtually coincided with the beginning of a sharp recession that deflated car sales everywhere. When the new model did not sell, Macauley lowered its price to $2,975, laid off employees, borrowed $10 million through a bond issue (it was snapped up in two hours), and ended the fiscal year $1 million in the red.[27]

One of Macauley's strengths was his readiness to admit a mistake, and the 116 certainly had all the signs of one. Packard, however, was small and centralized enough to respond to changes with a minimum of effort. When in trouble, Macauley had a tendency to retreat to the upper ranges of the market and await another chance to attack its lower regions. This was exactly what he did in 1920. He had his designers stretch the 116 out over 126- and 133-inch wheelbases and style a more attractive and less squarish body for it. The public responded by purchasing more than 26,000 of the restyled cars in the following sixteen months. From its

$1 million deficit in 1921, Packard rebounded—it showed a $2 million profit the following year.[28]

Throughout the 1920's, Macauley displayed his magic touch to the auto world. He could seemingly do no wrong as he played the market like a virtuoso, lightly and with finesse. For example, he wanted a luxury car that maintained Packard's prestige but enjoyed higher sales. Once again Vincent worked his own brand of magic with a new straight eight, really a 4-cylinder motor cut in half with another 4 inserted in the middle. The engine pumped out 85 horsepower, 15 more than Cadillac's V-8.

Packard was not the first to introduce the straight eight. Frederick Duesenberg had built and raced one with an overhead camshaft in 1920.[29] Macauley's stroke of genius was to take the more modest motor and install it in a chassis and body that gave the appearance of *more* power than even the Twin Six it replaced. Company stylists mounted the new eight on 136- and 143-inch wheelbases and lengthened the hood by ten inches, giving the new cars a long, lean, powerful look; they were stunningly beautiful. Years later, Lee Iacocca, at Ford and later at Chrysler, used the elongated-hood trick on his Mustang, Cougar, Lincoln Continental Mark II, and Cordoba.

Despite Packard's reputation for building luxury automobiles, 80 percent of its cars were sold in the upper ranges of the medium price bracket. Macauley's profits were greater on the eights, but his sixes paid the company's bills. His net profits rose from a low of $4.8 million in 1924 to a most satisfying high of $21.8 million in 1928. From another perspective, however, Packard in 1923 captured just 0.57 percent of the 4,034,012-car market.[30]

The auto industry was "shaking out" by the end of that decade, and it became clear that Packard ranked among the second level of manufacturers, the so-called major Independents, which included Hudson, Nash, Studebaker, and Willys-Overland. When Walter Chrysler, former General Motors president, chartered Chrysler, outbid GM for Dodge in 1928, and fielded autos from Plymouths to Chryslers, the Big Three had taken shape and the lines for the coming battles in the automobile marketplace had been roughly drawn. To make Packard's situation more difficult, Henry Leland, once general manager of Cadillac, formed the Lincoln Motor Company. He soon went broke and sold out to Henry Ford, who had the resources to challenge Packard in the expensive markets.[31]

Macauley found Packard's luxury image harder to maintain as the twenties wound down. Although the company appeared safe at the top of the market with its eights, the six, its bread and butter, was rapidly losing popularity and distinctiveness. A host of moderately priced cars also offered six cylinders, with many of the same Packard refinements, for much less money. Buick, Franklin, Chrysler, and Studebaker all built sturdy, dependable cars with thrifty 6-cylinder engines. A discerning consumer could put himself behind the wheel of a 6-cylinder Oldsmobile for less than $1,000 or of a Dodge for about $765. Even the lower end of the market was catching up to the leaders; Chevrolet introduced its first six in 1929, and Plymouth followed suit in 1933. Such general improvements compressed the entire automotive market, and as Plymouths, Fords, and Chevrolets became larger, more powerful, and more stylish, manufacturers in the middle ranges had to narrow the gap between their cars and the luxury vehicles. Moreover, family incomes rose during the 1920's and Packard's prices edged generally downward, making the marque appear less prestigious. Early Packards had sold for four or five times the average annual income; by 1923, the least expensive six was down to half that. All these changes posed serious threats to Packard.[32]

Packard's president, however, had only to look at his own competition to become alarmed. Cadillac stole a page from Packard's book in 1927 and introduced a new car, the LaSalle, to fill the gap between Buick and Cadillac. Styled by Harley J. Earl, head of GM's new styling and color studio, who would do so much to redefine automotive shapes in the industry, the new entry was powered by a V-8, built to Cadillac's quality standards, and priced at about $2,500.[33]

Macauley responded predictably to this new threat. Offering the public more car for the same money, he put a smaller straight eight in his lower-priced models. This new motor shared many components with the older one, and Macauley hoped to realize cost benefits. The fire sale of Packard sixes and the new eight in 1928 enabled Macauley to outsell the newcomer LaSalle by 50,054 to 36,480. These robust sales served as a springboard for 1929, when Packard had its best financial year ever. The firm manufactured 47,855 autos, of which 37,642 were the new Standard Eights, and reveled in a net profit of almost $26 million on sales of $107.5 million.[34]

That was the good news. The bad news was that the bottom fell out of the stock market on Black Thursday and would continue to fall erratically until the dark days of 1932, when the nation suffered almost 25 percent unemployment. Psychologically it was the single most devastating blow the nation had ever suffered. Americans, even those with jobs, postponed major purchases, fearing what the future might bring. Average earnings tumbled by almost one-third, from $1,405 in 1929 to a measly $1,091 in 1934; not until 1941 did average incomes return to their 1929 levels. In such hard times not many Americans looked at a $4,000 or $5,000 automobile and even fewer bought one. National auto sales plummeted from almost 4.5 million on the eve of the crash to only 2.8 million in 1930–and then they grew even worse. Sales fell below 2 million in 1931 and stayed under that mark until 1934, when they just barely cleared it. The only bright year in the decade was 1937, when 3.7 million Americans bought new cars, but even that faint recovery proved short-lived as the "Roosevelt Recession" again scared buyers off. New-car sales slipped back to about 2 million a year.[35]

Packard's sales in 1930 fell by 40 percent, as did Cadillac's and LaSalle's, but even so the firm posted a $9 million profit for the year, the sixth highest in its history. Production fell to 28,386 cars, and only 3,246 of those were DeLuxe Eights, the higher-priced models. Even the wealthy avoided the auto showrooms. Between 1930 and 1934, Packard lost $15 million. Money just hemorrhaged out, no matter how ingenious and clever Macauley and his colleagues were.[36]

One of the great ironies in American automotive history is that automobile companies manufactured some of their greatest motorcars at the moment when the nation's economic fortunes were at their ebb. Cadillac led off with its V-16 in 1930; Duesenberg brought out its super-charged SJ, which with its 320 horsepower could zip from 0 to 100 in seventeen seconds. Marmon, long touted as "The Easiest Riding Car in the World," in its last gasp in 1931 produced a beautiful V-16. Auburn made do with fewer cylinders and manufactured a new V-12 in 1932 that sold for under $1,000, which had to be the buy of the century. Its swan song, however, was the classic 1935 boat-tailed speedster, each guaranteed to have been driven over 100 miles per hour before delivery. Cord, the third company in Erret Lobban Cord's empire along with Auburn and Duesenberg, brought out a new V-8 in 1938 wrapped in a stylish Gordon Buehrig body that featured a unique "coffin nose." Peerless was a terminal case and went out of business in 1932 before it had a chance to put its V-16 into production. Pierce Arrow, Studebaker's subsidiary in Buffalo, brought out a 12-cylinder car in 1931 and won the award for the most expensive car introduced during the depression, a $10,000 Silver Arrow it exhibited at the 1933 Chicago World's Fair. Pierce Arrow breathed its last in 1938.[37]

Over at Lincoln, Edsel Ford brought out his Model K in 1932 with a V-12, another example of too much car for the market. The K's could hit an honest 100 miles per hour, but in those hard times not many people cared. Walter Chrysler was more conservative, introducing a straight

eight in 1931. He created more of a stir three years later when he unveiled his Airflow, with a unit body, flush headlamps, and strange aerodynamic styling, which cost only $1,300 but was too advanced for public
tastes and pocketbooks. Staid Buick stepped up to an overhead-valve
straight eight in 1931.[38] The market, however, even for luxury cars,
evaporated. In the 1920's about 10 percent of all cars sold were in that
range, costing more than $2,500. By 1932, when the twelves and six-
teens were coming off their assembly lines, that market had shrunk
to only 2 percent of new-car sales. Five years later, it would stand at an
almost imperceptible 0.5 percent. Dependence on the luxury-car market by any firm was fatal. In 1932 the major Independents, Packard, Hudson, Studebaker, and Nash, held about 10 percent of the national market. Their share fell precipitously to 6 percent and stuck there through
1935. On the other hand, the Big Three pushed their percentage of sales
from 82 in 1932 to more than 92 by mid-decade. Not only was Packard in
financial trouble by the early thirties but all the national auto trends
were running against it.[39]

It became patently obvious in 1931 even to the ever-optimistic
Macauley that the United States was deeply mired in its worst economic
catastrophe ever and that severe measures were called for if Packard was
to survive. Packard's president dusted off his old blueprint for pushing
Packard down into even lower price ranges and for bringing out a new
upper-level entry. He had done that several times before, but what made
his moves in the early 1930's different was his intention to spread his
product line farther than ever, down to well below $2,000.

Macauley wanted to invade Buick and LaSalle territory, but he
wanted to do so with a better car than those two offered. His new automobile, dubbed the "Light Eight," was anything but; it weighed in at two
tons, only about 600 pounds less than the standard Packard. It used the
basic straight eight engine and sported leather and wool broadcloth interiors and the firm's usual craftsmanship. The most noticeable difference between the new car and the rest of the Packard family was a new
grille that pinched in at the bottom and flowed out toward the front
bumper. Wags immediately dubbed it the shovel or snowplow grille. Introduced on January 9, 1932, and priced at $1,750, more than Macauley
had wanted, the car was not the panacea he had hoped for. By year's end,
Packard had produced only 6,622 Lights, well below the expected
30,000. Worse, Macauley discovered that his dealers were pushing the
cheaper car, rather than the more profitable Standards and DeLuxes.
Ruefully, he reported at the end of the year that Packard had lost more
than $6.8 million.[40]

The very day that Packard introduced its new Light Eight it also unveiled the new Twin Six, its first since 1923. Contrary to popular opinion at the time, the twelve was not an answer to Cadillac's V-16; such a move would have made no sense. In early 1929, Macauley dreamed of producing a superlative car with a technological edge in the medium price bracket. Specifically, he wanted a reworked Twin Six with front-wheel drive that he could sell for between $1,500 and $2,000. But things went wrong from the first. The new engine proved both dependable and quiet in the true Vincent style, but the front-wheel drive mechanism was a disaster. With a fortune already invested in the car, Macauley decided to cut his losses, mount the new engine in the DeLuxe chassis, and offer it in tandem with the Light Eight. At $3,650 for the cheapest Twelve, the car was not a big seller. Packard manufactured just 540 in 1932 and almost doubled that figure the next year. After that, the market for the Twelves fell back to under 800 a year. It helped refurbish Packard's prestige, eroded by competitors' twelves and sixteens, but did little for the struggling company's bottom line.[41]

Packard's sales in 1933 increased 10 percent to 9,893 units, enough to show a modest year-end profit of half a million dollars, but all self-congratulations disappeared the next year. Only 6,265 sales turned the ink in the ledgers red, to the tune of almost $7.3 million. The figures were scary, but they did show that Packard had a break-even point of about 9,000 to 10,000 cars per year, depending upon its product mix.[42]

Packard was far from broke in 1934. It still had ample cash reserves, harbored by its fiscally conservative management, and was free of debt. Many more years selling only 6,000 cars, however, and the company would have joined the other two P's in bankruptcy. That Packard escaped such a fate was largely due to Alvan Macauley's constant preoccupation with mass-producing a car that average Americans could afford. As early as the middle twenties, he had begun work on a Packard that would sell for about $1,000. Times were too flush then, but when the company's existence was threatened, Macauley's earlier proposal found ready listeners in the board room. Thus arose the irony that Macauley, never known for his daring or recklessness, spent millions of precious dollars in the depths of the depression to tool up for an inexpensive Packard, quite a corporate gamble. Macauley was not proposing another Light Eight; he wanted to sell hundreds of thousands of Packards.

To do it he was obliged to restructure his company's personnel and methods of doing business. The old conservative radically altered his firm and set it on a path from which it would never turn back. With all the new faces, machinery, and procedures, the public's perception of the company and its products also changed, but much more slowly. In the short run this differential between reality and Packard's reputation was a boon for the company. In the postwar world, however, this gap lulled the company into a fatal complacency until an industry outsider made one last frenzied effort to save the firm. It is a great story.[43]

Chapter 2

Model 30 landaulette, 1906

Episcopalian Cars for Methodists

I n January 1935, President Alvan Macauley announced a brand-new Packard, the 120, for sale at a shockingly low price of less than $1,000. The public's response was overwhelming; even before the first 120 rolled off its all-new assembly line, Macauley had 10,000 orders, each accompanied by a down payment. With a single bold stroke, he saved his company, turned a profit, and proved he could still work his magic. In retrospect, what appeared at the time to be a revolutionary change for Packard was actually well within the scope of its earlier marketing strategies. In the middle of the depression, pressured by the need to bolster his revenues, Macauley spread his company's products farther apart in the market than he had ever dared. He still employed 2,500 men handcrafting the beautiful Super Eights and Twelves, which sold for between $2,300 and $6,000 to the few Americans who could part with such sums. But with the 120 he had a car to appeal to the masses and built, he guaranteed, "as perfect as we know how to make it."[1]

To create his 120, a car that embodied Packard's traditional attention to fine detail, engineering, smoothness, and durability, Macauley had to drastically alter his company. He hired outside specialists, many from General Motors, and encouraged them to introduce new technologies, new accounting procedures, new costing methods, new language, new manufacturing processes, and a more diverse personnel mix into the firm's tight little family. This new management style was at odds with Macauley's tea-and-crumpets method of conducting business. Out on the plant floor, handcraftsmen were replaced with machines and a modern assembly line that moved briskly with pinpoint timing. Packard could thus manufacture more units per worker.

All signs indicate that Macauley knew exactly what he was doing and understood at least some of the far-reaching consequences of his actions. Years later, in 1952, when company managers looked back to the 1930's to get their bearings, they created a product flowchart that showed Packard's entries in the various price ranges. Someone labeled the 1935–40 era Macauley's "Five Year Plan." There is no evidence that such precise planning ever existed, but Macauley believed that once he had safely guided his company past the financial shoals into the mid-range Methodist markets, the new men could run Packard as well as he.[2]

Macauley repositioned Packard and transformed its manufacturing processes without serious opposition from within the company. It was ruled by a small group of old friends, like-thinking, long ensconced in their seats on the board, who knew each other's habits and who had close financial ties with the firm. In fact, in 1933 when the crucial decisions about the 120 were made, the board had only five members: two drew salaries from Packard, one sold its autos, and the remaining two had held their seats from the Joy and early Macauley years. In this clubby, intimate atmosphere, directors made the far-reaching strategic decisions that changed Packard's fortunes. The firm's size, gentlemanly business methods, and uniformly upper-class Episcopalian social orientation enabled Macauley to rule with a freer hand than he might otherwise have had.[3]

The president's position was so secure that even the 1929 stock market debacle had not shaken his control. His successful years in the 1920's pushed Packard stock up to $163 a share by 1928, and a year later the board voted a five-for-one split. The day before the crash, Packard stood at $23 per share; it bottomed out in 1932 at $2, a statistical performance no worse than that of General Motors, which fell from $73 to $8 in the same period. On the eve of the 120's introduction, Macauley's stock was selling for only $2\frac{1}{4}$. Within ten months it was up to $7\frac{1}{2}$, netting Macauley personally some $1.5 million and pleasing his stockholders as well. Packard paid dividends through 1932 and restarted them with the 120's profits in 1936. The two dividends Macauley announced that year were tangible evidence of the stockholders' wisdom: they had allowed the old man his head in refashioning the company to produce the 120.[4]

Packard's shareholders probably never understood how fundamental those Macauley changes were. The cheaper car demanded new skills that most Packard hands lacked. Macauley showed his understanding of this when he chose his own replacement. Max Gilman was so different from Macauley, it was hard to believe they were both hominids. Gilman combined an almost manic secretiveness with a glad-handing personality and flamboyant life-style, the very antithesis of Packard's tradition. Born on July 19, 1889, in Plymouth, Wisconsin, Gilman never talked to anyone about his early years, probably because his family was poor—a cardinal sin in his eyes. He attended the University of Michigan and dropped out, went to law school and left without a degree, and joined the Army Air Service in World War I and became a fighter pilot. In 1918 he joined Packard as a truck salesman in Brooklyn. This short, pudgy man, who would be bald by middle age and who seemed so out of step with Packard's corporate ethics and norms, prospered in New York. Gilman was direct, blunt, outspoken, and hard working. After Packard left the truck business in 1923, he switched to the accessories department and was soon named vice president for sales in the New York distributorship. Then he was tapped to come to Detroit as Packard's vice president of distribution, later general manager, and finally, in 1938, president.[5]

Alvan Macauley liked Gilman because he produced the desired results and manifested a common touch, an innate sense of American middle-brow tastes and culture; in short, Gilman was what Macauley thought a Methodist was. In a real sense Macauley was right, for Gilman loved to make and spend and live the good life. He bought a huge house in Detroit's Bloomfield Hills and, like Macauley and Vincent, was a golf addict and a bridge fanatic. He was an avid sports fan and frequently flew his two sons to football and baseball games around the country. At exclusive restaurants, he table-hopped rather than dining. Gilman was never hard to find in a crowd; his booming voice always betrayed his presence.[6]

Macauley wanted a "tough, shrewd, and aggressive" man, and he made Gilman responsible for Packard's new-car development. Gilman was a fanatic about squeezing costs out of the 120 to merchandise it at the lowest possible price. He pressured Macauley to bring Packard even farther down in the price range. Gilman had no intention of living and dying on the lap-robe trade; he dreamed of selling millions of Packards.

Packard also needed a man who understood mass-production techniques, had a reputation for being tough and meeting schedules, and could show a healthy profit on every car sold. Macauley was less interested in manners and good breeding than in getting his 120s out the factory door. He found his ideal man out on a farm in Tipp City, Ohio:

George Thurman Christopher, a real Methodist. Born to humble circumstances, he worked his way through Rose Polytechnic Institute, then went to Oldsmobile in 1927 as an inspector and approver of tools. His rise at General Motors was striking—in 1929 he was named vice president of manufacturing for Oakland Motor Car Company in Pontiac, and three years later he took the same position with Buick in Flint. In 1934, at age 47, however, he bought a 435-acre farm near Tipp City and abruptly "retired" to tend to his Hampshire hogs and Hereford cattle. Christopher's stint as a farmer lasted for 70 days, and then Gilman called him and offered him the challenge of building an assembly line from scratch. Christopher immediately accepted a position as assistant vice president of manufacturing at Packard. But he kept his farm, just in case.[7]

The new assistant vice president was the kind of man production workers loved. He was often out on the assembly line in his shirt sleeves, trailing billowing clouds of cigar smoke, talking over problems, giving encouragement, getting dirty, and comparing bowling scores. And his employees had little trouble understanding their new boss. Almost every other word he uttered was "Christ," and more than one observer noted that when Christopher unleashed his favorite machine-shop phrases in Macauley's presence, the old man blanched. Christopher used his easy relationship with his workers to cut down on labor troubles. When the Congress of Industrial Organizations (CIO) organized the auto industry, he presided over the unionization of his plants without noticeable trouble. Every Tuesday night he bowled in the factory's league, his shirt rumpled and soaked and his tie wildly askew. Christopher had a history of jumping from job to job and probably never intended to stay with Packard long; he rented a penthouse apartment on Jefferson Avenue. There, with his view of the river, he recreated Tipp City: in his rooftop garden he grew vegetables and flowers. He even tried to grow corn, a crop not often found in downtown Detroit.[8]

Behind the scenes, Macauley, Vincent, Gilman, and Christopher raided other car companies, especially General Motors, for technical people versed in the art of "costing" new cars. They hired so many of them away from Pontiac in 1934 that old-timers sneered that the 120's engine looked just like Pontiac's. The new "bean counters" were turned loose in a company that always designed, built, and tested a car before estimating its costs and final price. Macauley reversed the whole process and ordered his new hires to come up with an $850 car that was indisputably a Packard. It was a tall order, and it immediately set Packard's engineers and designers against the cost-conscious intruders. The General Motors veterans took away while the old hands put back. Ironically, when the 120's final design was approved, it bore improvements that even the "senior" models lacked—larger wheels, a bigger battery, and a new "Safe-T-Flex" front suspension that soon became standard on all Packards. But the new car also grew heavier, weighing in at 3,300 pounds, and its price edged up by about $150. The bean counters, however, won in the long haul. They introduced Packard to modern cost-accounting methods, and never again would the company produce cars the way it had.[9]

The cost accountants' jobs were made more difficult by personality conflicts that had long festered in Packard's tight little world. The company never had a policy against nepotism, and early in Colonel Vincent's tenure his brother, Charles Helm Vincent, joined Packard, also in its engineering department, and took over its new Utica, Michigan, proving grounds, complete with slate-roofed Tudor buildings. Charles's job was to find the weaknesses in brother Jesse's new creations, a source of friction for both men. Years later, Charles remembered that "Jesse was the genius who loved to create new things while I was the man who would make them work." Despite the fact that Charles always labored in his brother's shadow, he observed that "during the seventy-three years we were on this planet together, I do not think a harsh word ever passed between us."[10]

The two men rarely passed any words. A *Fortune* magazine writer noted parenthetically that "Colonel Vincent's brother Charles . . . indulges a savage anxiety to find flaws in every Vincent creation." Others inside the company put it more bluntly: "The Vincent brothers hated each other," said one. "Charles was jealous of Jesse's successes and was always denigrating him." Macauley was aware of the feud and took pains to see that Charles remained entirely independent of Jesse. The president realized that the enmity resulted in better cars, for Jesse would not send Charles an inferior design, and Charles would turn up every weakness in anything Jesse did send him.[11]

Packard's new ways of doing business affected employees outside East Grand as well. Macauley wanted to light a fire under his dealers, so he hired Bill Packer as his new sales manager, a man from the same mold as Gilman and Christopher. Well-spoken, friendly, portly, and full of energy, Packer had made a name for himself using hard-sell techniques at Chevrolet. His task was to teach staid Packard dealers, who for decades had operated upon the premise that Packards sold themselves, to cultivate clients. Macauley was under intense pressure to generate sales of the 120, and the 500 Packard dealers were not enough to make the car a success. Packer sought help over at Pontiac and hired Lyman Slack, sales promotion manager there, to the same post at Packard. The two men within three years signed up 1,200 new dealers. Packer also indoctrinated his dealers in "fast closing and intelligent closing pressure," how to sell on the installment plan, and how to tailor sales techniques common in Chevrolet's world to higher-caliber customers. Packer piloted his own plane, often carrying to his dealers such unwanted innovations as new-car quotas.[12]

First, however, Christopher had to build the new cars. When he accepted his job, he demanded a free hand in designing his assembly plant, and Macauley had made it easy for him. He had already moved all the senior manufacturing into one building and had gutted the old body-works building. With a budget of about $17 million, in a company losing $7 million a year, Christopher called upon his decades of machine-shop experience to completely equip the junior building with all the necessary machines, conveyor belts, and tools in just 90 days.[13]

Christopher laid out a production flow that was a marvel for its time; parts of it were so advanced, they were reintroduced 50 years later. On the lower floor, chassis, engines, transmissions, axles, and basic parts under the car were installed, and the upper floor was reserved for bodies, paint, upholstery, and trim. The two lines met at a drop where a finished body was lowered out of the ceiling onto a completed chassis pulled along on its tires. The timing had to be perfect, for one of Christopher's cost innovations was to have no spare bodies or chassis on hand. The job was more difficult because Packard also introduced a system of building cars of various models and colors as they were ordered, instead of assembling a week's worth of green phaetons (or whatever) as had been done in the past.[14]

The separate junior and senior assembly plants shared facilities such as the aluminum and iron foundries, woodworking shop, test grounds, engineering, maintenance, die shop, stamping plant, research offices, and power plant. Thus, Christopher had to spread his costs per vehicle across the senior lines as well, which infuriated him. As he pointed out to *Fortune*'s reporter, "that goddamned senior stuff," as he was wont to call the more costly Packards, employed 2,500 production men in 1936 who turned out only about 10,000 cars. On the south side of the street he had 2,600 men who built 55,000 of the 120s and another 15,000 of the new 6-cylinder cars.[15]

Although the 120s were not as cheap as Macauley had hoped, he could not have timed their introduction better. The depression eased a bit in 1935, and Americans responded by buying 3.3 million cars, over a million more than they had bought a year earlier. The prospect of better times prompted tight-fisted Americans to ante up the extra $200 to $300 for a Packard over what a Pontiac, Buick, Oldsmobile, or Hudson would have cost them. With a new, exciting product, Packard gained more than its share of increased sales after 1934. Christopher produced 52,045 cars on his lines in 1935, up from 6,265 the year before. Macauley must have smiled when he realized that without the 120, he would have sold only about 7,000 automobiles in 1935–instead of a $4.3 million profit, he would have suffered another splash of red ink amounting to $6 million or $7 million.[16] If 1935 was a good year, 1936 was a boon. Christopher built 80,978 Packards while his cost-cutting efforts warmed the company's accountants' and stockholders' hearts. When the books were closed at year's end, more than $7 million remained as profit. But the farmer from Tipp City was just getting started. In 1937 he ran two or three shifts per day with more than 13,000 employees and assembled 109,518 cars, setting the company's all-time production record. Christopher was anything but pleased, however. He had promised his shareholders that he would reach 200,000 units per year, and he had fallen far short. He became obsessed with the number. In contrast, Macauley was anything but displeased. He ended 1937 with a $3 million profit–even after a $766,844 fourth-quarter loss.[17]

On September 3, 1936, Macauley introduced yet another new automobile, the 115C. This car was proof, if any were needed, that Christopher and Gilman had prevailed in Packard's inner circle. The 115C was basically a downsized 120 with a 6-cylinder engine. The smaller car caught on like wildfire, selling 79,837 units in its first two years, setting a hotter pace than the 120 had. But the 115C's profit levels were lower and accounted for the firm's reduced 1937 surplus. The 115 was renamed the 110 in 1939, and as usually happens in the auto industry, both the 120 and the 115 grew in size as they aged. Nevertheless, the 115 put Packard in a brand-new market where it competed against 6-cylinder Pontiacs, Studebakers, and Dodges. By 1937, a frugal shopper could drive away in a new 115C for only $795. A well-heeled shopper could glide away in a 16th series Twelve after shelling out as much as $8,510.[18]

It was in the late 1930's that Macauley and Christopher charted a course that, owing to subsequent failures to modify it, harmed the company's hard-earned reputation for building luxury autos. When the bottom fell out of the new-car market again in 1938, Packard's cash and securities quickly melted away because of inventory buildups. Christopher knew exactly how to cut more fat out of the manufacturing process. He had for years been eyeing what he considered the inefficient senior production line. He shrank the larger cars, wrung the costs out of them, and sold them for less. He reversed Macauley's policy of widening Packard's price range, building the expensive cars on the 120 chassis and dropping the Twelve altogether in 1939. Macauley did not oppose this strategic move. Although the old man resigned as president in 1939 and moved up to chair Packard's board, he still commanded enough authority to stop Christopher cold.[19]

The decision to downsize the senior Packards made sense in the short run, but it eventually cost the firm its most valuable asset – its reputation for producing the finest-quality automobiles. The immediate manifestation of the policy change was to make the expensive Packards look more like the lower-priced ones. Company designers tried to maintain several separate lines. They introduced the 160, named for its larger 160-horsepower motor, and the 180, which had the same 8-cylinder engine. They both used the 120 body and chassis but offered different upholstery and exterior trim. Packard could sell the 160 for as little as $1,524 and the 180 for a bit more than $2,200; custom bodies and chassis, which could push the final costs over $6,000, were still available. The junior cars were not priced much below the new seniors – the 110 at $867 was the cheapest Packard, and a 120 could be had for only $1,100. Packard had become a mass producer of middle-priced automobiles.

By 1940, Christopher and Gilman were building Methodist cars for Methodists. Few Episcopalian cars left the factory gates anymore. From 1938 through 1940, the junior cars outsold the seniors by a ratio of better than seven to one, but that figure obscured a definite trend in favor of the Methodists. Before Christopher merged the lines, the juniors were leading three to one; the downsizing kicked that proportion up to eleven to one in 1939 and twelve to one the following year. Meanwhile, sales of the seniors dropped from 12,163 in 1938 to only 5,856 in 1940. Even at reduced prices, the company's best models were not attracting customers.[20]

Between 1935 and 1939, the struggle inside Packard between the bean counters and the purists was reflected in the company's advertising. Macauley had originally planned to present his new 120 as a practical answer to the new-car buyer's needs that carried with it decades of Packard research and prestige. At the same time he determined to continue to woo the Episcopalian lap-robe trade with advertisements that bordered on an art form. The approach confused the public – Packards could not be both practical and luxurious, cheap and expensive, exclusive and common. By the mid-1930's, Packard was clearly trading on the prestige and glamour of its stately Twelves and Super Eights to sell its junior models.[21]

Young & Rubicam, the firm's advertising agency, initially tried to separate Packard's two markets. On a $1 million budget the agency continued to place senior ads, most notably its famous "gateways" series that depicted entrances to the houses of families who had patronized

Packard for at least 21 years. These ads ran in such magazines as *Vogue*, *Junior League*, *Spur*, *Fortune*, *Canadian Homes and Gardens*, *New Yorker*, *Country Life*, *Stage*, *Yachting*, *Horse and Horseman*, and *Sportsman*. The admen introduced the junior line in the *Saturday Evening Post*, *Newsweek*, *Collier's*, *Time*, and like periodicals. This distinction made sense in theory, but it ended up blurring the company's image. This confusion was compounded two years later when Young & Rubicam coined its new theme, "For 1937 Get the Plus of Packard." Nobody was exactly sure what the "plus" was, although an account executive later admitted that it was prestige. Packard merged its advertising efforts with the new slogan and marketed all its lines from the 115C to the Twelves together, implying that the buyer could acquire the Packard "plus" for as little as $800.[22]

Packard's blurred public image, which stressed the uneasy combination of stylish prestige and an appealing practicality at budget prices, was not entirely Macauley's fault. It was true that the old man pushed hard to move his company down the price ranges and did at least sanction the ad campaigns, but it was just as evident that daily decisions were being made by the bean counters. Macauley failed to realize how totally they would revamp Packard. And it proved impossible to hide their changes from the public, especially after Macauley became chairman of the board of directors on April 17, 1939, and relinquished Packard's presidency to Gilman.

The new president wasted little time introducing yet another Packard model into the medium price range. Even though in a 1939 nationwide survey the public rated Packard the best-looking car, the company's styling was by 1940 at least five years old and was starting to look stodgy beside General Motors and Chrysler products. At the very top of the market, where Packard had contributed some of the world's most beautiful cars, often designed by private coachmakers such as Dietrich, Le Baron, Rollston, Brunn, Darrin, and others, the company's boast that it did not change its styling on a whim had real meaning.[23]

In the mid-price brackets, however, up-to-date looks sold cars, and it was in this market that frequent model changes caused Packard the most problems. In the middle 1920's, Alfred Sloan, Jr., General Motors president, used model changes as a sales tool. But John Reinhart, chief stylist for Packard from 1938, summed up his company's policy best when he remarked, "Packard never had any particular year when they'd decide to change a car, never had any cycles of any kind like the Big Three. They'd just carry on until sales started falling off."[24]

This philosophy evolved over the years when the firm dominated the top of the market, and it flowed from the personalities that guided the company. Packard's director of styling from 1930 through 1955 was Edward Macauley, Alvan's son, a man with a good eye for style, decent administrative ability, and a conservative esthetic bent, but absolutely no formal qualifications for the post. Ed was well liked by everyone who knew him, was the life of any party, played a great trombone, was always the gentleman, and despite the whispers about how he got his job, was respected—to a point. Packard in the twenties and thirties lingered behind styling trends but avoided the disastrous leaps that Chrysler made with its Airflow and Lincoln with its Zephyr.[25]

In 1940, Gilman decided that Packard had to have a more modern look and went outside the company for fresh ideas. He commissioned "Dutch" Darrin to create a new look that would embody the Packard distinctiveness. Darrin remembered that Gilman called him early in 1940, when "Packard was so afraid of GM they couldn't see straight." All Gilman wanted was a new car in ten days or less for which he would pay the designer $1,000 per day. Darrin's creation, which met the deadline, had front fenders sweeping back into the doors and disappearing, a roof flowing down and across the trunk, no running boards, and dimensions a foot wider than high. In short, Darrin brought in a beautiful car that, except for its traditional Packard grille, was quite unlike anything Packard had done before. Company stylists and engineers, especially Howard Yeager, did much of the detail work and made some major changes in Darrin's creation—most notably, adding vestiges of running boards and shortening the fenders' sweep across the front doors. They used the 120's chassis and motor, added a new front suspension, and called their new creation the Clipper. Sadly, Darrin never was paid for his work.[26]

The public loved the Clipper when it appeared in April 1941. Priced at only $1,420, it filled the gap between the 120 at $1,291 and the 160 at $1,795, further blurring distinctions between the junior and senior lines. It took Christopher until August to supply his dealers with an adequate number of the new cars, even though Packard rolled 16,600 of them off its assembly lines in 1941, roughly one-fourth of its total production. Plainly Packard had stolen a march on its competitors. With its streamlined styling, the Clipper was the wave of the future.[27]

The bombing of Pearl Harbor ensured that Packard would never find out just how well the Clipper would have sold. The company shut down its auto assembly line on February 9, 1942, victimized by a horrible case of bad timing that was wholly outside its control. It never reaped the benefits from its farsighted gamble, and by war's end its competitors had similarly styled cars. As Michael Kollins, a long-time Packard employee in the 1930's and again after the war, pointed out, several such examples of bad luck killed the Packard Motor Car Company.[28]

By the eve of the war, Packard had violated Macauley's marketing strategy of maintaining a perceptible distance between the firm's exquisite luxury offerings and its lower-priced cars. Gilman and Christopher compressed Packard's lines so much, the contrasts between the cheapest and the most expensive Packards were subtle. The marketing muddle enabled Cadillac in the late 1930's to take over Packard's position at the top of the luxury market. Cadillac had important advantages—as long as General Motors subsidized its losses, the marque could stay in that shrunken market indefinitely. Packard, however, was pressured to show a profit with its senior cars. Most observers believed that Cadillac lost money, lots of it, in the 1930's, but the company kept the division afloat because its officers loved to ride around in Cadillacs and because Cadillac prestige filtered down to the other GM offerings. Cadillac officials, who long chafed at being number two or lower in the luxury field, watched Packard take direct aim at the middle-price market. That strategy enabled Cadillac to outsell Packard in 1935 for the first time in the luxury field by a ratio of better than two to one. General Motors did it again the following year, but the race was much closer. Packard won in 1937 and 1938, but Cadillac almost regained the lead in 1939 as Packard downsized; General Motors was only about 1,000 vehicles shy of overtaking the East Grand automaker.[29]

Cadillac managers also watched Lincoln drop its Model K series to rely on the $1,300-to-$1,500 Zephyr to carry the marque's flag and noted that Chrysler was basically a middle-line producer as well. One by one Cadillac's competitors abdicated the fine-car field, prompting Cadillac's firm decision to concentrate on that market. Accordingly, it announced that it would cease making the LaSalle in 1940 and instead produce only higher-priced autos. It was a bold decision, since from 1936 through 1940 the LaSalle accounted for more than one-half of Cadillac's total sales. The results were almost immediate—Cadillac beat Packard in 1941 by a ratio of about two to one in the Episcopalian market and was on its way to repeating that feat the next year when war production cut deeply into auto manufacturing. From then on, Cadillac was the undisputed leader in its chosen field. And with the influx of wartime profits, the average family income almost doubled between 1939 and 1945. After the war, Cadillac was perfectly positioned to appeal to those who sought to display their newfound riches, but the public viewed Packard as a Clipper-LaSalle kind of company. The gamble taken by Cadillac's policymakers back in 1940 made them look clairvoyant.[30]

Gilman, Christopher, and certainly Macauley had no intention of sur-
rendering the upper reaches of the car markets without a fight. Packard
still had its premier engineering reputation, and those men in 1940 introduced such industry innovations as air-conditioning and power windows. The crucial question, however, was what would follow the 120.
The gossip in the late 1930's around the Detroit Athletic Club's bar, a
watering hole for automobile executives, was that "the new virgin is always the busiest girl in the harem. For a while. Sooner or later, she will
have to take her chances with the rest of us." Gilman knew that Packard
would have a hard time getting its costs down much lower and still produce a car that was uniquely Packard. He publicly said he expected to sell
many medium-priced cars "by the time the magic of the Packard name
has lost its special power." He admitted that he intended to wring the
name dry to buy time to ensconce the carmaker firmly in the middle-
class brackets.[31]

Gilman was thinking strictly in dollars and cents, but his policy was
ultimately fatal to Packard's image, which was built in part on relative
scarcity. When Packards cost three or four times the average annual income and sold in comparatively small numbers, they conferred prestige
upon their owners. The more frequently seen junior Packards, with their
similarities to other makes, lowered the senior cars' social value.

Packard's reputation was also built upon the notion that it symbol-
ized a life-style. Macauley's advertising agencies repeatedly fostered this
idea by depicting elongated, shining Packards, with their well-dressed,
happy owners, at country clubs, yachting basins, horse farms, estates,
and parks, scenes that subconsciously associated Packard with the fortunate few in the democracy who could afford to live that well. The 120, by
contrast, spoke to a depression middle class, affluent enough to afford a
new car that cost more than the lower-priced three, but whose members
still had to count their pennies. The juniors were built for professionals,
those who "earned" a regular wage and could calculate with some precision whether they could afford the down payment and the monthly in-
stallments necessary to procure such a luxury. It was the difference between buying Waterford crystal and Fiestaware during the depression;
crystal was more costly, but Fiestaware was tasteful and wore like iron.

The Fiestaware middlebrows who flocked to the junior Packards
knew that they were buying a mass-produced product. Gilman and
Christopher, with their money-saving machinery and techniques, had
forever ended any pretense that Packards were assembled with any more
loving care than, say, Buicks. The great Packards had not been hand-
assembled for decades, of course, but Packard had long taken pains
to advertise its craftsmen's careful attention to each of the expensive

cars before it was shipped. The buying public, even its Methodist component, was not stupid: when Packard manufactured more than 100,000 cars a year, people knew that the company used common mass-production techniques.

Even the rich and the famous who bought the expensive Packards in the late 1930's eroded the company's prestige. For years Packard had publicized its cars with the royals and the rich who were discerning enough to buy them. By the end of the depression, however, its expensive cars were increasingly purchased by Hollywood celebrities. Bob Hope, Al Jolson, Clifton Webb, and Gary Cooper, and even Franklin Roosevelt and his son, Elliott, were socially a cut below the earlier Packard loyalists. The new buyers were a tad too flashy and ostentatious by former standards, and the Episcopalians who had bought Packards had become much more private people. They were rarely seen riding behind their chauffeurs, and Packard's reputation suffered in proportion to their reclusiveness. On the other hand, people were seen everywhere driving their 120s and 110s to their offices.

The loss of the Twelve in 1939 and the decline in the number of custom-bodied Packards also hurt the cars' prestige. Twelve cylinders were fairly unusual on American roads in the 1930's, and so were extremely long wheelbase models graced with one-off, specially styled bodies. The yoked Packard hood never lost its following. In one form or another, it remained a company trademark until the very end. But that same grille at the end of the 110's stubby hood lacked the quality that conferred distinction and prestige.

Packard's prestige also suffered from Bill Packer's hard-sell techniques and the rapid growth of company dealerships. Macauley had worked closely with his dealers. He liked them well capitalized, willing to spend lavishly to display his Packards, often among Persian rugs, objets d'art, fresh flowers, and ornate furnishings. Macauley's dealers beguiled customers, sold to their social equals, and catered to the buyers' every whim. Bill Packer, however, was less interested in displaying Packards than in selling them. To that end, he preached the "fast closing" techniques that had proved so successful at Chevrolet. Moreover, in doubling his sales organization, he signed up new dealers with less capital and without the social standing that Macauley and the older hands preferred. Many would have been just as happy selling Mercurys or Pontiacs, but Packer promised a better deal than the Big Three could offer.

In terms of prestige and reputation, Packard stood at a crossroads by 1940, no longer what it once was, yet uncertain about what it was to become. Most observers agree that it was exactly at this point, between 1935 and 1940, that the critical decisions were made that sealed

Packard's fate. The company wrestled with a catch-22 proposition: the junior line allowed it to survive the depression, but the cheaper cars cost Packard its sterling reputation as the premier automaker after World War II. What the observers ignored, however, was that Packard was still a relatively small, wealthy company with room to maneuver – it had years to reposition itself in the industry. Macauley had always been flexible, but the men who followed, "scientific managers" in the modern sense, possessed not even half the old man's willingness to change. They played it safe, perhaps too safe. They built good automobiles, but not ones distinctive enough to justify the firm's existence.

Most writers agree that the junior cars were absolutely necessary, even if they reduced Packard to a common object with less intrinsic value and left it a medium-priced producer with only pretensions to being anything more. Richard Stout, however, argued that the 120 fatally wounded the company. Stout joined the product-planning department in June 1953, and as he struggled to bring Packard back into the luxury market to challenge Cadillac, he keenly felt Packard's loss of reputation. He concluded that things had started going wrong when Packard introduced the 120. Furthermore, because the Clipper was much the same car as the 120, Stout believed that the two of them "dragged the Packard name down" and compromised its reputation. By the 1950's, the company's image was so tarnished that its president, James J. Nance, was "overwhelmed" in his drive to refurbish its prestige.[32]

George Packard Lott, in his article "Why We Lost Packard – An Opinion," presented a slight variation on Stout's theme. Lott admitted that Packard would have died in the 1930's without the 120 and the 110, but he argued that if they saved the company, "they also killed it." The second great mistake the company's managers made, Lott contended, was shipping the senior car dies to the Soviet Union during the war at Franklin Roosevelt's request. Over the long haul, "the loss of the senior models *combined with* Packard's decision to penetrate the medium priced field cost" the company "its heritage in trying to seek a new image."[33]

Packard's last president, Nance, in an interview with Richard Langworth and George Hamlin in 1976, agreed with Lott. Nance looked at business as one large marketing puzzle and evaluated Packard's junior line from the salesman's point of view. Packard made a very bad mistake, Nance contended, in "bringing out their small car under the name Packard, which had a distinguishing front end design which was really the Packard trademark." He concluded philosophically that "you can always downgrade a name. That's easy in merchandising, to take a high-priced product and bring it down the price scale." He added, "In my judgment as a marketing man, they just turned the luxury car business over to Cadillac on a silver platter." [34]

It must have been easier for Nance, an outsider who came into the firm long after such decisions had been made, to pass judgment than it was for Owen Goodrich, who was with the company during all the years under discussion, to render such a detached verdict. Yet he fully agreed with Nance, if for different reasons. "Most of us who worked at Packard," he remembered, "felt that the One Twenty was the start of the company's downfall. It was the wrong merchandising decision." The 120 was a good car, but it was one you would see "on the other side of the tracks." [35]

Packard fell, Goodrich concluded, because its managers forgot the difference between "quality" and "luxury." "Mr. Joy, Mr. Macauley and all their associates (directors and board members) were of the highest quality up until about 1940," Goodrich wrote. In that year "those of us who were there at the time could feel the change. . . . The people brought in to build the 120 . . . ruined the firm." [36]

Others agreed. William B. Harris, in a 1954 *Fortune* article, stated that Packard "dominated the luxury market, both in volume and prestige, from about 1921 until 1935." Packard's problem was obvious, he thought. It "nearly wrecked itself by trading down its great name." The company made fewer high-priced cars, and the price of its trade-ins slipped. [37]

Lyman Slack, who had been "present at the creation" of the junior cars, disagreed. As sales promotion manager of the 120 division, he had a vested interest in seeing Packard successfully invade the medium-priced field. He emphatically asserted that "introducing the Junior line was NOT a mistake over the long run." He believed that into the early 1950's, when Nance was hired, "Packard's senior line of cars still led the group of prestige or high priced cars." His reasoning for this unpopular view was that "Cadillacs were being built at a *loss* to G.M.; . . . at least that was the 'gossip' in Detroit." Slack insisted that Packard undercut its own future right after the war when Christopher promised his dealers more cars. Operating on that promise, Slack beefed up Packard's dealer network. When Christopher failed to fulfill it, the whole corporate edifice began to crumble. [38]

Richard K. Phillips, author of "A Company Headed for Prosperity," the 120 chapter in Kimes's *Packard*, presented an even more spirited defense. The junior cars did not kill Packard, Phillips averred. Without them the company would have been destroyed by the depression. Packard was the only undiversified Independent to survive the hard times. He did wonder whether Packard was wise to use its traditional styling on the cheaper cars and whether they ought to have had another name. Packard's board debated calling the juniors Macauleys rather than Packards, but other companies' attempts to spin off newly named cars all failed: Studebaker's Erskine, Marmon's Roosevelt, Reo's Wolverine, Buick's Marquette, Olds's Viking, and the like. Phillips finally decided that use of the Packard name was probably wise in the 1930's, but postwar use of the name on its lower-priced offerings "was not so wise a choice."[39]

Phillips agreed with Arthur Einstein, who wrote his master's thesis on Packard's advertising efforts. Einstein believed that Packard's managers in the mid-1930's confronted a stark dilemma—compromise the Packard name or go out of business. "It would have been foolhardy to risk the very life of the Packard Motor Car Company by not trading on the Packard reputation, one of the major assets of the firm." But the new business "placed the destiny of the firm in the hands of the newly hired production and sales personnel," who burrowed deeper into the medium-priced field than its two major competitors. In the company's advertising, Einstein found abundant proof for his generalizations. He noted that Packard ads, right up to World War II, had no consistent theme to either the firm's traditional lap-robe customers or the larger audience who hungered for a quality-built, medium-priced vehicle.[40]

Robert Ebert took a much more detailed look at events in "An Economic Analysis of the Decline of the Packard Motor Car Company." After reviewing the shrinking luxury-car market and Macauley's reaction to it, he noted that Richard Naylor, who was in Packard's financial department at the time, reported that Macauley had talked about entering the medium-priced field back in 1927 and had set Vincent to work on a design. Naylor supported Packard's decision to build the 120, and Ebert agreed that it was a smart move. If blame was to be laid, Ebert implied that it should be placed squarely on Christopher for his refusal to retool the senior cars after 1935.[41]

Like Ebert and Naylor, Menno Duerksen was in accord that Macauley was "faced with the choice of joining the mass production market or else seeing the great Packard name wiped off the boards." He was joined by Robert E. Turnquist, who argued in *The Packard Story* that there was no question about whether Macauley's decision was a mistake. He and his colleagues had no other choice, and they saved the company for another twenty years.[42]

The class that bought the great Packard Twelves, however, disappeared under the depression's rubble, retreating behind the hedges of country clubs. Packard was compelled to court a new clientele, and its prosperity would depend upon what social reordering would emerge from the hard times. Events on the world's stage made Macauley's crystal ball even cloudier. The safest and most prudent course, Macauley and his new managers thought, was to stick to the medium-priced field and see what happened. Cadillac's executives, by contrast, gambled on the emergence of a new economic elite and set out to capture it.

Having guided Packard through the depression, Macauley turned the company's presidency over to Max Gilman. On paper, as chairman of the board, Macauley suffered no erosion of authority over the company's strategic policy-making, but the company suffered from managerial instability after him. Four men occupied Macauley's old office in the next fourteen years. This rotation did not lead to much change: subsequent presidents chiseled Macauley's policies in stone, and the company ossified.

By World War II, Packard had become a producer of cars in the $1,000 to $1,500 range. They were good cars, well engineered and well built, but realistically they were not what Packards had been in their heyday. Packard's Clipper proved that the company could innovate and assume styling leadership, and with the rather nice combination of the old hand, Macauley, and a coterie of energetic young manufacturing, costing, and sales personnel, the company was staffed with enough talent to succeed. When Packard ceased auto production in 1942, it stood at yet another corporate crossroads. The company needed a strategic long-range plan for the postwar automobile world that would ideally match its products with what was left of its sterling reputation.

Chapter 3

Model 18 "runabout," 1909

The Dogs
of War

T he decade after Pearl Harbor was not kind to Packard.
Virtually every problem that could beset a corporation plagued the auto
builders on East Grand, and as its rulers wrestled with the postwar world
they displayed none of the earlier, magical sense of corporate vision. Of
course, Gilman, Christopher, and later Hugh Ferry confronted a world
their predecessors had never imagined. They had honed their skills in
the struggle to survive the Great Depression and in the conflict to defeat
the Axis powers. In the sudden transition from depression to war, they
went from scarcity of customers to guaranteed government markets with
cost-plus clauses written into their contracts. Unfortunately, there was
not enough "plus" to ensure Packard a more secure financial future after the conflict was over.

War production proved to be easier and more stable than reconversion to building cars in peacetime. Despite years of forward planning,
peace in 1945 produced a host of conditions unfamiliar to the auto industry. Labor was unruly, inflation was a constant threat, government
controls remained, raw materials were in short supply, and new tools
were almost impossible to obtain at any price. Further, unemployment
was high, demand for new cars exceeded even the most optimistic
wartime estimates, and the industry's competitive picture was confused.

All the automakers brought out their warmed-over 1942 models and nervously eyed the competition to see what shape the first retooled postwar vehicles would take. Tooling was prohibitively expensive, and any misstep could be fatal, especially for the Independents. On the brighter side, the great postwar demand meant that the carmakers could sell everything they made, no matter how obsolete. But even that fact had its underside, which made everyone in the business nervous. When the seller's market evaporated, the manufacturers that had not prepared for the brave new buyer's world would not stay in business long. Packard officials could afford to manufacture the 1942 Clipper as long as the seller's market held, and it was to their financial advantage to do so. They just could not get caught with the prewar car when the market suddenly shifted.

At the start of that decade, the company had proved that it could radically change to meet wartime conditions. Even while it was planning the Clipper in 1940, its overworked engineering department, still headed by Vincent, took on the task of mass-producing sophisticated Rolls Royce aircraft engines. England had first asked Ford to manufacture copies of its Merlin engine. The Merlins were made by hand in England, where skilled workmen shaped each piece to fit the particular motor. After other companies declined to try to produce the engine, William S. Knudsen, GM's president, who served as Commissioner for Industrial Production, approached Vincent and Gilman.[1]

The challenge was exactly the sort of adventure that excited the 60-year-old Vincent. Under the intense wartime pressure, Packard built many of its own dies and machine tools, adapted what it had to fit specific needs, built a new factory wing dedicated to the Merlin, and at the same time brought out its new Clipper. By August 1941, Vincent had prototypes available for testing. They proved to be reliable and powerful, in the traditional Packard manner. During the war, the company manufactured 55,523 motors, which were used in the Mustang P-51, Mosquito, Lancaster, Warhawk, and Hurricane aircraft. In 1943, Secretary of the Treasury Henry Morgenthau, Jr., examined the operations and remarked that "only Packard had the nerve to tackle it, and the job I see done is remarkable."[2]

Packard also produced marine versions of the engine for wartime use. Starting in 1939, it began producing an 800-horsepower engine, which soon evolved into a 1,200-horsepower motor used in the U.S. Navy's 85- and 104-foot PT boats. A supercharged version of the engine produced 1,800 horsepower, and a PT boat with three or four of the motors was capable of hitting 47 miles per hour. By war's end, the company was working on a 16-cylinder, 2,500-horsepower engine for larger PT boats. Packard remained in the marine-engine business after the war and in its last years was still producing diesels for navy minesweepers.[3]

Under the company's cost-plus arrangements with the War Department, the government financed the machinery to build the Merlins, while Packard was responsible for tools, raw materials, and labor. By the middle of the war, more people were working for Packard than ever before, almost 36,000 employees, almost a third of whom were women.[4] For all its efforts, however, the firm did not enjoy much profit, earning only 1.2 percent on its war business from 1941 through 1945. That was less than the company could have made from investing its assets in war bonds. It was also hit hard by the excess-profits tax, a levy calculated on the firm's average earnings from 1936 through 1939, not particularly profitable years for Packard. Compared to its late 1920's earnings, Packard's wartime surpluses, which ranged from a low of $1.1 million in 1945 to a high of $4.7 million in 1942, were puny. Nevertheless, Gilman and Christopher pursued a very conservative fiscal policy during the war, and Packard retained a substantial part of its earnings. Not only did it keep its dividends at around ten to fifteen cents a share, but it set aside several million a year to fund reconversion costs. In 1945, Packard had no debt and almost $35 million in working capital, about $11 million less than before the war.[5]

Packard's upper management also changed during the war and did so in a manner that darkened the firm with its first scandal. The problems began when Gilman ran into a workmen's barricade on Woodward Avenue near Fourteen Mile on the night of January 22, 1942. He suffered a broken right leg and head injuries, and his passenger, Ruth Adams, broke her left leg. They were both hospitalized in Pontiac, Michigan. Adams was the wife of a fellow Packard executive. Detroit newspapers carried a brief announcement of the accident the next day, and then silence settled around the incident.[6]

Nothing more was said publicly for exactly three months, but privately a heated debate raged within the company. Arguments broke out among Packard executives over how to handle the embarrassing mess. One side wanted to let it blow over, since not much had appeared in the public press, and the other faction wanted to fire the president. Gilman, hurt quite badly, remained in the hospital, and finally on March 13 the forces in favor of restraint triumphed and his board appropriated $1,450 to convert a seven-passenger Packard to handle his wheelchair. But Macauley wanted Gilman out and, according to one source, sent a company executive to Gilman's hospital room to fire him. To protect Packard, the old man struck a deal with Gilman–in return for his silence, he would be allowed to resign and given a generous "separation allowance" later.[7]

No public announcement of Gilman's resignation was made until after the stockholders' meeting on April 20. On April 22, Gilman was given $50,000 to quietly vanish into the night, and the following day a careful Macauley told the press that Gilman had resigned "because of ill health dating from a January automobile accident" and that George Christopher was Packard's new president. Macauley had a long memory–he never spoke to Gilman again and blacklisted him at other auto companies. Gilman divorced his wife, married Ruth Adams, and took a job as general manager of General Tire and Rubber Company, later becoming its president. He retired with a General Tire distributor-ship in Los Angeles, and he lived in Beverly Hills, where his house was behind that of actress Joan Crawford. He died penniless in a hospital of heart trouble and cancer on February 28, 1965.[8]

Gilman's departure left a very different kind of person in Packard's driver's seat at a critical period in the company's history. Christopher's forte was things mechanical, and his newly added responsibilities for de-sign, advertising, marketing, public relations, and dealer relations were outside his previous experience. Christopher soon announced two gen-eral goals: he was "definitely committed to return to the automobile manufacturing business" and to some form of postwar diversification, which would grow out of Packard's wartime expertise. By the end of 1943, he was ready to explain the details. In his annual report, he pledged to produce more cars than before the war, vehicles that would be based on the 1942 Clipper. Moreover, he intended to find commercial markets for Packard's wartime engines.[9]

After Christopher's promise in his 1944 annual report that he would build 200,000 cars a year, the company revamped its dealer operations. Christopher went out to light a fire under them, established a deal-ers' advisory committee, signed up 267 new outlets, and negotiated a $30 million line of revolving bank credit to finance factory recon-version. On October 25, 1944, Packard's board authorized more than $2.8 million to begin the reconversion to auto production. The board continued to add to that amount until, by V-E Day, it had allocated about $4.5 million. And the heavy expenses were just beginning.[10]

Christopher did not mention building luxury cars again. Rumors were that President Roosevelt asked Packard during the war to give or sell its tooling for its big cars to America's allies, the Russians. Packard, in a spirit of wartime comradeship, happily obliged, and the Russians used the dies to produce the ZIS. The problem is that there is not a whit of supporting evidence—no letters, no eyewitness accounts, no mention in the company's annual reports or its board of directors' minutes. It seems queer that such a patriotic gesture could have passed unremarked. The postwar ZIS, when viewed from the front, is pure Packard, but its body differs in many important respects and could not have been struck from the old Packard dies. A more plausible explanation is that the dies were stored outdoors along with the rest of the company's machinery in 1942 and rusted in a vacant lot on East Grand, catercorner to what became Nance's office. They probably disappeared into a wartime scrap-metal drive. In any event, Christopher had only the Clipper's tooling to carry Packard into the postwar markets.[11]

Christopher needed all the help he could get, for all automakers were unprepared for the onslaught of reconversion problems. The litany he recited for his shareholders was daunting. After Japan surrendered, he said, the company had to terminate all its war contracts; to convert to auto production, which involved disposing of $35 million worth of raw materials and clearing government-owned machines worth $110 million out of its plant; to move some 3,200 Packard machines, stored outside for years, back to the factory floor for Clipper production; and to construct a new building for the final assembly line. The steel work for the addition started on September 13, 1945, but the building was far from complete when production began, albeit fitfully. Packard had to line up its suppliers, reconstitute its labor force, which had fallen from 41,000 to about 10,000, and rebuild its Utica test track. Chrysler had leased the track to test tanks and had destroyed it. Moreover, labor was restless as prices began to rise. Packard had endured 32 unauthorized work stoppages during the war and was facing a union demand for a 30 percent wage increase in 1945. That was postponed only because there was a strike at General Motors, and until the giant settled, none of the smaller companies dared make a move. Christopher could only hope that any wage increases would be offset by a rise in Packard's productivity, especially since the Office of Price Administration set new-car price ceilings that would not begin to cover the anticipated wage rise.[12]

It was amazing that Packard built any cars at all in 1945. A body dropped down on the first postwar Packard chassis on October 19, even before the roof had been installed over the body drop. From that date to the end of the year, the company produced just 2,722 cars, and Christopher warned his shareholders that parts and materials shortages would keep next year's production under predictions. He also said that Packard would have relatively high production costs which could not be offset by volume, and they should not look for "very satisfactory 1946 earnings." Packard was not alone in its predicament. George Romney, general manager of the Automotive Council for War Production, had been cautioning the general public all year that there would be no "volume production before late winter or early spring." Yet the *New York Times* discovered that the average car in the United States was over eight years old. American motorists were "running on well-worn equipment." [13]

The anticipated huge demand was the great lure for all automakers and especially the Independents. It was a seller's market, and Christopher hoped that Packard would get the "best possible volume of pent up demand for cars." He promised that Packard would produce 8,000 cars in 1945 and 100,000 the following year. Privately, however, Christopher was apprehensive about meeting the competition when the buyer's market reappeared. [14]

Manufacturing any cars was a lot harder than Christopher ever imagined. After his promise of 100,000 new Packards in 1946, he sat in his office overlooking his factory, which stood silent for 81 of the first 90 days of the new year, thanks to a strike at Packard's supplier of main and connecting rod bearings. The rest of the year was no picnic, either. Packard endured major strikes in the steel, coal, electrical, and transportation industries. Its own maintenance men struck for 7 days, and then the company lost another 67 days because of other vendors' strikes. Not the least of these was at Briggs, where 15,000 workers walked off their jobs and closed all Chrysler and Packard assembly plants. [15]

Packard's Briggs body contract had never been popular in the company's upper councils. William Graves, who became Packard's vice president of engineering, recounted how Briggs had convinced Macauley that he could make bodies more cheaply than Packard. Graves groused, "If we couldn't build bodies cheaper, we had no business being in the auto business." His fears were later borne out when Briggs raised the price of its bodies above what it would have cost Packard to produce its own. By then, however, the carmaker had disposed of its tools and machinery, and its start-up costs to get back into the business would have been very high. [16]

Christopher's goal of a 100,000-car year slipped away. He discovered that a shortage of raw materials, especially of cold-rolled sheet steel, threatened to close him down. The steel companies were in the same straits as auto producers were—they were stymied by labor troubles, worn-out equipment, rising wages, and a shortage of scrap iron. Packard even appealed to its dealers to "go through your business with a fine-tooth comb and get your scrap to a junk dealer as quickly as possible." Adding to Packard's woes, three of its prewar suppliers, which accounted for 60 percent of the company's steel requirements, sold their plants. Packard had to scrounge steel wherever it could, even as far away as Austria. Other Independents had their steel troubles as well. Henry Kaiser resorted to airplanes to bring steel to his Willow Run factory to keep the production lines rolling. Christopher worked around periodic steel shortages by using his work force in those periods to make more parts, especially those that required no steel.[17]

Through such methods, Christopher, in the first full year of peacetime production, turned out 42,102 autos, 62.9 percent of the company's 1941 production. Although that figure was disappointing, Christopher did beat the industry average of only 57.8 percent. But the company's bottom line showed a $3.9 million loss. Nevertheless, Packard's president remained upbeat, at least publicly. During a tour of Packard dealers and suppliers, he announced to the press that the company's $20 million expansion effort was about to bear fruit and that Packard was ready to turn out the by-now-fabled 200,000 automobiles per year. He also predicted that by the spring of 1947, auto companies would be at full production, making "it necessary for dealers to seek instead of dodge prospective buyers."[18]

Christopher tried to position Packard to meet the coming sales crunch. As early as possible in 1946 he expanded his model line and added 6-cylinder cars, primarily for use as taxicabs in New York City. In May he introduced the Super Eight with a 127-inch wheelbase, followed by the Custom Super Eight in June and a seven-passenger sedan. The cars, all with Clipper styling, put Packard entries into price classes from just over $1,000 to almost $5,000. A breakdown of sales, however, showed that 82 percent were in the $2,000-and-under range, hardly the "luxury class" Christopher liked to talk about publicly.[19]

Packard's 1946 marketing tactics may have been on target, but Christopher's plans for Packard's first new postwar car, the so-called bathtub Packard, did little to enhance the company's image. Preliminary estimates were that its tooling costs would run $8.5 million and that it could be introduced in September 1947. Christopher was so proud of the forthcoming Packard that he plastered a picture of the convertible version on the cover of his 1946 annual report, to give his stockholders a peek at its new styling and to announce that the company was going to build its first new convertible since the war. In fact, Packard rushed it to showroom floors in July 1947.[20]

The new car won numerous styling awards, but company stylists, like John Reinhart, were not enamored with it. He wanted to refine the basic Clipper, keep its vertical nose, and make the rest of its body more aerodynamic, to "sweeten the thing," as Reinhart later remembered. But Christopher wanted a fatter, lower version of the Clipper, and he got his way. Of all the cars that Packard produced, well over one million, the

22nd series caused the most controversy. In truth, a lot of bathtubs were sold, but to many people they were just plain ugly. Moreover, the car did not forge new styling paths, since it was patently a warmed-over version of the Clipper, and not a very good one at that. Tom McCahill, the most widely read automobile writer of the period, called the new Packard a "goat."[21]

If Packard had dominated any of its markets, the bathtub would have made little difference in the company's fortunes. But Packard was scrambling to survive in the upper-medium-price and luxury markets, and it could ill afford a "goat." What made the 22nd series look even worse was Cadillac's first postwar car, introduced in February 1948. A stunning creation, it was long and low from its restyled eggcrate grille and curved windshield to the biggest surprise of all, the pert tail fins that graced its rear fenders. It featured the aerodynamic styling Reinhart so badly wanted for his new Packards. Back in 1941, Harley Earl, who had become GM's styling vice president, had taken his designers to look at the still-secret P-38 Lightning fighter plane, a beautiful aircraft with twin tail fins. They took away a sense of line and shape that would dominate the car industry through the 1950's. Their early renderings, however, were not greeted with general applause—in fact, Earl returned from meeting with GM executives and told his stylists to "take that goddam fin off, nobody wants it." A week later, Cadillac's general manager told Franklin Hershey, who was in charge of advanced Cadillac design, to take the fins off or be fired. But Hershey stuck to his fins.[22]

Richard Langworth, noted automobile historian, observed that the new Cadillac's greatest contribution was to bring "product identity to the rear of the automobile." Traditionally such identity was limited to the grille, such as Packard's, which graced even its bathtubs. After 1948, however, a Cadillac was recognizable coming or going. By contrast, Christopher's new Packards displayed the weakest of rear-end styling.[23]

Worse, Cadillac in 1948 offered five different styles in its Series 75, priced from $4,479 to $5,199, against Packard's two top cars, which sold for a maximum of $4,868. The Series 75, however, still carried the prewar, traditional fine-car styling. It was the finned Cadillacs that sold faster than Cadillac could produce them. Priced from $2,728 to $3,820, they were more expensive than Packard's best-selling bathtub, the DeLuxe Eight, which retailed at a price from $2,125 to $3,425. But Cadillac had redefined the upper end of that market. A buyer who wanted a good $3,000 car went to Cadillac; one who wanted a good $2,000 car chose a Packard.[24]

General Motors increased the pressure on the East Grand Independent. In 1949, Cadillac introduced an overhead-valve V-8 that produced

160 horsepower. Although the new power plant was not all that much better than Packard's straight eight with its 145 horsepower, Cadillac identified its new engine with state-of-the-art technology, giving its dealers another edge. To make matters more difficult for Packard, Cadillac introduced at midyear a "convertible coupe," a Coupe de Ville that was a Series 62 convertible with a hardtop welded on it. Cadillac was not first with a hardtop. Chrysler had made a few the year after the war in its Town and Country series, and Kaiser-Frazer had tried it on its Virginian. But the hardtop Coupe de Ville was a hot item.[25]

Despite Cadillac's advances, Packard sales held their own; in fact, Packard narrowly outsold Cadillac from 1947 through 1949. But Christopher and his fellow executives could take scant comfort. Fully 30 percent of Packard's sales were 6-cylinder Clippers, which sold for well under $2,000. Cadillacs came only with a V-8. The situation did not improve much when the bathtubs went up against Earl's tail fins. Packard won in gross sales—98,897 cars to 66,209—but 70 percent were the cheaper Packards, which made the comparison unfair. When Packard celebrated its fiftieth anniversary in 1949, production topped the 100,000 mark for the first time since 1937, and it beat the General Motors division 104,593 to just 81,545. Cadillac was ensconced in the growing upper end of the market while Packard scrapped with Buick, Mercury, Oldsmobile, and Dodge for its customers.

Packard had become a vehicle for the fairly affluent middle class, and Cadillac was the younger money's car of choice. After Christopher kept the bathtub virtually unchanged for the 1950 season, he suffered a disastrous setback, selling only 72,138 copies against Cadillac's 110,535. Packard's executives had begun to understand that they had lost the race with General Motors and that Packard was in deep trouble.[26]

Chapter 4

Model 48, 1912

A Troubled
Packard

The chilling knowledge that Packard was sliding downhill toward disaster first penetrated its corporate offices in the late 1940's. It is impossible to pinpoint an exact date because the firm destroyed its papers after it abruptly closed its Detroit factory in 1956. Moreover, the minutes of the board of directors' meetings were carefully sanitized and often reveal more by what they omit than by what they actually say. Hugh Ferry, Packard's secretary, for example, never revealed conversations that took place around the table and often neglected to mention what topics were considered or whether the board voted. Given the board's clubby nature, however, that was not surprising. The directors rarely took the longer view of the market. They dealt with niggling matters, such as the cost of chrome trim around windshields or whether to build convertibles or station wagons, issues that managers should have resolved. If we read between the lines, it is clear that some time in 1947 the congeniality and comity that had long marked board deliberations began to disappear. The fractures began with Christopher's failure to make good on his pledge to produce 200,000 cars a year. According to Lyman Slack, the last surviving board member from that era, Christopher had promised that he would run two full assembly lines after the war and charged Slack with building a dealer network large enough to handle the

increased output. This Slack did, getting rid of many private distributorships and establishing a "direct dealer" method of shipping cars and
parts. A few privately owned distributorships remained, such as Earle
Anthony's Los Angeles operation, but most were purchased and set up
as company-run zone operations. Slack also recruited new dealers and
built the number of Packard outlets up to 1,800.[1]

By late 1947, Slack and the board knew that Christopher would never
meet his goal because of the critical shortage of sheet steel. Packard
dealers were screaming for more cars, and pressure on the board was so
intense that in June 1947 it began approving the purchase of steel wherever the company's managers could find it, even from other automakers
that had laid in a surplus. They paid premium prices which drove
Packard's cost per car up. By early 1948 the steel crisis was so bad that
the directors approved a $2.25 million loan to Detrola Corporation to
buy a steel mill being sold by the War Assets Administration. Slack dared
suggest to his fellow directors that Packard should buy a steel mill across
the river from Cincinnati, even if it meant taking a loss when the mill
was resold. The board ignored him. As Slack later noted, "the average
age of our Board members was seventy plus. I was not yet forty five and
my ideas were not considered mature or 'long range.'" The company
eventually contracted with seven different steel suppliers.[2]

The Korean War forced Packard to get involved in the steel business.
The automaker had just brought out its all-new 24th series in August
1950 when it discovered that there was not enough steel for the next two
quarters of production. The board first authorized overseas purchases,
but buying steel at premium prices on the open market was not the answer. The following year Packard loaned the Pittsburgh Steel Company
$2 million in return for a guaranteed tonnage over five years. The deal
indicated just how far the directors were willing to go to ensure an adequate supply of steel for Christopher.[3]

Despite these problems, Packard was fiscally healthy and showed a
profit every year but one from 1947 through 1953. But its profits were
small and, even after car prices were raised several times, never reached
the eight-digit range. Its working capital stayed stuck between $36 mil-
lion and $46 million. Luxuries that the public was coming to expect as
standard features, such as automatic transmissions, strained the resources of a company Packard's size. When the 1948 Cadillac offered a
hydromatic transmission, Packard had nothing to counter it. Vincent
had experimented with such devices as far back as the 1930's, but the
firm had felt no need to spend huge sums on such a project. Cadillac's
new option, however, galvanized Packard's board. On May 12, 1948, it
authorized the development of an automatic transmission, estimating

the cost at between $5 million and $7.5 million. But as Cadillac owners were shifting their cars into "drive" that fall, Packard was still tinkering with its own Ultramatic.[4]

In what must have been record time, Packard introduced its optional Ultramatic in May 1949. The new transmission featured a novel arrangement, a torque converter, like Buick's Dynaflow, attached to a direct drive mechanism that operated like an overdrive. Packard was the only Independent to build its own automatic transmission, and the cost was high. The company was forced to report a fourth-quarter loss in 1949 when the board decided to amortize the Ultramatic's tooling costs over only a fifteen-month period. Packard's costs did not end there. General Motors sued for patent infringements, and the case wound its way through the courts until Packard ceased to exist. The problem, as one wag put it, was that all torque converters looked alike, and therefore Packard had to be guilty. Richard Stout remembered that he heard Bill Graves, Packard's chief engineer, say that the technical development of the Ultramatic was too big for Packard to handle, so it copied Buick's Dynaflow. Whether Packard copied or not, the company had to stretch its resources to play catch-up with the competition.[5]

The East Grand manufacturer was still a company with many assets: modern production facilities, a talented engineering department, and the magic of its name. As other Independents looked into their crystal balls they realized that Packard had a lot to offer as a merger partner. And the fact that some well-placed Packard executives were seriously considering such a union in 1948 spoke volumes about the severity of the company's troubles.

The Independents' declining share of the car market after World War II intensified merger interest. Combinations among those firms with noncompeting automobiles looked sensible, for the merged companies could then whittle suppliers' prices, build a stronger dealer system offering models in several price ranges, and bring about economies of scale through compression of executive payrolls, interchangeability of bodies and parts, and shared production facilities. The Independents' creditors uniformly pushed for mergers. The Independents, however, were ruled by strong, willful men, each of whom enjoyed running his own show.

Packard's name was linked to all the other Independents at one time or another, but there were only two proposals solid enough to come before Packard's board. The first came in 1947 from the new entry in the automotive world, the Kaiser-Frazer Corporation. The company was a merger between Joe Frazer's Graham-Paige and Henry Kaiser, a California construction magnate fresh from his successes in wartime shipbuilding. Kaiser-Frazer appeared to be the postwar business success story–it made profits by 1947 and appeared ready to challenge the Big Three. But the company spent money lavishly, and the nearer its automobiles got to the end of the assembly line, the more costly they became. As finally priced, they competed directly with the lower and larger end of Packard's range, about $2,000 to $2,500, a field that was already overcrowded. In the summer of 1947, Kaiser approached James McMillan, a Packard board member, offering to purchase a large block of Packard stock with an eye to an eventual merger. Kaiser was lured by Packard's fiscal health, good name, and rather sluggish managerial team. If he could buy an entry into the upper-priced markets, he could achieve sufficient production to push downward and compete with the Big Three.[6]

Lyman Slack, who sat on Packard's board at the time, remembered that "the proposed Kaiser merger question didn't take much of the Board's time, because we all knew Kaiser didn't have the expertise to be a strong competitor in our industry." Without registering a vote in its minutes, the board decided "not to entertain the proposal." Although some of the board members' disdain for Kaiser may have arisen from a smug superiority that had enveloped Packard for decades, the board made the right decision. Although Kaiser-Frazer looked like a winner in 1947 when it outproduced Packard by almost two to one, it never made a profit after 1948 and had lost $78,341,369 by the time it built its last car in June 1955.[7]

The second proposal, from George Mason, president of Nash-Kelvinator Corporation, was more seriously considered at the East Grand headquarters. Mason was a man from the same mold as Gilman and Christopher, a type that appeared to fascinate the staid, aging Macauley. Mason attended the University of Michigan, where he studied engineering and business administration, and after graduation he went with Studebaker, Dodge, Maxwell, and finally Chrysler, where in 1924 he was put in charge of manufacturing. He left Chrysler to go into the refrigeration business with Copeland Products, from which he was lured to Kelvinator Corporation, whose sales he quadrupled in just eight years. Meanwhile, Charles Nash was looking for young, energetic blood to rejuvenate his company, and he spotted Mason, who refused all his overtures. Nash then bought Kelvinator to get Mason, who became president of the corporation.

The dry facts of Mason's career do not begin to do him justice; he was a colorful, flamboyant man who loved the outdoors, huge cigars, and good male company at some remote place where they could all shoot varmints and fish to their hearts' content. Oddly, Mason, the fervent sportsman, was also a conservationist–he founded Ducks Unlimited. One of his most copied photographs shows him with a cigar stub clenched between his teeth and a dozen more cigars sticking out of his pocket; he is wearing a broad smile and a fisherman's hat stuck all over with fishing flies. Like Macauley, Mason was a good golfer and, like most men who seemed intrigued with purchasing Packard, he was huge. Everyone described him as a happy man who never forgot a name, and donated his time to charitable causes such as the Boy Scouts and Finding Guide Dogs. If he had weaknesses, they were that he avoided anything unpleasant for as long as possible and that he was inarticulate in public.[8]

Mason and Macauley were old friends dating back to the 1920's. Mason probably suggested a merger of their two companies, and by September 1947 their informal discussions had proceeded far enough that Macauley brought Packard's general counsel, Henry Bodman, into the talks and the companies inspected each other's facilities. In October, *Business Week* reported gossip heard at the Detroit Athletic Club about the proposed merger. When Christopher announced publicly during Christmas week that Packard had made a deal that would get it enough steel to manufacture 50 to 100 percent more cars, most of the press assumed that the merger had gone through. *Business Week,* however, kept a cooler head and printed a small story in which it guessed that the "deal isn't dead; but there isn't much life in it."[9]

There may not have been much life in the deal, but it engendered a very lively discussion at Packard's board meeting. The fact that a detailed seven-point proposal made it to the board indicated that some important faction was in favor of the merger. When Nash had made overtures in 1929 and 1946, no such document ever reached Packard's directors. Evidence points to Macauley, still chairman, Bodman, and Robert Parker, the board's "old hands," as ardent supporters of the merger. Macauley knew that all was not well within the company. By 1948 he was disillusioned with Christopher's leadership but was equally unsure about who should succeed him. The most careful way around the conundrum was a merger that would open up all managerial positions, thus enabling him to ease Christopher out and replace him with a trusted friend from outside.

The deal Mason and Macauley proposed to Packard's board at a special meeting on February 3, 1948, was that Nash take over Packard through a stock exchange in which six shares of Packard would be traded for each share of Nash-Kelvinator. The most telling aspect of the plan, however, was that Macauley was willing to allow Charles Nash to become the new chairman of the board and Mason the president of the combined companies. There was no room for Christopher; his reaction to the plan could only have been negative. All five men in the boardroom that day–James McMillan, who had just assumed his late father's seat, Macauley,

Bodman, Christopher, and Vincent–are dead, and the surviving minutes of that meeting were sanitized. But it is clear that some members of
the board–certainly Macauley and Bodman–had pursued the union, for
six months must have expected the proposal, and knew its general outline before the meeting. Secretary Hugh Ferry noted in his minutes that
a motion was made on Nash's offer and that it was "duly supported" but
later "declined." [10]

Strong circumstantial evidence indicates that the board fight was furious and its repercussions long-lasting. Macauley and Bodman left that
meeting, and the chairman did not reappear until the April 2 gathering, two weeks after he had announced his resignation as chairman
and board member. Bodman resigned on March 17, along with Robert
Parker, who had been in ill health since the end of 1947. Their resigna-
tions caught everyone by surprise, evidenced by the confusion that followed. The annual stockholders' meeting was scheduled for April 19,
and Christopher and his supporters wanted everything cleared up before then. The actions taken in the five board meetings between turning
Nash's offer down and the stockholders' meeting were bizarre but revealing. At the meeting after the Nash vote, the board selected for a vacant seat Hugh Ferry, the genial secretary-treasurer of the company, a
man likely to support the president's policies. At the March 10 meeting,
the board filled the three new vacancies, and its choices were interesting. W. Tom ZurSchmiede, at 51, was a director of Crowley, Milner Company, a Detroit department store, chairman of the executive committee
of Federal Screw Works, and a director of the Grosse Pointe Bank. Henry
Bogle, who took Bodman's seat on the board, was also a member of
Bodman, Longley, Bogle, Middleton & Armstrong, Packard's legal
counsel. Earle C. Anthony, the company's second-oldest distributor and
second-largest stockholder, was not expected to attend many meetings
and did not disappoint his supporters. The board was still full of "insiders," but it had a more youthful cast. [11]

Macauley had been maneuvering behind the scenes since February
1948 to oust Christopher. He wanted George Romney, a man he had
been watching since before the war. In February 1948 he asked him
to join Packard as executive vice president with a seat on the board.
Macauley and Romney met with Christopher, and a contract, drawn up
by Bodman, offered Romney $50,000 a year and the firm's presidency
within two years. Romney was ready to accept, but Mason counseled him
not to, explaining that Packard's management had become flabby during the war with its cost-plus contracts and that he had heard rumors of
dissension among the company's elderly officers. Instead, Mason hired

Romney on a similar contract. Macauley thus retired from Packard with his plans for a merger and an able management team shattered. Ferry had the last word when he later noted that the Nash merger need not have fallen through: "We might have been agreeable to a 55 to 45 percent arrangement." So the basic problem was not with Nash taking over Packard, but rather with the division being "66⅔ to 33⅓ in favor of Nash."[12]

Curiously, Macauley, at age 76, left Packard the year before its fiftieth anniversary. His resignation induced the board to discuss the company's problems more openly. It was almost as if the old man's absence freed the directors for the first time to admit that things were very much awry at East Grand. The minutes of their meetings became more specific and noted the subjects they discussed. Their frequent return to the same problems every two weeks indicated the pressing nature of the problems and the directors' inability to solve them. The recurring topics also reflected the deep divisions over the company's future plans. Christopher's preoccupation with what could only be described as "crisis management" for the next twenty months, from April 1948 to October 1949, precluded any serious consideration of repositioning Packard in the automobile markets. Vital time was lost, and when sales of Packard's bathtub models began to sag, the company had no final plans for new cars on the drawing boards.

Of immediate importance to the company after Macauley's resignation, however, was to keep cars moving on the assembly line. Christopher could finally announce at the shareholders' meeting in April 1948 that he had enough steel to produce 104,000 new cars. In his annual report he boasted that the "better availability" of steel had enabled the company to earn its almost $10 million profit. Packard also enjoyed fairly stable labor relations in 1948. The UAW-CIO did close the plant down for half a day on June 17 in a wildcat strike, and a walkout at a Bendix brake plant shut Packard down the first week in July. Then a strike by Briggs guards closed Packard for fifteen days in September. Even with these interruptions, Christopher manufactured almost 99,000 new cars. He was more upbeat than usual, crowing that 1948 was the company's second-best production year and fourth best earnings year ever. He was running two assembly lines through his mile-long assembly plant, turning out 70 cars per hour with 10,848 employees, up almost 4,000 from the year before. Increased volume gave better economies of scale and still enabled Packard, he thought, to maintain its traditional quality. And he proudly pointed out that of the more than one million Packards produced since 1899, over 50 percent were still on the road.[13]

On the downside, Christopher complained that research, engineering, and development costs were running two and one-half to three times higher than they had in the prewar period and that tooling expenses had soared even more. He carefully neglected to explain how Packard was going to compete in an industry where three-year model changes were becoming the norm. Publicly, he gave the impression of business as usual and promised more of the same. He took comfort in predictions–such as one offered by *U.S. News & World Report* in November, to the effect that "backed-up auto demand" would remain high–to rationalize his decision to remain with the status quo.[14]

Even Christopher must have had the jitters, however, when he read *Business Week*'s January 1948 article on car sales. It said that the greatest demand was for lower-priced autos and the greatest weakness was in the luxury markets. In the $4,000-plus price range, where Packard had three of its thirteen models, sales were extremely soft for everyone except Cadillac. Worse, the magazine observed, it should not take long for "signs of saturation to show up in the next-to-the-top cars" if prices took another upturn, which they did that fall. Its prediction turned out to be amazingly accurate.[15]

The competition also threatened Packard. Buick was due out with a brand-new car late in the year, a "Riviera" two door hardtop. Chevrolet was scheduled to release its revamped models in the beginning of 1949, and although they did not threaten Packard, their new styling aped Cadillac's and would help entrench styling norms that worked against Packard's bathtubs. The new, boxy-looking 1949 Fords were introduced in June, and by the end of the following month Ford had 2 million factory orders on hand. Chrysler retained its square look and high roofline, but it was more significantly changed than Packard. *Newsweek* observed dryly that "both Hudson and Packard, having recently introduced wholly new postwar cars, are resting on their laurels."[16]

There were no great changes in the 1949 Packards. Even the press felt obliged to remark that Packard's "anniversary gold" cars, all 2,000 of them, looked just like last year's models, only in a different color. Christopher announced that he was biding his time, waiting for just the right moment to bring out a new Packard. According to *Newsweek*, that moment arrived in the third week of January 1949, when it headlined an article "Back to Normalcy–and Competition." If that was the crucial turning point in the postwar automobile market, it caught Packard asleep. The company had not even decided when it was going to retool or what its next model should look like. Yet by 1949 the buying public was beguiled by a welter of completely redesigned cars, and Packard dealers were still displaying a basic body introduced in 1941. Despite all the evidence that a seller's market was dawning, Christopher refused to authorize the design and production of a brand-new Packard.[17]

His dealers were also unprepared. Many of Packard's 1,563 sales agencies at the end of 1948 were undercapitalized, and for the first time Packard had to loan money to keep outlets in critical locations and to help with start-up costs. To make matters worse, Christopher's insistence that he was going to produce 200,000 cars per year had emboldened some dealers to spend lavishly in anticipation of the promised selling spree. When the outpouring of new Packards failed to materialize, they were justifiably angry. And Christopher introduced his 1949 models while his dealers still had their lots full of 1948s. When the factory began producing the 1949s, the assembly line did not even hesitate, but although the cars were almost identical, it was important to dealers not to get stuck with 1948s in the 1949 selling year. *Fortune* pointed out that in the 24 months of this jockeying between Packard and its dealers, 500 of the company's dealerships threw in the towel.[18]

Christopher, who begrudged every dollar the company spent, went before his board on March 23, 1949, to ask for more than $2 million in company funds to help his dealers dispose of their 22nd series cars. Six weeks later, the day after Packard introduced its anniversary automobiles, he announced price reductions that left year-old models in dealers' hands with higher price tags than the 1949s. The dealers howled, and Christopher had to spend $1.6 million in May to cover the deeper price cuts the factory had to make on the unsold 1948s. A customer could purchase a 1948 four-door Packard for as little as $1,558; Christopher, in a speech to 25-year company veterans, explained that Packard's average retail price had dropped 53 percent in 25 years, from $4,650 to $2,249, while its costs of raw materials had soared—steel was up 53 percent, copper 78 percent, iron 127 percent, and coke 311 percent. The press played it up as notice that Packards were now cheap cars, which was hardly the case, even with the company's recent price reductions.[19]

All automobile companies lowered their prices as the national auto market softened. Packard, however, with its smaller output, was hurt more than the larger firms. By May 23 its board was clearly worried. The directors granted Christopher his dealer-aid money but also ordered him to hire the Don Mortrude organization to help with future styling. Clearly the directors did not feel secure about competing in the changing marketplace with barely reworked versions of their products. Yet some time between late May and the middle of September, the directors' concerns notwithstanding, Christopher made up his mind to ride another year with the bathtubs and ordered his stylists to do a face-lift. By then, a coterie of upper-management officials, believing that Christopher was leading the company to an early corporate grave with his pinchpenny policies, had informally approached the directors. William Graves, Packard's chief engineer, George Reifel, vice president of manufacturing, Karl Greiner, vice president and general sales manager, and Eugene Hoelzle, vice president and comptroller, were among the leaders. These men, sensitive to market forces, were convinced that Packard had to retool for the 1951 season to beat the major auto companies, which were expected to introduce new models in 1952.[20]

Graves confronted Christopher directly, saying that he would not rework the bathtub design, and that if ordered to do so, he would resign. He then left town for a vacation. Aware that Graves spoke for others and that his board was becoming restless, Christopher capitulated. When Graves returned ten days later, Christopher ordered him to begin work on a 24th series car to be introduced in late 1950, just a year later. And Christopher must have been genuinely alarmed when, at the board's September 14 meeting, the directors established something called the "consulting committee." The members were Brodie from the board, and Graves, Greiner, Reifel, Hoelzle, and Milton Tibbetts, corporate counsel. The committee was formed for the express "purpose of counseling with the Board upon request, either in person or as a group."[21]

With this formal conduit to the board, Packard executives could run controversial corporate policies around the president, who was characterized by *Fortune* as "so much sand in the gears." The board was more candid at year's end when it reconstituted the group as the "Operating Committee," added another board member, Vincent, and charged the committee to bring "the combined knowledge of its members to bear on all important operating problems before a final decision is reached and recommended action agreed upon." The directors were determined to take a more active role in running the company, and with the creation of the consulting committee, they clearly compromised Christopher's authority. Further, they showed their support for Graves and his colleagues, who had, probably with some directors' tacit approval, stood Christopher down on the question of a new model. Christopher was not stupid; he understood what the board had done and the implications for his own position. The old engineer and manufacturing boss reacted by digging in and fighting the obvious.[22]

Throughout the summer of 1949, John Reinhart, the company's chief stylist, and his design men worked on the new Packard. By the board meeting on September 28, Reinhart and his people had mock-ups ready to display at Briggs. Prior to the viewing, however, the board met with its consulting committee over lunch and discussed the new car. Christopher was at that meeting and must have been anything but comfortable—his comments were sparse indeed. Someone mentioned that the tooling bill for the 24th series would be about $18.6 million. That would not pauperize Packard, with its $43 million in working capital, but it came just as the firm was writing off its $7 million investment in the Ultramatic. Christopher recommended that the tooling costs be amortized over two production years of 125,000 automobiles each, even though only four months earlier he had demanded a third year to write off the $8 million or so that the bathtub tooling had cost. Such a plan would have increased Packard's costs on the new car by about $75 each. No decision on amortization was made at the meeting, but after lunch the board went over to Briggs, inspected Reinhart's new cars, and authorized their production.[23]

When Christopher left the September 28 meeting, he was so outraged that he asked for a special board meeting to settle affairs. Presumably on the spur of the moment, the board met illegally on October 5, having forgotten to sign the necessary document to waive notice of the special meeting. Recognizing its oversight, the board drew up the required notice seven days afterward. This meeting merited even fewer lines than usual in the official minutes, but Ferry did leave a few clues about what transpired.[24]

Only five directors were there: Bogle, Ferry, Christopher, Vincent, and ZurSchmiede. For Vincent and Ferry, who had been around since Macauley's early days, the scene must have been disheartening. The five had what Ferry blandly described as "a discussion of the affairs of the Company." With Christopher's well-known penchant for speaking his mind in the saltiest language, the discussion must have been anything but polite. Secondary sources indicate that Christopher lost his temper, resigned as president, and stalked out. But that does not fit the surviving evidence. Lyman Slack, who had just left the board, was later told that the directors asked Christopher to resign at a special meeting held in New York. Although the special meeting was held in Detroit, the rest of what Slack heard fits more neatly with Ferry's note in the official minutes. Ferry and Vincent talked by telephone to Earle Anthony, the firm's second-largest stockholder and member of the board, *during* the meeting, and Anthony "concurred in the actions of the board." Had Christopher stalked out, there would have been no need to consult Anthony. Ferry could have telephoned him after the meeting and filled him in on the details. More likely, there were hard words, and with Anthony's agreement, Christopher's resignation was demanded. To save face, he was allowed to resign. He was later quoted as saying that "farming is a damned sight easier than the auto business—you don't have so many bosses on a farm." That could only have been in reference to the powers the board and its consulting committee held over him.[25]

Christopher's firing had certainly not been planned, for the directors had no successor in mind. They may have thought about the contingency, however, for although Christopher's resignation did not go into effect until December 31, the board at the same meeting appointed Hugh Ferry executive vice president, to serve until "his successor is elected." It is possible that the call to Anthony was to get his approval for Ferry's appointment. But it was doubtful that Ferry, even in that gathering of old friends, would have remained in the meeting while he was being discussed for his new position. Yet he and Vincent both conferred with Anthony, and there is no indication that two calls were made.[26]

Packard's former president was not tossed out into the cold. As it had when Gilman was fired in 1942, the company took care of its own. At the October 26 meeting, the board granted its former president his normal salary, almost $153,000 a year, until the end of 1949. He would then begin receiving installments of his $75,000 separation pay, which would be paid off before the April stockholders' meeting. The board also had a new Packard delivered to Christopher in January and charged him only the factory cost. He "retired" to his Tipp City farm and devoted the remainder of his life to bringing industrial techniques to his cattle, hog, and dairy operations. But he did not long enjoy his beloved rural ambiance; he died on June 7, 1954, at the age of 66.[27]

Christopher's ouster pointed up the weaknesses in the company's organizational structure and the profound changes that had shaken the corporation since the end of the depression. Like his successors, Christopher left his personal imprint on Packard. Its organization, methods of handling business, plans for the future, and position in the national auto markets were all the products of his temperament. Packard had always been highly personalized, and Gilman and Christopher had drawn more powers to the presidency. When the board lopped off its head, it may have slowed the relentless march toward the financial precipice, but the action also left the company without a strong force to move it in new directions. Unlike General Motors, where a decentralized committee structure weighed all decisions, Packard preferred the less time-consuming and more flexible stance of trusting such strategy choices to its chief executive. For an Independent, that structure made a great deal of sense, but it also demanded talent waiting to assume control when anything went terribly wrong. By 1949, when it was all going terribly wrong, the company's directors had to turn to Hugh Ferry, the arch-bureaucrat, who said publicly he did not have the talent to be Packard's president and did not want the job.

Nowhere were the changes that had convulsed Packard more apparent than in Ferry's dreary assertion to his stockholders that "Packard is producing automobiles of a character and price distinctly competitive with other makes of cars in the medium priced field, as much of our recent advertising and promotional activities have stressed." Ferry was only being honest, except that Packard was not quite as competitive in price as he would have liked, and it was technologically lagging behind its middle-priced competitors as well. Christopher had succeeded far beyond his dreams: his former company was now building Pontiacs and Buicks just like the ones he had manufactured before he came to Packard. Lacking the economies of scale enjoyed by General Motors, Ford, and even Chrysler, Packard's managers feared that they could not stay in business long in a truly competitive market.[28]

Before all this could be sorted out, however, Packard had to find someone with vision, a feel for the public pulse, an organizational genius, and a penchant for working miracles. The search took too long, over two and one-half years. Although the company already had its new car well under way and it promised to be a winner, the time lag meant that whoever was hired to replace Ferry would already be behind in planning for the next model. As the months stretched to years, the firm's managers and directors understood the dangers of dallying and tried to lay a groundwork for new corporate directions. Packard still responded best to a strong leader's hand on the wheel, and important decisions had to await the selection of that man.

Chapter 5

Model 326 "Opera Coupe," 1926

The Ferry
Years

Hugh Joseph Ferry, who presided over Packard's fortunes from October 5, 1949, to May 1, 1952, is the company's most underrated chief executive. His place in Packard's history, sandwiched between two more dominant personalities, the pugnacious Christopher and the flamboyant merchandising maestro Nance, was by most accounts a fateful interregnum during which the company's downhill slide accelerated. Ferry was noted for his lack of strong leadership; his most memorable utterance was his Hardingesque statement that he was unfit for the position of president.

In reality, however, Ferry was one of the most important men to rule Packard. In his own unassuming way, he left his indelible mark on the firm: he fashioned most of the policies that Nance followed until 1956. Almost every strategy that Nance claimed as his own, in his efforts to resuscitate Packard, originated in the Ferry years. Ferry planned the production of Packard's first V-8. Ferry bought the patent rights for the torsion-bar suspension system that Nance sprang on the public in 1955. Ferry contracted to build the Pan American, the forerunner of Nance's much-heralded Caribbean. Ferry pointed out that women were increasingly important in decisions about buying new cars. Ferry gambled the company's resources to tool for defense contracts, to bring in profits he could use to bolster Packard's sagging automotive fortunes. Ferry helped bring new blood into Packard's boardroom, men who had ties to national financial districts. Ferry started the firm's first executive pension plan, which Nance used to make room for his new managers. Ferry championed a merger to keep the Independents in business and brought George Mason, Chicago bankers, and Nance together to plan the formation of what they hoped would be American Motors. Ferry focused Packard's attention on its advertising efforts. Ferry brought in outside consultants to criticize and propose new corporate directions. And Ferry, the consummate Packard insider, in a bold stroke, entrusted Packard's fate to an industry stranger.

On paper, Ferry was the perfect man to lead Packard out of its doldrums. When he took over, he had been with the company for 39 years and had served Alvan Macauley, Max Gilman, and George Christopher faithfully. Ferry had a corporate perspective and knew everybody at East Grand and in the rest of the industry. He may not have been born with gasoline in his blood, but he spent his life inhaling the internal combustion engine's fumes.

The Irish lad, born in 1884, contributed to his family's larder with a series of menial jobs. He also had to hustle to stay in one piece in his rough Corktown neighborhood—when arguments became serious, the Irish kids would repair to "Cap" Finlayson's barn, where Cap had set up a boxing ring. Hugh did not have to go to the mat often, for his brother, Robert, was so good with his fists that he turned professional. Hugh collected his purses and developed a lifelong interest in boxing. He finally took a job at the Michigan Stove Works, where he was promoted to foreman. At age twenty, with a secure income, Ferry proposed to his longtime sweetheart, and the couple eloped. Soon after, Ferry's mother left him a small inheritance, and he went into partnership with a neighbor to make specialized plumbing equipment. The men gambled everything they had, and they prospered until an employee lost his hand in a machine and sued them. Ferry was in the hospital recuperating from hernia surgery and peritonitis, which left him using crutches and wearing a heavy metal brace. That was when he learned that the court had awarded the maimed employee $20,000. At 24, Ferry had a wife, a broken body, and a mountain of debts.[1]

The young man's problems were Packard's gain, however. He needed a job where he could sit down, and Packard was offering $60 a month for a cost accountant. Ferry dragged his 145-pound body, encased in its heavy brace, into Macauley's office and talked his way into a job, despite his decidedly spotty schooling. Ferry enrolled at the Detroit Technical Institute to take needed courses, and he was promoted to paymaster in

1912. In that post, he filled out 4,000 paychecks by hand and delivered them personally to the workers. In 1936 he was promoted to secretary and treasurer; nine years later he was made a vice president; and in 1948 he became a director. On January 1, 1950, he became Packard's sixth president.[2]

Ferry was perhaps the most likable man ever to work at Packard. With his rather square face dominated by a prize-winning bulbous Irish nose, bushy black eyebrows that wandered off at all angles, and a mouth that was amazingly straight when it was not smiling, he was endowed with all the physical manifestations of a friendly guy. Lyman Slack remembered him as "a jolly Irishman" who had "too many friends to count." As he rose through the ranks Ferry found himself close to the seats of power, and his wealth of inside information made him useful.[3]

The man from Corktown, however, never forgot that he had risen from humble beginnings. For years he drove a Nash to work at Packard, and his son remembered that Ferry was very hard on his cars and was lucky that the factory mechanics took care of them for him. His heritage also left him with some very strong opinions about nepotism. He groused constantly about the young Macauleys, Algers, and Joys on the payroll who did little to merit their positions. He would not even allow his own son to work at East Grand. When "Ping" Ferry needed a job in about 1930, he went down to the company's employment office and gave an assumed Irish name. He lasted until Milton Tibbetts caught him sidling out of the factory and reported him to his father.[4]

Privately, Ferry was proud that he was the first Catholic to become president of a major automobile company. But he preferred to keep his pride, like his strong opinions, to himself, and inside the company he was usually on the side of compromise. No corporate infighter, he kept a low profile in the disputes that racked Packard from 1948 on. Instead, he brought his wealth of contacts and knowledge to serve whoever triumphed. Slack alluded to this when he said that Ferry was "happy with his spot on the Board and with his responsibilities as Treasurer." Slack did *not* say that Ferry was happy as president. Nobody had ever accused the jovial Irishman of coveting the firm's top job.[5]

Ferry understood his strengths and limitations. He had achieved his successes through his financial skills, but he knew he was woefully weak in other aspects of the business. Although he was a hail-fellow-well-met type in person and in small groups, Ferry projected little charisma in larger ones and suffered from an almost total inability to demonstrate his warmth and friendly nature on paper. His annual reports and the few written documents that remain are uniformly ponderous, quite unlike the man.

Perhaps Ferry's greatest weakness, given Packard's increasingly desperate situation, was that he was not a take-charge kind of man. In a highly centralized structure, such as Packard's, a lacuna at the top in troubled times could be fatal. The directors, knowing that Ferry would not rock the corporate boat, expected him to provide a caretaker administration. Ironically, Ferry managed Packard much as Macauley had earlier. Even outsiders noticed this. *Time* in August 1950 observed that Christopher "had run the company pretty much as a one-man show for eight years," but Ferry "got the top brass working more smoothly." The new president, talented at conciliation and compromise, meshed the personalities and ambitions of the company's top managers.[6]

Ferry was the first Packard president to consciously share his power and responsibility. He gave the board's newly refashioned operating committee, which had given Christopher fits, more power over planning and daily operations. He cleared lines of communication between his board and the technical experts who understood the nuts and bolts of the business. Ferry attended the committee's meetings but does not appear to have dominated its deliberations.[7]

The triad of Ferry, the operating committee, and a more active board slowly steered Packard away from Christopher's policies. The impetus came from Packard's uniformly depressing statistics. If there was one thing Ferry understood thoroughly, it was numbers. And he could not have missed them, for even *Newsweek*'s announcement of his appointment as president was accompanied by the news that Ferry was taking over a firm whose share of the automobile market, a small 2.5 percent in 1948, had fallen a year later to only 2.1 percent. Before World War II, Packard averaged 2.33 percent of national auto sales, a figure that slipped to 1.7 percent in 1950. Even worse, Packard competed in just 11 percent of the market, and that segment had been shrinking. Packard's portion of the 11 percent declined even faster; in 1949 it won 17 percent but plummeted to a dismal 10.5 percent in the unpopular bathtubs' last year. The restyled 24th series propelled Packard back up to 16 percent of its market in 1951, but that brought little joy to East Grand. Even the bathtubs had done better.[8]

There was one positive note, however, behind the gloomy figures. *Consumer Reports* gave the new Packards fairly high marks. It had rated the bathtubs well below average in 1950 in the medium- and luxury-price classes, and had recommended Cadillac as indisputably the best buy. When *CR* road tested the 1951 Packard 200, its drivers waxed enthusiastic over the "all-round good dimensions of its body" and its new Ultramatic. *CR*, however, took a cursory glance at the Packard 300 and 400 and concluded that the 300 was not competitive against Cadillac's

Series 61 and that the extra $400 a Packard 400 cost was not worth it. Overall, in the $2,279-to-$2,555 class, the Packard 200 ranked as one of the three best buys; in the $2,568-to-$2,981 range, Packard joined Chrysler and Hudson as a smart purchase; and in the $3,402-to-$4,061 class, the Packard 400 was recommended with Chrysler and the Cadillac 62.[9]

Good cars, however, did not automatically translate into higher sales, especially when adverse outside events occurred. The Korean War, for example, could not have come at a worse time – just as Packard pinned its hopes on its redesigned cars. Defense contracts and a labor shortage beset auto executives, and Washington complicated matters even more when it instituted Regulation W in September 1951. A Keynesian measure designed to force Americans to save their money and prevent inflation, it required car buyers to pay one-third down in cash on a car and pay off the remainder in only 21 months. On the cheapest Packard, the 200 at $2,195, a consumer had to make a down payment of almost $732 and monthly payments of about $69 plus interest. The *New York Times* calculated later that under the regulation, the average family making $3,000 a year would have had to dedicate half of its income to making the first year's payments on a car. For Packard, which sold about two-thirds of its cars on credit, Regulation W was crippling.[10]

Regulation W made less expensive cars more desirable, but as a small producer up against giants, Packard had trouble getting its costs low enough that its models could compete vigorously in a cheaper market. Ferry had to amortize his tooling and advertising costs across production runs that were only about one-half of the 125,000 cars Christopher had estimated. Packards thus cost a few hundred dollars more than their competitors, and that was an important difference. The 1951 Packard 200, for example, cost $138 more than the Oldsmobile Super 88, and a Cadillac 62, the best-selling luxury automobile, could be had for $127 less than the Packard 400. In addition, Cadillac offered a greater variety of models.[11]

Worse, from August 1950 through November 1951, Ferry had to raise prices repeatedly. Three days after he introduced the 24th series, Packard upped its prices from $83 to $114 per car. Thirteen months later, when the Office of Price Stabilization allowed all auto manufacturers to raise their prices 5 to 6 percent, Packard was one of the very few to hold the line. But the company fumbled its opportunity to score a public relations coup. Instead of taking the higher moral ground, Leroy Spencer, Packard's executive vice president, told newspaper reporters that his company had slipped in under the regulations in 1950 and had raised prices on its 1951 models then. That rationale pointed out to Packard buyers that they had been paying higher prices all along. Prospective

Packard purchasers felt no better after November when the firm posted price increases from $59 to $105 on all its 1952 models. Packard had merely deferred its price hike three months to apply it to its 1952 models.[12]

Ferry was forced into the distasteful price hikes by a restive labor force whose members worried that inflation would outstrip their wages. He was hit by a strike on August 15, 1950, when Local 190 of the UAW-CIO called out 8,000 workers at East Grand, demanding higher wages, pensions, and cost-of-living increases. Unions also walked out at Ford and Chrysler that month, as well as at Briggs, Packard's body supplier, steel companies, railroads, and U.S. Rubber. Packard settled with its workers two weeks later. The package raised its costs per worker between 24¢ and 26¢ an hour, or $9 million a year. Under the wartime regulations, Packard had to absorb increased labor costs until it received permission to raise auto prices.[13]

Trouble seemed to assault Ferry at every turn. Only two months after he settled his strike, a steel shortage threatened to shut him down. He temporarily solved the problem by buying expensive steel on the spot market, only to confront a serious shortage of nickel, used to bond chrome to steel. For a time Packard had to omit nickel and cover its chrome with a clear synthetic enamel that looked fine until it started to chip and flake. In the meantime, the copper industry was also hit hard by unrest, and East Grand suffered through shortages of wiring harnesses, radiators, and other parts with copper components.[14]

Packard did enjoy a stroke of luck when the National Production Authority allocated metals for 1952. Despite the fact that the company had captured just 1.43 percent of the 1951 auto market, it was allowed enough metal to build 83,600 cars, 2.09 percent of 1952 estimated sales. But Ferry could not produce and sell that many cars—he fell 7,500 short of meeting his quota. The following year the NPA cut Packard back to 1.88 percent of the market. Ferry was lucky not to have suffered an even deeper cut.[15]

In the face of such a bleak business environment, Ferry tried on a number of fronts to arrest Packard's decline. He started with the problem of his dealers' inability to sell the cars he did produce, and he took a close look at the company's ad agency. Young & Rubicam had been with Packard since 1932, but by 1951 Ferry and some of his directors were upset over the quality and effectiveness of its campaigns. On June 27, 1951, the directors took up the matter and divided over a course of action. Eight years later, a Young & Rubicam employee, John Rosebrook, said he thought that the directors were looking for a scapegoat for the company's failures. Rosebrook remembered that "we defended ourselves as best we could, but finally a board meeting was held when a couple of our friends were absent; we were fired." [16]

Rosebrook's memory was not quite accurate. Only Bogle was absent from the meeting at which the directors left the decision on firing Young & Rubicam to Ferry. That was not a position Ferry liked, and during an off-the-record board recess, he struck a compromise in which Packard would fire the agency on December 15 and hire Maxon, Inc., to take its place. The choice of Maxon was most interesting. As Rosebrook explained, "It just so happened that Hugh Ferry's son, Robert, was a vice president of Maxon Inc. Maxon got the account." In good Packard tradition, Ferry was not really opposed to a little nepotism. Like Macauley before him, he placed the blame for lagging sales on the firm's ad agency, and Nance would do the same thing later. [17]

Packard made the switch public on November 11 in a news release that touted Maxon's forthcoming program, "the largest advertising campaign in the history" of the company. The media blitz, through newspapers, national magazines, network radio, television, and Sunday supplements, was intended to reach 199 million people within three weeks. It may have, but not many of them bought Packards. And the 63,000 who did each paid an advertising premium of $71.44, the company's costs per car. The following year, with sales up, its advertising expenses fell to $58.62 per unit. That was still almost $25.00 per car higher than Cadillac's costs, and the General Motors division spent a great deal more promoting its products. [18]

Ferry knew that to sell cars to the middle class he had to understand and appeal to that class. He, like Nance later, spent money to poll the public about its perceptions of Packard and tried to tailor his product to those expressed preferences. Ferry's surveys marked a turning point in the company's history. No longer content to sit in the confines of executive row at East Grand and decide what was good for the motoring public or to rely upon appeals to past glories to sell his cars, Ferry sent people out to assess the market and used what he learned in product development. He employed Maxon to run Packard's first consumer survey, polling those who bought new Packards in 1951. It verified many observers' impressions—folks who bought Packards were generally older and more affluent. Two-thirds were over 45 years old, and three-quarters earned more than $5,000 per year. Fully 51 percent bought Packards because of their looks, a sign that Packard would need large amounts of capital for major retooling every three years or so if it wished to stay competitive. Surprisingly, only 17 percent bought Packards because of their reputation. The Packard "plus" had little meaning left, even for the older generation. [19]

Buried in Maxon's report were numerous disquieting indicators for the East Grand carmaker. Packard buyers came from the ranks of those who had long owned the marque; as many as 55 percent had previously owned two to four of its cars. Packard was not wooing buyers away from other companies in any great numbers; it was courting the already convinced. Only 30 percent were first-time Packard owners. Seventy-five percent claimed that if they had not bought a Packard, they would have purchased a Cadillac. They opted for the Independent, they said, for a better trade-in allowance, availability, and immediate delivery–the one way that the high demand for Cadillacs along with Packard's tendency to overproduce worked to its advantage.[20]

On a happier note, Maxon found a very high degree of satisfaction among Packard owners. Eighty-nine percent rated themselves enthusiastic to moderately satisfied with their new cars. Only 6 percent were grumpy, complaining of small flaws, rattles, flecking paint, faulty locks, and the like. Seventy-five percent of previous Packard owners thought that their 1951 model was better than their other Packards. Another 10 percent rated it the equal of their former cars. Again, only 6 percent said it was inferior. Most of the specific complaints about the 24th series cited poor body work, which traced back to the fact that Packard did not build its own bodies. Packard carried its fine-engineering tradition into the 1950's, and owners found remarkably little of a mechanical nature to fret about. Instead, they reserved their most serious complaints for Packard's low trade-in value, high upkeep costs, and poor gas mileage.[21]

Maxon ran another survey in June 1952 to interview car owners about their engine preferences. The ad agency found that consumers were overwhelmingly in favor of V-8s over straight eights. Ferry was looking for the survey to confirm an action he had already taken. The previous November, Packard's operating committee had laid plans to introduce a V-8, and in January 1952 the committee approved spending $1.2 million for engineering work on a new, highly automated plant to build the engines. Packard may have been late in meeting the competition, but Ferry was not just sitting around. His V-8 program was well under way when Nance took over.[22]

Ferry demonstrated that he had something of a flair about him. He knew that Packard had fallen far behind automotive trends, even behind the low-priced three in some areas, and had to play catch-up. By early 1951, automatic transmissions, power brakes, V-8s, and hardtops were the necessary sales tools of the trade. Yet Packard offered only its Ultramatic and its vacuum-assisted "Easamatic" power brake. Its V-8 was still several years away, but in February, Ferry rushed out Packard's first convertible hardtop, the Mayfair, a classy-looking car available in two-tone paint schemes. No matter that they leaked so badly, Nance later ordered upholstery for them that would not show water stains. They satisfied a growing demand for sportiness and partially altered the public's perception of Packard as the car for old folks who drove slowly with the windows up.[23]

Packard's president wanted to do more than simply ape the competition. In his final year in office he gambled Packard's scarce resources on untried innovations that marked Packard's last few years of existence. He bought the patent rights to the torsion-bar suspension system, which Nance introduced in 1955, and he hired an independent body works to build Packard a futuristic show-car, the Pan American. That idea came from Charles Feldmann of Henney, which produced many of Packard's ambulances and limousines. He promised that he and stylist Richard Arbib could build a real Packard showstopper for the International Motor Sports Show to be held in New York on March 29, 1952. Arbib took a new convertible, sectioned it to lower the car's beltline, lowered the body on its chassis, removed the back seat, folded the top under a metal panel, cut a wide scoop in the hood, and covered everything inside with top-grain oyster white leather. To top off his creation, he installed round taillights to match Packard's parking lights and added a Continental spare tire. The car came away with the first-place trophy for "outstanding automotive design and engineering achievement."[24]

The public's reaction to the new car was so enthusiastic, Ferry considered putting it into production. But the cost would have been about $18,000 per unit. After turning out six Pan Americans, Ferry shelved further production plans, but a less radical version, the Caribbean, reached limited production in 1953. The Caribbeans, built until Packard closed its Detroit factory, gave Packard a high-visibility car whose patina rubbed off on the company's other products.[25]

The 1950's were marked by glitter, chrome, tail fins, and horsepower. Because Packard had to appeal to middle-class tastes, Ferry had to "smarten up" his offerings. He also understood that women were instrumental in making family decisions about what car to buy. Ferry hired a famous fashion designer, Dorothy Draper, to harmonize colors and fabrics in Packard's interiors. Her designs were not revolutionary, but they may have lured more women into Packard's showrooms. Draper's presence also indicated how important the automobile's "skin" was becoming in an era when mechanical differences were lessening and the distinctions between the lower- and medium-priced cars were shrinking.[26]

The Korean War aggravated Packard's troubles but also gave Ferry a heaven-sent chance to catch up. The Defense Department offered Packard $400 million worth of marine and jet engine contracts and subcontracts, which promised to bring in sorely needed cash. The difficulty was that Packard had to spend its own money to fill the orders. By the end of 1950, the company had won two major subcontracts for the J-47 turbojet engine and a $20 million order for diesel marine engines. In November the directors allocated $500,000 for marine-engine production; more important, they started spending most of their meetings discussing defense matters. In some gatherings, autos were not even mentioned. Given Packard's precarious standing in the auto industry, such a diversion of attention was dangerous.[27]

The company's initial investment was just the opening wedge. Packard purchased 55.5 acres next to its Utica proving ground to build a new parts warehouse, which would free up space in Detroit for defense work. It also bought a manufacturing plant in Mt. Elliott, Michigan, for almost $2 million and spent another $500,000 refurbishing the facility to make jet engine forgings. At the close of the year, Ferry announced to his shareholders that defense contracts would reach $200 million per year, but Packard would have to spend about $17 million to facilitate the orders. He admitted that the firm had not yet made any profit from the war work—he had no idea what the earnings would eventually be.[28]

Ferry gambled that those earnings would be large enough and would last long enough to enable him to finance retooling his cars. The wager meant that for several years he had to plow automobile earnings into war work, which was why Nance reported in 1952 that the company's working capital was down. Actually, it had merely failed to rise. Christopher's conservative fiscal policies increased it to about $45 million by 1950, but Ferry's heavy outlays for new plant and machinery dropped it by about $5 million, where it stayed until the merger. But Ferry was financing the firm's future, and the promise of continuing federal dollars emboldened Nance to gamble on expanding Packard's automotive facilities.[29]

Hugh Ferry also helped bring new men to Packard's board, men who later allowed Nance the freedom to revamp the company. Christopher's removal left a vacant board seat, and his replacement, Edwin Blair, elected director on February 9, 1950, was something of a surprise. Just 49 years old, the cum laude graduate of Yale Law School, partner in his own New York City law firm of Hughes, Hubbard, Blair & Reed, had important legal and financial connections. As a director of the Union Bag and Paper Corporation, he was acquainted with Henry Bodman, Packard's former director, who was active in that firm. And when Packard's board decided to increase its size a year later, it selected 60-year-old Homer Vilas, a member of a brokerage firm who was also a director of Union Bag and a governor of the New York Stock Exchange. The two men broadened the board's geographical representation, introduced new business contacts, and came highly recommended by Packard insiders.[30]

Circumstantial evidence indicates that the new directors were selected with an eye toward supporting Nance for Packard's presidency. Within a month of Christopher's firing, Ferry, Bogle, and McMillan talked over some internal candidates, including William Graves, the vice president of engineering, and Leroy Spencer. Eight months later, Nance was invited to Detroit, where he explained that Hotpoint did not offer him the future Packard did and that he was willing to come to the automaker. Nance made some rather harsh demands, however. He wanted $50,000 a year (his salary at Hotpoint), a pension fund for Packard executives and himself, an option on 25,000 shares of Packard stock, and the company's presidency as soon as possible. He could not assume office immediately because the stockholders had to elect him to the board, which only then could elect him president. And the next stockholders' meeting was not scheduled until April 1951. In the meantime, Nance wanted to be named vice president for merchandising, advertising, and distribution, a job that would overlap Vincent's. Ferry suggested that Vincent could be named executive vice president of operations.

Ferry discussed Nance's demands informally with each member of his board, and they invited Nance to come to Detroit on June 19, 1950. They all met at the Detroit Athletic Club. Ferry characterized Nance as being "very frank" at the meeting–perhaps too frank, for the proposal was simply dropped. Years later, Frederick Rush, a Packard executive until 1954, claimed that Nance and his public relations man, Patrick Monaghan, had engineered Nance's approach to the auto industry. Rush believed that the two had hired a Chicago executive placement agency to scout possibilities. Meanwhile, Monaghan hyped Nance's name in the press, and as Rush put it, "The 'bite' came from Packard." Even after the talks fizzled out, the Hotpoint executive still had devoted supporters at East Grand who were determined to bring him aboard. Vincent resigned as executive vice president on December 27, 1950, and accepted a position as a $12,000-per-year consultant; that removed one obstacle. In the meantime, on September 13, 1950, Packard's board had granted management the same pension rights that union members had won; that met another of Nance's demands.[31]

Nance had not lost interest in Packard either. He put one of his employees to work quietly investigating the company. His April 16, 1951, report was less than encouraging. Of Packard's 1,600 dealers he found that perhaps only 350 were any good. Packards' trade-in prices were low and, combined with the fact that the cars were overpriced in the first place, placed them at a disadvantage in the marketplace. Further,

Packard made a bad mistake hinging its advertising efforts on the "prestige angle," because, as Nance's aide advised, "you know there just isn't any such connection with the Packard name as of now." [32]

Nance met with a "group of Chicago bankers" who favored Packard's merger with other Independents. George Mason had been preaching that such combinations were inevitable, and by 1950 everybody knew that Hudson was "being shopped" because Queen Wilhelmina, who owned 11 percent of the automaker, was anxious to sell. Ferry, seeing an opportunity to achieve two objects at once, arranged a meeting between Nance and the president of the Harris Trust Bank of Chicago, a friend of Mason's, to discuss Mason's plan. Harold Vance, Studebaker's president and chairman of the board, hated Mason and refused to entertain the proposal, so Mason dropped the difficult Vance into Nance's lap. Publicly Nance always stated that he agreed Packard would join Studebaker while Mason merged with Hudson, and the two new entities would later combine into a company to be named American Motors with Nance as president. The scope of Mason's grand design appealed to Nance, a man who always thought in the larger context. In fact, he candidly admitted later, "I would not have gone into it just to take over Packard." [33]

By February 1952, Nance was hooked, but he was still careful. He approached Ferry, and he and ZurSchmiede talked to Nance as early as March 20, 1952, and later to their fellow directors. Six days later the board met, agreed to Nance's stipulations, and set May 1 as the date for a special meeting to confirm him. The meeting began on a somber note as the directors authorized $1,800 to have a small sculpture made of Macauley, who had died on January 16 in Florida. After that quiet moment, Nance signed his contract, was elected a director, and took his seat for the remainder of the proceedings. Nance's inaugural board meeting set the tone for the next few years. The directors voted to reestablish the position of chairman of the board, and Ferry assumed the post, which carried no powers. The directors then elected Nance president and general manager and strengthened the authority of both positions. The board in effect returned to the organizational chart the company had had during its greatest successes, a highly centralized structure that enabled a talented president to exploit market opportunities and gave him virtually a free hand to manage the company's internal affairs. The directors also retreated from the fray when they decided to meet monthly instead of semimonthly. And they were most generous with their new top executive. They awarded Nance a five-year contract that paid him more than $168,000 per year and guaranteed him $40,000 annually for fifteen years after he retired. In addition he was given options on 100,000 shares of Packard stock. [34]

Not everyone at Packard was thrilled about Nance's arrival. In September 1950, after the board's negotiations with Nance were put on hold, Earle Anthony promoted Leroy Spencer as his favorite-son candidate for Packard's chief job. A University of Illinois graduate, Spencer had joined Anthony in 1928 as a retail salesman. By 1935, he was vice president of Anthony's Packard distribution organization and administrative head of all of his operations, including KFI, his radio station. When Ferry's search for a successor stalled, Packard's board appointed Spencer executive vice president of the company. Michael Kollins remembered that everyone at Packard assumed that Spencer was the heir apparent. He was not, however, and he sat frustrated on the sidelines when "Hotpoint Jim," as his detractors liked to call him, was brought in. Three months after Nance's appearance, and perhaps with a little nudge, Spencer resigned as vice president and asked for an appointment on the West Coast.[35]

Nance's policies were dictated less by personalities within Packard than by a set of consultants' reports. Circumstantial evidence indicates that when Nance first interviewed Ferry back in 1950, he suggested that Packard hire someone to analyze the company's structure and needs. Ferry and his directors contracted on November 13, 1951, with the Chicago consulting firm of Booz Allen & Hamilton to conduct an internal review of the company's business and to outline a strategy for its survival. At a cost of at least $238,000, Booz Allen delivered six fat volumes, covering all aspects of the business, to Packard on June 30, 1952. Unlike most such documents, this one became important. Nance, who thrived on such surveys, read his copy thoroughly. He used it as a general introduction to Packard and as a source of ideas on what to examine and change, to destroy and rebuild. Many of his later memos—and the man could produce such documents with machine-gun rapidity—referred to the report by name or elaborated on one of its themes or ideas.[36]

The picture Booz Allen drew in its report was not a pretty one, and its authors painted it in vivid, primary colors. The authors pointed out that "Packard has not really been successful for many years" and for the last two decades "has drifted along on a static basis." They laid the blame squarely on the presidents. While "other companies in the industry have expanded and prospered through mergers, new product lines, and improved merchandising, Packard has tried little in the way of major policy changes that might have brought an improvement in its position." They agreed that the company's case was not hopeless, for "Packard could continue to perform at this level for a long time to come," but it was "a mediocre showing" because Packard was not making "enough money to represent a fair return on capital invested, the assets used or the effort put forth." Yet, they admitted, the firm "has not lost money."[37]

That was the fundamental conundrum. The evaluators saw a company in what they called a "sound position" with "substantial net worth, adequate working capital and a sound borrowing position," but facing a clouded future. They feared that Packard's earning prospects would decrease, and reversing this trend would require "major" improvements— not just "polishing up" here and there. They agreed with George Mason and others that a major Independent was too small to succeed against the Big Three, with their cost efficiencies and capital resources.[38]

Taking the need for change as given, the consultants listed Packard's choices, and there were not many. The company could stay the same or grow slowly through internal economies, or it could emerge from its lethargy, transform itself, and become a major player in the automobile markets once again. The advisers outlined two avenues to bigness: build its own low-priced, high-volume car or merge with another Independent. Gliding along on the company's outdated sense of prestige was not enough. In fact, the consultants disabused Packard hands of that when they observed that "Packard's name is good, but not up with Cadillac."[39]

Booz Allen found at East Grand what could only be described as a moribund company, staffed at the top with complacent men who conducted business much as they had since the introduction of the 120. The advisers reminded Packard's managers that they worked for a big company but were using procedures more suited to a little one. Executives saw to it that incompetent and aged employees were kept on, like old family retainers, in easier jobs. There was much to be said for the sense of family and decency, but Packard seemed unable to continue it and prosper. To reverse the decline, according to Booz Allen, the firm had to portray itself as vital and aggressive. It had to devise a hard-hitting public relations campaign to "get across to industry and to the public that Packard has come to life." Such a program, the consultants mandated, had to convince the public that the company had a "young, able, aggressive management team and an upward trend in sales and profits" to give the impression "that here was a big outfit on the move." That public image would set Packard up for a merger.[40]

The authors also advised Packard to snare all the defense contracts it could, to "provide the time and money needed to permit the new management team to improve the automobile business." They also warned that its jet engine contract was vulnerable to design changes and suggested that the company seek "more stable defense items." The consultants failed to notice that Packard was more a defense contractor than an auto manufacturer. In 1953 the company expected to complete about

$235 million worth of government work and sell only about $200 million in automotive products.[41]

Packard had to strengthen the auto side of its business if it was to survive, and, most important, it had to reinvigorate and expand its dealer organization. It must develop its planning capabilities and create an "over-all long-range guide" for company growth. Packard should, the writers thought, develop the product line (a mix of autos, defense matérial, diesels, and so forth) it needed to be more profitable. Lastly, they urged Packard to make full use of its facilities by selling automotive parts to competitors. Booz Allen reminded Packard managers of the mistake they made when they did not sell their Ultramatic to other companies, especially Lincoln, which bought its automatic transmission from General Motors. They hoped Packard would remember that experience when it built its new V-8.[42]

Overall, the report called for heroic measures from Packard's top managers to resuscitate the company. Nance had to become a public figure to symbolize the firm's new mood and "aggressiveness," one of the consultants' favorite words. The advisers assumed that he would have breathing room, owing to the Korean War and government restraints on car production, to enable him to revamp his product line, raise needed capital, build new plants, complete a forward planning campaign, and convince the public that Packard was once again on the march. Nance was to be Packard's lightning rod, its most visible figure–indeed, almost a cult personality. He took credit when things went well at Packard and bore the blame when they suddenly turned sour.

Chapter 6

2-36 "Sport Model," 1925

"Hail to
the Chief"

Packard had never seen the likes of Jim Nance. Observers, inside and outside the company, exhausted their vocabularies trying to describe the man. Owen Goodrich, who did not like him one bit, labeled Nance a "one man gang" after he barged into East Grand. Dick Stout, there at the time, admired Nance's efforts to turn the firm around but later admitted he "shook the place up." Even Ferry, who was not given to colorful oratory, introduced Packard's new boss as a man of "aggressive ability and drive." *Time* called him "one of the ablest salesmen and shrewdest analysts of new markets in U.S. industry." Lyman Slack, who was long gone from the Packard scene but watched events there closely and did some consulting work for Nance, concluded that he was a "good man." He also remembered that a dealer once told him at a National Auto Dealers' Association convention that Nance "insisted" that the band play "Hail to the Chief" when he entered a meeting, but Slack thought the story apocryphal. Mike Kollins did not think so. He characterized Nance as a man who "read his own press releases and believed them." Nance's South Bend secretary, Margery Warren, a woman given to careful understatement, remembered her boss as "eccentric."[1]

Whoever was correct, Nance shook things up at East Grand, and that was exactly what Ferry and his board wanted him to do. They desperately needed someone to put Packard in the public eye and promote its products. So they gambled on Nance to break with established canons and burst out of the long, dark halls at East Grand to stir public emotions. They were looking for what they called a professional "merchandiser." They got one of the best. *Fortune*, back in 1950 when Nance was Hotpoint's president, counted him among the nation's top four "sales bosses" and described him as a "sensation."[2]

That Nance had never been in the automobile business mattered less to Packard officials than his never having failed at anything. Indeed, he had been successful on a national scale. Skillfully, he merged his flamboyant personality with his selling techniques to make himself a household word. His face and his career were splashed across newspapers and magazines. He was noted as a man who emerged from the depression convinced that selling was a science, a practical application of known techniques that, if done correctly, got consumers to buy anything. Packard, if its sales record and the Booz Allen report were any indications, lacked even elementary knowledge of the new "science" of merchandising.

Nance was not a total stranger to Packard, however. He was born in Ironton, Ohio, a few miles from Warren, two years after James Ward Packard built his first car. Born of solid Midwestern stock and imbued with his parents' tough Methodist principles, Nance early learned that success was the reward for hard work. The young boy was a high school football star, an experience that left him an avid sports fan, long an informal requirement for holding Packard's top job. He went to Ohio Wesleyan, where he played halfback on the football team and pursued his prelaw studies until his junior year, when his father died suddenly. Nance dropped out of school, and when he returned he changed his major to business. He graduated in 1923 and was voted the outstanding man in his class. The following year he attended Ohio State University for postgraduate work but was lured away from his studies by the man who would become his mentor.[3]

The National Cash Register Company in Dayton, Ohio, trained many automobile men through the years, including Alvan Macauley and others at Packard. In 1924 it was still the top sales training school in the country, and Nance joined its program under Richard Grant, who became Nance's hero. While Nance was still learning the rudiments of the new "science," General Motors built a brand-new Frigidaire factory almost across the street from the company and in 1927 hired Grant to run it. He took a few men, whom Nance would later call "comers," with him. The hoary stories about Nance's early career recount that Grant paid him peanuts at GM, but he was grateful to work under the great man's tutelage. Besides, when the depression struck, higher-paid executives were fired to hold down costs, and Nance kept his job. By 1931, making a grand total of $75 per week, perhaps three times the average wage, Nance was in charge of all Frigidaire's merchandising and advertising. In 1936, when Frigidaire was reorganized, Nance became manager of the air-conditioner and commercial refrigerator division. It was a heady rise for a man only 35 years old.[4]

Conventional Nance lore related that he was tired of working for a large corporation and left GM for Zenith in 1941, just before Pearl Harbor. With the outbreak of the war, Nance headed Zenith's wartime production and held a seat on the War Production Board's industry advisory committee. One of the other members was Charles E. "Electric Charlie" Wilson, president of General Electric. Wilson liked the young man's hustle and afterward brought him to GE's subsidiary, Edison General Appliance Company, which made Hotpoint appliances. As Edison's president, the first thing Nance did was to change its name to Hotpoint.[5]

Nance and Hotpoint were in a rather odd corporate position in 1945, for they made household appliances that competed with the General Electric brand of the parent company. Moreover, Hotpoint was a minor player in its market, ranking tenth among appliance manufacturers when World War II broke out. Nance made his national reputation as a supersalesman by boosting Hotpoint to third in the industry. He accomplished this miracle by applying marketing principles that became part of his arsenal at Packard. He surveyed wired homes, and from those figures he created what he called a "rainbow chart," perhaps the origin of his well-known penchant for charts on everything. From this chart of market saturation, he decided that Hotpoint should avoid the replacement market and concentrate on selling appliances to those who had none, exactly the opposite of what the rest of the industry was doing.[6]

To implement his "rainbow" marketing strategy, Nance borrowed money, lots of it. Unlike many other businessmen, he was not afraid to. His big advantage at Hotpoint was that he could borrow from parent GE, which he did to the tune of $15 million to build an electric-range plant at Cicero, Illinois. He borrowed another $11 million to refit a Milwaukee war plant to make hot-water heaters, but when the Korean War erupted, he landed a turbocharger contract from the Defense Department and made them instead. With his tax write-off, Nance expanded the plant and, by late 1951, was making hot-water heaters there as well. It was the first instance in which he piggybacked production of civilian goods on defense contracts' profits, an idea he would bring to East Grand. Nance thought big and borrowed another $20 million to build a refrigerator plant. In the meantime, Hotpoint won a contract to make Pratt &Whitney jet engine components, and he diverted those funds to this contract.[7]

At the same time, Nance devised new methods to sell his products. One of the lessons he learned from Grant was that everyone connected with selling Hotpoint products, from the factory to the showroom floor, had to hew to the same sales line. Hotpoint held training seminars, produced films extolling its products, and coordinated national and local advertising to hit the same themes hard—and Hotpoint sales soared. Nance also always took the larger view of his business. He noted that since hired girls in the home were now unusual, American housewives would be attracted to coordinated appliances. Nance introduced "ensemble buying," obviously pitched at women, in which they could select an all-electric kitchen with every Hotpoint appliance styled and colored to match. Late in life, Nance said that he would like to be remembered as "an emancipator of women" because he marketed the first home dishwasher and all-electric kitchen.[8]

To create such ensembles, Nance relied on his sales department to find out what attracted women, what colors they preferred, and what options they wanted, and then to pass that information on to Hotpoint's engineering department. This procedure was exactly the opposite of that used at other companies. Nance firmly believed that the point of sale was the heart of any business, and nobody knew better than the salespeople what gave them an edge in the market. Booz Allen's report recommended that Nance's design scheme be transferred to East Grand, and Nance saw no reason why it should not also work in the auto business.[9]

By the time Ferry approached Nance about taking Packard's top job, the appliance man had Hotpoint well in hand. In more normal times, Nance might not have been attracted to the automaker, since he seemed to be on GE's inside track toward bigger and better things. After Ferry's tender, however, Ralph J. Cordiner, GE's president, reorganized the company and proposed to do away with a great deal of his subsidiaries' autonomy. Nance would become an executive vice president at GE, a staff position, and he would not receive as much publicity and credit for his successes. For a man of his temperament, such a position held no allure. This probably explained why he was willing to reconsider Packard's offer in 1951.[10]

For all his public reputation for impetuous and bold strokes, Nance was something of a careful, cold, calculating man who knew exactly what he wanted to accomplish and how he was going to do it long before he took his first step. Sometimes his penchant for caution showed. For example, he wrote Packard's director of advertising and public relations,

H. W. Hitchcock, a memo in which he cautioned that "we must crawl before we can walk, and . . . not indulge in an elaborate promotion program." Ralph Watts, the automotive writer for the *Detroit News*, recognized Nance's conservative streak, noting that Packard's newly elected president was "making haste slowly." And Nance was quite candid about it. He told a *Newsweek* reporter, "I was what you might call a cautious man in a hurry. Now our program has jelled."[11]

Nance was a big believer in teamwork. Stout remembered Nance's having told him that he wanted to operate the business like a coach ran his team. Nance filled his public exhortations with football metaphors and held a summer camp for his "key men" up in the Michigan woods at Houghton Lake. It was just like fall football practice. He mixed serious presentations of Packard's new models and plans for the coming year with vigorous competition among teams of overweight, cigar-chomping Packard executives. Nance tried to instill in Packard's managers a unity of purpose and give them experience in working together under rough circumstances. Like everything Nance did, the camps were organized down to the last minute. The program for the 1954 outing consisted of thirteen typewritten pages.[12]

Packard's new "coach" was not a physically imposing man. Of only average height and perhaps a few pounds over his optimal weight, he looked like anything but an athlete. His rather oval head, whose features turned increasingly fleshy as times worsened in Detroit and South Bend, was topped by thick black hair that had receded well up to the top of his head. His deep, inset, sparkling blue eyes had enough crinkles about them to lend a hint of underlying mirth. He sported an unremarkable nose, until one noted that it was triangular when viewed from the front, rather like the classic Halloween pumpkin's nose. It was his mouth that revealed the most about his complex personality. Thin lips, always pursed in photographs, made him seem a man hard to deal with, which many thought he was, but the prominent crescent-shaped smile lines indicated his deep-seated playfulness and his enjoyment of the basic pleasures of everyday life. Nance tended to dress like a salesman—he had a proclivity for double-breasted suits with pointed lapels, and, according to his photographs, he preferred a bit of sheen in them. Unfortunately, they made him look thicker and shorter than he actually was. At the same time, he was not afraid to wear neckties that were a tad loud for an executive in his rarefied position, and occasionally he liked a pocket handkerchief drooping out of his breast pocket. He was no dandy, but neither was he the classic man in the gray flannel suit.

His appearance honestly reflected a man with a complex personality and myriad contradictions, which was one of the reasons why everybody who ever met him left with strong opinions of him. Nance was a publicity hound, often arranging for his own write-ups in magazines and newspapers, and he was at the same time a quiet, private man. He kept his wife, whom he married in 1925, Laura Battelle, and his two children, James Battelle and Marcia Lou, out of the public eye and squeezed time out of his hectic life to be with them often. He brought his work home with him, though, and frequently scheduled business meetings at his home in Bloomfield Hills on Saturdays and Sundays. He habitually started his Monday implementing decisions made during the weekend. He maintained a summerhouse at Torch Lake and a 180-acre dairy farm in northern Michigan that somebody said he ran like a business.[13]

Everyone agreed that Nance was a driven man, bordering on being a workaholic. His mind was always working, always asking questions, always seeking a plan of action to attack some problem. Until things turned really sour at Packard, he hit the banquet circuit at least once a week, eating chicken and peas, touting Packard's revitalization program, and speaking on industry-wide concerns. All agreed that Nance was a spellbinder at the podium: with his gravelly voice, he could move even his dealers' stone-cold hearts with his yearly spiels introducing the new models, which he gave all over the country. On the stage he was witty, cogent, persuasive, homespun, and warm, a persona he projected in smaller groups as well.

On the other hand, Nance had a furious temper that frequently bubbled to the surface. Stout remembered that Nance got really angry over big problems and let the smaller ones slide by. The president's internal correspondence shows otherwise. When he thought a member of his executive team had goofed, he would send withering memos, admonishing him for his transgressions and sometimes implicitly threatening him if he did not mend his ways. Occasionally, several days of such memos would flow from his office, excoriating various folk, indicating that he was not immune to rather lengthy sour moods. He had detractors, like Goodrich, who emphasized the bleak side of Nance's personality and his ruthlessness, citing the 400 old Packard hands Nance fired when he took over, and Kollins, who said that Nance "could be horribly insulting." Even his supporters, like Stout, admitted that the former appliance man "could be pretty ruthless" at times.[14]

A major part of Nance's reputation for ruthlessness originated when he "retired" about 385 Packard executives, a housecleaning recommended by the Chicago consultants. The remainder derived from his managerial methods. Taking a page from Franklin D. Roosevelt's book, Nance had a tendency to order two subordinates to do the same job and watch them compete for his approbation. It was an old ploy in managerial circles, but in Nance's case it also had to do with his being a devo- tee of the game, any game; business was the ultimate game to prove one's personal worth. Clara Brown, who worked in the executive office pool at South Bend, told her interviewer that during the World Series, her job was to listen to the games on the radio and be ready to give Nance the scores whenever he called. "He just had to know," she said. Nance be- lieved that internal competition was good for the company. It identified the real "comers" among his subordinates and presented him with a greater number of strategic options. As one of his former colleagues ob- served after Nance retired, "He did not like little surprises." Stout had another explanation for Nance's treatment of subordinates. He thought that such competition fed Nance's love of "mystery and intrigue." No doubt he loved the play of corporate politics, and he vastly increased its complexity at East Grand.[15]

Yet Nance also had a reputation for loyalty to those who worked for him. He may have yelled at them and showered them with invective, but he also backed them in tough times. Stout thought that Nance stood foursquare behind his team members as long as he had confidence in their abilities; once he lost that, he did not necessarily fire them, he simply ignored them, which was worse. He demonstrated his loyalty when he brought a team from Hotpoint to Packard in 1952 and 1953. And after Studebaker-Packard collapsed in 1956, as he later said, "to show my appreciation for the loyalty of these management associates, I maintained an office in Detroit, and devoted my time and effort in help- ing these executives get placed with other companies." After he retired, he was inordinately proud of the "warm greetings and personal notes" he received "from these men" whom he had helped.[16]

The wonder was where Nance found the time to do it all. He was swamped with daily details. As a public figure, he drew correspondence from every quack in America who had an idea or who wanted something, and he was always pleasant to those who importuned him. Packard own- ers who had a complaint, no matter how niggling, often felt obliged to explain it to the president, along with their personal histories of Packard ownership. Nance replied to each and kept a mental tally of their prob- lems. Occasionally he fired off memos asking underlings to remedy the defects at the factory.[17]

Nance had little trouble finding details to fret over—the master of the big picture always noticed the little things. He objected to the fact that new Packards on display outside company headquarters were not lighted at night, so he had spotlights put on them after 5 P.M. He updated the decor in the lobby, complained of antique and outdated offices, reviewed the size of the print in Packard's ads and of the buttons in its upholstery, complained of limp ropes on the backs of front seats, sent flowers to dealers, wrote notes to recent widows of employees and purchasers, advised on color combinations (he hated Packard's yellow), investigated thefts in the factory, watched the quality of the executive cafeteria's food, and once wrote a general memo about a "coffee Klatch" each morning that was "well attended after 8:30 A.M." Nance believed that careful attention to the little things in the business world made bigger achievements possible. Such attention, however, cost valuable time and sapped some of his manifold energies.[18]

Packard's president needed all the time he could muster because the sheer volume of reports that he perused daily made for anything but quick reading. He had a mania for information that went unrequited until the day he resigned. He regularly received figures on ten-day car sales for the industry; daily counts of his own sales; a mass of dealers' statistics, especially those concerning open points, lost sales opportunities, and dealers' profits and losses; production targets for the month, week, and day ("bogies," he called them); actual production figures; running tabulations of cost per car; defense business figures, especially monthly production; an overview of the company's employment statistics for various periods; a tally of Packard's working capital reported on a daily basis when times were rough; a liquidity statement; and detailed reports from zone managers. If Nance helped kill off Packard, he certainly did not do so from a lack of information. He knew at all times just about anything of importance that was happening in his corporate domain. He often noted that he plowed through these compilations while being chauffeured to or from work or while on an airplane.

Nance's penchant for details extended down to his personal office. His South Bend secretary, Margery Warren, remembered the first time she met him. He brought in a "package . . . that the secretaries in Detroit had made up" and proceeded to show her that "this was the only kind of pencil he wanted, these were the only kind of papers that were to be on his desk, and all this kind of goofy stuff." And some of it was strange. Nance wrote all his internal notes with a blunt, smeary pencil. When he had read something, he put a check across the whole front page with the same pencil. He used only green memo paper, and most of the time he cut it in half. When he had a lot to say, he wrote on the back rather than use a second sheet. He loved to scribble indecipherable marginalia that were so smeared, only a cryptographer could have unraveled them. He actually wrote a clear hand, when his pencils were halfway sharpened, but he preferred them well worn. His secretaries would type up his notes, on green paper, before they were sent out.[19]

Packard's president also liked an informal office atmosphere. He called everyone by his or her first name and insisted that the Mr., Mrs., or Miss be dropped. That may well have been the tradition at Packard, although it strains credulity to believe that office girls ever called Macauley "Alvan," at least to his face. Studebaker, on the other hand, for all its trumpeting that it was a family business, insisted that everyone be addressed with a title. When Nance hit South Bend, he ordered the folks in his office to drop all that nonsense. His secretary refused, noting that "Mr. Nance was Mr. Nance." [20]

For all his stress on informality at work, Nance could lash out at those close to him. Warren remembered that "he swore at me once" and discovered he had riled the wrong woman. She told co-workers, "I don't take that from anybody." She never said a word to him, just "shut the door, and when I shut the door he knew it was shut. And I must have looked fire. . . . Out of my office, I didn't care whether they fired me or whether they didn't." She recounted that the master of Studebaker-Packard stayed in his office about twenty minutes, "and when he came out he was a different man." He never swore in front of Warren again, but neither did he apologize. She said, "He didn't have to—he looked sheepish." After that, old Studebaker hands noticed that Nance treated Warren differently than he did "the girls in Detroit." The incident illustrated that Nance was not insensitive; he chose to make peace with her on her terms. Ever the Studebaker loyalist, Warren was never overly fond of Packard's Nance, but she did admit that "he was nice to me." The man hired at Packard to turn the company upside down hated to have his office details and routine disrupted. He needed some things to remain as they were, anchors in an otherwise chaotic corporate world. [21]

The man *Newsweek* called "a fast-moving, manufacturing and merchandising wizard" may have moved slowly on a number of fronts at Packard, but he made some vital personnel changes with lightning speed. At a special board meeting called just three weeks after Nance arrived, Ferry resigned as treasurer and Nance's man, Walter Grant, from Hotpoint, was named financial vice president and treasurer. At the same meeting, Frederick Walters was brought in from Oldsmobile to be vice president of marketing. A scant two weeks later, Milton Tibbetts resigned as Packard's general counsel, and Patrick Monaghan, also from Hotpoint, took over the company's public relations office. Nance believed in compensating his top executives. The directors voted Grant and Walters each an option on 25,000 shares of Packard stock, and Grant a salary of about $50,000. Monaghan joined the firm for $20,000 annually. [22]

By mid-July 1952, Nance stepped up his reorganization of Packard's management. He hired Gordon Van Ark to run management development, accepted the resignation of the company's secretary, and appointed Packard's Wilmer B. Hoge as comptroller. As chief of procurement, Albert Behnke, an old friend who had been vice president of Hotpoint's Chicago division, was brought in, effectively replacing Leroy Spencer, who resigned at the July 23 board meeting. And for vice president of Packard's industrial relations Nance reached into his color-coded files and selected C. Wayne Brownell, who had been with Packard since 1944 as legal adviser and personnel manager. After Nance's fast and furious start on building his own "key man" group, it was another year before he completed the circle of men with whom he felt comfortable. In September, Robert Straughn was added as merchandising manager, and Robert Blythin left Hotpoint to become Packard's general counsel. Replacements slowed until February, when Blythin was elected the company's secretary and Roger Bremer was hired at $30,000 per year as director of purchasing. Nance rounded out his circle on July 1, 1953, when he hired Ray Powers from Lincoln-Mercury to be his vice president for manufacturing. George Reifel, who held that position, was undone by Booz Allen's recommendations. When Nance completed his new management team, he admonished it to "make no little plans." That kind of thinking, he said, lacked "the magic to stir men's souls." [23]

Before Nance and his team could worry about stirring men's souls, they had to get automobiles out of their factory. That task became more complicated when steelworkers walked off the job in the second week of July 1952. Inventory grew so tight that *Business Week* announced, "Cars Back in Seller's Market." When the strike was over at the end of the month, Nance was preparing the public for the firm's third-quarter statement, which would probably be bleak. The outlook did not improve when the National Production Authority announced the metal allocations for 1953. The Big Three and Studebaker received increases, but Packard was dropped from 2.09 percent to 1.88 percent of the market. Nance, hoping to increase his volume, was less than pleased, but in November the NPA granted leeway to companies with a "carryover." The NPA agreed that Packard could build 10,000 cars a month during the first quarter, but would be restricted to a total of 23,500 the second. By then, however, Nance was less upset about the restrictions. He was having trouble getting enough bodies from Briggs to meet his allowable targets; by November, Briggs was 8,700 cars behind schedule. But that was not all the bad news. Packard dealers were having trouble selling the cars they had, and the company's inventory had dramatically risen. To add insult to injury, the *New York Times* announced in December that Cadillac had a backlog of 90,000 orders for its 1953 models. Nance must have been apoplectic.[24]

Despite difficulties with the day-to-day operations, Nance worked on Booz Allen's recommendations. On September 5, he shot off a terse memo to Grant, telling him to read the consultant's report on manufacturing "and glean from it some objectives and bogies for improvement that we can set up." When manufacturing budget projections for 1952 were blasted by an overrun of $6.2 million, Nance fired another succinct missive at Grant, ordering him to formulate a plan to attack the problem, reminding him that they needed figures "that can be put on charts, etc., so that we can follow the trends as we used to do at Hotpoint." There were also smaller problems that were driving Nance to distraction. By Christmas Eve, 1952, he was sick of customer complaints about leaking Mayfairs. In a confidential note to Graves, Nance grumbled, "I know you have changed the upholstery so it won't show, but it's like putting linoleum down when you have a pup in the house." He was in no mood for long-range study of the problem. "Fix the Mayfair and get a body engineer," he ordered.[25]

By the end of his first year at Packard, Nance was not all that dispirited, however. He had initiated plans to target cost savings, he had survived the steel strike and the government allocations, he had his men in place, and he took pleasure in watching one of his favorite projects, the Caribbean, go into production. On October 30, Graves signed an agreement with the Ionia Manufacturing Company of Ionia, Michigan, to produce 500 of the sporty Packards for 1953. Nance, ever the salesman, understood that those special editions would help move his more traditional autos. Until the very end, he had a soft spot for the Caribbeans, even though they were costly to produce and his salesmen never had enough of them. Long after he retired, Nance wrote Stout about the prices Packards commanded, noting with pride that "you will be interested to know that the Caribbean of our vintage is rapidly becoming a favorite. And it is still a good looking car."[26]

Packard's president was much better at merchandising than at production. In 1952, as he planned for Packard's future products and ad themes, Nance operated upon two basic suppositions about the future. He was convinced that the buyer's market would return (although he little knew its magnitude) in the second half of 1953, when Packard must be ready with an "aggressive" organization to survive, and he sensed that a recession was coming, probably in 1955. In light of his hunches and the consultant's report, he worked diligently to revise his product lines, revitalize his ad campaign, coordinate public relations, and hone his competitiveness. Nance left few doubts about the thrust of his plans to fight for the luxury market. Privately he told a gathering of his "key men" in June that "if we are going to abandon the field, then Jesus let's do it for *honor*, not by default." But Nance had no intention of relinquishing sales to Cadillac. A month later, he told the *New York Times*, "Packard is going after a lot more of the quality car market it once dominated and lost, through default." And in September he repeated that threat when he said to a *Newsweek* reporter that there would be a new "custom" car for the "carriage trade," a reference to the new formal sedans Derham had agreed to produce for Packard. To mount his assault on Cadillac, Nance followed Booz Allen's advice and raised his advertising budget for 1953 to $3.87 million, which was $800,000 more than the company had spent the previous year. With expected sales at 85,000, the expenditure averaged a little more than $45 per vehicle.[27]

By the end of 1952, he was dissatisfied with Maxon's "sales point" that over one-half of all Packards were still on the road. Nance's question was whether it was lively enough "to combat Cadillac." Instead, Nance suggested that the agency "take a leaf out of Cadillac's advertising" to "sell the people who are buying this class of car that it is the smart thing to do." Three weeks later, Nance wondered why so many people bought black Cadillacs and concluded that it was because GM advertised black Cadillacs. Impressed, Nance dropped a letter to Maxon, admitting that "Cadillac is so far in front selling our Packard market that I am inclined to follow them until we better learn how to sell this class of buyers." He was nervous because he still did not have a hard-hitting ad theme, and by December 10 his owner relations department was telling him "that the first flush of Presidential 'newness' is slowly wearing off."[28]

The advertising muddle was created by Nance's product differentiation philosophy; it did not lend itself to simplification. In what Nance grandly labeled his "New Packard Program," he promised to improve Packard's "traditionally fine products" and to separate the Packard and the Clipper, giving each its own identity. The idea was to return to Packard's philosophy of 1935–36, when the company pitched a cheaper car to the masses and retained its cachet for its more expensive offerings. Nance wrestled with the distinctions that separated the cars and floated his ideas by Monaghan. After admitting that "I have not succeeded very well insofar as the verbiage is concerned," he opined that the Clipper was a quality car for "the man who likes good things . . . but who must watch his investment in a car." The Packard, on the other hand, was a "fine car in the true Packard tradition." This was pretty dull stuff by Nance's normal standards, and he knew it. As usual, though, he resolved his uncertainties with action: he announced in November 1952 that he was going to expand his Packard line to seven models, as his consultants suggested, ranging from a two-door sedan at $3,000 to custom-built limousines that sold for $7,000 and more.[29]

He was quieter about the Clipper because he did not know what kind of car it should be. Nance had created a ten-man Clipper program committee, and its first estimates were frightening–to retool the Clipper, exclusive of a new V-8, would cost $21 million. Since Packard could not afford that, the committee started working out compromises, and it began to fuzz the sharp distinctions between the Clipper and the Packard. It decided, for example, to cut costs by using a common body for both cars and, harking back twenty years, mandated a 120-inch wheelbase for the Clipper and 126-inch one for the Packard. After many such concessions, Nance was moved to speak at length of the necessity for "curbstone identity" for the Clipper and its bigger brother. Otherwise, Nance could not effectively distinguish the cars in his advertising. The committee, however, compromised and delayed, and the whole process of design for the 1955 Clipper ignored Booz Allen's suggestions. Packard relied on its engineering division to provide the crucial information that determined styling and sales.[30]

Having reworked the 1954 Clipper and settled on the retooling for the following sales season, Nance turned his attention to the Packard. In this case, he reversed the planning procedure and started with the sales department, asking C. E. Briggs, his general sales manager, to recommend specifications for the 1954 Packards. Nance peppered Briggs with questions ranging from whether Packard was "going to hit Cadillac on the nose, or bracket them" to whether the cars needed new dashboards. "You fellows take the initiative in writing specifications for the engineering department," Nance told Briggs, for "you know enough about costs to keep your suggestions on a practical basis." Nance honestly believed that having his sales department specify what the new cars should look like would revolutionize the automotive business. But he had to pump up Briggs, an old Packard hand, who had never been asked to do anything remotely similar in his career. Nance promised him that this was a great opportunity for "the Sales Department to start setting their own sales strategy in the Packard Company." Lest Briggs miss the point, Nance added grandiloquently, "This can be the birth of a nation." Briggs had his work cut out for him. Just two weeks earlier, a *Fortune* survey had shown that 1.9 percent of its subscribers would buy a Packard but 13.1 percent of them wanted a Cadillac. Moreover, the well-heeled *Fortune* readers thought the Clipper was an "also ran" in terms of its looks, value, and desirability.[31]

The *Fortune* survey was no news to Nance. Back in August 1952, he had bluntly admitted to his "key men" that "Packard is 'blighted' with the stigma of failure" and that the company had to combat the belief that Independents were "dead ducks." Packard's case was more severe because the public thought its "management has not kept up with the parade–is old–gone to seed and non-aggressive and non-sales minded." The company had so many shares outstanding, their selling price was low, "in the 'cat and dog' category." The firm's reputation, Nance said, was about in the same echelon, its luster gone; the public was confused and believed that Packard no longer built a quality car. Most important, the company's lack of objectives and market targets hurt sales "because the public doesn't know what they are getting in purchasing a Packard." [32]

The key to turning that around, Nance argued, was a publicity blitz to keep Packard in the public eye until it could adjust its product line to counter these beliefs. Nance ordered his public relations department to emphasize the new management team, rising sales, and Packard's contribution to the nation's defense needs. He hoped at the end of the year to publicize the more favorable earnings record he was certain would follow. To combat the problem of being an Independent, he wanted to steal Studebaker's approach, which was to present itself as a "happy *compromise of craftsmanship and mass production.*" For a quick increase in sales, however, he initiated a "new approach to the woman as a factor in purchasing a car." [33]

Monaghan had already drawn up an ad campaign aimed at women. Its list of innovations that made cars easier to drive included an automatic transmission, power steering and brakes, and "advanced springs," and touted Packard as the only car "especially emphasized to make a woman's automobile." He wanted the campaign extended to dealers' showrooms and service departments so "a woman won't object to going in"; this was presumably a reference to taking down girlie calendars. The executive committee at its December meeting suggested that the company publish a booklet entitled "Recipes for Car Care" and asked for a careful "working out of color charts, fabric harmonies and numerous other 'housekeeping' ideas" to be published in newspapers and "farm paper women's department pages." Nance was serious about attracting women to his showrooms and thought that by offering them dealers' teas and "vanities" such as Kleenex holders, he could sell cars as he had washing machines. More realistically, however, he was looking for a "quick fix" to tide Packard over until he could improve his dealer network and realign his product mix.[34]

Although a whirlwind in other respects, Nance was very careful in approaching his dealers. His plan was simple: following Booz Allen's advice, he set out to increase the number of Packard dealers and later to weed out the weaklings. The first part of his plan was under way by

September 1952, when he reported that he had increased the number of dealers from 1,360 to 1,427. But that number was still less than satisfactory. To make Packard "depression proof," Nance thought he had to sell at least 150,000 cars a year, and that "bogie" required at least 2,250 dealer outlets. To reach his sales goal, Nance needed to know what kind of cars his dealers wanted. He commissioned Briggs to poll the dealers and in the meantime ordered Walters to "develop a real sales training program." Walters was to look at historical sales methods in the industry and "go back to Handy and ask for the original sales training program used by Chevrolet in the late 20's." James Handy, who won a gold medal in the 440-yard breaststroke in the 1904 Olympics, organized a company (named after himself) in 1911 to give motivational training. Chevrolet, and later Nance, thought this was the essence of good salesmanship. Nance, for all his merchandising self-confidence, knew his own abilities and was willing to consult outsiders, provided that he retain control over the final product.[35]

Nance appeared to be doing things backward when he ordered a sales program before he received the dealers' survey results. He had seen the preliminary findings in late September, however, and knew that his dealers were not as helpful as he had hoped. They agreed that a merchandiser in the president's office was a good idea, although a few grumbled that an insider who knew the business ought to have been promoted. They talked about the need for "new blood" at East Grand and the necessity for a "shot in the arm" to get the company going again. What they needed on the showroom floors, they reported, was a prestige car called Packard and a low- or medium-priced car bearing another name, which was precisely what Nance had proposed. A few curmudgeons called on East Grand to return strictly to the luxury field and emphasize the prestige inherent in the firm's name—the dealers did not think that Packard's image was all that fuzzy. Salesmen agreed that Packard's quality engineering could be taken for granted, the bathtub models were styling "duds," for the last two years styling had sold Packards, and Packard's Ultramatic was "outstanding."[36]

The dealers evinced fair satisfaction with the Packards but were decidedly unhappy about the company's advertising and promotion, which were, they grumbled, of low quality and out of date. Like dealers everywhere, they wanted more advertising help, increased print exposure, discontinuance of TV advertising unless "it is of top drawer quality," closer ties with local ads, and a national campaign to draw the public into their showrooms.

Most of what his dealers had to say reinforced Nance's preconceptions. His salespeople loved the Ultramatic, the device Booz Allen

thought was overpriced. Nance left the transmission alone. The dealers'
pleas for more powerful engines were harder for Nance to answer. In reality, Packard's old, reliable straight eight was as powerful as its competitors, but Packard's engineers had tweaked just about all the horsepower they were going to get from it while maintaining its reputation for
reliability. Worse, compared to the new V-8s now crowding showroom
floors, the straight eight looked dowdy. But Nance listened, and the 1953
models emphasized increases up to 180 horsepower in the Packard series and 135 to 160 horsepower in the Clippers. The horsepower race was
on in earnest, but Packard dealers would have to wait a couple more
years for their promised powerful V-8.[37]

In the time it was going to take to turn Packard around, Nance had to
support his public relations attack with some solid financial figures as
evidence that Packard was on its way back. He looked into raising dividends to lift the price of Packard's stock and had Grant do a historical
survey of the company's dividends. He discovered that during the eleven
postwar years, Packard had returned anything from zero to 13.3 percent
on its stock's market value, for an average of 4 percent. Grant made
"a conservative estimate of what volume and earnings might be over
the next five years." He projected production figures from 75,000 to
125,000, a clear indication that he was not optimistic about hitting the
targeted 150,000. He calculated that "dividends should not exceed 25
cents a share," a 5 percent return. Fiscally, Grant was more comfortable
with four percent, but he counseled Nance, "You may want to show some
improvement to the stockholders during the next five years."[38]

No doubt Nance was anxious to appease his shareholders, but his expansion program called for cash outlays that would require massive borrowing. He was in a money bind from the day he took office. By July 1952,
Nance could publicly boast that second-quarter sales were up 16 percent, but investment in the plant to handle defense contracts had cost
more than $7 million, which had drawn Packard's working capital down
to about $43 million. Only a week later Grant wrote a confidential
memo, asking Nance to think about contracting for "some long-time
loans." Grant noted that Packard had "these splendid lines of credit"
with its bankers, but he wondered "if they could stand up in times of bad
business or recession when we might need them." As a clincher, the treasurer mentioned that GM and Studebaker had already set up such loans.
Although Grant promised that "there is no great rush about this," he
was obviously planting the seed in Nance's mind and making a politic argument that Packard's financial resources would not permit high dividends to appease stockholders.[39]

For the first time, Grant and Nance could not borrow from a parent organization. They were going to have to parry the Wall Street sharks to put together a banking consortium or a group of insurance companies to revamp Packard. Further, Nance habitually thought more in terms of cutting costs than of raising money and concentrated his early efforts on shaving expenses everywhere. His eye missed nothing, no matter how politically sensitive. He asked Grant, for example, to look into the history of directors' compensation and to make recommendations. The finance man reported that each director received $5,000 per year, a fee established in 1925. Grant discovered that the directors had reduced their fee in 1947 to $2,400 a year, after stockholders complained. But after firing Christopher, they raised the fees to their former level "because for a period of time the directors were running the business and men like Mr. ZurSchmiede were spending a tremendous amount of time on company problems." The $5,000 compensation, Grant thought, was high, especially in light of the Pennsylvania Railroad directors, who were paid exactly nothing. "This is, of course, a ticklish subject," Grant reminded his boss, and it was probably too ticklish for the politically pragmatic Nance, but the inquiry indicated the way Nance approached Packard's financial problems.[40]

In the back of his mind, he hoped that he would not have to deal with bankers, that he could finance expansion from internal profits earned from his defense business. He made this crystal clear in a confidential memo he wrote George Reifel in July 1952. Nance reminded the manufacturing man that Packard had to stay "in the defense business indefinitely to provide us the additional volume to help absorb our overhead over the next few years while we make an attempt to improve our position in the car business." He implored Reifel to bring more defense work into Packard's shops and to beat "Studebaker on performance on the Jet engine so that we can become the solid #2 supplier to the Air Force and thereby insure our continuance in business at the time the schedules are reduced." Nance knew that defense contracts would soon be cut back, by which time he had to have revitalized Packard's auto business.[41]

Nance was unrelenting in his efforts to bring more contracts into his factories to help cover his overhead costs. From the very first, the new president also looked into bringing Packard's body production back to East Grand. Nance was bothered that he did not make his own shells, a car's most important selling point. And he received scads of complaints about Packard's bodies—they rattled, they fit badly, and they leaked—which he blamed on lousy workmanship at Briggs. In addition, Briggs, faced with rising labor and materials costs, passed its increased expenses on to Packard and to Chrysler. Packard might have been more willing to bear the rising costs, but Briggs was beset by constant labor troubles, and fell behind in its contract every year. That played havoc with East Grand scheduling.[42]

Several years earlier, George Brodie, vice president of coordinating operations (mostly defense work), had done a study of what it would cost Packard to bring its bodywork home. His estimate must have been daunting, but Nance was anxious to see whether Packard could at least make a start and build some of its own cars: "We are in the clutch with Briggs right now on the hardtop, where their costs are completely out of line against the competition." Brodie's "offhand thinking" was that such limited production would result in no appreciable savings, but Nance was determined to "solve" this problem.[43]

Nance sent Brodie's earlier study to Reifel, asked him to incorporate it into his "new program" to "manufacture . . . our own bodies," and urged Reifel to set his sights even higher: "We should also [study] other components with a view to establishing the volume to which it would justify Packard doing their own manufacturing rather than buying on the outside." Nance specifically nominated steering-gear assemblies as a possibility for in-house work. Packard's president kept hammering on the subject. "As I see the situation," he said, "the greatest problem facing Packard is to get more labor content in to the end product."[44]

Long before Reifel's report was ready, Nance took the issue to his board on October 29. The upshot of the unrecorded directors' conversations was that they authorized Nance to shop for a body-stamping plant. This became Grant's responsibility; a week later, Grant proposed that Packard trim its Briggs bodies starting in 1954 in the building space south of East Grand. To make any money from doing its own large stampings, Grant estimated that the company's volume would have to reach 200,000 cars per year, a figure nobody at Packard thought realistic. Furthermore, Packard had a shortage of floor space as long as its defense work continued at the same level. Grant wanted to maintain Packard's "flexibility in defense and civilian production," and he warned that if Packard purchased an outside stamping plant and defense orders were curtailed, the company would find itself with a costly excess of unused floor space.[45]

Nance presented Grant's findings to his board at a long December 20 meeting. The figures for finishing out Clipper bodies showed that the company would save about $30 to $35 per car. The board authorized Nance to start work on the operation, but before he did he heard rumors that Briggs might be sold. At his directors' behest, Nance put in a bid. But all his forward planning was dashed when the government suddenly cut his defense contracts and the bottom fell out of the car market. Nance was forced to turn his attention to cost reductions and possible mergers.[46]

The quickest way to bring the body stamping in house, Nance reasoned, was to follow his consultant's recommendations to merge, and Nance's preferred partner was Nash. Early in June 1952, Brownell wrote his boss, suggesting that Packard build V-8s for Nash and expand the relationship to include "dualing" dealers. As Brownell pointed out, it "would be a natural for Nash and Packard dealers to dual because Nash does not have a large car and Packard does not have a small one." Booz Allen had recommended that Packard build parts for others, and, faced with an outlay of $9 million to tool his new V-8 plant, Nance warmed to Brownell's idea. Grant reported that the total costs for the engine facility would run closer to $12 million. He also concluded that Packard would make a pretax profit on Nash's business of only about $500,000 to $600,000 per year, not enough, he thought, to justify "the commercial risk." If, however, Mason was willing to help defray development tooling, to the tune of $3 million, "an entrance fee so to speak," Grant said, Packard "might" be interested. Grant also talked with Nash about buying Packard's Ultramatic.[47]

Nance sat through Grant's presentation and then said that the committee members should keep Packard's future programs in mind. He told them that Packard was not contemplating any merger "now or in the future" and that the company should be positioned for a merger but be "fully capable of acting" on its own as well. It was Nance's version of a preparedness campaign. He wanted to push the 1953 Packard hard and to bring out a lower-priced 1954 Packard, which would help achieve his goal of 150,000 sales.[48]

Nance was fascinated by his consultant's suggestion that Packard build a lower-priced car, and he kept turning the idea over in his mind. Only three months after taking office, he ordered Clare Briggs to send him a report on Packard's efforts to build lower-priced cars since 1937, a date he must have chosen because that was the year Macauley brought out his 6-cylinder 115C. Then Nance sent a long memo to Reifel, complaining that Packard could not survive with 17 percent of the market, particularly at the upper end. Nance obviously thought that any possible mergers that could bring Packard a lower-priced car were either dead or far in the future. He therefore leaned toward Booz Allen's recommendation to build his own small car. So he told Reifel that "we must have a car that will come down one or more notch in the market price" to give Packard market coverage of about 28 percent. That meant Reifel had to carve out about $125 in costs from Packard's 200 sedan to create what

Nance wanted to call the Packard 100. The Clipper would be available in the 100 and the deluxe 200 model.[49]

In a November 1952 product-planning meeting, the committee decided to bring out a retooled 1954 Packard and face-lift the Clipper. The following year it expected to introduce its V-8, an entirely new Clipper, and face-lift the Packard. The pertinent questions still unanswered were the degree of interchangeability between the two models and how inexpensive the company could make the Clipper. Nance, obsessed with making Packard "depression proof," wanted the Clipper's costs reduced as "far as possible . . . without stripping the car of necessary selling and operating features." If Reifel could not get the costs out any other way, Nance proposed offering a 6-cylinder Clipper for less than $2,400, on which Packard would make no profit, "in order to give the dealer merchandise which would permit them to stay in business during any recession." In an ironic turnabout, Nance asked Graves to look into purchasing 6-cylinder motors from Nash and to estimate the costs of manufacturing them in Packard's own plant.[50]

Nance's preoccupation with building a cheaper car caused him to make suggestions that must have startled some of his colleagues. For example, in December Nance told Grant that he was thinking of purchasing the Austin Company, "or at least their American operations," and wanted the firm's financial statement. Austin had for years manufactured the Bantam, an aptly named car, which was about as small an auto as Nance could hope to get. Grant politely informed his boss that Austin had not made a Bantam since it started building Jeeps in World War II; the company had lost $2 million in 1950 and was in "reorganization" under Chapter 10 of the Bankruptcy Code. If Nance could not buy a sub-compact, he was willing to build one. He asked Briggs to talk over the possibility of building a car to compete with the Nash Rambler, a vehicle Nance thought was a "sleeper" for "a two-car family and the novelty car market." Part of the underlings' jobs was to quietly disabuse their boss of his wilder notions, and Briggs noted at the bottom of Nance's letter, "Discussed with JJN. Nothing further." Nance also briefly considered acquiring Willys-Overland and had Grant work up detailed balance sheets comparing that firm with Packard, but did not follow up.[51]

The new president hit Packard like a whirlwind in 1952. His emphasis on forward planning and merchandising was new to East Grand, and the frenzy with which committees and executives churned out reports for their boss must have exhausted the lot of them. Nance floated all manner of ideas, possibilities, and solutions to the company's problems, some of which were patently unworkable, and asked for further information. But in the final analysis, he was a careful, conservative manager. His intentions, clear by year's end, were to split the two lines, spread their retooling over two years, cut costs, keep his merger options open, and search for cheap ways to bring out the equivalent of Packard's old 120 and 110. Nance's strategic plans were not revolutionary; they were at best evolutionary.

If he did nothing else in those eight months, Nance questioned all the verities that Packard hands held dear. He asked everyone what he or she was doing and why. He questioned decades-old procedures even in the sacred engineering department. He brought a vigor and an enthusiasm to his job that wore others down. He appeared to be everywhere, and the green memos fluttering down on managers' desks reminded them he was watching and expecting something for the company's wages. Lights at the East Grand offices began flickering on before dawn, when executives came in early to catch up on their work, and blazed late into the night. Nance set Packard into motion. It was not always clear where the company was going, but it was going somewhere.

Nance's approach was a fresh one, but the older executives, lacking the stamina or the inclination to keep up with the new pace, fell by the wayside or were eased out. Many left angry, certain that Nance was bent on destroying the edifice they had devoted their lifetimes to building. The fresh faces, however, many still in their thirties and forties, sensed that Packard offered them an opportunity to do something different in the auto industry, a chance to work for a man who was open to new ideas and the hope that Packard could be what it once was. To some, Nance was a miracle worker sent to save the company; to others, he was the Antichrist who would destroy Packard.

The new president made mistakes in 1952, but they were errors of ignorance or presupposition. Perhaps the most glaring was his inability to appreciate just how intractable automotive costs really were. Nance thought it perfectly reasonable to demand that Reifel cut $125 out of a car the company sold for $1,800 to its dealers; Reifel found it impossible. Nance failed to understand that many of his costs, especially ones that hurt the most, were outside his control. He was helpless in the face of materials costs, shortages, and inflation. On the other hand, Nance thought it wise to spend money to save money. For the first time since Macauley tooled for the 120, Packard opened its pocketbook and spent lavishly. Nance argued that he was catching up on capital expenditures that should have been made years previously. Others thought he was spending Packard into bankruptcy. And finally, Nance did not realize just how little time he had to turn Packard around. He guessed that he had until 1955, when a recession would ravage the auto markets. In reality, he had only about one year of grace before a buyer's market reappeared with a vengeance. As it squeezed Packard's profits, all Nance's other plans became more difficult to execute. When the red ink began to flow, he threw all his forward planning out the window and struggled desperately just to keep Packard alive. That was his fate in 1953: he had too much to accomplish and too little time.

James Ward Packard, shown at the wheel with Alvan Macauley in this early
1917 photograph, founded the company that later bore his name in Warren,
Ohio, in 1899. He never devoted full attention to his automotive creation, however, and within a decade lost control of Packard to Henry Joy and his fellow investors. (Courtesy of the *Packard Cormorant*)

The car that started it all: an 1899 Model A Packard, here seen with Packard's second president, Henry B. Joy, at the tiller. The Model A boasted a single-cylinder
engine that pumped out 9 horsepower at 800 rpm. James Ward Packard built five
copies of this car. (John A. Conde collection)

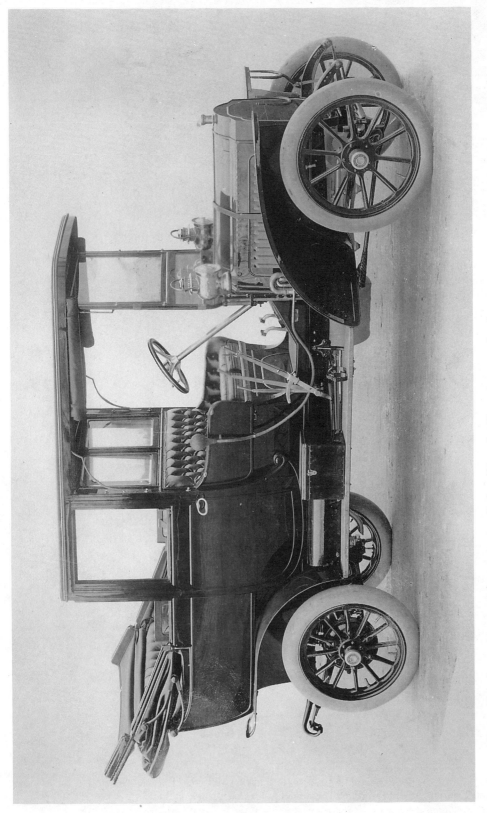

The Model 30, introduced in August 1906, was Packard's first "mass" seller at 9,540 units. It was available in several versions: touring, runabout, limousine, and the popular landaulette, shown here. The 30 was powered by a massive 432-cubic-inch 4-cylinder engine that reached a maximum of 30 horsepower at only 650 rpm. (John A. Conde collection)

Packards were not only for the staid rich. This 1909 Model 18 "runabout" was a dashing piece of machinery powered by a 4-cylinder "T" head engine that put out 18 horsepower. The auto was not for the impecunious, however; it sold for between 3,200 and 4,400 pre–World-War-I dollars. (Ed Mark's collection, Packard Museum, Niles, Mich.; © 1990 Packard Industries, Inc.)

Packard repeated its success in 1912 when it introduced its new Model 48, a car that remained in production through 1915 and sold 4,649 units. A huge 525-cubic-inch 6-cylinder engine rated at 74 horsepower enabled the 48 to keep up with growing automobile traffic on U.S. streets. (John A. Conde collection)

When Packard introduced its first "Twin Six" or 12-cylinder engine in May 1915, it stole a march on all its competitors in the luxury-car class. The brainchild of Colonel Jesse Vincent, the Twin Six was an engineering marvel. It was capable of putting out 85 horsepower from only 424 cubic inches and, more importantly from Vincent's perspective, it was the quietest and smoothest motor in the world. (Author's collection)

Packard advertised its new, powerful Twin Six to appeal to its traditional buyers. The company emphasized the motor's smoothness, quietness, and economy, with just a hint of its exhilarating speed, for those in the lap-robe set with an urge to live a little dangerously. (James Pearsall's collection)

The new Packard Imperial Limousine, seven passengers

Why do men ski?

In free flight—down the long incline he sweeps at the speed of the wind—unhampered by that resisting force—*vibration*.

Slivers of wood and flakes of snow supply the means of obtaining the thrilling sense of unfettered power.

Smoothest speed is not only desirable from the standpoint of pleasure—but it is always most *efficient speed*.

Because the Twin Six engine has min- imized vibration—it not only adds to the exhilarating joy of motoring—but conserves the stored-up power of gasoline.

Twelve balanced and sprightly cylinders divide the stresses—and develop great, smooth, *economical* power.

"Beauty of motion" is in this splendid Packard accompanied by a beauty of design that surely adds to the delight of the fine sport of Twin Six motoring.

Seventeen distinctive body styles in open and enclosed cars in the Third Series Twin Six—3-25 and 3-35

A s k   t h e   m a n   w h o   o w n s   o n e

Packard Motor Car Company, Detroit

Alvan Macauley, "the gentleman's gentleman" of the car industry, was Packard's president from 1916 until 1938. He was responsible for making the company the premier marque in the luxury-car class. For his efforts, he was featured on *Time* magazine's cover twice and was often a spokesman for the industry. (Courtesy of the *Packard Cormorant*)

During World War I Colonel Vincent applied the lessons he had learned from designing Packard's Twin Six to develop a 12-cylinder "Liberty Engine." The 905-cubic-inch, 710-pound airplane engine was rated at 335 horsepower but was capable of attaining almost 405 horsepower, a horsepower-per-pound ratio that was very efficient for the times. Packard produced 6,500 of the engines, which were used in the DH-4 fighter plane. (Ed Mark's collection, Packard Museum, Niles, Mich.)

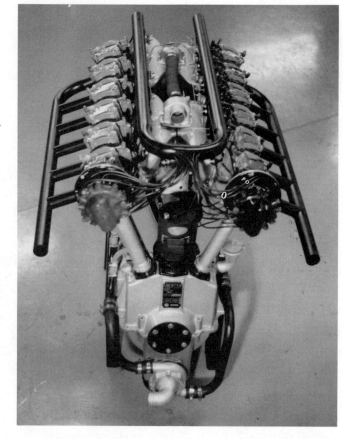

Packards always enjoyed a reputation for durability and speed. Here Colonel Vincent, Packard's masterful chief engineer, is shown driving a 1919 Packard Twin Six pace car to get the Indianapolis 500 started at the famous brickyard. Ralph DePalma, driving a Packard with a Liberty aircraft engine in it, finished sixth in the event that year. (John A. Conde collection)

Alvan Macauley, long the brain behind Packard's success, obviously took pride in his own creations. This photo of him behind the wheel of a 1921 Packard Single Six Model 116 touring car was shot in front of his home. The five swells accompanying him are unidentified. (John A. Conde collection)

All auto manufacturers adopted the popular postwar boxy styling, as this Packard 1926 Model 326 "Opera Coupe," one of two extant, illustrates. The 60-horsepower car was more reasonably priced than some earlier Packards at between $2,585 and $2,785. Even at those prices, however, it was far from an inexpensive car. A Model T Ford of the same year could be purchased for less than $300. (Ed Mark's collection, Packard Museum, Niles, Mich.; © 1989 Packard Industries, Inc.)

The famous general Billy Mitchell preferred a more stylish Packard. Here he is shown taking delivery of his new 1925 2-36 "Sport Model" in front of the East Grand Boulevard Packard factory. (Original Packard Motor Car Company photograph; James Pearsall's collection)

On the eve of the depression Packard stylists were on the verge of designing some of their most beautiful offerings. With its 106-horsepower straight eight motor and quiet luxury, the 1929 Packard Town Car, Model 640, was favored by many in the lap-robe set. (Ed Mark's collection, Packard Museum, Niles, Mich.)

Colonel Vincent never lost his interest in aircraft engines, and in the 1920's he tinkered with new ideas. He was always convinced a diesel engine was practical for aircraft, and just before the depression he tested this 9-cylinder rotary diesel engine, the DR-980. It was never a commercial success, and the depression temporarily ended Packard's interest in the project. (Ed Mark's collection, Packard Museum, Niles, Mich.)

Many manufacturers, including Packard, offered their finest products in the midst of the country's worst depression. Illustrated here is a 1930 Custom Eight phaeton with its telltale radiator screen guard in front of Packard's signature radiator shape. (Author's collection)

This 1931 Model 8-40 phaeton illustrates Packard's continuing refinement of the automotive stylists' art during the depression. (Photograph by James Pearsall)

Packard's trademark "yoked hood" looked good from any angle, as this photo shot across a 1930 and a 1934 attests. (Photograph by James Pearsall)

This 1932 Standard Eight Model 902 illustrates that the company continued to build large, quality cars for its conservative clientele well into the depression years. (Photograph by Bill Mayes; James Pearsall's collection)

PACKARD
Individual Custom Built Cars

The vehicles in this advertisement for custom-built 1932 Packards were costly for Americans, who earned an average weekly manufacturing wage of $17.05 in that year. (James Pearsall's collection)

About the only people who could afford Packard's depression-era classics were royalty. This 1934 dual-cowl Twelve with a custom Rollston body was built for the king and queen of Yugoslavia. The car was photographed on Fifth Avenue, across from Central Park, in New York City. Note the LeBaron hood ornament. (John A. Conde collection)

Even some of the Packards built for commoners in 1934 commanded royal prices. This Twelve sold in the $4,000 to $8,000 range. Today, restored, the car could fetch well into the six figures. (Author's collection)

For Americans who wanted a big, powerful, fast family car, this 1934 Super Eight Model 1103 five-passenger sedan, riding on a 135-inch wheelbase, was just the ticket for slightly under 3,000 depression dollars. (Photograph by Gary Roberts; James Pearsall's collection)

Mr. W. K. Jewett *of Pasadena*
is one of more than 1000 distinguished owners through whose gateways
Packards have passed for 21 years or more

Packard Twelve Cabriolet with Body by LeBaron

HERE is perhaps the greatest tribute that could be paid to the quality that Packard has maintained through the years . . .

. . . more than 1000 distinguished families have owned Packards continuously for 21 years or more.

Such a record is the greatest possible proof of the luxury Packard affords, the service Packard gives, the prestige Packard carries.

It is proof, too, that Packard has succeeded in its greatest aim —to make each new Packard finer and more beautiful than the one before.

And America is agreeing with that opinion. Since the introduction of these brilliant new cars, Packard has received a greater share of the fine car business—both here and abroad—than ever before in its history. And while it may be a coincidence, more people have been buying fine cars during these months than at any time in years.

If you, like so many of these people, have driven your present car far longer than usual, why not join them now in the joy of owning a new 1935 Packard? . . . Just telephone your Packard dealer—he will gladly bring one of these new cars to your door for a trial.

PACKARD EIGHT · SUPER EIGHT · TWELVE

⁂ *Ask the man who owns one* ⁑

Before the Fall: As the One Twenty Debuted to save the Company, ads for seniors continue to stress the "distinguished owners."

Despite hard times, Packard continued to run advertisements that were artistic masterpieces. This example of the company's "gateway" series featured a LeBaron-bodied Packard Twelve designed to appeal to someone with Jewett's tastes and money. (Courtesy of the *Packard Cormorant*)

Opposite. With Packard's profits plummeting in the early 1930's, Alvan Macauley tried to move the company into the middle range of the market without sacrificing traditional Packard quality. The result was the ill-fated 1932 Light Eight shown in this advertisement. (James Pearsall's collection)

The New PACKARD LIGHT EIGHT

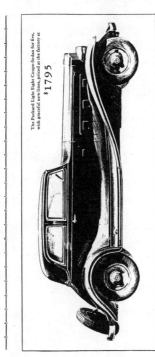

The Packard Light Eight Coupe-Sedan for five, with graceful new lines, priced at the factory at
$1795

The Packard Light Eight Five-Passenger Sedan, a large, roomy, comfortable car, priced at the factory at
$1750

THE new Packard Light Eight for the first time introduces Packard quality in a current model at a price less than $2250 at the factory. This could never have been done before without a reduction of quality—a thing Packard's thirty-two-year-old policy would never permit.

These sensational prices are possible now only through Packard's taking full advantage of the most unusual circumstances since before the war. Prices on fine materials are at or near pre-war levels. This, combined with advanced engineering and production methods and the assurance of a very substantial volume, makes motor car history by greatly broadening the fine car field.

The new Light Eight Packard line comprises the four beautiful, completely modern models illustrated on these pages, all with 110 horsepower and on a new chassis of 128 inch wheelbase. New cars throughout, designed to fit today's economic conditions—to reflect the new purchasing power of the dollar—these Packards offer many improvements never before available to Packard buyers.

Most important of all are the new Packard Synchro-mesh Transmission, *quiet in all three speeds*, and the new Finger Control Free-Wheeling. These two features together revolutionize all conceptions of driving ease, effortless control and *safe* free-wheeling results. The new Angleset Rear Axle and double-drop frame permit a lower center of gravity, and the low, modern design of the body.

Other improvements, just as found on the larger, heavier and more costly Packard models, include Ride Control, dash-adjustable hydraulic shock absorbers; complete equipment of shatter-proof glass, and body insulation which excludes outside heat and cold and adds silence to the other interior luxuries. Six-ply tires and bumpers, front and rear, are standard on all models.

Packard is proud to give the Packard name to these aristocratic new Light Eights. They uphold the Packard tradition of engineering leadership and supremacy in beauty of line and luxury of transportation. You will be proud to own one of these new Packard cars. A demonstration will make you dissatisfied with all you have previously experienced in acceleration, ease of control, power and comfort. You will be unfair to yourself if you do not see and drive the Packard Light Eight before buying *any* car at or near its price this spring. You *can* own a Packard.

The Coupe-Roadster for two or four, $1795 at the factory

Finger Control Free-Wheeling permits the advantages of free-wheeling or conventional operation at the instant choice of the driver.

Shatter-proof Glass, standard equipment in windshield and all windows, affords complete protection to passengers as well as driver.

The Coupe for two or four, $1795 at the factory

Synchro-mesh Transmission, quiet in all three speeds, brings a new ease and convenience in gear shifting, a new quietness in operation.

Ride Control, dash-adjustable hydraulic shock absorbers, provides restful riding comfort whatever the road, load, speed or temperature.

ASK THE MAN WHO OWNS ONE

OF A DISTINGUISHED FAMILY

The Light Eight Model 900 is shown here. The car enjoyed all the usual Packard refinements, even a straight eight rated at 110 horsepower, but sold for as low as $1,795. Even that was too expensive for hard-pressed Americans, and the Light Eight still had too much Packard quality; the company made no profit on the model, which was only offered in 1932. (Ed Mark's collection, Packard Museum, Niles, Mich.; © 1992 Packard Industries, Inc.)

Max Gilman was one of the men Macauley hired to build and sell an all-new Packard priced in the middle-market range. It was a desperate gamble to save the luxury-car builder that had watched its market all but disappear. Gilman and other new hires revolutionized the way Packard built and sold automobiles and altered the company's internal culture. Gilman became president of Packard in 1939 and departed three years later to avoid public scandal. (Courtesy of the *Packard Cormorant*)

The gruff-talking and often profane George Christopher was lured from Pontiac to become Packard's vice president for manufacturing. He applied mass-production techniques to Packard's new medium-priced cars, the 120s. Christopher replaced Gilman as company president in 1942 and was forced to resign in 1949. (Courtesy of the *Packard Cormorant*)

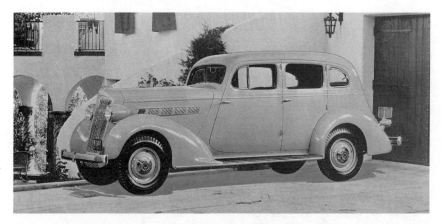

The car that saved Packard from bankruptcy in the depression. A 1935 Model 120 five-passenger sedan offered a lot of car for about $1,000. The 120 featured an 8-cylinder engine with 110 horsepower, a 120-inch wheelbase, and most of the usual Packard niceties. The public responded by purchasing almost 25,000 of the bargains in their first year. (John A. Conde collection)

Max Gilman and other advocates of mass production at Packard pressured President Macauley to step down another notch in the market. The result was this 1937 Packard 115C, brought out in 1936, priced as low as $795, and powered by a 100-horsepower, 6-cylinder engine. Despite its 115-inch wheelbase, it looked remarkably like the more expensive Packards. Note the company's advertising pitch toward middle-class professionals in this photo. (John A. Conde collection)

The junior cars may have been Packard's bread and butter after 1935, but as this 1936 Twelve, a Model 1407 Convertible Victoria, illustrates, the company had not lost its touch for building handsome large cars. For his $6,435, the discriminating Packard buyer could select from thirteen standard colors. (Photograph by R. Tyler Bland, Jr.; James Pearsall's collection)

Just because the Packard 120s were relatively inexpensive did not mean they were dowdy or dull, as this 1937 convertible shows. With its Packard styling, side-mounted spare tires, and "Goddess of Speed" radiator ornament, this 120C was quite the sporting auto. (Author's collection)

More photographs follow page 195.

Chapter 7

Model 640 Town Car, 1929

"God Save the King— and Packard!"

The year 1953 was a turning point for Packard, every bit as crucial as 1935 had been to its prewar survival. At the start of the year, Nance sat down and listed his short-range goals and his long-range targets. Imbued with a sense of neatness and balance, he outlined exactly ten general "bogies" and another ten for his "New Packard Program." It was a measure of Nance's year that he met none of them.

The paradox was that as Nance sat at his desk, cataloging his ambitions, Packard's future had never looked brighter. He was confident that he could double his company's car sales, maintain or even increase his defense orders, and continue his public relations blitz, backed with hard evidence that Packard was "on the march." Even his adjectives illustrated his buoyant attitude toward the future. He proposed to develop a "lean, imaginative management team with plenty of 'fight'" to convince the public that Packard was a "hard-hitting, aggressive and successful company." He scribbled as if he were a man fully in control of his destiny, who knew what he was doing and was confident of success. The first-quarter results did little to disabuse Nance of his dreams. He had hoped to capture 3 percent of an estimated 5 million car sales, and a manufacturing run of 150,000 autos would have solved most of the company's problems. Nance thought he had a fair chance of reaching that goal, although he more realistically set 134,000 as his target. The government had dropped its auto production quotas at the end of 1952–automakers were free to produce all the cars they wanted. The Korean War was still raging, but with Eisenhower's election and his promise to go to Korea to end the conflict, Nance had every reason to believe that consumer confidence would be high.[1]

At the end of the first month, Packard was on its way to a record-setting year. Fred Walters reported that dealers had delivered 8,003 retail sales, breaking the company's all-time January sales record. Walters was so elated that he listed the February and March company sales records and promised to try to break them too. Nance's cryptic, smeared reply was to send his "letter to key men." The factory was running full tilt with two shifts, and Packard's dealers, for once, sold everything delivered to them.[2]

Packard actually had a shortage of cars by early March, but not entirely because of a sudden surge in demand. Nance could not get enough steel to maintain his output: the materials market was chaotic after the government lifted its restrictions. He suggested to his board that Packard ought to loan money to steel companies in return for a guaranteed percentage of their product. He wrote the vice president of U.S. Steel, with whom he had done business at Hotpoint, pleading that "we need help and need it badly" and promising larger orders once he had rebuilt Packard. He also advanced another $2 million to the Pittsburgh Steel Company to enable it to expand its production. In return, Pittsburgh Steel agreed to share its production of slab and sheets with Packard and Chrysler. The arrangement was a flop, and Pittsburgh Steel eventually repaid all the money Packard had advanced.[3]

Briggs felt the steel shortage most acutely and could not keep up with Nance's assembly line. Nance was losing a golden sales opportunity and was furious. On the basis of the upsurge in demand, Nance had increased factory hiring–by Groundhog Day, Packard was staffed to manufacture 540 cars per day. Five weeks later, Nance was begging Briggs for 600 bodies a day and was only getting 480. He fretted that Briggs was costing him 5,000 sales in the first quarter. By mid-April the situation had not changed. Lower production rates forced Nance to lay off 19 percent of his hourly workforce. Even with those efficiencies, Nance noted that his overhead was $19 per car higher than the industry average. Briggs was hounding him for a $30 to $35 increase per car. When the quarter's figures were tallied, Nance discovered that Briggs had fallen 6,000 bodies short. Nothing must have rankled Nance more than losing sure sales.[4]

There were other clouds gathering as well. Although Packard still had no corporate debt, the new V-8 plant at Utica and the Ultramatic's redesign were costing millions of dollars. The company was also faced with high tooling costs in 1955 and 1956. Worse, the first postwar cutbacks hit the company in March when the Defense Department canceled one-third of its contracts for jet engines, which cost Nance $42 million in anticipated revenue. Capitalizing on Packard's rising sales volume, Nance received his board's permission to set up a $25 million credit line with banks and ordered Grant at the end of March to see to it.[5]

It was, with the dark exceptions of the defense cancellation and the body and steel shortage, a heady first three months for Packard and Nance. Nance crowed that his $3 million first-quarter profit was the company's best ever and was three times greater than the previous year's. While he was at it, he plugged his new program and the progress he had made at East Grand, putting 400 supervisory employees "out to pasture." He bragged that he had beefed up his dealer organization, weeding out 200 weaklings and adding another 400 new outlets, to raise the company's total to 1,685. He had stepped up production of the Packard to 15 percent of his total output to regain dominance of the prestige market. Nance predicted that eventually 35 percent of Packard's cars would be in the upper price range. With 30,378 autos turned out in the first quarter, Nance guessed that Packard would reach his goal of 120,000, a little lower than his private ambition. The only caveat was his warning that the industry was producing 7 million cars annually while dealers were selling only 5 million. But Packard, he noted, was in better shape than most companies because its dealers' inventories were down from eleven cars in January to only six per dealer at quarter's end.[6]

At that instant, Nance stood at the very apogee of his career at Packard. "Hotpoint Jim" was well on his way to pulling off a miracle for the old automaker, just as he had for General Electric's junior appliance division. Moreover, Nance had inextricably intertwined his own reputation with Packard's fortunes, and he basked in the aura of continuing success in the spring of 1953. But even at that shining moment, Nance, who never had his ear far from the ground, could discern the rumblings that portended trouble. He had no idea, however, how severe it would become and how it would affect Packard's future. Even before the Defense Department cutbacks, Nance had some forebodings as he tallied each month's figures. In the midst of Packard's best financial quarter ever, he saw that his profits were below expected levels by $300,000 in March, $400,000 in April, $340,000 in May, and almost $500,000 in July. Most of the first quarter's impressive showing was owing to January and February sales, and they slowed down as Packard entered what was usually its peak selling season.[7]

Nance did not have to look far for the reason behind the decline: the feared buyer's market had returned, and Nance was one of the first in the industry to recognize it. As early as April 13, he fired off a memo to Walter Grant, warning that he was "deeply disturbed" that Walters had reported a 55-day supply of Packards and that April orders for the senior car were down. Grant noted on the bottom of Nance's memo that he was cutting Packard's April production "so our stocks should go down slightly." The softening in the upper price range was a hint of things to come at East Grand. The market malaise spread so quickly that Nance reported to his directors at their May 27 meeting that the long-awaited "competitive period" had arrived.[8]

Little did Nance know just how competitive that period would be or how long it would last. Over at Ford headquarters in Dearborn, Henry Ford II decided to challenge Chevrolet for number one. In all of 1952, Ford had produced just over 777,000 cars, enough to give it 17.6 percent of the market, and Chevrolet, America's best-selling car since 1946, put out 877,000 units and gained a healthy 20 percent of the market. The perennial third-place producer, Plymouth, manufactured about 500,000 autos per year, good enough for 10 to 12 percent of the market. These shares had remained fairly stable in the years after World War II.[9]

Traditional market patterns fell apart in 1953 after the government freed producers to run flat out. Ford's and Chevrolet's assembly lines operated around the clock, and Plymouth increased its output to hold onto third place. Factories forced their dealers to digest the glut, even after midyear statistics showed sales lagging far behind production. Dealers did everything to unload the autos that overflowed their lots. They cut their profit margins, even sold at cost, to move them out. The faster they sold new cars, however, the more rapidly their used-car lots filled up. Some dealers resorted to wholesaling used cars after fifteen days; others tried gimmicks, such as offering free acreage with mineral titles with each car. A few dealers, even more hard-pressed, sold their newly minted cars straight to used-car lots, a practice known as "bootlegging." Manufacturers condemned the practice but did nothing to curtail the conditions that forced dealers to resort to such shady deals.[10]

The financial community was nervous and, by July, began to restrict auto credit. Finance companies had routinely loaned up to 90 percent of a new car's price in 1952; by mid-1953, they demanded that prospective purchasers put 40 percent down on older used cars and one-third in cash on new cars. Lower prices and sales gimmicks attracted marginal buyers. By midyear, New York lenders were reporting new-car repossessions at

10 percent, a rate unheard of since the depression. As used-car prices continued to fall, lenders became wary of loaning money on them, further clogging the automotive pipeline.[11]

After the summer selling season wound down, the Big Three continued to overproduce. As late as October, Ford and Chevrolet were manufacturing 5,000 to 6,000 cars per day, approximately Packard's monthly rate. Even Chrysler pushed Plymouth production up to about 3,300 daily. At the end of the year, Chevrolet still held first place with almost 1.5 million cars, its best year since 1950. Ford remained in second, with about 1.2 million units. Plymouth retained its hold on third, with an output of a little more than 660,000. Most striking, however, was that the lower-priced cars gobbled up 62.79 percent of the entire car market, up ten points from one year earlier.[12]

The low-priced three's increased market penetration came directly out of the Independents' pockets. The percentage of sales in the luxury market tumbled from 3.71 in 1952 to 2.09 by October 1953, and Packard's share of that segment fell even faster. The next-highest price bracket went from 4 percent to just 2.76 percent, dampening sales of Nance's 300s. And the market where Clippers battled with Buick, Chrysler, and DeSoto dropped from 11.59 percent to 7.43 percent of all cars sold. Although Packard competed in almost 20 percent of the market in the heady days of January, its percentage had shrunk to 12.28 by Halloween, with no end in sight. It was scant consolation at East Grand that it was not alone in the bloodbath. South Bend, Kenosha, Willow Run, and Hudson all saw their total market penetration crash from 13 percent in 1952 to 6.77 percent in October 1953. Compared to the 20 percent market share the Independents enjoyed in 1948, the 6-plus percent was disastrous.[13]

Nance's initial reaction to the chaos was to intensify his sales efforts. Packard's president, who, if his April memos are any indication, was becoming decidedly grumpy, called in Fred Walters and read him the riot act, demanding that he ignite Packard dealers to actively pursue customers. Packard's dealers, however, were woefully unprepared for the buyer's market. Many could not order cars from the factory because they lacked capital for floor-plan financing. Unfortunately, the banks and the finance companies were beginning to tighten up, and the dealers' capitalization problems grew worse. Many dealers did not even have a Packard demonstrator, and Walters promised to get 800 cars out in the field, still not enough to give all dealers one; some dealers did not have even one auto to show customers. None of this was news. Back in March, when he was still emphasizing separating the two lines, Nance wrote a lengthy memo to Clare Briggs, complaining that "we are starting to

112
=====

*"God Save
the King—
and
Packard!"*

tread the same route that has always been the case when two lines of cars are featured by one company," namely, "the dealers take the line of least resistance and sell the low priced cars." Nance had found some dealers who "will not even discuss a Packard." He fired off a testy letter to those dealers he called "goose eggs," reminding them of their Packard quota.[14]

For all his emotional outbursts, Nance was not sanguine about achieving dramatic results. Even in better times, fully one-third of Packard's outlets were undercapitalized and more than one-fourth of them lost money. In any protracted buyer's market, many of his dealers, especially those in larger towns and cities, lacked the resources to survive. Yet Nance always showed the best possible public face. In April he warned the American Marketing Association that "tough selling" times were ahead, but he assured the luncheon guests that he had Packard ready for them.[15]

Nance did more than pressure his dealers, however. He looked at what he was selling and, in April, commissioned a public survey to evaluate his cars. He listened to his dealers' long recitations of Packards' defects and passed them on to manufacturing. Clare Briggs had restaffed his sales department, hiring at least two new managers from Ford. In July, Nance completed his key-men group when he hired Ray Powers at $60,000 a year. As Nance watched his sales dwindle during the second quarter, what should have been his peak selling season, he sensed that he no longer had the luxury of following his own timetable. His actions were increasingly determined by outside forces, and he became testier.[16]

For the first time, Nance began to doubt whether his corporate strategies could save Packard. Although he continued to push his capital-improvement projects, even if they drained Packard of precious funds, he lost his focus on the merchandising side. He questioned why all the old verities were not working. His mind ran in some strange channels— he asked, for example, for data to show whether car sales rose and fell with the Dow-Jones average. Looking at the company parking lots, he saw that most Packard workers drove other makes of cars. He dashed off a memo to his personal assistant, Paul Shine, whom he had lured away from the FBI to handle spying activities at the plant and to ferret out information from other auto companies. Shine was to pressure men at the foreman level and higher to take advantage of Packard's employee discount purchase program, which put the Clipper within the Ford and Chevrolet price range.[17]

Privately he fretted about the term "Independent" and what it did to Packard's image. In June he sent a thoughtful note to Monaghan, observing that "Ford is just as much of an Independent as is Packard," unlike GM and Chrysler, which were amalgamations of one-time Independents.

Three months later, Nance returned to the tormenting subject. In an uncharacteristically long two-and-one-quarter-page letter to Clare Briggs, Nance wrestled with exactly what it meant. Convinced that the word was killing his company, he nevertheless noticed that "the paradoxical aspect of it is this word 'independent' has one of the finest acceptances in the English language." That may have been true in a more general sense, he thought, but "in the automotive trade it has come to mean a dog." His attention to etymology may have appeared academic to his colleagues, but Nance understood the power of words, especially in the marketplace. He believed that the despised "i" word bred a "lack of confidence in the future of the independent company," and he blamed "the Big Three dealers [who] promote this idea." Nance's approach to his semantic problem was characteristic—he ordered Clare Briggs to take it up with Maxon and have the ad agency run a public survey.[18]

Nance's toying with the "i" word, however, indicated a much deeper soul-searching. By the autumn of 1953, he was no longer certain that he knew what Packard stood for either publicly or inside the halls at East Grand. Thus he had no good ideas for a hard-hitting advertising theme that might reverse his fortunes. Back in late April, he had surprised his key men when he asked them to outline what they thought Packard stood for. They advised Nance to return to Packard's glorious past for solutions to its conundrums. The dead hand of the company's history held them fast, and their suggestions were of little practical help to Nance. Six months later, he was becoming desperate to find out, as he wrote Briggs, "what Packard stands for with the public (and what we would like to have it stand for)." He asked his sales manager to hire Maxon to "find out what they think Packard stands for. Maybe they can tell us better than we can tell ourselves." Nance was so troubled that he stood his whole selling philosophy on its head. Instead of telling the public what he wanted it to know, he was asking it to define his business for him.[19]

In the midst of the 1953 debacle, Nance did not spend all his time dithering about in the realms of the ethereal. He ordered a number of practical attacks on the deteriorating situation. He asked Briggs and Walters in June to study how Ford's Lincoln-Mercury division successfully marketed two cars in different fields. Mercury was gaining market shares on Nance's Clipper, and he wanted to know why. At the end of the month, Nance ordered Walters to draw up a direct-mail "strategy" so the company could target Packard prospects, an idea he stole from "Lincoln [which] has done an outstanding job in this area." In his desperate search for a selling miracle, Nance even investigated advertising Packards as the cheapest car per pound on the market. After discovering that it was not so, he quietly dropped the idea.[20]

Right after the Fourth of July, Nance learned that the sales department projected a huge inventory of unsold cars by the 1954s' introduction date. After a series of meetings on the subject, Nance laid out a set of draconian measures on July 8 to try to save the situation. He ordered an immediate production cutback to 300 cars per day, a figure he admitted was "60 cars below the basis at which our standard costs are set." The lower production level necessitated laying off the second shift and shutting the factory down for three weeks. Even if he delayed new-car introductions to January 1954, Nance estimated that his dealers would still have 6,600 old cars and 12,000 to 14,000 new ones on hand on New Year's Day. He accepted the fact that Packard could not make money at those production levels, but he was sure about his decision. He told his subordinates, "The schedule is now firm. There is no leeway left . . . this is 'IT'—from which there is no deviation or withdrawal." By Labor Day, Nance was convinced that "in retrospect it is perfectly obvious that our production schedule should have been cut way back in April" because "not since February have we been traveling in terms of retail deliveries at a rate to justify the schedules to which we have been producing." [21]

As unsold Packards began to fill dealers' and factory lots, Nance agreed to give dealers rebates of $300 on Packards and $200 on Clippers to move them out. Red ink was seeping across the company's ledgers, and in October the deficit was more than $500,000. Nance was so concerned that he ordered his sales department to cancel all newspaper advertising for November and December and all radio ads for December, actions that violated every merchandising tenet he held dear. The times, however, called for harsh measures. [22]

Cost reductions everywhere were instituted; even the product would have to be cheapened. In the face of a measly third-quarter profit of $55,000, most of which was earned early in the quarter, Nance ordered Grant to pare costs on the carefully developed plans for the 1955 and 1956 models. The original tooling estimates for both lines by 1956 had been $18 million, with a goal of establishing greater "curbstone identity" between the cars. With the same front fenders, grilles, bumpers, and bonnets, however, Packard could save almost $2 million. Grant also proposed to eliminate the planned Packard hardtop, while retaining the Clipper version and the Packard convertible, to make much of the chrome and trim on both models similar; to dump the eight-passenger sedan and the Caribbean; and to bring out a plastic sports car predicated on the Panther. The total savings would be $6 million, but the cars would seriously jeopardize Nance's campaign to separate the Clipper from the Packard and further cloud his blurred vision of exactly what Packard stood for. [23]

After a $750,000 November loss, there were no sacred financial cows at Packard, not even the engineering department. Byers Burlingame, responsible for counting the corporate beans, tackled Grant in finance with a forceful reminder that Graves had taken "no action to reduce expenses" and had not submitted a 1954 budget "that will meet the bogey established for them." Engineering had a fairly severe one; Graves had to cut his expenditures 15 percent for the coming year. Burlingame suggested that the department fire at least 100 employees, almost one-quarter of its engineers on the automotive side of the business. To support his "recommendations," Burlingame attached figures showing that Packard's engineering costs had been exactly $31.73 per car from 1946 through 1952, but had risen to $48.03 per unit in 1953. Its goal for 1954, depending upon sales, was between $45.58 and $60.77. Part of that increase reflected the heavy tooling costs for the all-new 1955 and 1956 cars and the V-8 and Ultramatic plant, as well as Nance's efforts to bring recent college graduates with fresh ideas into the department.[24]

By year's end the disastrous selling conditions had forced Nance to cut into the company's infrastructure because Packard was running out of money. Starting in July, he began each directors' meeting with a summary of the company's cash position, something he had not done in balmier days, and as of July 7 it stood at $40 million. Throughout summer and into fall, the till grew progressively emptier, falling to $24 million on August 25 and then dropping to a dangerously low $18 million by Christmas.[25]

Nance exhibited no Yuletide cheer when he met with his directors four days before the holiday. Scrooge-like, he reported that Packard would lose $5.5 million in 1954 if it sold 60,000 units, and an increase of 20,000 sales in 1955 would cut the firm's losses by only $700,000. He thought 1956 looked a little brighter predicting that 80,000 units would bring East Grand a profit of $3.5 million. To survive long enough to enjoy those profits, Packard would have to postpone product development plans for at least two years. The company would instead do a "major facelift" for 1955 and 1956 at a cost of $8 million and save a complete change for 1957. He still wanted to build an inexpensive Packard, and he reported on his discussions of a body program with Studebaker to bring out such a car, dubbed the "PS model" (Packard Studebaker) at East Grand. He estimated that it could be done for between $6 million and $10 million. Nance wanted to expand Packard's niche at the lower end of the mid-priced arena and take on Mercury.[26]

Packard's president was rather upbeat at the board meeting, considering what he had in hand. Grant's financial forecast reminded him that there had been "a complete collapse of our dealer organization in the face of competitive selling," which developed "about 9 months earlier than expected." And that was only the beginning. Packard had also endured rising costs from wage and pension adjustments of $20 per car, from Briggs of $24 per unit, and from vendors of $100 per unit. Moreover, it faced the problem of how to manufacture its bodies after Chrysler bought Briggs, how to pay for anything after it lost its defense contracts, and how to raise $37 million to pay for corporate modernization. Grant forecast that Packard would lose a pretax $11 million on 60,000 automobiles in 1954, and he was "not very sanguine . . . of obtaining much in the way of further budget reductions." The biggest threat of all, he thought, was that Packard's executives "are still going along on the basis that all is well and will not face up to the seriousness of the situation." [27]

Grant may have been a doomsayer, but Nance listened to him. He knew that Packard was going to have to borrow money for working capital. Its revolving $25 million loan was solely for defense business, but Nance needed money quickly to stay in the auto business. His directors gave him authority to borrow $20 million to carry the company until the market returned to normal. He had no trouble raising the money through short-term loans, but when he tried to interest a syndicate of insurance companies in a fifteen-year line of credit, it balked. Nance and his key men suffered from their lack of contacts in the national money markets, a flaw that haunted Packard until its very last days. [28]

The early arrival of the postwar selling spree was not the only ill wind that buffeted Packard. Ferry's and Nance's whole turnaround at East Grand was predicated upon the continuation of the Korean War and assurances that the Cold War would force the United States to maintain huge standing armies and a gigantic air force. Defense subcontracts for the J-47 turbojet engine and navy diesels were Packard's form of diversification, and its government billings often were larger each month than its net automobile profits. Nance was well aware, as he said in his inaugural speech to his key men, "that this defense business is a very precarious business, because it's run by politicians. . . . They can turn the spigot on or off." He urged his managers "to get on target with this Defense business for two reasons. First we need the business. That's reason enough." Nance made no bones about it: "We need the billing, we need the profit." He warned in 1952 about problems with the upcoming presidential election, which made defense contracts "a damn precarious business." [29]

The irony was that Nance's man, Dwight Eisenhower, won the presidency, but Packard suffered as much as it would have under Stevenson.

The new administration, influenced by the conservative policies of Robert Taft, abandoned the Democratic linchpins of foreign policy by containment, maintenance of huge conventional forces, and high levels of foreign aid to allies. Secretary of State John Foster Dulles disabused the nation of these aims as early as January 1954, when he announced that the country was going to rely on "the deterrent of massive retaliatory power" rather than conventional forces. The nation was going to emphasize air power and nuclear weapons and shrink military spending. The new administration put teeth into Dulles's worldview when it cut the defense budget for 1954 by $8 billion. The reconceptualization of America's place in the world boded ill for Nance's attempts to rejuvenate Packard's fortunes. The Korean armistice, signed on July 27, 1953, after 33,629 Americans had been killed, brought the war to a halt. This released some of the pressure on Eisenhower to maintain an engorged military establishment. As Nance watched political support for maintaining defense production levels soften, listened to Dulles, and looked at the new people he had to deal with in the Defense Department, he knew Packard was in trouble.[30]

Journalist Richard Strout labeled Eisenhower's cabinet "eight millionaires and a plumber." It was Ike's selection of Charles E. Wilson, GM's president, as the new secretary of defense, however, that sent shudders through Packard. For once, Nance found himself in agreement with Adlai Stevenson, who, upon hearing of the selection, quipped that "Americans had taken government away from the New Dealers and turned it over to the car dealers." Wilson entered the Defense Department determined to run it like a business, to wrest full value from every dollar. The department, he thought, was not a social agency for communities or corporations, and he immediately enacted what he liked to call, perhaps enigmatically, a "narrow-based procurement policy." To Wilson, the businessman, that meant fewer suppliers and lower costs; to Wilson's detractors, that meant GM would get the lion's share of the defense business; to Nance, that meant trouble.[31]

By late summer 1953, Drew Pearson was attacking the secretary, charging that he "has proceeded to pile up important arms output in a few big factories, many of them General Motors plants." Down at South Bend, Harold Vance was appalled when Studebaker was forbidden even to bid on a new order of 2½-ton trucks, leaving little Reo Motors to bid against GM for the contract. At the same time, Wilson cut Ford out of the bidding on the M-48 tank, accepted bids from Chrysler and GM for its production, then ordered Chrysler to close its tank line, and awarded the whole contract to his former company. Vance clipped several articles from the newspapers and sent them on to Studebaker chairman Paul Hoffman, a bridge-playing buddy of Eisenhower's, with a note asking, "How long are you going to let this continue to go on?"[32]

Wilson's ax fell sporadically at East Grand, but his cuts were deep enough to almost bankrupt the carmaker. And Wilson worked fast. In June, Nance had Brodie tally Packard's defense business since 1952 with the value of all remaining firm contracts. Brodie indicated that Packard had commitments for 4,000 jet engines and 572 marine diesels at $323,293,554; in addition, the government owed Packard almost $4 million for "facilities contract funds."[33]

The March defense contract cut of $42 million, severe as it was, was just the beginning. In August, Nance complained to Roger Kyes, deputy secretary of defense, about a 50 percent cut in his production of jet engines and the Defense Department's insistence that Packard lower the price of each unit. Packard had charged the air force $46,481 per engine, less spare parts. By August, Nance was pleading to retain what was left of his contract and offered the government a unit price of below $35,000.[34]

It was not low enough to hold the contract. On September 17, Nance heard that Packard was about to lose most of its defense business. He wrote Grant to revise his financial forecast for the company, informing him that "we'll soon have cutbacks on jets, and the car business" and adding unnecessarily that "1954 begins to shape up as a very rough year." Nance asked Grant to recalculate break-even points so that they could set some reasonable cost targets.[35]

The feared telegram from the Air Material Command, which ordered Packard to cut back to pilot line production of only 25 engines a month and stretch it out through mid-1955, arrived on September 30. The changes meant that Packard lost 975 engines, or roughly two-thirds of its 1953 contract, with the remainder stretched over 21 months. Nance was lucky to have gotten that much. When he discovered in August that Packard was likely to lose the contract completely, he went to Washington and lobbied the assistant secretary of defense to at least establish a pilot line so he could keep his work force intact. His success in selling the idea was not much solace, but he remained a step ahead of Studebaker, which lost all its jet contracts at the end of 1953.[36]

Navy work at Packard was not in much better shape, but its loss did not hurt quite as much because diesel billings had been only about 40 percent as large as the jet business. At lower levels of production, however, the navy's orders became proportionally more important. Originally the navy contracted for 406 motors and spare parts for $65,210,981, but cut that back to 310 engines for $36,757,064. The loss of almost $30 million in billings in 1953 was painful, but it was partially offset by orders for 175 engines in 1954 for almost $27 million. Brodie had budgeted his department on the expectation that Packard would build 1,735 diesels in 1954.[37]

The Defense Department's cutbacks severely weakened Packard. Nance ruefully reported to his board that the company lost $40 million in expected profits on its defense business in 1953; actually, he was $1.8 million low. Worse, the trend line was down sharply. In October 1953, Packard billed the government $10.5 million; grossed only $7.3 million on new-car sales. For the last half of 1954, the company hoped to bill the Defense Department $1.5 million a month, and Nance expected that Packard's need for cash in that period would be much greater. By 1955, Packard's billings were projected to fall to only $11 million. Like the buyer's market, the military contracts ended sooner than anyone expected, and for a company that had gambled on the Pentagon's dollars to retool its automobiles, the loss was catastrophic.[38]

By the last half of 1953, Nance must have felt like a juggler with too many knives in the air. Simultaneously he was negotiating mergers with Nash or Hudson or Studebaker, was investigating sharing parts and body stampings with other Independents, was lobbying for defense contracts, was eyeing his declining cash position, was exhorting his weakened dealers to greater efforts, was reporting monthly losses to his directors, was trying to make some sense of product development plans, and was attempting to hold his work force together in hopes of a better 1954 selling season. The last thing Nance needed was to lose his Briggs contract.

Since the 1941 Clipper, Packard had relied on Briggs for all its bodies, and although Chrysler and Hudson also bought their shells from Briggs, the arrangement was awkward for Nance. He and his executives knew that they could build their own bodies at East Grand and reduce some of the costs that overpriced their cars in the marketplace, but the high start-up expenses for machinery prevented them from bringing all their manufacturing and assembly operations back home. Nance intended to return stamping operations to East Grand someday, after he had built up the company or found a merger partner. Under no circumstances would he have chosen to tackle the problem late in 1953; the issue was forced upon him. He had precious little time to plan, arrange, and move machinery from East Grand in time to bring out his 1955 Packards.[39]

The farther back Nance went from the point of sale, the less sure he was of his abilities and the more apt he was to lean upon the advice of others. In the Briggs difficulty, he listened to his vice president of manufacturing, Ray Powers, who assured him that modern, one-story plants were best and that the cavernous, multistory East Grand factory buildings, although much larger, were inefficient. This made sense to Nance, a man attuned to contemporary trends, which in all facets of urban and suburban architecture deemed the single-story low profile "modern." The new suburbs were crowded with "ranch" houses, debased Frank Lloyd Wright offerings for the masses, and department stores moving to the edge of towns abandoned their multistory downtown buildings in favor of sprawling one- or two-story emporiums featuring chrome and off-white interiors. New auto dealerships springing up further illustrated this trend. They opted for single-story operations that enabled them to park their new and used cars around the building. Nance, whether he was aware of it or not, absorbed the physical manifestations of modernity. So when Powers suggested that contemporary cars were manufactured in such places, Nance readily agreed.

The supreme irony of Packard's move to Briggs's Conner plant was that it called for a George Christopher in the president's office, not a Jim Nance. Christopher, with his innate fiscal conservatism and experience in setting up manufacturing lines, probably would have re-created the old body stamping and assembly lines that existed in the 1930's at East Grand. It was Packard's misfortune to have had Christopher when important styling and marketing decisions were made in 1947–48. Nance would have saved the company from the bathtubs, but revamping Packard's manufacturing facilities almost overnight and without much money taxed the appliance man's abilities to the limit.

The truth was, Nance had eyed the Briggs plant for some time. Ever cautious, however, he instructed Grant to proceed on the assumption that Packard would continue to buy its bodies from Briggs in 1954 and trim them out at East Grand. The following year he wanted to buy Briggs stampings and assemble them in his own factory. To prepare for bringing all body operations under the company's own roof in 1956, he ordered Grant to visit Briggs's Conner plant and estimate its value, with a view to making Briggs an offer.[40]

Nance was pushing up his timetable because Walter O. Briggs, the founder of the body company, had died on January 18, 1952, and his family, which held substantial interest in the works, wanted to sell out. By midsummer 1953, the rumors of Chrysler's purchase became stronger, and Nance understood the threat to Packard. The rumor proved true. On October 23, 1953, "Tex" Colbert, Chrysler's president, announced that his company was going to pay $35 million for all eight Briggs plants, which employed more than 27,000 workers. As soon as the news broke, Nance talked with Colbert to ensure that he would not sign "any contract that would not give adequate protection to Packard on their bodies." The upshot was that Colbert agreed to provide Packard with its 1954 cars but that was all. The timing put Nance in a real bind: it would be prohibitively expensive to move the tools and dies for the old bodies out of the plant and set them up at East Grand to make the 1955s, which were going to be warmed-over 1954s, and then pay millions more to retool for the expected complete 1956 changeover. If Nance had been able to stick to his original product development plan and bring out a wholly new 1955 Packard, the arrangement with Colbert would have been more attractive and would have allowed Packard about a year's lead time. Nance's only other option was to buy the Conner plant and stamp his own bodies for two more years with the tools, dies, and machines already there.[41]

Nance had Powers and Grant rush an assessment of the Conner purchase, to have it ready for Packard's November 18 board meeting. The directors were swayed by Powers's presentation of the cost savings in the Conner plant over Packard stamping its bodies somewhere else. Powers, backed by Nance, had the only proposal that made any financial sense and was workable in the short time available. The directors authorized Nance to offer Chrysler $7.5 million for Conner. No mention of assembling the entire car at Conner was entered into the official record.[42]

Colbert and Nance found themselves locked in delicate negotiations. Nance had sent him a "proposal to purchase this plant" on November 12, almost a full week before his board gave him formal approval. After the board dutifully authorized the money, Nance met with his financial people to take a long, hard look at what they called "Program A," the acquisition and rearrangement of facilities for the entire company in light of the need for Conner. They concluded that the overall Packard modernization plan would cost $44,926,000 and "decided that our cash and working capital positions were not adequate to meet the full impact of this program." With everything else already under way, the only item that could be postponed was Conner. Thus, on December 31, 1953, Nance sent Colbert a letter withdrawing his offer and submitted a tender for an option to purchase. Packard did not have $7.5 million, and until Nance could get a loan he could do little but string Colbert along and hope he did not sell the factory to someone else.[43]

While Grant raised the money, Nance and his committee worked to show "good faith" to Colbert after they withdrew their purchase offer. They decided that a 5 percent increase in the price, to $7,875,000, would be sufficient to cover the carrying charges for "any funded indebtedness that may be required"—presumably, Chrysler's cost of buying the takeover money. As usual, more was going on than met the eye. As Bremer noted, Packard decided on a hefty "inducement" because "there was a known possibility that Chrysler did not want to sell at the original price of $7,500,000." It was a dicey proposition. Packard could not raise either amount of cash and was not sure that Colbert was willing to part with Conner even for the higher price.[44]

Grant was having problems raising the funds. Although Packard furnished financial firms with a two-page plan that showed costs, square footages, and approximate completion dates, the moneymen were interested in physical details, what went where and what was to be done with abandoned space, both north and south of the boulevard. The bottom line was, as Grant indicated, "that for Packard to spend $37,000,000 in 1954 would, in their opinion, be very hazardous and a physical impossibility."[45]

The whole imbroglio was further muddied at the December 1953 board meeting when Powers for the first time suggested that at lower production levels Conner might be used for assembly operations as well as body stamping. After that meeting, several Packard executives, including Nance and Bremer, stayed in the boardroom and hashed out the details of "Program A." They discussed whether the Conner factory with its 769,000 square feet was large enough to house both assembly and body stamping. They concluded it was not. In the final plan $1.5 million was allocated for a 150,000-square-foot addition to Conner, scheduled for completion at the end of 1955. Those dollars were incorporated in the $44,926,000 figure Nance used as his baseline. Nance and Powers debated only two choices, Conner with the addition or no Conner. Nance did not want both assembly and stamping crowded into a small plant, and Powers also thought the building had to be enlarged. Moreover, the day after Nance received Bremer's estimates with the Conner addition, he wrote Grant that they ought to calculate final costs based on the acquisition of Conner with the addition and on the use of Studebaker's East and West Coast plants (in case the two companies merged).[46]

The proposed Conner addition evaporated some time between January and late March 1954 in a haze of cost estimates, suppositions, hopes, bad news, and semantics. When Grant pulled together calculations on stamping and assembly costs at Conner he "discovered" that at 80,000 units per year, or 25 per hour, it was unnecessary to expand Conner. If Nance agreed to that lower target, some 40,000 less than the president hoped, Packard could move its assembly operations into Conner a year early. The smaller plant, the treasurer further averred, would lower Packard's break-even point, and he promised that "sufficient land is available at Conner Street to add more capacity if it were required long range." The figures Grant attached were compelling. If Conner were used for body manufacture alone, the company would save $103.22 per car at 80,000 units, or $8,257,600 per year. The break-even point would be only 30,000 cars, and even at 40,000 in 1955 the company would save almost $2 million. If Packard combined both body and assembly operations in the small factory, savings would soar. At 80,000 autos, Packard would realize an additional $147.71 per car for an almost $12 million bonus. Even at 30,000, a level no Packard executive took seriously, the firm would still cut $46.45 from each car, for a $1,393,500 savings. Grant saved the best for last, however. He estimated that the total costs of buying Conner at the option price, acquiring its inventory, rearranging its body operations, and transferring assembly operations from East Grand would be $12,625,000. But, Grant crowed, at a reachable level of 80,000 units in 1955, Packard would recover almost all of its out-of-pocket costs within one year.[47]

Grant knew exactly how to approach his boss. The document was based on hard data with only two major suppositions: that Packard could sell 80,000 units in 1955 and that it would merge with Studebaker. More important, Grant left Nance all his options. He could recover his costs without expansion and still remain poised to reach his long-term goal of more output either by increasing production at the two Studebaker facilities or by using the savings generated by the smaller plant to finance a later expansion.

The major hitch was that Nance had to raise the money to enjoy the savings. Colbert agreed to hold the Conner plant, pending Packard's negotiations for a long-term loan, but Packard's losses of about $500,000 a month made the bankers chary. By early May, Grant called off his search. After John Hancock and Massachusetts Mutual turned Packard down, only Mutual Benefit Life agreed to loan the company any money. Its limit was $7.5 million, far below what Packard needed. To make matters worse, Colbert finally demanded $8.75 million for Conner, almost $1 million more than Packard's offer. It was also mid-May, and Nance wanted to manufacture 1955 Packards in the new facility. Time was running out as fast as money.[48]

Nance was a master of fall-back plans, a talent he called upon numerous times from 1953 through 1956. He approached Chrysler with a compromise plan whereby Packard would lease Conner for five years, retaining its option to buy during that time. The new plan drastically lowered the price Nance would have to pay to get into Conner. Instead of more than $12 million, the yearly lease payments would amount to only $758,568. With moving expenses, Packard's first-year costs would come to only a mote over $3 million.[49]

The end of the Nance-Colbert negotiations was not without its snags. Colbert was able to wangle almost $500,000 more out of Packard's depleted coffers. Nance was desperate, however—he needed the plant immediately if he even hoped to have a chance of bringing his 1955s out of

124
===

"God Save
the King–
and
Packard!"

it. He agreed to pay Chrysler $4,172,000 over the five-year lease. The *Detroit Free-Press* played the story as another of the planned pieces in Nance's revitalization program. The following day the newspaper reported that Hudson was shutting down its Detroit assembly operations as a result of the American Motors merger and was moving its operations to Kenosha and Milwaukee. The Kenosha plant boasted 3,195,000 square feet, and the Milwaukee body plant, 1.6 million square feet. With a capacity of 350,000 cars per year, the American Motors facilities dwarfed Packard's new Conner Street operation.[50]

Despite the inordinate amount of time Nance spent dealing with the acquisition of Conner, he and his key men pushed ahead on all fronts, including forward planning. In early April 1953, Nance had written his product planning committee that "we will button up the specification of our 1954 line of cars" on April 2. The only question was whether to build a Clipper hardtop "by sawing off the center post of a 2-door model." If he could not have it in 1954, he demanded it the following year. Longer-range product planning was more iffy, however. He and the committee had planned to retool at least one of the lines in 1955, but that was no longer possible. Packard's new body shell, desperately needed for it to compete effectively, had slipped a full year.[51]

The massive retooling costs placed in doubt a successor to the basic Reinhart 1951 body, but Nance's flair for publicity kept special-edition Packards rolling out of the factory until the very last. In the tough year of 1953, two such surprises emanated from East Grand. The Balboa, a car that won *Cars* magazine's award for design, safety, and comfort, also won the Classic Car Club of America's gold trophy for "outstanding contributions to the classic car concept of styling and design." It featured a Caribbean body with a hardtop welded to it, a precursor of the hard-top Caribbeans manufactured after the merger. What made the Balboa noteworthy, however, was designer Dick Teague's reverse slanting back window tucked under an overhanging top, a feature Mercury would adopt several years later.[52]

Packard's other exotic offering had a more convoluted history than the Balboa. The original Panther was a Reinhart-designed model built for Ed Macauley with standard 1951–53 body parts. It featured a very short "greenhouse" and an abnormally long deck. The 1953 Panther, however, was an attempt to update the Pan American. The assignment was again given to Teague, who wanted to call it the Gray Wolf II. He dourly noted later that since "some of the gray wolves at Packard didn't like that, the name was changed to 'Panther.'" What made the Panther unique, aside from its styling, was that it was built of fiberglass. The idea was not new. Back in 1941, Clyde Vandeburg of Packard's public relations department had written a piece for *Esquire*, touting fiberglass as a replacement for steel in times of national emergency. Across town, Chevrolet in 1953 brought out its fiberglass Corvette, while "Dutch" Darrin was using the material in his Kaiser-Frazer sports car.[53]

Teague farmed the Panther's construction out to Creative Industries in Detroit and Mitchell-Bentley in Ionia, Michigan. His car was a low-slung, two-seat roadster with a front-end design that could only have come from Packard, and it featured the Clipper's "sore thumb" taillights. The surprise was under the hood. Packard engineers crammed in their largest 359-cubic-inch straight eight topped by a McCulloch centrifugal supercharger, which raised the motor's horsepower to a hefty 275. At Daytona Beach, a Panther scorched the sands for a measured mile at 131 mph, the fastest ever for its class. Four Panthers were constructed, and the last two were modified using 1955 parts, principally cathedral taillights and a V-8. Nance knew how to milk the car for all it was worth. After the speed record, the company's public relations people noted that the Panther used a standard 212-horsepower straight eight engine "which can be raised to 275 horsepower" by "forced draft carburetion." Although that was not untrue, it was misleading.[54]

It was entirely understandable that Packard would continue to tout its straight eight. The new V-8's birthing process was slow, difficult, and expensive. In March 1953 the directors had approved a total V-8 budget of $18,428,000, about $2.5 million less than its final cost. Fitting the Utica plant with automatic machinery, which would make Packard's V-8 facilities state of the art, was unbearably time-consuming, and Nance tried to hurry the whole process.[55]

Nance had never been enthusiastic about the new engine. He thought that the straight eight was every bit as good as any V-8 on the road, but the public believed that it was outdated and underpowered. In the middle of October 1953, he wrote Graves that he feared the new engine was not "going to put Packard back in any position of prominence." After all, he pointed out, "our V-8 is going to be just another V-8." Nance wanted a sales gimmick and asked his chief engineer why Packard could not have overhead camshafts like Mercedes-Benz, reminding Graves, "We've got to get out ahead some way in our development." Nance, looking to the company's history for an idea, asked Colonel Vincent to write an essay on Packard's experiences with V-type engines. Clare Briggs passed Vincent's report to Nance with a covering memo that admitted, "It occurs to me that there is not enough here on the advantages of our new motors over present V-8s." Briggs promised to work with engineering to find out what they were.[56]

Graves, however, was more interested in testing his engine in the time-honored Packard tradition. Contrary to the accepted lore, Packard did not rush the new V-8 to its dealers untested. By June 1954, the engineering department was experimenting with seven prototypes, one of which already had 58,000 miles on it, although Graves admitted that it was "slightly different in size and design than our present engines." Nance still had no advantages to tout over Oldsmobile and Mercury.[57]

In the early part of 1953, Nance asked Vincent, an advocate of the Twin Six, to investigate manufacturing both V-8s and V-12s at the Utica plant and to rough out the statistics for both motors. Vincent responded on May 27 with plans for a 287-cubic-inch V-8 of 150 horsepower and a 430-cubic-inch V-12 with 225 horsepower. The motors shared the same bore and stroke and many components, though major exceptions included the blocks and cylinder heads. The colonel concluded that both would fit under existing "bonnets," so the V-12 would not be excessively costly. Tooling expenses for both "should not be greatly in excess of the tooling now under way."[58]

The two new engines would have enabled Nance to draw a distinct line between his two cars and score a public relations coup for having the largest motor in the industry. The V-12 would have given Packard bragging rights over hated Cadillac, but bad timing once again subverted Nance's plans. By the time the engineering and finance departments roughed out specifications and costs, it was June 1953. Nance met with Vincent, Grant, Graves, Walters, and Bremer on June 15, just as the suicidal sales race was spreading gloom over East Grand, to decide whether to go with the V-12. They agreed that the big engine would "serve as a sales stimulant and put Packard's name in the foreground as a leader in engine development." But tooling for the V-12 and needed axle changes would cost $7.5 million, and there would be a $1 million loss on finished tooling. Despite being stacked with individuals who were emotionally in favor of bringing out the V-12 if humanly possible, the committee regretfully decided not to "because of the delay in introduction time, excessive tool and piece cost, higher fuel consumption and a shrinking market for expensive cars," almost the exact arguments that ended production of the company's Twelves in 1939. History kept repeating itself at East Grand.[59]

That was not the end of the V-12, however. It was such an integral part of the company's tradition that it would not die. About a year later, Nance brought the subject up with Bremer, who checked to see how much of the straight eight's tooling and parts could be used in a V-12. In an encouraging memo of June 18, 1954, Bremer told Graves that many of them could be adapted to build a V-12 of more than 400 cubic inches that could be ready for the 1957 model, or even for the 1956 Caribbean. Bremer's proposal disappeared in all the hullabaloo over the Packard-Studebaker merger. Once that settled down, Nance in October asked Graves to find out whether Vincent was still working on a V-12. Graves replied that the work was suspended, but Vincent hoped to get back to the V-12 in about a month. Nance penciled a scrawl to Bremer, "Note—and keep alive." It was kept alive, but just barely.[60]

Packard engineers were also working on an improved version of the Ultramatic to give the new V-8s some additional zip. The original transmission with its torque converter was a smooth unit but hardly fast off the line. Some changes were made for the 54th series, but the new motors due in 1955 required extensive reworking of the old model. The project was costly, about $4.5 million for the tooling and for moving the transmission facilities to the new Utica plant. Unlike the V-12, however, the new Ultramatic made it off the drawing boards. Designed by engineers Forest McFarland and a new hire from Chrysler, John Z. De-Lorean, who would go on to make his name with Pontiac's muscle cars, the new transmission featured a gear start that shifted into direct drive after the car was moving. The redesign gave Packards more acceleration, but it also proved the weak link in the new drivetrain. The V-8's torque was too much for it, and if the Ultramatic was not properly maintained, it was prone to failure. On another front, however, Packard received some good news on the Ultramatic in June 1953 when a lower court ruled in *Specialty Equipment & Machinery Company v. Zell and Packard* that Packard had not infringed on GM's torque converter patents and awarded Packard damages. The company's legal department estimated that those damages might run as high as $6 million, but also warned that "on appeal the Court of Appeals might not fully understand the situation due to the fact that time for presenting the case to them is extremely limited."[61]

Despite all the major challenges at Packard, Nance still kept track of details. He was very curious, a man who tended to look at conditions through the eyes of a fly, full of facets and images that suggested multiple solutions, sometimes bizarre, sometimes not. So when Nance in early 1953 had lunch with Murray Corporation's president, who mentioned that George Christopher had approached Murray to build bodies for a very small Packard back in 1949, Nance returned to his office and ordered Graves to dig out information on the project. The engineer found the car's specifications, which made it "similar to the Henry J," but not its cost data. Called a "Packette," the design was a two-door hardtop sedan with a wheelbase of only 102 inches and a curb weight of one ton. Riding on 12-inch tires, it was powered by a 4-cylinder valve-in-head engine of 135 cubic inches that put out 60 horsepower. The price was only $1,000. Someone realized that "a used Ford, Chevrolet or Plymouth would be more desirable than the small car we were working on," and the project was shelved. Nance likewise abandoned the idea.[62]

Instead, Nance focused his efforts on the upper echelons of the market. On March 11, 1953, Packard announced that it was offering three distinctive custom cars "for the motorist who is not concerned with easy installment buying." That was probably the understatement of the week, for Nance introduced a custom limousine at $7,095, an executive sedan at $6,985, and a formal sedan at the bargain price of $5,771. Nance always looked for superlatives to give his top-of-the-line Packards distinctiveness. At their New York City debut in late April, he bragged that the limousine and the executive sedan each seated eight and rode on a 140-inch wheelbase, the longest in the industry.[63]

In that March announcement, Nance reported that the company was not seeking merger partners and was on a record-setting earnings pace. Back in his office, however, documents boldly stamped "CONFIDENTIAL" indicated that he was trying to cut his costs through cooperation with other Independents short of merger. His most pressing desire was to sell Packard V-8s to Nash and have George Mason pay some of the engine's burdensome tooling costs. As those expenses rose in early 1953, Nance became more anxious, but Mason wanted Packard to buy parts from Nash. Back on November 17, 1952, Graves and Grant had met with Mason, Romney, and Nash's chief engineer to rough out the swap. Packard was willing to consider using the Ambassador's untrimmed front seat and adjustment mechanism, a Nash rear axle assembly, and perhaps its 6-cylinder engine. The most interesting conversation, however, was about Nash building Packard's bodies. Packard representatives vetoed the idea because the costs of shipping bodies in white, or with their prime coats, from Milwaukee would be prohibitive. As Grant explained to Nance, "We would be shipping a substantial amount of air." Mason countered that if Packard decided to assemble its own bodies, Nash would do its large stampings and ship them "nested" to Detroit. Packard turned down all these proposals and instead demanded that Mason pay "a fair share of the initial common tooling" for Packard's V-8. The talks snagged on what constituted a "fair share."[64]

Packard's future might have been altered or its demise at least postponed had Nance bought his bodies from Mason. That he did not may have been because the Nash Ambassador competed with the Packard Clipper, which would have created problems. Had such an arrangement for body stampings been made, however, it would have changed the merger alignments. Nance would have found it difficult to join Studebaker if Nash supplied his bodies. On the other hand, such an arrangement might have made it easier for all four Independents to join together in their quest for survival.

They all trailed histories of willfulness and reputations for being led by men who left their personal stamp on their firms and products. The 1947 or 1953 Studebakers spoke volumes about that company's daring to set its products off from the mainstream styling trends. The Hudson Jet and the Nash Rambler, with their "step down" bodies and reclining seats, were attempts to create distinctive styles and market niches. Of the four, Packard remained the most conventional, gathering attention to itself, not because it forged ahead with innovations, but because it determinedly remained at least a step behind, firmly rooted in the conservative ways of its past. It was the old great-uncle in the business, always there, always conventional, and always solvent and proper.

The people who bought the Independents' products were the neighborhood oddballs. They lived in houses on the corner, their families marched to different drummers, they did not look for their friends' approval, and they probably dressed funny. They took a lot of kidding about their 1950 Studebakers' front ends, their Nashes, Frazers, and Packards that looked like bathtubs, and their "roller skate" Henry Js. And there were not quite enough of them to keep all four Independents in business. On East Grand feelings of panic and hopelessness took hold of Packard officials. Even Nance's mask of self-confidence and optimism slipped a bit when he discovered that his favorite Packard, the Caribbean, was not selling. He wrote Fred Walters on August 31, 1953, that it was obvious that "they are not going to move through ordinary channels, with ordinary procedure," and asked him to get some good men to devise a solution. Nance revealed the depth of his despair, however, at the end of his otherwise routine memo, when he added, "This situation was a shock. God save the King–and Packard." [65]

Chapter 8

Custom Eight phaeton, 1930

"Rapidly Approaching Bankruptcy"

Everywhere Nance looked in 1954 conditions were rapidly moving from bad to worse; no matter what he tried, it failed to bring the desired results. At the bottom of his troubles was that he had predicated Packard's budget on a 60,000-unit production year. The final tally showed, however, that Packard sold only 27,593 cars, in one of the worst years in its history. Red ink flooded Grant's financial ledgers, and expenses for modernizing the company rose. The search for new capital to enable Packard to completely retool its cars for 1956 became more difficult.[1]

Nance had been aware as early as September that "1954 begins to shape up as a very rough year." He did not realize, however, just how rough it would be. During the first weeks of the new year, he was so engrossed in putting out fires that threatened to engulf his kingdom that he could not find the time to sit down as he always did in January to chart his twelve-month goals. When he finally did so, he forgot to date them, but internal evidence indicates he drafted them in early February. Not only was he late, but the whole exercise must have seemed futile, even to the normally ebullient appliance man. Of the dozen objectives Nance laid out for himself in that winter of Packard's despair, he achieved two, perhaps three, by year's end.[2]

Nance's goals were more modest than they had been earlier. He even reduced his production bogey from the sacred 120,000 to 150,000 cars per year to 75,000 "sold to dealers," as he put it. On the financial side, he abandoned his constant race to better his figures each quarter. He modestly asked to "break-even–financially," and failed. He was determined to strengthen his dealer organization, and it almost collapsed. He hoped to bring his 1955 cars out on schedule and missed by months. Somewhere he picked up the idea for a smaller Clipper in 1954, though no solid forward planning had been done for it. Perhaps he was thinking of working with Studebaker to bring it out. In any case, showroom salesmen never glimpsed such a car. Nance's sales and marketing plans went by the wayside as his marketing division became demoralized by the competitive pressures. Nance's evaluation of his sales personnel, never very high, plummeted. At one point he became so angry, he cut off payment to Maxon until it improved Packard's ads. Nance hoped for more government business, but he was soon threatened with a shutdown of even the jet engine pilot line. He only met his objectives to move into the new facilities and to merge with somebody. Even at that late date, however, he still talked of putting off a merger until he had "Packard on a solid basis" so he could "consolidate advantageously." He did make some progress on a few other goals, to strengthen Packard's organizational structure and to initiate a new employee relations program. Thanks to the publicity about Packard's deteriorating financial position and its merger, he did maintain public relations at a "high pitch." But that was a Pyrrhic victory at best.[3]

Packard's fundamental problem, however, was outside its control. The furious race between Ford and Chevrolet for number one continued unabated in 1954 as the two companies sold 2,809,114 cars of the year's 5.5 million total. They continued to squeeze the medium-priced field where Packard earned what Nance liked to call its "bread and butter." But Packard's percentage of that reduced market also slipped because its offerings (as its sales department admitted) were "off year" cars. And Packard had to amortize its costs across smaller production runs, so its cars remained overpriced. Nance was constantly amazed at how well the Mercury, a car that did not even exist in Packard's heyday, was doing. It was competing against the Clipper, and people drove 256,000 Mercurys home in 1954. If Nance could have sold half that many Clippers, he would not have had any major problems. Befuddled by the Mercury's success, Nance had Bremer run price comparisons with the Clipper, and he found that the Mercury was about $500 cheaper.[4]

These problems further depressed Packard sales and crippled its dealers. Nance told his directors in February that Ford and Chevrolet dealers had no clean-up problems with leftover 1953 models, but other manufacturers, including Packard, still had a glut of 1953s on hand as they pushed their new models. Banks and finance companies became more reluctant to loan dealers money, and Packard retailers, whom Nance described as "exceedingly weak," were in trouble. The board had reduced factory prices on 1953 autos back in December, but dealers still could not clear their lots. Worse, Nance warned his bosses, sales of 1954 Packards were "not satisfactory." He entertained hopes that sales would improve with better weather, but by mid-April he could not see an upswing. He told the board that Packard's production was as low as he could keep it, but dealer and factory inventories were still high. A month later, Nance knew that Packard would have no spring, so he reluctantly lowered his estimated annual sales to a measly 40,000 units. Little did he know that his projection was still 30 percent too high.[5]

Most frustrating to Nance was that he did not have direct control over his dealers. They were independent businessmen. If they could borrow easily and move their cars, they ordered well in advance of sales and kept East Grand's assembly lines humming. When times looked difficult, however, they cut back on their factory orders, refused to assume new credit obligations, and hunkered down to await better days. By early October 1953, Nance realized that this was what his salespeople were doing. He confessed to his directors that even Packard's bigger dealers were "refusing" to stock large numbers of cars. Their conservatism had a built-in multiplier effect. Fewer cars on showroom floors drew fewer customers, and a smaller inventory meant less pressure on dealers to hustle new business.[6]

Nance made dealers the scapegoat for Packard's sales woes. He was so angry with them by winter, he would not support their entreaties for factory aid. Aware of their difficulties, he took their requests to his board, but he argued against loaning them any money, citing Packard's own financial troubles. Although he objected to helping dealers who he believed would not help themselves, Nance did not live in a fairyland. Factory sales figures worsened, and almost $15 million worth of unsold cars stood on factory lots by January 1954. He held a series of meetings to pep dealers up for the hoped-for selling season, and he looked into dualing those in smaller towns and rural areas with Studebaker dealers, a loud hint that merger talks were under way. Some Packard dealers were already dualed with Studebaker, Nash, Hudson, and other lesser nameplates. Terrified by what he perceived as the imminent collapse of his sales outlets, Nance in February asked his board to help specific dealers. But with the factory losses, Nance was in no position to bail out many such retailers. By early May the company had lost 7.4 percent of its outlets, leaving only 1,221 dealers, far below what he knew it would take to sell 120,000 cars per year.[7]

Ever the salesman, Nance preferred going on the offensive to sitting and complaining. He ordered a study of Packard's sales outlook through 1965. That document warned that Packard was going to have to greatly expand and strengthen its sales force to compete for its fair share of an 8-million-car market in the mid-1960's. Lacking the funds to do anything drastic, Nance and Clare Briggs instead tinkered with the company's distribution system and came up with something they labeled "local market autonomy." It was difficult to tell exactly what that meant, but Nance stated that it aimed to raise Packard's dealer outlets from 1,400 (a number he must have manufactured) to the 1,600 deemed necessary for the 1960's. Nance also announced that Briggs had lured Dallas's largest Ford dealer into the Packard fold by making him a distributor for the city.[8]

President Nance was a wizard at extracting the maximum mileage from any tidbit of good news. Stockholders reading his 1953 annual report must have thought that he had assembled the world's greatest sales force. He bragged of new marketing practices, aggressive sales management, realignment of products, broader marketing perspectives, strengthened dealer organization, greater sales training, and more forceful merchandising. He boasted of 3 nationwide dealers' meetings, 122 retailing schools for salesmen, and a 60 percent increase in Packard ads. His best rhetoric, however, no matter how enticing, could not move a single Packard off the showroom floor, nor could it, Nance became convinced, light a fire under his dealers. As their inventories rose, despite East Grand's severe production cutbacks, he recommended to his directors in July 1954 that the factory give them financial help.[9]

By midsummer, Nance knew that the public did not think much of East Grand's 1954 offerings and that the sales declines were not all the dealers' fault. As part of the planning for the 1955 models, Nance had commissioned several surveys to find out what his dealers and the public liked and disliked. In a March opinion poll, which elicited replies from 405 dealers and 131 sales managers, the salesmen overwhelmingly wanted greater differentiation between the Clipper and the Packard. Most liked the "sore thumb" Clipper taillights, but less than half thought that the new Clipper dashboard was an improvement. A whopping 64 percent of Packard's dealers thought that the Oldsmobile 98 hardtop was superior to Packard's two-door Panama hardtop, and 73 percent thought that Oldsmobile's interior was better as well. Only 11 percent rated the Clipper Special's upholstery as "good," and 60 percent rated it as "poor." When asked what improvements they needed to sell more cars, they chose, in order, V-8s, lower prices, and improved interiors. Robert Russell, Packard's manager of organization and analysis, wryly observed to Nance that "these rankings provide an excellent clue to the areas where we may need to give immediate product attention." [10]

When Russell sent Nance his results from a concurrent survey of 843 new Packard purchasers in late May 1954, the picture was considerably muddied. A high percentage of owners, just over 20 percent, were "not pleased" with their new Packards, although 53.1 percent of Clipper owners and 59.8 percent of Packard purchasers were "very pleased." Buyers had a long list of complaints—low gas mileage, rattles, poor dealer service, the Ultramatic's lack of acceleration, faulty paint, water leaks, shoddy workmanship, impaired rear visibility, cheap chrome, dull upholstery (only 3.2 percent of Clipper owners and 1.6 percent of Packard owners), valve trouble, sticky door locks, lack of leg room, reflections in the windshield, and on down the list. Dealers and consumers were not talking about the same problems. Russell also found that Nance's new Packard program had not attracted a different buying public. The Packard owner's average age was 47 and the average income was $9,802, almost three times the 1953 average. Clipper owners were a little younger and poorer, at 44 years old with an income of $6,729. More than half of the respondents traded a Packard in on their new car, Buicks being the second most common trade-in. Packard's market was still the older, more affluent previous Packard owners who remained loyal to the make. [11]

Nance knew what his product problems were, but he was severely handicapped by the company's $574,000 loss in October 1953 and $775,000 loss the next month. At the end of 1953, Nance predicted that losses would continue through the 1955 selling season. He hated to even think about what would happen with his warmed-over 1954s. Thanks, however, to the selling boom at the beginning of 1953, Packard showed an overall profit for the year of almost $5.5 million. Nance milked the last bit of favorable publicity from that news. But the profit curve was running strongly against him, and he had no idea when it would bottom out. [12]

Company finances improved only marginally in early 1954. Packard's January loss was about $240,000, rising to $420,000 in February. Nance still put the best possible face on the numbers. He released a long article to local newspapers, touting the fact that Packard was spending $47 million to move portions of its operations to Utica, where 3,500 of the company's 11,000 hourly employees would be working. He hedged on exactly where he was going to get this money, explaining instead that the company was free of debt. Even though he pointed out the firm's short-term $20 million line of revolving credit, the reporter inferred that Nance was going to finance his modernization program from accrued earnings.[13]

In the face of his continuing monthly fiscal woes, Nance tried to find ways to address the looming catastrophe. He asked Burlingame, a member of Grant's staff who would later become president of Studebaker, to make projections for the year and take a hard look at the company's manpower costs. Burlingame's reply was anything but upbeat. He reminded his boss that falling sales and income were overtaking the planned cuts. Production, he told Nance, was only about two-thirds of the budgeted level of 60,000 cars. Even if Packard did produce and sell its targeted goal, the company would lose $10,740,000 before taxes and $5,155,000 after. If Packard cut its manufacturing force and lowered output to anticipated sales, it would lose more money than expected. If it kept employees and produced more cars than the market would bear, it would also lose huge amounts.[14]

In this obviously deteriorating situation, Nance resorted to cooking the books. To keep the bad news to a minimum, he announced to his board that Packard lost only $380,000 the first quarter, a figure the *New York Times* still characterized as a "sharp setback." This was after he had already told his directors that the company had lost more than $600,000 in the first two months. There was no board meeting in March, so losses for that month were not divulged. It is highly unlikely, however, that Packard showed a $220,000 profit in that 31-day period, especially since it lost $696,000 in April. Nance could no longer hide the full extent of the bad news from his directors. In May he dropped the twin bombshells that Packard would not be able to introduce its 1955 models until January of that year, months after the other companies, and that it would lose $10 million in 1954.[15]

The only good financial news early in the year was that Packard's cash position stabilized, a tribute to Nance's budget cutting and perhaps to his accounting. From a low of less than $18 million in December 1953, the cash account rose to more than $27 million in January and then dropped back to $20 million in February and March. The figures were not divulged every month, but when the next cash figure was revealed in July, it showed that the company was back to where it had been in December, around $17 million, dangerously low by historical standards. For years, it had hovered around $40 million.[16]

In public, Nance put the best possible face on things. Privately, he was becoming discouraged. Early in March 1954, Grant sent him a brutal report in which he hedged none of his statements, bowed to no aspects of the modernization program, and gave Nance nothing he wanted to hear. "Basically," Grant said, "the company is rapidly approaching bankruptcy." From there, the news got worse. Sales had so "dwindled," he wrote, that it did not pay Packard to manufacture cars. The company's working capital was rapidly being depleted, its cash position was "deteriorating," and the "substantial expenditures" that lay ahead to finish the V-8 and body plants meant that Packard would have "no working capital left by June 30th, 1955." Packard's dealers were overloaded with unsold cars; in early February they had a 60-day supply, with another 30 days' worth of unsold 1953s and 1954s gathering dust in zone warehouses and factory stocks. At an annual rate, Grant estimated, Packard could sell about 40,000 cars in 1954, but even that low figure was in jeopardy because dealers were having trouble getting financing. Again, Grant resorted to the verbal sledgehammer. "It is my opinion that our dealers, with some notable exceptions, are practically out of business." [17]

Conditions were little better at the factory, Grant continued. Because everyone counted on the spring selling season, Powers was reluctant to furlough workers. Instead, he went to an interrupted production schedule, producing flat out one week and closing down the next, a very expensive solution. Grant must have also stunned Nance when he predicted that Powers "cannot obtain competitive costs in either the present *or new* [Grant's emphasis] facilities at our present production rates." The fault was that "basically our car is already too expensive in relation to sales price and the trend is continuing." Grant did not spare Colonel Vincent's former fiefdom either. "I think it is safe to say that the present line of cars is engineered with little regard for manufacturing economies." The moneyman hurled specifics at his boss. Packard's methods of trimming cars were expensive, its hydraulic window lifts cost more than three times what competitors paid, and the new automatic transmission was 38 pounds heavier than "some competitive designs." Engineering had to become more cost conscious and, Grant added, must learn to meet production schedules. "Frankly," he predicted, "I do not believe that either problem [sales or costs] can be fixed without a merger with one of the two remaining independents." Such a union would increase the number of retail outlets and "shake Packard dealers and Packard personnel out of their lethargy and make them realize they have to perform to keep their franchise or jobs." Grant then recounted examples of costly stupidities that had crossed his desk that very morning and quoted Powers as saying, "The only way to eliminate so many mistakes is to eliminate people so that there is no one to make them." [18]

Oddly, Grant, who was already deeply involved in the Studebaker merger, was not sanguine about formalizing such a deal in the immediate future. He told Nance that "if the merger cannot be affected (*sic*) quickly," then "drastic steps" had to be taken to "cut our payrolls to the bone." "In a fight for existence," he warned, "we should coldly analyze the benefits against the costs and eliminate all functions not necessary to the bare operation of the business." He boldly suggested eighteen economy measures, some of which were indeed drastic. He called for closer scrutiny of the firm's warranty work, citing a Grosse Pointe dealer who had collected from Packard for differential work he had never performed. The bean counter also went after Nance's sacred cows, sales and merchandising. He suggested cutting ad costs by one-third and sales promotion material to almost nothing. In a more direct assault, Grant advised Nance to eliminate all market and consumer surveys and instead "get necessary data through contacts with larger companies who can afford it." And he attacked fellow officers by name, pointing out that Al Behnke's purchasing department was doing a lousy job. "Inventory control is not working," Grant charged, and he wanted an investigation into why the department had not cut inventories more. "I still feel Bill Graves can eliminate at least 20 people," he said, adding that "I am sure you noticed the rather modest tempo at the Proving Ground last week." Grant hacked at sales, contending that the sales promotion manager could be eliminated. He suggested that promotional items and corporate contributions be stopped and that Packard quit loaning cars on consignment, which meant that Nance's alma mater, Ohio Wesleyan, would lose its Patrician.[19]

Talk of bankruptcy, cash depletion, catastrophe, and survival frightened Nance. He ordered Clare Briggs to tell his struggling dealers that they had "to assume responsibility for firm orders for us to operate." Otherwise, the factory would go bankrupt, and so would they. His doomsday approach was to emphasize that the factory's products, facilities, and future prospects were "the only things that the dealer has in his franchise that is worth anything." Further, the dealer had an obligation to help ameliorate East Grand's financial problems.[20]

Nance was not yet ready, however, to give up on Packard's chances of going it alone in the savage automobile marketplace. It would take a few more months of devastating losses to make him do that. But the increasingly desperate edge in his notes and letters suggests that he had begun to seriously consider a merger. He had lackadaisically investigated such unions since 1952, but it was the 1954 financial debacle that prodded him to discard all his conservative, go-slow instincts. He rushed willy-nilly toward Harold Vance and Paul Hoffman, who were at a loss about how to revive Studebaker's fortunes. The paradox of the whole merger effort between the two companies was that although they both sought salvation in a merger, the path they trod was anything but straightforward. The old wagon-makers in South Bend and the tarnished luxury marque from East Grand entered the marriage with hesitation and deep doubts and fears.

Chapter 9

Model 8-40 phaeton, 1931

"The Shotgun Wedding"

From his first day at Packard, Nance had investigated mergers with all the Independents, but his failure to follow up indicated that he thought a corporate union was not immediately necessary. He was not interested in any combination that would not give him control of the new company. His personality and employment history showed that he disliked playing second fiddle to anyone. The other Independents, with the exception of Hudson, were dominated by men with similar personalities. Only Mason, who had long been serious about the need for all Independents to merge, pursued consolidations before the smaller automakers suffered their sharp reversals in 1953. As their sales nightmares continued, however, they all began a helter-skelter dash to find financial solace in union, any union.

Packard's erratic moves toward merger with Studebaker, in the eighteen months before the final papers were signed, fell into three stages. From early 1953 until February 1954, Nance and his directors were lukewarm toward the merger and investigated unions with all the major Independents. In March, after Smith, Barney & Company proposed to combine the Independents into one company, Nance and his board concluded that they *had* to merge to survive and began to lean toward Studebaker as a partner. From then on, an inexorable magnetic attraction pulled East Grand and South Bend toward their corporate covenant. Ever afterward, Nance referred to the merger as a "shotgun wedding," on account of its unseemly haste.

The merger scenario did not play out the way Nance had envisioned. He was too calculating to make a precipitous corporate move, especially one that could cost Packard its independence and Nance his corporate control. As conditions worsened throughout 1953 he evaluated possible merger candidates, labored to keep his options open, and tried to strengthen Packard to attract a merger partner it could dominate.

The process of creating conditions for such a union was as intricate and subtle as a courtship dance, but the stakes were higher. It required a familiarity with the personalities involved, as well as a cold assessment of the merger's chances for survival. Nance had kept up with South Bend affairs. When Paul Hoffman left the presidency of the Ford Foundation to return to the chairmanship of Studebaker's board in February 1953, for example, Nance asked Brodie "to try to get the low-down on what the setup is to be between Hoffman and Vance." Nance also invited gossip from the outside, taxing Harry Alexander, who owned an industrial consulting service, for news about that new managerial setup. In early March, Alexander wrote that folks at Studebaker were not too happy to see Hoffman back, but then they discovered that Hoffman was only going to work part time and would continue to live in Pasadena. Nance also asked about Vance's intentions, for Vance had agreed to take over as director of defense mobilization and was splitting his time between South Bend and Washington, D.C. Alexander heard that Vance "had no intention of leaving his job," which probably dampened Nance's enthusiasm for pursuing the merger much further.[1]

Nance was not sure, however, that Studebaker was the appropriate bride; he kept looking at the others. On March 17 in a confidential memo to Brodie, Nance asked whether he had ever inspected Nash's and Studebaker's facilities. Brodie was not familiar with Nash's physical setup and was only "partially acquainted" with Studebaker's layout and he did not think much of it: it "is a scattered operation . . . with certain semi-up-to-date buildings" that "generally speaking, are older than those of Packard." Brodie thought that "their layout would not tend to promote efficient low cost operation."[2]

Packard's president was even open to an offer from the more "minor" Independents. He asked Alexander to talk to officials at Kaiser and Willys, who were scheduled to merge April 28, 1953, about Packard joining the new company and what role Nance would play in such a three-way merger. Alexander talked to Bob Elliott at Kaiser, who admitted that the merger was "a tax deal" to save face and greater losses. Alexander told Elliott that "Mr. Nance will never consider anything except to be the top manager of any business to which he was assigned." Alexander then wrote Nance, "If you see a thought in this for yourself or yourself and the Packard Company, or Packard, I know that I can steer a good course for you in a quiet way to have them the aggressor."[3]

Nance never seriously considered merging with Kaiser-Willys and quickly returned to the possibilities at Studebaker, especially after Alexander hinted that South Bend's officials might be interested, too. Alexander went to Colorado Springs, where he met with George Asterita, a merger expert for Lehman Brothers banking house, which held a seat on Studebaker's board. Asterita had worked on a Studebaker-Packard deal before Nance arrived at Packard, and he was intrigued by the fact that Studebaker "was the big earner" and Packard "had good book value." When Nance took over at East Grand, Lehman Brothers had dropped the idea, but Asterita now thought it might be time to take a new look. He suggested that Nance or Alexander contact Frank Mannheim, a Lehman partner who was "an aggressive merger man." Clearly intrigued, Nance asked Alexander to look into the possibilities. Ten days later, Alexander reported that he should get in touch with the Lehman people and firms such as Merrill Lynch, warning that "there is always a lot of froth about deals but there is also a lot of bulls eye people, as you know."[4]

Nance pursued the question with Wall Street moneymen. On June 11, he asked Grant to study the possibility of a reverse split in Packard's stock. The company still had 15 million shares outstanding. Nance told his treasurer, "I am advised by friends in financial circles that this problem is one of the major obstructions toward bringing about a merger." He added that "one of the biggest objections to such a reverse split is that it would leave thousands of stockholders with fractional shares of Packard that would be a nightmare for the company to service."[5]

At the same time, Nance interrupted his courtship of Studebaker to ask Grant for detailed histories of Packard, Nash, Studebaker, and Hudson from 1936 to 1952 and for an examination of the "possible bases of merger" with each. Grant bought from Duff, Anderson & Clark a study that included these companies as well as Kaiser-Willys, Chrysler, and General Motors. Written in late 1952, the report contained a wealth of statistical information. It noted, for example, that Nash, because of its Rambler, enjoyed a high postwar market penetration, whereas Packard "has not yet regained either its industry position or former prestige." Studebaker, the largest Independent, achieved high postwar sales, but its ratio of working capital to sales was, along with Chrysler's, the lowest of the seven companies.[6]

Although Packard looked less attractive as summer wore on, Nance remained as coy as ever. On August 10, he wrote Grant, asking just how bashful Packard ought to be in its initial pursuit. He wanted to know "if it is better strategy for Packard to take the initiative in our approach to Studebaker." Nance let his indecision show when he also suggested, "Let's ask the same question on Nash." Nance was seriously thinking of getting married but was not yet sure to whom.[7]

The pace of his merger thinking quickened in early fall as rumors of the Nash-Hudson merger became more insistent. The *New York Times* on October 7, 1953, ran a piece about that prospective union, explaining that all the Independents were having a hard time, and that some analysts thought mergers among them were "inevitable." Nance was quoted as observing that "the going would be particularly rough for some of the independents," but that "his company was not at present involved in any merger talks," a statement that was, strictly speaking, true–if a little misleading. In fact, Nance had already talked to Hudson officials. They contacted him, probably in early August, and asked to explore a Hudson-Packard combination. Nance dutifully reported his conversation to his directors, who were less than enthusiastic, but asked whether Hudson could be purchased at "substantially current value." If it could, then the board promised to rethink the matter. Nance was interested because he thought it possible that Hudson's highest-priced car would make a good low-priced car for Packard. The board indicated its true sentiments toward the end of the meeting when it unanimously voted that Studebaker would make the best merger partner.[8]

Privately, Nance was still not sure. He wanted more information, and by fall he again was surveying public opinion, collecting financial information, and soliciting gossip. Russell ran another of his consumer surveys, probably in September, in which he asked 475 auto owners which Independent had the best chance to compete against the Big Three. The survey unearthed good news and bad news. The good news was that Packard fared pretty well in comparison with the other Independents; the bad news was that the Independents did not fare well against the Big Three. Almost three-fourths of the respondents thought that bigness was "very important" in the auto industry. The item that caught Nance's eye, however, showed that almost 38 percent of the owners thought that Studebaker was in the best position to compete with the Big Three (Packard trailed with 22.7 percent, followed by Nash with a meager 14.5 percent). Studebaker ranked just behind Packard on most questions, but Nash and Hudson were also-rans, far down the list. This public opinion poll strengthened Nance's resolve, especially in light of the Nash-Hudson merger rumors, to look more closely at South Bend.[9]

Both companies' financial positions had deteriorated in 1953. The *New York Times* reported that Studebaker's profits for the first three quarters fell 56 percent from $9,299,511 the previous year to only $4,171,498. Studebaker was having trouble competing in the lower price brackets just as Packard was in the middle- and upper-market segments. The longer Nance waited, the less attractive Studebaker became. On the other hand, the Kaiser merger and the impending creation of American Motors pressured him to pursue the union. In October, Nance asked director Edwin Blair for advice, and in a "personal and confidential" note, the board member replied that "the Packard interest, if possible, should end up in control." He thought that "the easiest way to do this is to have Packard sell its fixed assets at an agreed price . . . for common stock in the other company." In this manner, East Grand "would end up as the largest stockholder in the other company with practical working control," and Packard would become "in substance" a holding company. Blair did not mention any specific "other company." [10]

By Thanksgiving, all the Independents were engaged in an elaborate two-step and were publicly denying it. Mason, long a merger fan, told a reporter on November 5 that it was "ridiculous" to think that the Independents had to merge to survive. Even after the *New York Times* pointed out that the Independents' market share had plummeted from 12.8 percent in April to 4.1 percent in October, Mason declared that Nash was the strongest Independent and could go it alone. Seven days later, *Newsweek* quoted Hoffman as saying that Studebaker had been approached by another company and "if it were advantageous to Studebaker, we'd buy." He, too, was determined to control any merged entity. Nobody was rumored to be about to merge with General Motors. It had just reported $8 billion in sales for the first three quarters, a company record. [11]

The flurry of merger rumors and the chaotic state of the car market increased Nance's anxiety to join the merger dance, lest Packard be left out after the couples paired off. On November 18, he flatly told his directors that Packard had to merge. He reminded them that he had studied the possibilities, and he wanted the board's authorization to enter into preliminary discussions with "other companies." [12]

Then, nine days later, Robert Barit of Hudson announced "strictly exploratory" discussions with another company, which the *New York Times* revealed was Nash. Nance responded with a closer look at Studebaker. On December 3, Graves sent Nance a proposed product lineup in which Packard dealers would sell Champions, Cavaliers, and Packards and South Bend's dealers would handle Champions, Commanders, and something Graves referred to as the "X-Car." His estimate for retooling the whole Studebaker line, including the "X-Car," was a robust $16,445,000. Several weeks later, Nance and Studebaker officials hesitantly approached substantive merger talks under the guise of negotiating the interchangeability of parts. Graves met with Vance and Harold Churchill, and they agreed that the 1956 Champion would remain unchanged while the Commander and the Clipper would be built on the Commander platform and the Clipper would use a modified Commander body. The Packard would be "an enlarged version of the Clipper," possibly using front fenders and grilles from the mid-priced cars. Later, Graves had another meeting in South Bend and returned with a proposed Packard shrunk to a 122-inch wheelbase. "I believe this is livable," Graves grumbled.[13]

The stumbling block to more substantive negotiations came from South Bend, where Studebaker officials were still not convinced that they had to merge. Whereas Nance knew by May 1953 that Packard was in trouble, Vance and Hoffman did not begin to get nervous until September. Even then, they thought the disruption of the "normal" markets was only temporary. The reason for the delay was that Studebaker had a selling year vastly different from Packard's. In the first quarter, when Packard was doing record-setting business, Studebaker lost almost $1 million because of production problems with its redesigned models. But then Vance reported a $1.5 million profit for April. Just as Studebaker increased its production to satisfy its car-hungry dealers, however, Borg-Warner Corporation, which furnished Studebaker with its automatic transmissions, went on strike. South Bend cut production in half on May 25 and did not resume normal output until July 8. Its dealers' stocks fell to about a 45-day supply, and the company lost at least 44 sales outlets because they could not get new cars. It was June before executive vice president Kenneth Elliott even mentioned the difficult market to his board, but he assured his directors that Studebaker's dealers would have no trouble selling everything the factory produced. After the walkout was settled, South Bend raised its production to 1,040 cars per day. The summer of 1953 looked fairly normal. The company showed monthly profits, the 75¢-a-share dividend was issued as usual, and working capital rose to about $52 million.[14]

The business-as-usual facade cracked in September when Elliott revealed that Studebaker sales fell 21 percent for the second ten-day selling period of the month. Everything was crumbling, Elliott reported, the market "was completely demoralized," and since Studebaker dealers had not made their normal profits in the first quarter, they lacked money to stock adequate inventory and meet the price cuts. Elliott finally released the July and August sales figures, which showed that dealers sold about 12,000 fewer cars than Studebaker shipped. The board cut 19,400 autos out of the year's production, approved greater sales efforts, and concluded that the company would suffer operating losses for the balance of the year.[15]

Whereas Nance, in anticipation of hard times, had immediately started cutting costs and production, Vance confidently predicted that 1954 would bring a return to "normal conditions." His optimism carried into October and November, when Studebaker produced its 1954 models at a rate of more than 1,500 per day. Just before Thanksgiving, Vance predicted that the company would break even in the fourth quarter, though production was lowered to 720 vehicles a day. He was a bit nervous about production costs, but he was sure that he could cut $50 out of each 1954 car and give the factory a profit of $250 per unit.[16]

By Christmas, Vance was decidedly less jolly. Studebaker had lost $500,000 in November and, Vance said, would "almost certainly" lose money again in December. For the first time, Vance and Elliott began to look for money-saving possibilities, especially in the company's high factory piece-rates. Union officials demanded that the company cut indirect production expenses before talks could begin. By year's end, Vance was ready, but it was going to be a tough sell. Studebaker historically had not confronted its union, preferring to accede to wage demands, and its labor costs were the industry's highest. Vance was still not willing to face his union down. He hired Anna M. Rosenberg Associates, a New York City labor relations consulting firm, to make recommendations.[17]

Studebaker executives had not yet pushed the panic button, although the company posted only a $2,687,000 net profit for 1953, down from a $15,201,000 surplus in 1952. By January, its plants were on a four-day week, producing only 600 cars per day. Studebaker's subcontract on the Curtiss-Wright jet engine expired in January 1954, cutting off another source of funds just as the company raised its outlays for sales promotions, dealers' schools, and nationwide meetings. At the January board meeting, Vance and Hoffman argued for the usual quarterly dividend, to "restore confidence in Studebaker." Their directors agreed but cut the payout.[18]

Nance, however, judging that it was time to move, made a tentative proposal to his Indiana counterparts that they merge. He hated to make a premature overture, thereby putting himself in the position of a supplicant and he kept in mind Studebaker's public statement that any merger would be on its own terms. Nevertheless, on New Year's Day 1954, Nance approached Hoffman about a corporate union. Later he remembered that "Hoffman [was] willing" but unable to convince Vance. Nance, however, had planted the seed; it would just take a few more disastrous months to germinate. In the meantime, Packard continued to talk with Studebaker about sharing body and chassis parts, and Nance put Bremer to work on a report entitled "Merger Possibilities for Greater Integration," a copy of which has not been located.[19]

In the midst of this corporate dithering, the *New York Times* broke the news of the Nash-Hudson merger on January 15, just two days after Packard finally introduced its 1954 models. Mason was to become chairman of the board and president of the new American Motors, but Nance, when contacted by reporters, reiterated that he had undertaken "no serious negotiations . . . and none was contemplated." He was at least half honest. The merger announcement raised the question of what the last two Independents were going to do, which also bothered Nance. Four days later, he took it up with his board. A merger with American Motors was not beyond the realm of possibility, and Mason had carefully left the latchstring out for Nance. Later that month Mason ran into John L. McQuigg, vice president of Lennen & Newell, the advertising agency, with whom he discussed creating a larger company composed of Nash, Hudson, Packard, Murray, Borg-Warner, and Auto-Lite. McQuigg wrote Nance that "George indicated to me the other night that the current set-up might be regarded as 'Step No. 1,'" and promised that after dining with Mason the following week, he would pass more information on to Nance.[20]

Other negotiations were going on behind the scenes to bring the last two Independents into the American Motors fold. By early February 1954, Nance was warily cooperating with them. William Harding, senior merger partner with Smith, Barney & Company, proposed that all four Independents merge. Vance and Hoffman passed the information on to Lehman Brothers and told Harding that Studebaker would be interested only if the merger involved more companies than Packard and resulted in a new firm with a healthy "capital position." Nance's exact view of the proposed four-way merger remains something of a mystery, but he could not have ignored it if the alternative was a three-way merger leaving Packard to go it alone.[21]

Nance continued his delicate balancing act at Packard's February 17 board meeting. He reported that his informal contacts with McQuigg and Harding had borne fruit; Mason had approached Nance and asked him to bring Packard into American Motors. Mason wanted Nance to have Dillon, Reed & Company examine the financial arrangements. Nance balked and instead asked for copies of AMC's future plans. He would not see Dillon, Reed until he had analyzed the costs and benefits of the merger. Nance was stalling, but Mason pressed the issue, asking that AMC officials be allowed to talk to their counterparts at Packard. The two presidents also haggled over the terms under which Packard would sell Nash its new V-8. Indeed, Nance's hesitation on the larger merger question may have been a tactic to pry V-8 tooling funds out of Mason. But he must also have figured that since Mason held the top two jobs at American Motors, there would be room for him there. There was, of course, the heir apparent at AMC, George Romney, to consider, and there was little love lost between Romney and Nance.[22]

Within 30 days of that meeting, conditions at East Grand and South Bend changed dramatically. The bottom fell out of Studebaker's sales. The company laid off all 12,000 of its production workers for the week of March 8, the first public admission that it was in deep trouble. Hoffman, speaking to reporters, did little to put the shutdown in a favorable light. He admitted that auto sales were "far below expectations so far this year" and blamed it on "an atmosphere of 'pessimism and distrust.'" Juxtaposed with Hoffman's remarks was Henry Ford II's comment that "things look so good at this point that . . . Ford may outsell its old rival, Chevrolet."[23]

Top managers at both companies finally realized that a merger was their only salvation. And despite Nance's hesitation, Packard initiated the formal request for negotiations. All earlier such discussions had adhered to the unwritten rule that such talk be restricted to officers of unequal rank. This time, in the second week of March, Packard's chairman went to see his counterpart, Hoffman. Ferry found his task a most unpleasant chore. The man from Corktown disliked Hoffman, a flamboyant and liberal West Coast politician who spent evenings playing bridge at the White House. Years later, Ferry complained that Hoffman misrepresented Studebaker's affairs to him at the meeting, but the two men did set the formal process in motion. On March 16, both companies' representatives met in the Lehman Brothers offices in New York City with officials of Glore, Forgan & Company (who looked after Packard's interests) and Kuhn, Loeb. Nance and Ferry represented Packard, and Hoffman and Vance spoke for Studebaker, although Hoffman stayed only about an hour. They agreed that Lehman Brothers "would make a survey for the purpose of sending to the respective representatives of Packard and Studebaker the feasibility and suggestions as to how the possible merger of the companies could be accomplished . . . at the earliest possible moment." The elaborate courtship was over.[24]

Frank Mannheim, the "aggressive merger man," moved swiftly. Within three weeks he had worked out a financial plan. By mid-April, the principals were back at Lehman Brothers with factual data on the

union's advantages. Nance admitted to his board that merger partici-
pants usually hired outside firms to collect such information, but everyone was in such a hurry that preparation of the "Benefits of Merger"
report was assigned to Grant and E. C. Mendler, a Studebaker vice
president.[25]

The merger pace was accelerated because Studebaker was collapsing faster than anyone expected. It suffered a first-quarter loss of
$6,431,000 on sales that were only 45 percent of those in its depressed
1953 first quarter. Vance slashed managers' salaries, taking almost
$900,000 out of administrative expenses. Studebaker's board even
talked about getting tough with labor. After reading Rosenberg's report,
the directors decided they were willing to take "whatever action may be
necessary and (although the desirability to avoid labor difficulties was
recognized) to assume whatever risks may be involved."[26]

George Mason's invitation to Packard to join AMC was lost in Packard's and Studebaker's rush to embrace. Mason knew about the negotiations, but gamely showed up at East Grand to make a formal presentation to Nance and Ferry. At its conclusion, Nance promised to take
Mason's offer to his board. But since Mason was not allowed to pitch his
case before the directors, his grand dream of uniting all four Independents was clearly dead. The board postponed action on Mason's proposal
and instead discussed what transpired during the two meetings at
Lehman Brothers. Not until a month later, at a special May meeting
called to wrap up the details of the Studebaker merger, did Packard's
board turn Mason's invitation down.[27]

The real merger work, however, was done outside the financial offices
and corporate halls. The meetings were off the record, and only tantaliz-
ing glimpses remain. Two weeks after the first Lehman conference,
Ferry talked again with Hoffman at the California Club about the rough
outlines of the arrangements. The results of their discussion surfaced in
the Lehman Brothers financial plan, which evinced hard bargaining.
With each company determined to be the dominant partner, financial
arrangements had to be compromised. By mid-April 1954, Lehman
Brothers had finished work on the merger's expected benefits, but the
"arrangement of shares" was still disputed. On April 22, Nance flew out
to Los Angeles to talk to director Earle Anthony, who was still a power
within the company. Six days later, Hoffman, on one of his frequent trips
east, sat with the members of the merger committee to "review [the]
CEO's operations." The shuttling continued at a frantic pace until the
end of April, when Nance flew back to California and spent the weekend
at Hoffman's.[28]

The upshot of all the discussions was the issuance in early May of two position papers, "Benefits of Merger of Studebaker and Packard," by Grant and Mendler, and "Studebaker and Packard, Part II: Suggested Basis of Consolidation," written by Lehman Brothers. They were curious documents. Grant and Mendler's offering had all the earmarks of having been thrown together in haste–they even admitted that it was a "brief, preliminary . . . somewhat cursory study" based on "a volume of sales . . . which appear reasonable of attainment" and "is consequently conservative." They carefully pointed out that they were not judging the relative financial strength of the two companies, nor were they suggesting "a satisfactory financial basis for a merger." Those much stickier problems were left to the bankers.[29]

Grant and Mendler turned out to be dead wrong when they suggested 120,000 Studebakers and 72,000 Packards a year as reasonable sales figures. So their estimated savings were anything but "conservative." Using those figures, however, the two men forecast that Packard-Studebaker could save $15,573,984 in operations, tooling, and sales. Plus it had the potential of additional gross profits of $4.2 million to $8.4 million from its larger dealer network. The biggest savings, they thought, more than $8 million, would come from merging operations. In producing these figures, they made some questionable assumptions. First, they supposed that Packard could assemble its bodies in Studebaker's Los Angeles and New Jersey plants. Those factories were relatively small, however, and both companies already had capacity far in excess of sales. Second, the projected $1 million in annual savings in the combined engineering departments must have struck Graves, at least, as visionary. Third, the $4 million savings in tooling was predicated upon the companies' sharing parts. This was a realizable goal, but not in the first couple of years. Only at the very end of the 27-page report did Grant and Mendler warn that "many of the benefits and cost reductions would not immediately become operative."[30]

Overall, the benefits report was a sophomoric effort. It evinced no hard data and was based on optimistic guesses. It was loaded with generalizations designed to gloss over difficult decisions. Its financial estimates were, at best, "soft." And it was more a political treatise than an economic game plan; it was carefully hedged to leave all important options open. If both parties had not been forced headlong into the merger, the benefits analysis would have raised eyebrows in any sane boardroom.

That document was a model of clarity in comparison with the Lehman Brothers report on the suggested financial basis of consolidation. Their recommendations determined, in effect, who was going to own the combined company. The bankers were honest from the very start, stating that their plan was "a compromise," an "opinion of the banking group," which took "the form of an acquisition by Packard of Studebaker's assets." The crux of their proposal was that Packard was going to buy Studebaker but would not own it–a feat of financial legerdemain.[31]

The financiers proposed a stock swap that was complex because Packard had almost 15 million shares still outstanding while Studebaker had only 2,361,458. The bankers therefore suggested that Packard "reclassify its capital structure" and issue 6,440,455 new shares of common stock, some of which would be traded for the outstanding Packard shares at one-fifth of a new share for each old share. This one-for-five reverse split would give Packard owners 2,898,268 shares in the merged firm. Packard would then buy Studebaker's assets with the remainder of the new stock, issuing 3,542,822 shares to Studebaker stockholders at a ratio of one and one-half shares of new Packard stock for each share of Studebaker stock. A holder of 100 shares of Packard would own 20 shares in the new company, but a Studebaker stockholder with 100 shares would end up with 150 shares. Studebaker stockholders would control 55 percent of Packard-Studebaker. The whole exchange was designed so that stockholders held about the same book value in new stock as in old. Studebaker, for example, had a book value at the end of 1953 of $45.93 per share. This would fall to $44.58 in the new concern. Packard shareholders, on the other hand, would see their $5.72 Packard shares rise to $5.94. Market values, however, were another story. A Studebaker shareholder's 100 shares, worth about $1,500, would increase to about $2,000. A Packard stockholder's 100 shares, valued at $350 before the merger, would only be worth $270 afterward, which made the deal a tough sell for Nance.[32]

When the plan was brought before Packard's board in a special May 13 meeting, the discussion was lively. The board's minutes did not reflect this, but a copy of the proposal used at the meeting was amended in the discussion, and the insertions indicated that the directors were not happy about the 55–45 percent split. Although that figure might have been historically accurate, they argued, first-quarter results showed that Studebaker was crashing much faster than Packard. Thus, the financial comparisons from 1948 through 1953, which had provided the basis for the plan, were no longer applicable. In sales volume, for example, Studebaker had historically outsold Packard by 69 to 31 percent, but at the beginning of 1954, even with Packard's horrible performance, the ratio was down to 56 to 44 percent. Net earnings changes were even more startling–they were large enough to have driven off all but the most ardent suitor. Historically, Studebaker held a 65 to 35 percent edge, but in 1953 Packard's earnings outdistanced South Bend's by 2 to 1. Packard's first-quarter loss in 1954 of $380,000 was only 6 percent of Studebaker's. So the board suggested issuing only 5,850,090 new shares, retaining the 1–5 Packard reverse split but swapping with Studebaker stockholders at a ratio of 1.25 to 1. Studebaker shareholders would then control 50.5 percent of the new company. Realistically, however, the directors did not think they could sell that deal. They ordered Nance to continue negotiations on either a 50–50 or a 55–45 basis and to return with a contract as soon as possible.[33]

Nance lost. The final proposal kept the 55–45 percent split, and the new board's composition reflected Studebaker's majority. Studebaker directors held eight seats on the fifteen-man board. The nature of Nance's compromise became clear when the officers of the company were named: Nance and his "key men" controlled the daily corporate workings. Hoffman was named chairman of the board and was not expected to take an active role in running the company. Vance, who already was down to half time at Studebaker, accepted the chairmanship of the board's executive committee, a position that also took him out of the firm's daily affairs. Nance was named president, and there was no doubt in anyone's mind that he would bring in his Packard team to run the company. Industry observers agreed that one of Studebaker's weaknesses was its dearth of managerial talent. Like Packard, the South Bend company was highly centralized and middle-management levels were very weak. One of Nance's first tasks was to weed out Studebaker executives who could not perform under the pressures he liked to put on his underlings.[34]

Studebaker's board met May 28 and Packard's on June 17 to ratify the agreement. Packard's directors also accepted Mutual Benefit Life's offer of a $9 million long-term loan, far below what Grant had hoped to borrow. The rest of its meeting, however, dealt with the details of the merger, including approval for the new firm's name, Studebaker-Packard. The initial question had been whether to keep both names or dream up an entirely new one, as American Motors had done. After looking at many possibilities, including "United Motors," they stuck with the two well-recognized corporate names. The question then became which should come first. Nance and his executives naturally preferred Packard-Studebaker. Somewhere in the negotiating process, however, Packard lost its preference, despite the fact that it was purchasing Studebaker. In so doing, the company lent ammunition to Packard stockholders who argued that Studebaker had emerged as the power in the new company. Actually, Studebaker-Packard sounded better.[35]

Even after the details had been hammered out, Studebaker officials were not certain that the deal would go through. The directors feared that their company's loss of at least $3 million "may make it difficult to sell deal to P. stockholders." Moreover, they feared a possible appraisal, which was "dangerous because their firm had a high book value but a low net value." Worse, they figured that Packard stock would go up with the reverse split and Packard would demand an appraisal on the basis of that rise. They finally concluded that Delaware, where Studebaker was chartered, did not require appraisals of assets being sold, so they were under no legal obligation to have one. Left unmentioned at that meeting and Packard board gatherings was the need for an independent audit of both companies' books. Nor did either firm bother to audit its finances for operations in the first three months of 1954. The pressure for a speedy resolution of the merger led officials on both sides to accept each other's financial renderings on faith, an oversight that came back to haunt S-P.[36]

In retrospect, the lack of an audit was stupid. On the very eve of stockholder approval in mid-August, Nance did not know how large Studebaker's losses were. He knew that Packard had a $2,790,000 deficit for the first half of the year and guessed it would lose $24 million before taxes or $10 million net. When he tried to bring Studebaker's finances into perspective, however, he was not sure what it had lost in the first six months. Studebaker announced a $8,925,000 loss for the period, but Nance did not believe it. For one thing, the company did not release that figure, even to its own directors, until the last possible minute–August 16, the day before the special meetings to approve the merger. For another, Studebaker's board argued for two meetings over what number it should release; the figure depended upon what accounting procedure was preferred. If the board continued on its "present basis," the figure was horrendous, $17,259,748, including almost $4.5 million in June alone. Two weeks later, the board looked at the figures under the "new basis," and they showed only an $8,949,748 deficit with a profit of $1,557,000 in June.[37]

Nance told his board in July that Studebaker was losing money "with no end in sight" and guessed it might lose $33 million before taxes. But Nance had no faith in those figures either, and he sent Grant to Indiana to work on the numbers. All Grant could divine was that conditions there were bad. He told Nance that "it was apparent . . . that the Studebaker picture is deteriorating rapidly," and he thought that the company's monthly losses might be 40 percent above its first-quarter deficit. Grant took Mendler's figures, adjusted them, and concluded that Studebaker would lose $38,889,000 before taxes in 1954. Moreover,

Studebaker would use up its carryback credits by September, which would mean almost a $24 million loss after taxes for the year. Grant thought that S-P might lose about $58 million before taxes. But if Packard applied its tax credits to some of Studebaker's losses, the final figure might be in the range of $29 million after taxes, $3 million over the company's actual 1954 loss.[38]

Twenty-two years later, Nance reflected on Studebaker's condition and admitted that Packard ought not to have linked itself with Studebaker. He remembered that "Studebaker was in much worse financial shape than even Studebaker was willing to admit" and, he could have added, than Packard knew.[39]

The truth was that both Nance and Studebaker officials were still interested in joining American Motors, and everyone knew it. At the end of June, *Business Week* reported that S-P officials wanted to form what they called the "Big Fourth," by bringing AMC into their union. The magazine editorialized that such a follow-up merger would be difficult. Nance and Mason could "never see eye to eye because, as some say, both men wanted the top job in any merged company." Two days later, *Time* reviewed S-P affairs and also mentioned that a union with AMC was in the works. Nance favored expanding the S-P deal if he could, but his workload left him less time to look at the larger picture and he was not going to make the first move. Instead, he wrote Grant on July 21 to "take a look" at AMC "to determine the extent of our interest should we be approached on their merging with Studebaker-Packard Corporation."[40]

Grant spent almost three weeks ferreting out information on AMC before he recommended that Nance look into a merger with the company. As was Grant's wont, however, he painted a bleak picture of both companies. Mason was ruthlessly cutting costs, but AMC was losing lots of money–$6,774,667 in the second quarter alone. By contrast, Grant pointed out that Packard lost $5 million in the same quarter, including $1.5 million incurred in the company's modernization program. Overall, however, AMC was healthier than S-P because it had not suffered "the financial collapse that Studebaker had witnessed during the past few months," and it had $91 million in the bank and in insurance company loans. Although AMC was more heavily in debt than Studebaker, it was not depleting its working capital as fast. And after Packard borrowed the $5 million to $10 million it needed to complete its modernization and added that to Studebaker's $7.5 million debt, S-P and AMC would be carrying about the same debt loads.[41]

AMC's operating strength lay in diversification, a word that was creeping into Nance's vocabulary. AMC had its Kelvinator line of appliances and its Refrigerator Discount Corporation, which, Grant assumed, was profitable. On the debit side, AMC's 1955s were warmed-over versions of earlier models, and the company had to buy its V-8s for its larger Nashes from Packard. Nevertheless, Grant noted, even the warmed-over Nashes were selling better than Studebakers. South Bend had historically outsold Kenosha, but by late summer 1954, Nash and Studebaker were almost even in sales. As for quality of physical facilities, Grant's ranking was Packard (after modernization), Nash, Studebaker, and Hudson.[42]

"The very rapid deterioration of the operating picture of all independents," Grant cautioned, made it mandatory to look into a merger with AMC. There was room in the auto business for only four companies, he believed, and the government would look favorably upon another combination. The Independents' failures would bring political pressure on Washington to regulate the Big Three more closely, to save the Independents. Grant "felt [that] both GM and Ford are secretly cheering the mergers that have been undertaken to date in the hopes that this would remove the plight of the independents from the public and governmental eye." Grant suggested in conclusion that if S-P and AMC merged, they "would be in no worse position than either is individually at present, and might lay the groundwork for a grouping of additional companies within the corporate structure." He warned that negotiations should begin immediately, to take advantage of common body tooling for the next scheduled model changes. AMC already had six months' start on working together and would look better "operating-wise" in 1955 than would S-P with its high probability of "a year of heavy losses." Grant did not bother to add, for he knew that Nance understood, that S-P would be at a great negotiating disadvantage in such a state of affairs.[43]

That might be why when Romney wrote Nance on June 24 to congratulate him on the merger, Packard's president gave him the cold shoulder. Actually, Romney in his own way was inviting a dialogue when he pointed out that the merger would "make cooperative relationships of the type we are currently developing all the more beneficial to both organizations." In diplomatic language, Romney was saying, "Talk to me, work with me." He caught Nance on a bad day, however. He had just received a gossipy letter from McQuigg, who had talked to Romney about the S-P merger. McQuigg had told Nance that he thought he detected in Romney "a definite note of 'sour grapes.'" He quoted Romney as saying that S-P was "a swell deal for Studebaker. . . . They got a premium for their stock in a ratio of $7\frac{1}{2}$ to 5." When McQuigg acted amazed that Romney and Mason were not after Studebaker, Romney snorted that "they had their hands full now." McQuigg concluded that Romney thought that Nance "had more or less stolen their thunder with such a fast follow-up to their own merger." Nance's bad mood allowed only a 48-word response to the AMC executive. That was about one-fifth the length of a letter he had just written complaining about his photograph in *Time*. Worse, Nance slammed the door on any chance to reopen discussion of an AMC merger. Three and one-half months later, Mason died suddenly and Romney assumed AMC's reins. All hope for a four-way merger was gone.[44]

In Nance's defense, when he received Romney's letter he was also distracted by some of his Packard stockholders, who wrote to tell him, often in insulting terms, that he ought not even venture into the Studebaker merger. Many of the letters that flooded Packard headquarters indicated that the shareholders were an uncommonly informed lot. Those with a little age on them, like a writer from Great Neck, New York, warned that "the Studebaker people manipulated Pierce-Arrow so it's no more, so be careful." Many did not like Paul Hoffman, a liberal Republican who headed the Fund for the Republic and opposed Senator Joe McCarthy's tirades, coming into the corporate fold. "Mr. Hoffman is friendly toward the reds and pinks," one New York correspondent scribbled. More careful shareholders watched Studebaker's fortunes collapse just before the stockholders' meeting and wondered, as one from Detroit did, "what exactly Studebaker has to contribute to this merger." Many were angry about the 55–45 stock split and Studebaker control of the new board. A Delmar, New York, shareholder felt compelled to tell his president that "those who managed the details of the merger deserve the thanks of the holders of Studebaker stock." And some were furious about the reverse split. From Chicago, a disgruntled shareholder wrote Nance accusingly that "someone in Packard must be getting a big cut on this deal. Why should I lose $\frac{4}{5}$ths of my stock and go into a company that can lose money three times as fast as Packard."[45]

Frederick Rush, who worked in Nance's office soliciting proxies, broke with his boss and organized something called "The Packard Majority Stockholders Committee," which made fourteen demands upon Packard before it would agree to support the merger. In light of later developments, some of their requests, such as publishing the "true financial condition of both" companies, made good sense; others were petty and called Nance's probity and abilities into question. Stockholder resentment resulted in a number of lawsuits against the merger, but 89.9 percent of Packard shareholders and 99 percent of Studebaker stockholders cast their votes for the union on August 17.[46]

The stockholders had a point. Their new firm was threatened by bankruptcy even before it was born. The companies were losing money at an unbelievable rate in the third quarter of 1954: Studebaker's loss was

$13,825,000, and Packard, when production ended on the 1954 models on September 16, failed to meet its expenses by $11,755,000. Worse, renovation of the Conner plant postponed the resumption of production until November 17.[47]

As the October 1 date for S-P's start-up neared, Nance, Grant, and others must have approached the challenge with only scant hope that they could make it work. Nance's inability to strengthen Packard, even in the short run, called into question whether he could take over another company he knew little about, one in worse condition than Packard, and make it profitable. By late September, he would have been less than human had he not asked himself whether he had done the right thing in taking Packard into the merger.

Once again, as in the Conner decision, Nance had been victimized by haste, bad timing, and outside events. He believed that the Independents had to merge to survive, a conclusion that Booz Allen had reinforced, but he had uncharacteristically rushed into it. Nance always listened to public opinion and believed in its power to make things happen. As public merger fever became intense with the 1953 union of Kaiser and Willys, he became convinced, and his surveys confirmed, that Packard's lagging sales were partly the result of the public's queasiness about Packard's survival. He was sure that the positive publicity about the S-P merger rumors would counteract that fear and buoy public confidence.

In the days between stockholder ratification of the merger and the S-P start-up, Nance's mind must have drifted back to those early meetings he had had with Mason, Ferry, and the Chicago bankers, in which they discussed bringing all four Independents together, and Mason's assertions that Vance was the problem. Well, Nance had brought Vance around—or, rather, Hoffman and market conditions had. It was Nance who was unable to bring himself to join the two recent mergers. Perhaps it was because Nance, whose schedule increased exponentially with another company to run, became bogged down in the daily minutiae at East Grand and South Bend and lost sight of the larger picture. His surviving correspondence indicates that he became less of a public figure, less given to grand pronouncements about the industry, and less apt to promote his own image within it. Whereas he had sought public-speaking engagements in 1952 and 1953, he began to duck them in the following years, perhaps because he had so little positive to say about his companies.

Nance found himself running two firms that offered cars he knew were overpriced and out of the styling mainstream. After he saw the new 1955 Studebakers, he went back to Detroit and told his directors that "they did not look any better" than they had before. Packard was not in much better shape. Nance had hoped for an all-new body shell for 1955, but that dream was postponed to 1956 after the selling slump. When S-P started operations, he talked about retooling for 1957. In the tough 1955 selling season, Nance sent his Packard dealers a seven-year-old body design. By contrast, the Big Three were poised to introduce smart new cars throughout their lines for the 1955 season.[48]

To make his automobiles more competitive required money, lots of it, and that was exactly what S-P did not have. Nance spent his first days in office at S-P trying to cut costs, raise loans, and keep the company afloat. He had to merge two management structures with many duplicate positions, select the best men, and wrest economies from his indirect production costs. Managerial reshuffling was not always Nance's strong point, but his troubles were compounded by Studebaker's labor problems. Precious few of Nance's hours at Packard had been spent on union problems, but Studebaker had allowed its costs to get out of control. Nance spent an inordinate amount of his scarce time in South Bend, browbeating the unions to lower Studebaker's break-even point.

Obviously, Studebaker-Packard was born not of promise and hopes, but of desperation, as Grant put it, to stave off liquidation. It fell to Nance and his "young, aggressive" East Grand coterie to take up additional responsibilities and make the consolidation work. They had little time to try, really less than sixteen months, before they lost all hope. But theirs was a valiant effort to disprove the conventional wisdom that there was no room for a smaller company in the capital-intensive auto industry.

Chapter 10

Model 900 Light Eight, 1932

Slow Off
the Line

October 1, 1954, Studebaker-Packard's first day, was normal in South Bend. Studebaker workers straggled into the cluster of red-brick buildings west of Main Street and south of the railroad tracks. Fathers, sons, and sometimes grandfathers, bearing surnames such as Gegax, Kruszewski, Grohowski, and Nadolny, arrived together and scattered to their respective departments as they had done for 20, 30, or even 40 years, to earn their daily bread. Up in Detroit, 170 miles as the crow flies, the other half of the company was shut down to reconvert the Conner plant. Had it been open, thousands of men, almost indistinguishable from those in South Bend and also bearing Central European names, would have been silently filing into the company's new factory. On the workshop floors, nothing changed; wages, hours, and working conditions remained the same. But in the offices at both plants, nervous middle- and upper-management officials awaited news of what the merger would mean for them. Their worlds would never be the same.

Many would have a long wait, because Nance, despite his earlier vow "to hit the floor running" on merger day, was still undecided on how to shuffle the two firms together to realize the savings that Grant and Mendler had promised in their premerger report. Nance had worked on a new S-P organization chart as early as June and had hired the firm of

McKinsey & Company to lay out his options and advise him on specific changes. Ewing Reilley, McKinsey's agent, presented Nance with two general options on June 28, 1954. The new company could be organized on functional lines, grouping similar jobs in both companies, or on divisional lines, keeping both organizations intact and adding a central coordinating staff. General Electric, GM, and Ford had adopted the divisional setup, and Nance favored it for S-P.[1]

In June the new president took out his well-dulled pencil and wrote his organizational objectives on torn notepaper. He wanted the "divisional setup" because he did not want to destroy the advantages that separate identities brought to S-P. Mostly, though, he wanted to "go after the big chunk of money first from [the] organizational standpoint," then steal a page from GM's structure and "substitute committees" for centralized authority. Reilley agreed that S-P needed to maintain "the identity of the two present companies" to minimize "the disruption that comes from a major reshuffling." But he pointed out that to accomplish the "prompt exploitation of the benefits of consolidation," the company must provide for "some sort of unification by function between the present companies." Reorganization would not be easy because of "the scarcity of proven general management talent" in S-P.[2]

Grant and Mendler had promised immediate savings of almost $1 million through the consolidation of management functions, yet Reilley's suggested "modified plan of functional organization" added management costs, required duplication of staff effort, and called for the creation of "corporate functional staff positions." This would, he admitted, "make more difficult the achievement of economies" elsewhere in the organization. From Nance's perspective, the consultant's suggestions would place "a greater load on corporate top management."[3]

That was as far as the overall reorganization planning had advanced by October 1, but Nance had given some thought to specifics. In July he had decided to ape GM and create a centralized styling studio. Two days before the merger, he brought Studebaker styling under Bremer. Studebaker's consulting contract with Raymond Loewy, who had styled the classic 1953 Studebaker Starlight coupe, however, was a stumbling block. Nance did not like Loewy and warned Bremer that he was merging the departments early so that "Packard styling won't be taken over by Loewy (in the latrines)." The move also signaled Nance's penchant for promoting old Packard hands.[4]

Nance was not unmindful of the delicacy of dealing with South Bend executives, especially in the budgeting process. Early in September, he warned Grant "to be careful not to create the impression in South Bend that we are trying to take over" and followed with the suggestion that he assign a Studebaker official as his budget director. Treating both companies' personnel equally was not going to be easy, and Nance early hinted at how he would handle such problems when his two chief engineers, Harold Churchill and William Graves, recommended that both proving grounds be kept. Nance fulminated that no auto company could afford two test facilities, but then he equivocated and suggested that one be used for experimentation and development work and the other for testing. Finally, in exasperation, he ordered the engineers to solve the problem. Two months and five letters later, S-P still had two proving grounds.[5]

Nance tipped his hand at the first S-P board meeting when he explained that he would not move hastily to create a merged corporation and that he favored an "evolutionary method" of reorganization. He laid out the advantages of the functional and divisional organizations and said that he wanted to pursue a "hybrid," which would operate the company on a "profit center" basis, an ironic choice of words. The directors granted him authority to change all job descriptions except those of the chairman of the board and of the chairman of its executive committee. Nance had the power, he was just not sure what to do with it.[6]

That was obvious the same day when he wrote Reilley a "Dear Zip" letter asking for more concrete plans, pleading that "to capitalize on merger offerings, we must quickly develop a pattern." "Zip" had met with Nance several times since June and had sent Nance another set of organization charts he referred to as an "interim plan." He wanted to keep the companies' integrity intact and "coordinate" them with a centralized staff. In some areas, such as finance and styling, that was possible, but in the larger management context, his recommendation was complex and unworkable. He proposed to create, for example, vice presidents for Studebaker and Packard operations, attached to Nance's staff but without line authority. That meant that South Bend and Detroit each had two men responsible for divisional policies. Ed Mendler, who later broke with Nance and criticized his policies, told his boss in November 1954 that responsibility for the two plants could not be "split in two pieces." Nance disregarded his financial man's advice, and the result, as Mendler later remembered, was that S-P "had a headless production monster in South Bend, and doubtless also in Detroit."[7]

By opening day, Nance confronted pressure from every direction–it was almost impossible for him to do anything without taking some risk. The bankers upon whom he was dependent for loans and credit advised him to do as little as possible, so as to preserve morale in both companies. Nance also understood that S-P had few men with general managerial experience and was, as Reilley told him, sorely pressed for money, so

Nance would have to gamble on untried men. Nance also had to grapple with S-P's geographical split, which meant that some measure of autonomy would have to be accorded each division.[8]

Nance understood that both Packard and Studebaker had long evaluated their executives on the basis of how well they carried out directives. To expect these men to assume what Reilley liked to call an "entrepreneurial spirit" was asking a lot. He recognized this in his "interim plan" when he noted that "emergency management," which he defined as that "required in the period immediately ahead," had to be "of a relatively authoritarian nature."[9]

Nance's "evolutionary" plans meant that he was going to make changes slowly. His hybrid-interim organization would be modified into a full-fledged divisional structure only after S-P became profitable. In the meantime, confusion arose because each division kept its own engineering, sales, styling, and finance departments. The plan cost money, upset everyone, and frustrated managers by giving them responsibilities but no authority. Worse, it overloaded Nance with daily burdens; after October 1, he had two troubled companies to run instead of one.[10]

That was probably the way Nance preferred it, however. He assumed and exercised authority with ease—that was the only way he knew how to operate. S-P was Nance's company, and it would have been difficult for him to be comfortable anywhere that decisions were hammered out through compromise in committees. He had a chance to create such a system at S-P, and he refused. Instead, he shaped the kind of centralized organization he wanted and used McKinsey & Company to give it legitimacy.

Nance was not exactly running when he hit the ground on day one, but he was ready to start choosing men to fill new positions. As he promised, he was not fast—it took him more than three months to name his vice presidents. The majority of men who exercised power at S-P were old Packard hands with whom he felt comfortable. To lessen antagonisms in South Bend, Nance started with a less important consolidation, the export divisions, and gave them to an old Studebaker man, R. A. Hutchinson. Packard won the next appointment when Nance made Ray Powers the new vice president in charge of operations. His position was fraught with problems and complications, but if S-P did evolve into a divisional setup, Powers would become, after Nance, the most powerful man in the company. In the middle of December, Ed Mendler, whom Hoffman wanted in Powers's job, was rewarded with the vice presidency of the service, parts, and accessories division. Then Nance chose as sales manager a new hire from Lincoln-Mercury, W. W. Keller, who for years had outsold the Clipper. During the holidays Nance decided on a plethora of appointments: Grant, vice president of finance; Bremer, vice president of product planning and programming; and Graves, vice president of engineering. Studebaker people were not entirely left out, however. H. L. Misch was appointed chief engineer, Paul Clark took over Blythin's job as corporate secretary, and A. J. Porta was made comptroller. Heads rolled at South Bend; four Studebaker vice presidents resigned as their jobs were melded into the new structure.[11]

Thinness in S-P's managerial ranks delayed selection of division managers for almost a year. Harold Churchill, formerly Studebaker's chief engineer, was selected in August 1955 to head operations at South Bend. Packard, however, took longer. Nance passed over everybody at East Grand and chose R. P. Laughna from Lincoln-Mercury. Laughna had started with Ford in 1938 in the stockroom and worked his way up to manager of manufacturing administration there.[12]

Lesser central administration appointments came more easily. Brodie became vice president of government and industrial products; Courtney V. Johnson, of Studebaker, was named S-P's lobbyist in Washington, D.C.; and C. E. Briggs was demoted to vice president and group executive, responsible for coordinating policies with S-P's Canadian subsidiary and directing the company-owned sales branches in the United States. He stayed just long enough to find another job, as vice president of Chrysler sales. Albert Behnke became S-P's vice president of procurement.[13]

By February 1, Nance had rounded out his list of S-P's top eighteen officers from chairman of the board through assistant secretary. It was a neatly balanced affair, nine Packard and nine Studebaker men. But looks were deceiving. Of the ten vice presidents, seven were Nance's key men from Detroit; only Churchill, Hutchinson, and Mendler were from Studebaker. Instead, Studebaker personnel held staff positions, as secretary, treasurer, and comptroller.[14]

Nance had gained working control of S-P but had achieved none of the promised immediate merger economies. Mendler charged that the Studebaker and Packard divisions were forced to share the cost of a "grossly top-heavy, expensive Detroit corporate staff." He thought that as the staff grew and the chains of command became less distinct, managers got busier and accomplished less. Almost two years later, Mendler opined that "if charts, graphs, forecasts, committees, heavy staff organization and meetings were the only techniques and requirements of success, Studebaker-Packard should have been declaring record dividends."[15]

Nance understood these problems, too. In mid-January 1955, he wrote seven of his vice presidents, asking for lists of "surplus" personnel in their departments, "especially at the supervisory and upper salary levels." He complained that he had been "going along" with their requests to hire "new Blood," but he reminded them they had promised that the new hires were replacements. Nance checked the executive payroll and discovered that was not the case. He complained that they were "all put on and none going off." [16]

As S-P's losses increased, pressures on his ramshackle managerial creation increased. Salaries were frozen, and in May, Nance instituted a drive to cut $15 million out of overhead expenses. Tensions in company offices were palpable by midyear. Nance told Grant and Porta that his managerial edifice had clearly led to a "lack of financial planning," which made it impossible "to allocate responsibility for performance and profit." In his notes of this discussion, Nance wrote that S-P's management system "was a serious mistake on my part" and was "responsible for much of our trouble and lack of progress." Conditions at South Bend and Detroit were so bleak that he could not realign corporate responsibilities. Instead, he fell back on the rhetoric of old. He told his financial men that management "must move aggressively and positively to correct" the problem, and that "if biz. is to be saved—we will have to provide the leadership." Even after S-P was one year old, Nance did not understand that he had neither a functional nor a divisional organization. It was a straight hierarchical arrangement in which he overrode the weak lines of command to get things done. [17]

Nance kept mulling the problem over and, in early 1956, changed his mind about evolving toward a divisional structure. Instead, he sought to create something he called "a centralized functional organizational structure." This would eliminate S-P's division and staff organization and save the company $4.5 million. Nance combined Studebaker and Packard sales into one office but continued the "manufacturing and assembly" divisions. Combining the sales departments was projected to save $2,740,000, and the remainder would come from firing 685 of the 7,070 nonmanufacturing personnel. [18]

The changes further blurred the philosophical distinctions Nance tried to maintain, but he was desperate. His key men were leaving for more lucrative and less stressful jobs—Grant left in December 1955, and Bremer and Graves were preparing to depart within the month. The staff was cutting itself back. The new plan called for only eight vice presidents, and since both sales departments were in disarray by May 1956, a consolidation could only help. Despite its name, the proposal was a step toward a divisional structure. Gutting the functional staffs threw more responsibility upon the two divisions. Nance recognized this a few days later when he called it "the new Divisional setup." [19]

Privately, however, he realized that the changes and the confusion were the result of constant losses and the company's dwindling pool of talent. In a meeting with D. C. Borden, a former First National City Bank vice president hired by S-P's board for advice on financial problems, Nance told the banker he had picked men from Packard and Studebaker, companies that had "gone to seed," and "picked up more from within the industry," but S-P had lost some "*good* men" who had "jumped ship." He thought they had "dropped out" because the jobs were "too tough." By February 1956, Nance was convinced that "GM & Ford men can't function in our climate–too rough–can't take it." [20]

S-P's organizational flaws were the direct outgrowth of its financial weaknesses. Nance had known when he took over that Studebaker was "collapsing," but not that it was almost impossible for South Bend's automotive operations to show a profit. Its manufacturing costs were the highest in the industry–but nobody seemed to know just how high. South Bend officials contended that they had not attempted to deceive anyone when they asserted during the merger negotiations that their break-even point was 165,899 units. Mendler, who had made the esti- mate, later denied that any specific break-even guesses were made by ei- ther company prior to the merger. He remembered that the numbers were calculated for the insurance companies that provided S-P with its $25 million in long-term credit. Mendler may have been correct that no formal break-even estimates were made until September 1954, but there had been earlier guesses that Studebaker's number was around 165,000 because Nance was stunned when it turned out to be much higher. [21]

East Grand officials, however, did not question Mendler's figures be- cause, as Grant explained in June 1955, "the whole philosophy of the merger was that each of the parties was to accept the book figures of the other without examination." More amazing, nobody figured out Stude- baker's real break-even point until long after the merger. Grant spent two days in South Bend on September 11 and 12, 1954. He returned with an inkling that 165,899 cars was too low, but he had no idea what the real number was. In October, Studebaker manufactured 14,000 cars, which put it at an annual rate of 168,000. Nance told Grant that this "should give us a break-even point," showing he still accepted the Studebaker es- timate. When Porta and Mendler told Nance that a continuous run of 14,000 cars per month at South Bend would saddle the Studebaker divi- sion with a deficit, Nance was understandably confused. He wrote Grant, "I am at a loss to understand why we are projecting a loss," and ordered him to get together with the Studebaker financial men and "determine just where the problem exists." [22]

Two weeks later, Grant hazarded a guess that Studebaker's real break-even point was most likely 286,256 vehicles, a number that must have come close to giving Nance a coronary. Packard's break-even numbers, 64,000 cars per year before the company began to write off its expansion expenses and 80,000 for 1955, when added to the new Studebaker figures meant that in the ferocious buyer's market, S-P did not stand a chance to make a profit in the near future.[23]

The immediate effect of the mistaken break-even estimate was to impel Nance to slash costs everywhere. Its long-range effect, however, was more devastating: Nance and Grant had borrowed from banks and insurance companies using the 165,899 figure. By mid-1955, Nance was preparing to ask for new tooling money and would have to explain the faulty figure. Grant calculated that had Studebaker's original estimate been correct, S-P "would have been slightly in the black for the first five months of 1955."[24]

The 73 percent increase in South Bend's break-even point was a terrific blow to S-P's chances for survival. Packards, at least in the early months of 1955, were selling at a rate close to 80,000 annually, but South Bend's sales were not even near its projected break-even figure. Studebaker was bleeding the company to death, and it terrified Nance. He struck out in two directions—he pestered his financial people to come up with some reliable cost estimates, and he dedicated a major portion of his personal efforts in 1955 to cutting labor costs out of Studebakers.

At least the labor problems at 635 South Main were a little less opaque than the elusive break-even point. Nance explained to his directors as early as November 1954 that the 90.5 hours of production labor and the 50.4 hours of indirect labor in each Studebaker were much too high. Studebaker had remained on piece rate long after other automobile manufacturers abandoned the practice. Rates were established at model introduction time, when the factory was under intense pressure to get the new cars out quickly. Management often agreed to rates as much as one-third below the norm, just to get into production. The lowered rates meant either that workers received additional pay to meet what should have been a normal quota or that additional manpower was hired. Even the union admitted that the lowered rates led to a great deal of loafing and goofing off as workers played cards or slept after they had made their pay.[25]

Nance faced a union already made hostile by Hoffman's earlier attempts to cut labor costs. Studebaker workers averaged $2.39 an hour when the industry average was $2.03 an hour, a tolerable differential as long as Studebaker held its traditional market share. With the sales race, however, that 18 percent increment became important. In September

1953, Hoffman and Vance laid off 5,000 workers, dropping their labor force to 15,000 men. The continuing sales decline led them to lay off another 3,000 hourly employees in February 1954 and to put the plant on a four-day week. Finally they scheduled intermittent shutdowns to allow dealers to catch up with production.[26]

As prospects for the Packard merger brightened, Hoffman got tougher with his workers. He wrote Louis Horvath, president of UAW-CIO Local no. 5, which represented Studebaker workers, to ask that those who produced in excess of their low piece rates forgo their incentive pay. The company promised to pass the savings along to the public in lower car prices. Local no. 5 was a feisty group that often operated independently of the international and was noted for its free-swinging internal politics. On August 5, the union turned Hoffman down. He threatened to close the plant—rumors circulated that Studebaker would move its production to Detroit. Horvath met with union members to explain Studebaker's plight, and Studebaker took out ads in the local newspapers and on television. On August 12, 6,000 members of Local no. 5 rallied at a football field to listen to union officials explain the plan and exhort them to vote for it. Their choice was to take a 10 to 15 percent pay cut or lose their jobs. The next day, the rank and file voted by an eight-to-one margin for the plan. Horvath, however, lost the local's presidency in June 1955 to Bill Ogden, who ran as an anti-administration candidate promising to be tough on Nance. Even with the wage cuts, Studebaker's labor costs remained about 3 percent above the industry norm.[27]

The workers believed they had done their part to make Studebaker competitive again. Nance knew full well that only 6,000 employees voted and that many of the 5,000 who stayed away were against the voluntary pay cut. Yet he was convinced that the incentive-pay waiver was merely the first step in squeezing the excess costs out of South Bend's factory. His urgency increased in November when Grant showed that Studebaker was headed for a fourth-quarter loss of $10 million and could not possibly show a first-quarter profit in 1955.[28]

Nance may have been something of a novice in labor affairs, but he was quick to see that Local no. 5 and the UAW did not see eye to eye. He suspected that Walter Reuther would be more sympathetic to Studebaker's plight than to union members. In late December or early January, Nance and Powers went to see the UAW president. Nance's appeal was simple: if he could not cut his labor costs, Studebaker would not stay in business and nobody would have a job. He proposed a course "of adjusting standards in the shop," a change he admitted would be "a rough one." He showed Reuther that Studebaker produced 16,500 cars in November, more than its original break-even estimate, and lost

$2.5 million. He explained that Powers had changed some factory standards in October. The local responded with slowdowns, and in some departments the workers sat down whenever a "methods man" came in to time their operations. Nance told Reuther that the issue was "the right of management to manage," but that he was "perfectly willing" to adhere to standards determined by "a competent union time study man."[29]

S-P's president was also willing to take unilateral action. In January he reported to his board that Powers had taken 140 men off the line and cut the man-hours per car by four. The firings had made conditions in the shop, Nance said, "exceedingly difficult." That was an understatement. A day earlier, Local no. 5 had authorized a strike, the first in its 22-year history. Nance believed that they were serious, and he told his directors that it might be better to liquidate the company than to have its assets "liquidated through impossible labor costs." Hanging over the tense situation was the UAW's threat of a national strike against one of the Big Three. If it was at GM, S-P's directors were warned, that "would tie up Studebaker-Packard quickly."[30]

The local did not want a strike any more than Nance did. The union members were swayed by the fact that even their own Hoffman was at the end of his patience. When they met with him on a "social" visit in Los Angeles in late December, he lectured them "to quit griping and instead start counting their blessings, particularly the blessings of having not only forty hours of work but fifty-four hours in many departments." Hoffman was hardly anti-labor. The "Memorandum of Understanding" signed on February 3, 1955, established new standards, withdrew disciplinary action against workers who had resisted the company, set shift-pay differentials, regulated the posting of new jobs, and even promised new shower heads in the foundry locker room.[31]

The agreement defused the confrontation, but neither side operated in good faith. The company calculated the agreed-upon new work standards, but implementing them would cause layoffs and would precipitate a strike. Porta guessed that a South Bend walkout would cost S-P $5 million per month. Nance admitted in March that all he could do was try to educate employees and win acceptance of new contract standards, scheduled to take effect August 1; he called it his "milk toad" policy. In the meantime, Nance and Powers relied upon attrition to take about 13 hours out of each car by May, although they knew that was not the way to reach their target of 104 hours per car. Nance estimated by Memorial Day he still had 1,100 excess workers in the factory. He was becoming impatient—monthly losses were mounting, and he was preparing to force the new standards. By June, he was sure that the number of excess workers was closer to 2,300 or 2,500. The plant's break-even point was still somewhere between 240,000 and 250,000 cars, a level he thought "unbearably high."[32]

Nance shrewdly chose the timing for his next move. He announced on July 7 that Studebaker was going to lay off 1,700 workers indefinitely to implement the new work standards. At a mass meeting two days later, "thousands" of Local no. 5 members "shouted authorization of a strike vote for the coming week." Nance, however, predicted that the union would not strike—its factions could not agree on what policy to follow. With Ogden just voted in, Nance had no reason not to push the confrontation; if he did not, Ogden would bring it to him. Even as Nance discussed strategy with his board, 6,000 Studebaker workers, in a dispute over seniority, walked off their jobs on July 14.[33]

Nance got tougher. He refused to talk until they ended their wildcat strike and returned to work. Moreover, he stipulated that the 1,700 laid-off workers would not return and announced the plant was going to speed up the assembly line to 66 cars per hour, 9 more than the prelayoff rate. On July 20, talks resumed on seniority and bumping practices. Nance had won his point—he was going to reduce the number of men on the assembly lines; the union was reduced to quibbling over which workers were going to lose their jobs.[34]

Local no. 5 voted strike powers, but *Business Week* doubted that the strike would occur because Ogden was "an old hand at bargaining." A source at S-P told the reporter that the company "found him reasonable and responsible." In reality, Nance and Ogden were watching the larger labor picture. The UAW did not strike Ford or GM and by mid-July had negotiated new contracts with both. At the end of the month, the union was close to a contract with Chrysler and ready to begin talks with AMC and S-P. Both Nance and Ogden preferred to keep the assembly lines running while they talked.[35]

Traditionally the UAW parleyed with the Independents only after it had signed agreements with the major auto companies. The contracts with the smaller firms usually were "pattern plus" accords that gave workers additional benefits, such as higher wages, shorter working hours, and broader seniority rights (a worker with seniority could bump into a job anywhere in the plant, not just in his department). In 1955, the UAW was pushing for supplemental unemployment pay, a guaranteed annual wage, and better health benefits, and it expected the Independents to bargain in good faith on its new demands.[36]

S-P was in no condition to give anything away, and Nance was determined to whittle down the "plus" agreements. He faced no easy task.

Studebaker workers, objecting to his demands for departmental bumping, closed down the plant for eleven of the last thirteen working days in July. To get production restarted, S-P caved in on August 1. The company allowed 55 complainants to bump men plantwide and recalled 500 laid-off workers who had more seniority than some still working. The tactical retreat lasted exactly one week, until more seniority conflicts closed the plant for three of the five working days in the second week of August. A pro-management local newspaper editor warned of liquidation if Studebaker did not stem its losses and advised South Bend workers to give the new managers a chance to turn the company around.[37]

His pleas fell on deaf ears. While Nance anxiously awaited word on details of AMC's contract, Studebaker workers walked out on September 1, the day their contract extension expired. It was Studebaker's first strike since the Knights of Labor closed its plants back in the 1880's. The next day Nance learned that AMC had settled for a pact similar to the ones the Big Three had signed. He talked to Reuther, and the international's board ordered Studebaker workers back to the plant. They returned, and talks were restarted. Nance stated that he was ready to go farther than AMC in agreeing to supplemental unemployment pay and a guaranteed annual wage, but he expected major changes, especially in occupational seniority and the right to set work standards. Nance would have liked to put East Grand's work rules into effect at South Bend, but with Reuther's backing he moved Studebaker talks to "the back burner" and settled with Detroit first, hoping to use that contract as a model for Studebaker. Detroit negotiations were completed by November 10, and although Nance admitted that S-P's contract was not as good as GM's, he was happy with it.[38]

Work continued in South Bend, although as Nance said, "we are trying to operate the plant as we think it should be, which of course, violates the old contract in many respects." He had been violating the contract since July and had taken wildcat strikes to bring his labor costs down, but production had been so intermittent that the factory turned out only 3,000 Studebakers in July. Nance had no clear picture of how much the new standards had lowered his costs. On the upside, however, curtailed production meant Studebaker dealers had few "clean up problems" with the 1955 models.[39]

Eventually Nance wore the union down. Just three days before Christmas, the local and the company announced that an agreement similar to Packard's had been reached. Local no. 5 gave up plantwide bumping and made concessions on seniority, cleanup time, and relief work. It was problematical, however, whether the rank and file would ratify the contract, despite news reports that S-P had lost $29 million in the first nine months of 1955. Nance told Hoffman they were lucky that the international had arranged for a secret ballot, or the company would have lost the pact on a voice vote. Nance flew down to South Bend the next day to plot strategy. He had company officials concentrate on workers' wives to make sure their husbands voted after work. Nance explained to Hoffman that "it's an old axiom that wives don't like strikes." With a sigh of relief Nance reported, "It worked, and saved our bacon." The company won ratification with 53 percent of the vote.[40]

Although Nance claimed that "we have won a beachhead," it was smaller than he hoped. S-P took a beating in reduced output and higher costs throughout the year-long fight. Even though the new contract reduced man-hours in every Studebaker by 33 percent and lowered the factory's break-even point by 40 percent, Nance had fallen short of his goals. If the new contract lowered the labor in each car to 104 man-hours, he told his directors, the plant's break-even point would fall to about 175,000 cars, still almost 10,000 more than Studebaker had estimated before the merger. A couple of days after the contract was signed, he wistfully wrote Laughna and Churchill that "if we had the volume that we enjoyed last March with today's costs, we would make over $3,000,000 net."[41]

The great irony was that S-P could not achieve profitability in the banner year of 1955 when the industry broke all records and produced 7,950,051 cars. The two companies combined, from 1946 through 1953, had never controlled less than 4.05 percent of the market. Their more normal penetration had been in the 5 percent range. The merger year had been an anomaly–they dropped to only 2.16 percent. The clairvoyants in S-P's analysis department predicted that the company would control between 3.07 and 3.11 percent of the industry. But 1955 was so good that even though both Packard and Studebaker outproduced their minimal expectations, they nevertheless had a minuscule 2.2 percent of the market, with no chance of making a profit.[42]

S-P had a good year in 1955, manufacturing 182,060 cars (69,667 Packards and 112,393 Studebakers). Despite all the disruptions, it managed to assemble 69,214 more cars than the two individual companies had made the year before. But not only was that number insufficient to blot up the red ink, the timing of production hurt profits and sales. When demand for Packards was highest, the Conner plant could not get any out. Later in the year, as demand fell, Conner was up to full production. Studebaker muddled along all year, its performance usually below expectations but somewhere near market demand. From Nance's perspective, however, the decent production levels were a disaster. In December 1954, Grant had told his president and the board that S-P could break even at a minimum run of 301,648 vehicles.[43]

Nance probably never expected to reach that figure, and by Christmas 1954, he despaired of getting any production out of Detroit. Packard had not manufactured a car since September 16 and did not get a 1955 model out until some time in November. Five thousand cars were scheduled for that month, and when Nance found out, he wrote to Graves, "This must be speeded up—please." All the pleading in the world could not get Packards out of Conner more quickly. By mid-December, Nance complained that even though the 1955 Packards had been "received better than expected," Powers was getting only about half the scheduled production out. S-P's president put a great deal of pressure on Powers and Laughna to build new Packards fast—he needed the money. In January, Nance warned Powers that Packard was going to show a $5 million loss for December, over twice the forecast. That miserable showing, Nance complained, "is practically all attributable to the fact that we produced only 2,200 cars instead of our budgeted 5,000." And he reminded his vice president, "We are going to take another bump of the same kind in January." With everything awry at South Bend, Nance was not in a good mood. He ordered his production man to hit February "with a full head of steam" and push 10,000 cars out of the plant.[44]

It was a tall order. Just a week earlier, Grant had calculated that Conner, running full tilt, could produce 30 cars per hour. With two shifts a day, Powers could manufacture 480 cars per day, or 8,784 a month, 105,600 per year. Nance thought that the "tardiness" at Conner was caused by building a "new" automobile. As winter snows melted he changed his tune. "Production acceleration at Conner" was slower than expected on account of the new engine, transmission, and suspension, as well as the transfer of the labor force to Conner, an unfamiliar assembly layout. Privately he explained to his directors that it was all "very disappointing" and had occurred because "we tried to do too much."[45]

The company had a backlog of orders as late as April 12 for 17,000 unbuilt Packards. Nance was especially pleased that 46 percent of them were for the higher-priced Packards. Production managers were running two shifts of ten hours each and working three Saturdays a month, and the factory assembled 8,381 cars for all of April, but Laughna estimated that it would still be short 1,171 cars. A week later, Nance remonstrated with Powers because he had lowered his projection to only 7,816 cars for the month. Nance had just promised his directors 8,400, which, Nance explained, "brought us to slightly better than break-even." He again ordered Powers to get the 8,400 cars out somehow.[46]

The new Packards were so shoddy, however, that they were quickly getting a reputation for being dogs. Dick Collins, the plant manager, remembered that he could build 25 cars an hour at Conner "but none would pass inspection" because of "defects of workmanship, poor assembly, poor quality on every aspect of the automobile." Powers heard about the problems from the sales department and wrote Neil Brown, his manufacturing manager, that "such things as loose wires, loose assembly, non-functioning items such as radios, clocks and windshield wipers and generators, are a little hard to understand." His complaints did not translate directly into action, an inherent flaw in Nance's corporate organization. The defects were so numerous that any reduction was heralded as a triumph. In February, Gordon Van Ark tried to assuage his boss with a note that began, "Here is good news." Defects were down 50 percent from the previous month, and he thought Nance would be pleased to hear that "by this time two out of five cars are up to quality typical of the industry." Van Ark cheerily concluded, "We hope that this helps to brighten the remaining portion of your week away."[47]

Nance was keeping the pressure on Powers. On March 7, he wrote his vice president that the cars Conner was shipping were still horrible. "One Patrician was so bad I couldn't begin to itemize all the things wrong with it, but suffice it to say it was literally necessary to use a crowbar to get one of the rear doors open." Ten days later, Nance was again complaining to Powers that "23 cars out of 44 delivered to Bankston yesterday had to go into the shop before they could be delivered to either dealers or the customers." Worse, the cars "were loaded with inspection slips indicating what was wrong, but the corrections had not been made." It was costing distributors an average of $85 per car to fix them. Nance's much-maligned dealer force was doing the factory's work.[48] Detroit even tried to comply with Nance's demands for haste by scheduling batches of identical cars. Dealers howled. One in Chicago received six blue Patricians and only one of another color. He was lucky—most complained that they received only green cars.[49]

Nance's unrelenting pressure to produce also led to a temporary breakdown of Packard's parts program. Demand for 1955 models was so great that cars were sent out missing vital components. Dealers assumed they could purchase the parts from Packard and finish off the cars themselves. But the move to Conner, the many mechanical changes made after production started, the new paperwork, and vendors' slowness created a tug of war between the parts department and the factory. When things were at their worst, there were 2,000 emergency requests each day, and the parts department was forced to steal from Conner's assembly bins. Everyone hoarded scarce parts. A physical search at Conner yielded many parts in foremen's desks and "other out-of-the-way places." Merging Studebaker and Packard parts depots did not help, either. But by September, the parts crisis was resolved; the parts division had only 31 items that it could not provide, a number that was its historical average.[50]

Under pressure from Nance and Powers in late March, plant managers established a short "conditioning" line at the end of the assembly process where each car was touched up, tuned, checked, and repaired. It was no solution, and it was expensive – like putting waterproof upholstery in the leaking Mayfairs. Packard's warranty expenses continued to run twice what they had in 1954.[51]

Quality at Conner improved by April, but Nance was chary. With his penchant for detail, he kept an eye on the problem. He liked to drive factory-fresh cars home at night to test his product and occasionally drove other makes for comparison. On Friday, June 10, he picked up a Patrician and drove it for the weekend. On Monday morning, he shot off a memo to Laughna with a list of complaints, beginning, "The quality was not good," and continuing, "The rear left-hand door could hardly be closed. The trunk leaked. The gear shift was not positive – you had to jiggle the lever to get it to take hold in the correct steps." When Frank Mannheim of Lehman Brothers, a new S-P director, ordered a Packard 400 hardtop, Nance had Paul Shine, his personal assistant, follow the car through the factory. He was to report on the way it was checked and road tested by the company's retail sales and service managers.[52]

Many of the Conner plant's problems resulted from defective engineering. Nance's list of recurrent troubles cited carburetors, clutches, the new Ultramatic, air conditioners, rear main bearings, torsion bars, and power-steering pumps. But the biggest defect was oil starvation in the V-8s. The new motor's hydraulic lifters were oiled by a pump that used a vacuum booster. At high speeds or after the motor had some wear on it, the booster could leak and create air bubbles in the oil. This caused noisy lifters and, eventually, abnormal lifter wear. The factory improved the oil pump during the production run and cured the problem. But this serious flaw had somehow slipped by Graves and his staff during all their testing procedures.[53]

The Conner plant finally produced cars at least as good as those Packard had built in the early 1950's. But despite Nance's constant badgering of Conner's managers, he still did not get the level of output he wanted. For example, his beloved Caribbeans did not go into production until May 1955. Nance told reporters that they were delayed so Conner could fill orders for the rest of Packard's line, which was partly true, but the main reason was the engineering department's tardiness. Dan

O'Madigan, Packard's general sales manager, put the best face on it when he coupled the Caribbean's late introduction with the news that Conner had reached full output. He told the press in mid-May that Conner was turning out 8,000 vehicles a month. That was news to Nance, who asked Grant to check the numbers. His treasurer replied on June 3 that it was indeed possible.[54]

Nance probably would have preferred actually seeing that many cars roll off the assembly line. Packard's sales continued strong, but S-P's finances made it necessary to lay off 1,000 men at Conner. Just as the plant was getting up to speed, however, demand for Packards slackened. In August, Nance reported that Packard's July sales were "extremely disappointing." In fact, they were so bad, dealers were already demanding rebates. Nance was convinced that they had stopped selling cars in anticipation of the money. Conner slowed production, but the glut of Packards soon forced the cut of another 1,500 from its production schedules.[55]

The 1956 face-lifted Packards were scheduled to come down the assembly line on September 12 to avoid the disaster of the previous year's late introduction. That date slipped several weeks because the grille manufacturer did not ship his parts on time. When the 1956s finally appeared, they did so at a snail's pace after an October vendors' strike, and "headlining difficulties, body side quality, and other problems" cut output to 4,674 cars for the month. Nance reported that the quality was much better, but he worried that he would not have enough cars by new-model introduction time.[56]

Quality problems and production delays could not have been more ill timed, for Nance in 1955 had a competitive car for his dealers. And the competition was rough. Mercury brought out revamped autos, Buick reworked its whole line and added fresh touches, Oldsmobile, with its Rocket 88 series, was flashy and fast, and even staid Pontiac introduced an overhead-value V-8 with a new body shell sporting GM's tail fins. Packard offered the old Reinhart body shell again, but in 1954 had turned it over to a new hire in the styling department, Richard Teague. Teague was the type of man Macauley and Vincent would have hired in a moment. At five years of age he had starred in five episodes of *Our Gang*, appearing as Dixie Duval, a girl. Exempt from World War II because of an eye injury, he landed his first job at Northrop Aircraft Corporation. In 1947, Teague joined GM's design team and worked on Oldsmobiles. After GM fired him, he went to Packard during the Korean War, where he worked for Ed Macauley and William Schmidt.[57]

Schmidt recognized Teague's talent for the felicitous line. When it came time for the 1955 face-lift, Packard made its styling studio compete with outside companies' designs, and Teague's renderings won. He grafted wraparound windows in the rear and front onto the old shell, redesigned the grille to jettison the "fish mouth" look, and put an overhang on the front and rear. Perhaps his most brilliant design, however, was the 1955's taillights. As Teague told the story, Nance and Powers wandered through the styling studio the week before Easter. Nance's eyes fell on the 1954 taillights, which he liked to call "bull's nuts," and he burst out, "Godammit, Teague, you're a bright guy, why don't you come up with something and I'll see you next week." In about four hours, Teague sketched out the "cathedral" taillights, a Packard trademark for the next two years. "Godammit, that's it," Nance exclaimed when he saw the sketches. "Put that sonofabitch on the car." He immediately raised Teague's salary by $250 a month and sent him to the Turin automobile show in Italy. One hundred twenty days later, the taillights were in production. In any other automobile company, a move like this would have taken months and dozens of committee meetings.[58]

The new car's skin may have been simply face-lifted, but its mechanicals differed radically from those of earlier Packards. Under the Clipper's hood nestled the company's long-awaited new overhead-valve V-8 with 327 cubic inches. The Packard had a large-bore version of the engine that at 352 cubic inches produced 260 horsepower, the highest in the industry. The Caribbean was even hotter–Packard's engineers extracted another fifteen horses from the mill and redesigned the Ultramatic. All the cars held their own with anything on the road. They also rode better. Their innovative and complex suspension system did away with traditional coil and leaf springs and replaced them with torsion bars. The idea had been around for a long time, but the system Packard finally adopted came from outside the company. William Allison had worked on the idea at Hudson as early as 1941. When he showed it to Packard engineers ten years later, he found a ready audience. Eventually a dozen experimental Packards were built with torsion bars before Nance, always looking for an edge in the marketplace, ordered them put on the 1955 models.[59]

The innovative suspension created a great deal of interest. Even staid *Business Week* devoted a lengthy article to its mechanical intricacies and promised that "the shopper will hardly feel the bumps even if the salesman is smart enough to pick the roughest road in town." It was complex, but with the sole exception of some corrosion in early control boxes, it worked well. Its soft ride and load compensator, which adjusted the car to level when it was evenly loaded, led Chrysler to introduce torsion bars on its front ends in 1957.[60]

Packard's immediate problem was how to sell torsion bars to the public. They were complicated and hidden under the cars, where few buyers ever looked. The company produced several bare-chassis demonstrators, which could be turned on their sides, for use in showrooms; some dealers held general clinics conducted by "trained engineers"; and Packard invited vocational-school instructors to bring their students and welcomed "Boys' clubs and other clubs" to free demonstrations. By the end of the 1955 model year, however, Packard's advertising agency gave up and highlighted such minor amenities as courtesy lights. Richard Stout recounted that his torsion-bar presentation to the ad agency just "could not get that idea across." Afterward he thought that the idea did not catch on because its timing was wrong. The device to smooth out dangerous bumps and potholes was twenty years too late – the United States had already vastly improved its road system.[61]

Despite S-P's myriad production, sales, and financial problems, Nance retained his taste for sporty, special cars that whetted the public's imagination. Early in 1955, Teague suggested that he create something with the traditional Packard grille for the Chicago auto show. Nance was intrigued and told his stylist to "put one of those old grilles on it, but you gotta keep the fenders, you gotta keep the pickle, keep the onion, bread, and lettuce . . . make it look like a Packard." Teague took a Packard 400 and, in another of his "quickies," added Caribbean side-trim, wire wheels, dual antennas, and a special bronze-and-white color scheme. With the beautifully reworked front end, featuring a tall traditional Packard grille and a special bumper treatment, Teague created the Request. Everyone loved it, and Teague's ideas lingered in the styling studio, where preliminary sketches for the all-new 1957 Packards retained the old vertical grille, though much narrowed.[62]

Teague needed more lead time to prepare something special for the 1956 Chicago auto show because he and Schmidt wanted to look ahead to what Packard might bring out, rather than rework old designs. Eighty people labored practically around the clock on the car, tagged the Predictor. Teague, its principal designer, allowed his imagination to roam. The fiberglass beauty was built around a Clipper chassis and mechanicals, but it was a low, sleek auto. The windshield curved up into the retractable, "T-top," "tambour" roof, an idea that Teague, an antique collector, got from his rolltop desk. The Predictor also boasted swivel seats, retractable headlights, sculptured sides, a powered and reverse-slanted rear window (similar to the Balboa's), narrow whitewall tires, and the classic Packard grille. He also added a pair of tail fins because "the chiefs would keep dropping by and say 'put some fins on it' and on they went." Until the day he died, Teague disliked tail fins.[63]

The Predictor was built by Ghia in Italy and was shipped to the United States during the Christmas holiday in 1955. It was an instant sensation, but it was too late to save Packard. The company ran out of money before the Predictor's refinements appeared on production models. The styling studio's clay models for 1957 and one crude prototype, Black Bess, however, incorporated the Predictor's rear end, with fins, an elongated, low silhouette, and a flattened version of its front end. Teague's car almost lived up to its name.[64]

All the special cars showing all the novelty in the world, however, could not overcome the public's growing perception that Packard no longer built high-quality, reliable automobiles. A confluence of factors had left Packard staggering. As a small company, it had inherently higher production, advertising, and materials costs; in a normal market, where sales margins were fat, the few hundred added dollars were not critical. But the auto industry had changed in the 1950's. Three-year retooling schedules became the norm, tooling costs escalated, and the buyer's market pushed retail car costs down, pinching dealers and factories.

The fundamental idea behind the Studebaker-Packard union was to cut overhead costs, produce a full line of cars using interchangeable parts, and sell through a combined dealer network capable of competing with the Big Three. Under excruciating financial pressures, Nance tried to make it all work. Everything he tried, however, cost money he did not have. He could not create the organization he wanted and instead temporized, adding a thick layer of central office staff. This costly alternative would, he hoped, mitigate hostilities within the company. Stout remembered that Studebaker men "did not much like us–these were older men–and we were all young." And even corporate social graces differed. At South Bend, Stout remembered, when Studebaker officials entered an elevator, the underlings exited to make room for them. Everyone there called each other Mr., but Packard executives called each other by their first names. It is worth noting, however, that Nance in his memos always referred to others as Mr., so a degree of formality was still observed at East Grand. Stout said that he "felt like an invader when he went down" to South Bend, and in that case Nance's organizational compromises made some diplomatic sense.[65]

The key, as Nance knew, was the bottom line. He had to raise large amounts of cash quickly to buy the time he needed to "turn the thing around," as he liked to say. With his continuing losses, his only chance to raise the funds was to sell more cars, hustle defense business, and borrow money from outside lending institutions. Nance knew more about selling and leaned hard on his sales and marketing departments in 1955. If they could generate enough sales, his other two options would be easier. He also took a more direct hand in soliciting defense business, but that too cost him money. He was confident, however, that the banks and the insurance companies would not let the company fold. Nance and his key men were sure that they could make the merger work; the company had been slow off the line, but it was moving.

Chapter 11

115C, 1937

"Life or Death for Packard in 1955"

Nance made a risky announcement four days after the merger: S-P expected to double its market share in 1955 and manufacture 300,000 passenger cars. It was a bold declaration for a company that built only 112,845 cars in 1954, but he hoped for a more normal selling year, which would enable South Bend to produce to its 1953 level (186,000) and Packard to turn out 90,000 to 100,000 vehicles. His overall plan called for a heavily face-lifted 1956 Studebaker to carry the company's sales banner until Packard could be completely retooled for 1957. Nance also planned to push inordinately hard to win direct Defense Department contracts and subcontracts with prime manufacturers. Such business would increase S-P's prestige and provide badly needed cash to tide it over until it could bring out its new cars.[1]

The key to Nance's whole scheme was to achieve sales gains in 1955 that, coupled with his plans to slash expenses, would cut S-P's monthly losses and perhaps even allow a modest profit. His promised 300,000 production figure looked profitable to him, given Studebaker's estimated break-even figure of 165,000 units. The irony was that although he fell far short of his rash predictions, he managed through herculean efforts to squeeze 61 percent more vehicles from his factories than they had built a year earlier—and still lost money at a frightening rate.

184

=====

*"Life or
Death for
Packard
in 1955"*

To prepare for the 1955 selling season, Nance had C. E. Briggs explain
Packard's failures in 1954. Briggs grimly pointed out that the company
would have little problem with its cleanup of 1954 models; it had not
manufactured many. The new Clipper looked good, he said, and Packard
had a new hardtop, the 400, that would make the line more competitive
in 1955. The new motor, suspension, and transmission, Briggs predicted, "will put some real sales tools into the hands of our field organization." He also thought that the new cars would be more competitively
priced and attractive after the reams of merger publicity had effectively
removed the "orphan" stigma from them.[2]

Briggs's report was an upbeat document and gave Nance hope for a
better year. He fired Packard's ad agency, and by September 13, Lou
Maxon's letter of resignation was on his desk. Within a week, he
had shifted Packard's account to Rauthrauff & Ryan, an agency H. A.
Wichert had told him at Camp Packard was a "'hard hitting' outfit"
whose "greatest growth has come during hard times." Wichert, who had
left Rauthrauff to join Packard, guaranteed Nance that the agency knew
the "hard sell," just the kind of language that appealed to the old appliance man.[3]

Nance had also overhauled Packard's distribution system just before
the merger. He reminded Briggs and O'Madigan that the dealers' failure
to "measure up to expectancy" cost the company $20 million in 1954
and put its bank loans in jeopardy, and then he zeroed in on Packard's lax
zone operations. He told the two that "in 30 years in business, I have
never seen such an irresponsible and undisciplined organization" and
authorized the creation of 103 special distributorships, located in the
larger towns and cities. They would be allowed $70 off on each Packard
they bought and an additional $70 on any they ordered for other dealers.
Nance expected the new distributors, who included Earle Anthony, to
promote Packards with greater enthusiasm and heavier local advertising. His move was also calculated to hold major dealers in Buffalo, At-
lanta, and Kansas City, who threatened to leave the company.[4]

Nance's carefully laid plans began to unravel almost immediately. He
was decidedly unimpressed with his new ad agency's campaign for the
fall selling season. His truculent memo to Briggs complained that "such
a mediocre job by those responsible for the handling of advertising and
merchandising is inexcusable." After all, it was "life or death for Packard in 1955." Nance was so upset that he cleared his calendar for the rest
of the day "to try to get some basic thinking done."[5]

He had plenty of time to think. Production delays at Conner pushed
Packard's introduction date to January 4, 1955, the very doldrums of the
selling season. Even then, many Packard dealers still had no cars and

could not take advantage of the publicity blitz. Briggs advised his dealers "to take advance orders and use the shortage psychology as a selling tool." Moreover, Nance discovered that the first cars off the assembly line were stripped models. He was so dismayed that he called friends at Ford and Pontiac to ask how they equipped their early cars. The response was that for the first two months' production they were loaded "to the hilt." Nance did not have to remind his chief salesmen that S-P made large profits on accessories. He was also peeved because the factory persisted in building only single-color cars. When he called O'Madigan to complain, he discovered that O'Madigan "was unfamiliar with the schedules." Nance wondered, "How can this be–a sales manager not even knowing about this vital subject affecting his dealers?" [6]

The production and sales snafus drove Nance to distraction. To O'Madigan and Keller he sent a pointed reminder in mid-February that S-P had targeted 100,000 Packards for the year, and he had promised the company's financial backers 6 percent of the car market. But, Nance continued, what had been estimated as a 5-million-car year was beginning to look like a 6-million-car year, and that presented a great opportunity. Nance believed that the public did not want GM to have more than 50% of the market, "so it's ours for the taking." [7]

But Nance needed a grand theme to spark Rauthrauff & Ryan's creative energies and capture the public's imagination. As the selling season approached he was still dissatisfied with the agency's efforts. "Advertising, promotion, and sales planning is," Nance charged, "the most desultory I have ever seen." Everything was "always late," and he never saw any "forward planning." He had become heated when his admen came to see him on March 3 to discuss Packard's ads for that month. "Isn't that awful?" he asked O'Madigan. "With your General Motors training you know the value of forward planning." But he saved the bulk of his wrath for his advertising manager, Macke. "Bill Macke's performance is inexcusable, for he was personally trained by Ed Taylor and me. . . . So I suggest laying on the whip, because Macke is lazy." [8]

Going before the old appliance salesman with ad copy was an ordeal of major proportions. In April, when Macke and O'Madigan sent proofs of the June Clipper ads, Nance tersely responded that "it is some of the weakest, most ineffectual ads I've ever seen. It literally has nothing–no selling copy, poor art." Almost as an afterthought, he added, "We have advertising managers–Macke and Remington–What does each of them do?" [9]

For Nance, advertising was more than an exercise in public persuasion. He was trying to sell two separate car lines, he had a shoestring budget, and he needed to milk every ounce of effectiveness from his copy. The Independents were at a great disadvantage because their advertising costs per car were much higher than those of the Big Three. In fact, S-P's ad costs per vehicle were the highest in the industry. In 1955, after Nance cut every other budget in the corporation, he raised his advertising outlays to more than what the two separate companies had spent in 1954, from roughly $8 million to $10 million. At that level, S-P's 1955 ad costs per car stood at $67. In contrast, GM flooded the media with $81.5 million worth of promotional material, but its cost per vehicle was only $22.50. Even AMC had lower advertising costs than S-P, although at $50 per car they were still higher than the industry average.[10]

One of Nance's great hopes was to reap sales advantages by "dualing" Packard and Studebaker dealers. Grant had promised big savings, and Nance wasted no time. In S-P's first six weeks, he dualed 500 dealers. The merger publicity also lured 200 new Packard dealers into the fold. Nance wanted to use dualing to expand Packard's sales in rural areas, where Studebaker was strong. In big cities, where Packard dealers were larger and where Studebaker already had outlets, no dualing was allowed.[11]

Nance and Grant assumed that most of S-P's 4,000 original dealers would be combined, but after the initial 500 were dualed, the pace slackened, in part because of confusion out in the field. The high turnover of zone managers and district representatives was a serious problem, and Nance's constant carping about zone inefficiencies had helped cause it. He did not let up in 1955, either. He griped to O'Madigan that zone officers "have not established the feeling between factory and dealers that is, in my judgment, our main corporate asset–, namely being accepted as a friendly factory, but also as smart, alert, knowledgeable, and aggressive." The only way to settle his dealers down, Nance thought, was to create a dealers' council, "not to let the dealers dictate," but to "let them feel they are being heard." Although Nance believed that Packard had the "fairest and best contract of all manufacturers" with its dealers, he asked O'Madigan to get together with the company's lawyer, Robert Blythin, to sell the dealers on their contractual advantages.[12]

The dualing process was also slowed by corporate infighting. The Studebaker division would not gain many outlets. Furthermore, drawing up the procedures took almost thirteen months. And no wonder–they were ponderous. For example, if a Studebaker dealer wished to dual he had to go through his zone officers first, then through the appropriate Packard zone officials, and finally through the Studebaker division's central office, completing all the proper paperwork. Dealers seeking both franchises had to prove adequate working capital, wholesale financing, service facilities, and manpower; in some cases, S-P demanded a separate showroom and sales force for each line.[13]

Privately, Nance admitted that the dualing policies were designed to boost Packard sales to the 80,000 level needed to justify his revitalization plan. Even with all the procedural safeguards against abuse and stupidity, dualing sometimes violated common sense. In early December 1955, for example, Nance learned that the leading Packard dealer in Milwaukee had been given a Studebaker franchise. Nance was livid; he wrote Churchill, general manager of the Studebaker division, that "our whole policy is crumbling." What really bothered Nance was that Packard and Clipper dealers were already having enough problems getting the credit to buy cars from the factory. Adding the Studebaker line further stretched their financial resources. Nance ordered Churchill in no uncertain terms to stop "this policy of promiscuous dualing."[14]

Packard and Studebaker dealers largely escaped Nance's wrath in the first half of 1955 because he had so many problems elsewhere. In July, Packard's sales slumped badly, and Nance suspected that his dealers were waiting for factory rebates. He complained to his directors in September that Packard dealers had never understood volume selling and were, in effect, nine-month dealers. Nance had leveled that charge at them for years, but his dealers understood their business better than he did–72 percent of them were showing profits. By year's end, after Packard's sales had dwindled, the dealers no longer enjoyed "satisfactory profits," but most were still sticking with the company.[15]

When the news broke in December that S-P had lost almost $30 million in the first three quarters of the year, the immediate public reaction was seen on the company's showroom floors–they were deserted. Customers became wary of investing in what could become an "orphan" car, without dealer service, parts, or trade-in value. The news could not have come at a worse time. S-P had just introduced its 56th series, and dealer stocks industry-wide, as Nance explained to his board, were almost double what they had been a year earlier. Bankers were reluctant to give Packard dealers floor-plan financing, so the dealers predictably cut back their factory orders. By mid-January, Nance reported that sales were "seriously below projections." Paul Hoffman interjected that the company's sales organization was a wreck. He recommended that S-P create a holding company to build a wholly new dealer organization, which he estimated would cost at least $10 million. The board was so worried that it authorized Nance to present the undigested plan to the company's bankers and insurance companies.[16]

S-P's sales debacle was not entirely of its own making; the company was a victim of the industry's success in 1955. Record sales left the two Independents fighting for crumbs in the marketplace. The great boom was fueled by consumers' unprecedented willingness to shoulder additional credit burdens, automobile overproduction, and salesmen's eagerness to deal. In the more normal year of 1953, only 59 percent of new cars were financed. In 1954, the percentage rose to 70, and by the third quarter of 1955, fully 72 percent of new cars were sold on the installment plan. Moreover, auto dealers attracted buyers with marginal credit ratings by stretching the length of their loans. Twenty-four-month payment plans had been the industry norm for years, but to lower monthly payments, dealers and banks in mid-1955 were advertising 30-month options. As sales slowed at the end of the year the average credit sale was extended to 36 months. Americans responded in 1955 by assuming $4.5 billion more debt, nine times as much as in 1954. The Federal Reserve Board watched this credit expansion with alarm and, at the end of 1955, tightened up the banks' reserve requirements, thus reducing their ability to loan funds. Consumers, already anxious about their debts, slowed their new borrowing in October and focused on repaying their obligations—just as Nance desperately sought sales increases to impress his bankers. Many people bought Clippers only because liberal credit terms enabled them to buy into the upper-middle-priced field. Stretched the tightest, they were among the very first to pull back.[17]

Throughout the 1955 sales boom, Nance watched AMC with an interest that bordered on obsession. Early in the year, AMC and S-P sales were about even. In April, however, AMC took a commanding lead, which thoroughly upset Nance. He shot O'Madigan and Keller another of his biting memos, professing amazement "at the sales American Motors is getting out of the Hudson dealer organization." Nance, like most other automakers, assumed that Hudson was a sure loser, and when its dealers began to sell almost as many cars as the Studebaker outlets did, he was both stunned and furious. His figures showed that "Nash is equaling Packard and Clipper with their Statesman and Ambassador," and when Rambler sales were added to AMC's mix, "it is obvious American Motors is currently outperforming Studebaker-Packard and the implications of that fact are not good."[18]

A week later, Nance wrote a hurried letter to Earle Anthony, whom he was always careful to appease, to prepare him for a forthcoming story in the *Saturday Evening Post* on whether S-P or AMC could survive long enough for the two to merge into a "fourth full line company." Nance was worried about an "epidemic of such stories," which were "very damaging to our cause." He promised Anthony that he had ordered Hill & Knowlton, S-P's public relations firm, to quash future articles or furnish material "to help us come off as well as possible."[19]

The press kept harping on the comparison between AMC and S-P. In the middle of December, the *Wall Street Journal* reported that in 1955

S-P outproduced AMC, 168,411 cars to 150,632 – that was the good news. The downside was that Nance had not approached his predicted 300,000 automobiles, and the *Journal* discussed the demise of the other Independent, Kaiser-Willys. If one Independent could fold, it was possible that the other two could as well. By contrast, GM had another banner year. Its output of 3,789,868 cars dwarfed the Independents and put their struggles in stark perspective.[20]

Nance and his board gambled on winning more defense contracts to provide the cash flow needed to offset their automobile losses. Nance was frank about it: "My intention is to establish Studebaker-Packard as a primary contractor for defense business." It was, he thought, a way to tide the company over its "off" years and would help insulate S-P from the cyclical nature of the automobile marketplace. S-P's officers wasted no time. The company put on a huge public fete in South Bend on September 26, 1954, to celebrate the merger, unveil the 1955 Studebaker, and welcome Nance. The site was the Notre Dame football stadium, and Washington notables were invited. Fifty-seven thousand cheering workers, families, and townsfolk listened to Horvath ask Harold Talbott, secretary of the air force, for contracts to build "aircraft engines, guided missiles, and military vehicles." Talbott promised only that the "Air Force would be delighted if it could find a contract to place with the new Studebaker-Packard consolidation." The crowd roared its approval, which the "if" did not dampen.[21]

The biggest stumbling block to S-P's defense aspirations was Secretary Wilson's policy that prime contracts should be concentrated among the nation's largest corporations. The day after S-P's party, Senator Henry Jackson, Democrat from Washington, unleashed a barrage of criticism against Wilson. In the first eighteen months of Eisenhower's administration, GM's defense business had increased by $1.7 billion while all other auto producers' contracts had dropped by $395 million. Romney complained that AMC had not received its fair share, but Hoffman was caught between being an Eisenhower intimate and the chairman of a struggling company. He proclaimed that he knew of "no policy that prevented his company from obtaining a fair share of defense business." But he admitted that it "could use some defense business" and expressed confidence "that it would be obtained when it becomes available." Nance must have had apoplexy when he read his chairman's statement. S-P was entering a political minefield.[22]

Nance, unsure about Senator Jackson's figures, asked Grant to check them. The treasurer's rendering proved that the senator knew what he was talking about. After the Republican administration took office, procurement patterns changed dramatically. From January 1953 through

June 1954, GM picked up another $1,700,430,000 in business, while Studebaker lost $244.9 million and Packard $84.7 million. Chrysler and Ford were also big losers. Nance, however, must have choked on the information that AMC gained $80.9 million in Pentagon contracts during the same period.[23]

S-P had few resources to devote to defense business but was well connected politically. Hoffman, who knew everyone in the Republican party and who frequently had Eisenhower as a guest in his house, made many initial contacts for the automaker. Nance, who was also a friend of Eisenhower and Vice President Richard Nixon, occasionally attended their Washington dinners and White House stag parties and handled the more formal corporate diplomatic duties. Vance did little except try to get out of the company. Despite the firm's connections, its defense contracts were relatively small and had the unpleasant tendency to fade away. In 1954, Studebaker and Packard had firm commitments for $72,235,834 worth of work; at the end of the year, S-P had only $19,087,868 in contracts. Those won late in the year were small, ranging from $4,000 up to $1 million.

Courtney Johnson, S-P's Washington lobbyist, had already submitted bids by December for a production study of a new jet engine and an overhaul contract for older jets. He had much broader goals, however. In March 1955, after a lunch with the assistant secretary of the army in charge of procurement and logistics, Frank Higgins, Johnson told Nance that he wanted the company to start building $2\frac{1}{2}$-ton trucks again, bid as a second source for the Jeep, manufacture eight-inch shells, build JATO rockets, work on the DART missile, convert marine diesels for tanks, design something he called a snow train, and contract for the LCM-8 transport.[24]

Nance had Grant search out small electronics companies with skilled designers for S-P to purchase. He and Nance zeroed in on Aerophysics Development Corporation, a private company. It was unique in that almost all its assets were its 200 employees, including 75 engineers. Nance estimated that the firm was worth no more than $100,000, but its talent was worth $700,000 to $800,000. S-P bought the company in November 1954 for $600,000 in cash, and it turned out to be a profitable subsidiary. Its biggest contract, almost three-fourths of its billings, was the DART missile. By the end of August 1955, it had secured more than $6.5 million in defense business and increased from 200 employees to 330. In early January 1956, the little firm won a $3 million subcontract from General Electric on the Atlas missile program. Overall, it did not add much to S-P's coffers, especially since the purchase agreement assigned

ADC's former owner, Dr. W. Bollay, a percentage of the firm's net profits, but it was a consistent bright spot in S-P's defense efforts.[25]

S-P also had some success in its quest for the contract for the $2\frac{1}{2}$-ton trucks. The company had an advantage because larger firms would not maintain a separate assembly line for intermittent truck contracts and their civilian truck lines were too busy to fit the military vehicle into their schedules. Johnson suggested that South Bend investigate assembling Jeeps on its truck line, and then Johnson said that S-P should perhaps buy the business from Kaiser. He thought it could be acquired without a cash outlay and, as a prod, mentioned that "there is a rumor that Edgar Kaiser has approached George Romney recently just as he approached us a number of times in the past." Nance drew a thick line in the margin beside that news and added a check for emphasis, but did not follow up on it.[26]

By spring, Johnson had submitted firm bids for several defense requirements, the most important of which were a $1,762,200 contract for $2\frac{1}{2}$-ton trucks (267 of them) and a $4.5 million contract for 20-mm cannons (1,640 of them). Brodie admitted to Nance that the company's "greatest weakness is the lack of facilities," but he gently suggested that "possibly a word to C.E. Wilson might be beneficial." Nance scrawled across the top of his letter, "Not Wilson – get Courtney to see Sec. Higgins"; Nance preferred to avoid petitioning his old competitor from GM.[27]

The truck bid turned out to be a nightmare. Johnson talked to Higgins, and the specifications he gave S-P differed from those GM used for the same truck. S-P had to use Timken axles at $1,700 each, but GM could use its own, which cost $1,200. The S-P truck had to have a Reo engine that cost $605.12; GM could use its own engine. Moreover, GM only bid on the army trucks, which were easy to build and returned a greater profit. Johnson complained to Higgins that it was not "fair for one company to elect to bid on the tenderloin of the beefsteak with the idea of leaving the lean meat, the bone and the gristle for its competitor."[28]

Higgins talked to General John Medaris, chief of the industrial division of the Ordnance Corps, before Johnson went to see the general. Medaris told Johnson that the Pentagon might buy at a higher price from a second company to maintain industrial capacity, in case of an emergency. But, the general warned, "the preservation of smaller companies by allowing them a share in the Defense program is a sociological question and is not a matter in which the Army can assert itself." He strongly hinted that GM would get the contract for more than half of the truck order. Johnson concluded that in the future S-P should find out what GM intended to bid on and refrain from bidding against the giant.[29]

192
===

*"Life or
Death for
Packard
in 1955"*

On June 29, Johnson happily informed Hoffman that S-P had been awarded 1,022 trucks at $7.5 million; GM won the other 1,182. Johnson thanked Hoffman for his "conversations" with "many people in government" and observed that the contract "serves to get us back into the Ordnance Corps Family." Johnson feared that the army was going to continue its "drastic policy" of awarding contracts to the lowest bidder, however, and suggested that S-P work at "the highest level of government" to change this practice.[30]

S-P's attempts to rebuild its jet engine business were less successful and demanded a great deal more effort. Packard still operated its jet engine pilot line and Nance had high hopes that he could become the prime contractor for the new J-57 engine to be used on the B-52 bombers. Realistically, however, S-P never had a chance. The Pentagon split the contract between Ford and Pratt & Whitney. When news of Ford's $195 million contract for the J-57 was published, Nance clipped the article and sent it to Hoffman with a penciled note: "Don't cry—but think what this would have done for S-P." It quickly became clear that neither prime contractor was interested in subcontracting much business to S-P. Brodie talked to Roger Lewis, assistant secretary of the air force, to try to get him to intercede on S-P's behalf. Lewis said that Brodie's "key people," such as Hoffman, should discuss the matter with Pratt & Whitney's president because "direct personal contact between the organizations might remove some of their objections."[31]

Nance worked every political angle he could to pressure the two companies to throw some business his way. Homer Capehart, Republican senator from Indiana, contacted Defense Department officials on S-P's behalf and advised Higgins on appropriate strategies. Such personal contacts had their costs, however. When Capehart went to Europe, S-P paid for his car and chauffeur and set his itinerary and made reservations for him in the United Kingdom. Company officers also spoke with the captain of the *SS United States*, ensuring the senator the best possible service while at sea. Edwin Blair, an S-P director, worked his contacts inside Pratt & Whitney and took the matter up with his friend, Attorney General Herbert Brownell. Capehart gained an admission from Harold Talbott, secretary of the air force, that he was in favor of "the need for expanded subcontracting by both prime sources." Talbott made it clear to Pratt & Whitney executives that if they increased production, the secretary expected the company to "increase its subcontracting by an equivalent to the dollar increase."[32]

By July, Nance was fairly sure that S-P would get a subcontract from Ford but would get little from Pratt & Whitney, which, he told his directors, was anxious for S-P to "withdraw pressure" on the air force. In

August, S-P won a parts contract from Ford for $46 million. Hoffman was still hopeful about the Pratt & Whitney prospects, although when Lewis and Talbott left the air force, S-P lost two of its staunchest allies. Hoffman was working on the new secretary, Donald Quarles, and thought that S-P could "reasonably hope to get [its] foot in the door" there. Hoffman's suasion worked—early in 1956, S-P finally was permitted to bid on $10 million of the Pratt & Whitney contract. S-P needed about $100 million a year in defense business to break even, and by November 1955 it had only $57 million in "firm contracts." The company was under pressure from its banks and insurance companies to get its defense orders up to the $100 million mark. But if Nance counted on reaching that goal by building jet engines, he was sorely disappointed.[33]

Nevertheless, his dreams of using the defense business to salvage his automotive fortunes died hard. Late in 1955, after Brodie and Nance had soured on jet engines, they concentrated on winning a foothold in the atomic energy business. That idea had first come up when the Atomic Energy Commission sent Nance a registered letter in January 1955, asking if S-P would be interested in participating in a new reactor program. The AEC warned that companies would be expected to pay for "necessary research and development work," which made Nance less than enthusiastic about the proposal. But he asked Grant and Brodie to "review the matter" anyway.[34]

Although S-P had no expertise in the nuclear field, Vance held a seat on the Atomic Energy Commission and was friends with one General K. B. Wolf, president of Oerlikon Tool and Arms Company in Switzerland. Wolf, who had an office in Asheville, North Carolina, sought nuclear work for his firm. Vance asked Hoffman to talk to Wolf about selling S-P a 60 percent interest in his business, to ease the auto company into the atomic energy industry. Hoffman met with Wolf in November and then went to see Wilber Brucker, former governor of Michigan and now secretary of the army, to discuss "working out a deal with Oerlikon." The Swiss company lacked a security clearance and so could not bid on defense contracts. Hoffman hoped an alliance with S-P would solve each company's problems. Brucker was not interested in helping a Swiss company—he had enough political problems parceling out defense work among domestic corporations—and he told Hoffman so on November 23. Quarles was willing, if a new company was formed from a merger of Oerlikon and S-P, to allow the firm to bid on contracts, but he was unwilling to give it preferential treatment. Hoffman passed all this on to Nance, who advised Brodie that "we ought to consider the Oerlikon deal dead."[35]

Brodie thought S-P could bid on subcontract items or propose "Studebaker-Packard developed equipment" that would "accomplish

some new and unique function of interest to the AEC." The latter would
have to be projects "we would carry out on cost-plus contracts for the
Government." He suggested that S-P develop a nuclear-heated-gas turbine engine because the company had a good chance to win a $50,000
study contract for it. Brodie was trying to dovetail the nuclear contract
and the company's ongoing work on a marine gas turbine, for which it
had the technical experts in-house.[36]

Nance and Brodie both sensed that the AEC would be a future gold
mine. In February 1956, when Nance was eyeing daily cash balances to
keep S-P afloat, Brodie hired ten new men to work on the turbine study
contract. He also prepared his boss for the front-end costs required to
enter the field. Brodie submitted a three-part plan for working S-P into
the business—his long-range strategy was adapting the nuclear subma-
rine reactor for civilian purposes. He was horribly overworked, however, and when Nance, desperate for immediate cash, asked Brodie in
April for a rundown of his short- and long-range defense probabilities,
Brodie did not even list atomic energy.[37]

Even if Brodie had realized all his hopes, the company's billings
would have remained far below what they had been during the Korean
War, when defense work accounted for 42 percent of Packard's gross
sales and 35 percent of Studebaker's. Brodie hoped that a contract for
five thousand $2\frac{1}{2}$-ton trucks would bring in a total of $30 million. If the
contract was awarded soon enough, as much as $9.8 million of that
amount could be realized in 1956. Jet engine parts would gross S-P another $12,245,000 in 1956, and if he won a contract for the jet's rotor
blades, he would add $1,602,000. The problem with that small contract
was the $2,084,800 S-P would have to spend on preproduction and tool-
ing before it could charge the government a cent. Navy contracts were
steadier but smaller, and a new engine contract would bring in $2.5 mil-
lion by year's end. The DART missile looked promising and could eventually mean $300 million to $400 million, but not very much of that was
in the immediate future. Brodie promised Nance that if the DART and a
prime contract for the J-57 both materialized, S-P could have between
$700 million and $900 million in defense business, which "would be a
major attraction in any consideration of our corporate stability."[38]

Brodie had touched on S-P's basic problem. The constant barrage of
newspaper and magazine articles that detailed S-P's growing losses and
questioned its survival made the Pentagon leery of awarding it contracts. Cash was scarce in South Bend and Detroit, and S-P was unable
to fund facilities to help win a greater share of the nation's defense
contracts. Moreover, S-P was a high-cost military producer. Unable to
achieve the volume it needed to lower its per-unit costs, S-P was forced

to plead for contracts on the ground that the government should maintain manufacturing plants in case another national emergency arose. S-P officials sought to use the Pentagon as a cash cow—they wanted the contracts that paid the quickest return with the least development and tooling costs, a form of direct government aid for their company. They pursued that short-sighted policy because they had little choice. S-P was losing so much money that by the end of 1955, only fifteen months after its birth, it was dangerously close to insolvency. Without some kind of outside help, the firm had no future.

Packard stuck with its basic 120 body style until the start of World War II but face-lifted its styling to keep its lines fresh, as this 1940 120 illustrates. Headlights moved down onto the fenders, Packard's famous grille was "modernized," the shift was moved from the floor to the steering column, and Packard adopted the split windshield. This 120 body also graced the 1940 Packard 160. (Author's collection)

For those in 1940 who wanted to set themselves apart from the common Packard owner, this 180 Model 1807 Cabriolet with a custom body by Rollston was more than adequate. (Photograph by James Pearsall)

To achieve desperately needed economies of scale, Max Gilman and production man George Christopher used as many common components as possible in the 120s and the company's larger, more luxurious cars. It became harder to differentiate between the "junior" models and the more expensive "senior" cars, especially from a distance. The 1940 Packard Formal Sedan, Model 1807, perched on its 138-inch wheelbase, illustrates that Gilman and Christopher never succeeded in completely blending their models. This was clearly a car for the elite few, especially since it sold for as much as $6,300. (Ed Mark's collection, Packard Museum, Niles, Mich.; © 1988 Packard Industries, Inc.)

Many purists believe that Packard's 1941 and 1942 "senior" cars, such as this 1942 Model 160, marked the company's apogee. Undoubtedly, they represented the final refinement of the original 120 styling. (Author's collection)

By the end of the 1930's, Packard needed a new model to meet the competition, especially from General Motors. Gilman turned to "Dutch" Darrin, an outside stylist, and in a remarkably short time he created what became the 1941 Packard Clipper, a fresh, new approach to automotive design. Although the new "skin" was stretched over standard 120 mechanical components, the new Clipper was an instant hit. Unfortunately, the war intervened and stopped production in 1942, the year this Clipper was manufactured. (Author's collection)

A Packard on a family outing: Lee Greenfield of Los Angeles with a 1941 One Ten Touring Sedan in Santa Barbara in 1946. The car was owned by Adolf Greenfield, a sheet metal contractor, and his wife, Irene. (Elsa G. Stewart collection)

During World War II Packard adapted modern production methods to the manufacture of Merlin aircraft engines, which Rolls Royce had built by hand in Great Britain. (Ed Mark's collection, Packard Museum, Niles, Mich.)

The name Packard made for itself during World War II manufacturing marine engines enabled it to secure defense contracts that helped keep it financially solvent long afterward. The example here is a 1943 version, the 4M-2500, which produced 1,200 horsepower. When three or four of these power plants were installed in 85- and 104-foot PT boats, the craft were capable of doing 47 miles per hour, or 41 knots. (Ed Mark's collection, Packard Museum, Niles, Mich.)

AMERICA'S MOST *POWERFUL*, MOST *LUXURIOUS* MOTOR CAR

—ONE GUESS WHAT NAME IT BEARS!

THIS page needs no signature.

Even the car itself dares to carry no name-plate. For there is no mistaking the identity of "America's most *powerful*, most *luxurious* motor car."

No other car built in America today offers you the performance of a precision-built, 160-horsepower engine.

No other car offers you such delightful smoothness, such roadability, and so broad a range of luxury appointments.

This car shares its distinctive styling and engineering with no other car of lesser name. It is the proudest achievement of America's oldest builder of fine motor cars.

At home, and in the far corners of the world—for 49 years—its famous "face" has been the symbol of the very finest expression of American craftsmanship.

One guess what name it bears!

ASK THE MAN
WHO OWNS ONE

130-HP-EIGHT   145-HP SUPER EIGHT   160-HP CUSTOM EIGHT

THE 1948 CUSTOM COULD ONLY BE A PACKARD, SAID PMCC. SEE PAGE 16.

Packard admen attempted to trade on their earlier "gateway" successes. The 1948 models, however, were driven up to the ornate front doors—probably by their owners. Unfortunately, many people in Packard income brackets preferred Cadillacs. (Courtesy of the *Packard Cormorant*)

Opposite. Packard, like all auto companies, started its postwar production by building its prewar designs. Packard concentrated on the Clipper. Rushing to turn them out for a car-hungry public and facing severe raw material shortages, Packard did not modify the Clippers much between 1941 and the end of 1947. They were still beautiful cars, as this 1946 model suggests. (Ed Mark's collection, Packard Museum, Niles, Mich.)

Unlike the other major auto companies, Packard chose not to completely restyle its autos when it made its first major postwar changes in its 1948 models. What some have dubbed the "bathtubs"—a 1949 model is shown here—were the result. All beauty may be in the eye of the beholder, as this publicity shot suggests, but the bathtubs were stylistic dead ends. (John A. Conde collection)

Cadillac's 1948 redesign set styling trends for the next decade. The upswept rear fenders, adapted from the P-38 aircraft, soon became the rage. Cadillac also pressured Packard with its automatic transmission and attractive hardtop coupes. Packard, with its bathtubs, struggled to attract newly affluent buyers to its showrooms. (Courtesy of the *Packard Cormorant*)

The three men who controlled Packard's destinies at midcentury. On the left, Leroy Spencer, a man many thought was heir apparent to the company's throne; in the center, Hugh Ferry, the unwilling occupant of the firm's presidential office who diligently sought a successor; on the right, Colonel Jesse Vincent, the born engineer responsible for many of Packard's technological triumphs, such as air-conditioning in 1940, the Ultramatic (the only automatic transmission manufactured by an Independent), and, of course, Packard's renowned engines. (Courtesy of the *Packard Cormorant*)

Packard finally abandoned its bathtub styling when it brought out its 24th series cars, shown here, in August 1950. These basic bodies would continue to adorn all Packards and Clippers until the Detroit factory ceased production in May 1956. Unfortunately, as with the Clipper in 1941, wartime restrictions limited Packard's ability to manufacture and sell these new models. (John A. Conde collection)

Packard was late offering the public hardtops. Even the low-priced three beat Packard into production. The wait may have been worth it, however, for as this 1952 Mayfair hardtop illustrates, Packard could still build attractive cars. (Ed Mark's collection, Packard Museum, Niles, Mich.)

Hugh Ferry tried to bring back some of Packard's former luster by creating special cars, such as this 1952 Pan American. The Pan American was an eye-catcher and garnered much publicity for the firm, but the huge amount of hand labor involved in its creation made it unsuitable for commercial production. (John A. Conde collection)

In the early 1950's Packard made more money from defense contracts than it did from car sales. The J-47 jet engine was one of Packard's major subcontracts. The 6,000-horsepower engine was used in the 2,200 B-47 bombers of the Strategic Air Command. Packard built the jets under a license from General Electric and charged the U.S. government $65,600 for each engine. (Ed Mark's collection, Packard Museum, Niles, Mich.)

By 1955, when this publicity shot was taken, James John Nance was showing the physical ravages of trying to keep Studebaker-Packard afloat. Standing in front of his company's twin-engine Beech-craft, however, Nance could still project his personal magnetism. Note the battered briefcase he habitually carried. (Studebaker National Museum, South Bend, Indiana)

The 1953 Balboa, another striking Packard creation, had a Caribbean body with a special hardtop welded on. Its reverse-angled rear window originally was designed to roll down to increase air circulation in the car; it did not, but Mercury later picked up the idea for its Turnpike Cruisers. (Courtesy of the *Packard Cormorant*)

Celebrating the formation of American Motors in 1954 were its principal architects. Edward Barit, on the left, president of Hudson, was pleased to ease into retirement. George Mason, president of Nash, shown in the center with his ever-present cigar, was the prime mover behind the merger and wanted Packard and Studebaker in the combination as soon as possible. George Romney, once offered a high position at Packard, became president of American Motors and helped keep Packard out of the new combination. (Courtesy of the *Packard Cormorant*)

Richard "Dick" Teague was Packard's master of styling. He was responsible for the 1955 face-lift of the Packard bodies that had been in production since 1950. He also practiced his considerable skills on Packard's special cars, such as the Balboa, Predictor, and Panther. He finished his career as styling chief for American Motors. (Courtesy of the *Packard Cormorant*)

Even though the commercial artist stretched the new 1955 Packard Patrician in this ad to minimize its high beltline, the new Packards were attractive by any standards and boasted a number of technological refinements. If only Packard could have built enough of them to quality standards. (Courtesy of the *Packard Cormorant*)

The NEW PACKARD
with the fabulous Torsion-Level Ride

THE MAGNIFICENT PACKARD PATRICIAN—"ASK THE MAN WHO OWNS ONE."

More Engineering Advancements than any Automotive Achievement of Our Time

America has a new choice in fine cars — the great *new* Packard . . . the result of years of planning, designing and testing to build an individually distinctive automobile embodying more engineering advancements than any automotive achievement of our time. You will find it the finest, most luxurious car in a long line of history-making Packards.

NEW TORSION-LEVEL RIDE automatically levels the load . . . smooths the road. Imagine not knowing or caring whether the road under you is rough and pitted or boulevard smooth! Incredible? Yes! You see, in the *new* Packard, instead of using conventional coil or leaf springs in an attempt to "cushion" the bumps, full-length torsion bars absorb road shocks automatically *before they can reach you.* And an ingenious power-controlled levelizer keeps the *new* Packard on an even keel. Compare this *new* Packard with the car you think is the finest made in America today. Then let the ride decide. You'll find driving the *new* Packard is easier, less fatiguing, and much safer.

POWER-PACKED PACKARD V-8 . . . DELIVERS MORE DRIVING FORCE to rear wheels than any other American passenger car engine . . . a sweeping surge of power to master any situation . . . 260 horsepower in the Patrician and Four Hundred models . . . 275 in the Caribbean.

NEW TWIN ULTRAMATIC TRANSMISSION. Actually two automatic transmissions in one — with a choice of two starts. Simply select the start you want. With either instant take-off or cruising glide, you'll note the difference on the open road or in traffic.

ADVANCED GRACEFUL STYLING. Long, low lines . . . massive grille . . . distinctive rear deck . . . every detail of design, like the exclusive Dual Courtesy and Safety Light, forward of the rear fenders, bespeaks Packard distinction and good taste. Breath-taking colors and textures reflect the decorator-smart fashions of today's finest homes. Your Packard dealer will be pleased to demonstrate this *new* kind of fine car.

Nothing on earth rides like the <u>New</u> Packard
Visit your Packard Dealer ... LET THE RIDE DECIDE

If the 1956 Clipper line did not sell well, it was not for lack of marketing ideas. The company gave away free postcards of its cars, such as the Clipper Custom Hardtop shown here. (John A. Conde collection)

This Packard Executive Hardtop was Packard's last-ditch effort in March 1956 to reposition its line in the marketplace. The Executive was designed to fill the gap between the Clipper and the Packard. It sold well but not many were produced. (Ed Mark's collection, Packard Museum, Niles, Mich.)

Opposite. Dick Teague's "concept car" for the 1956 auto show was this Packard Predictor. The futuristic creation embodied some novel concepts in addition to the reappearance of the traditional Packard grille. Teague added swivel seats and retractable roof panels, ideas that later found acceptance with other automakers. (John A. Conde collection)

The idea for Dick Teague's "cathedral" taillights, used on the 1955 and 1956 Packards, came to Teague while he was sitting in church. (Courtesy of the *Packard Cormorant*)

Presenting
The New

PACKARD
For 1956

THE APPEARANCE of the first Packard on the American scene marked the beginning of a tradition, among discriminating buyers, that one cannot buy a better motorcar.

NOW, for 1956, another fine Packard is making its bow. Your dealer will be most happy to place the keys to a *new* Packard at your disposal, confident your own good taste and knowledge of what a fine car should be will confirm this as *the greatest Packard of them all.*

The 310 h.p. Caribbean . . .
America's Most Exclusive Convertible

PACKARD DIVISION • Studebaker-Packard Corporation
Where Pride of Workmanship Still Comes First

[33]

Even as late as 1956, as this ad illustrates, Packard was still trading on its former reputation for building luxury motorcars. It still produced a few, such as this Caribbean, but most Packards were mid-priced automobiles. (Courtesy of the *Packard Cormorant*)

"Black Bess," the prototype for what the 1957 Packards would have looked like had they made it into production as planned. Instead, the 1957 Packards were manufactured at South Bend using mostly Studebaker components. Black Bess was cut up after Packard closed its Detroit factory. (Courtesy of the *Packard Cormorant*)

The 1957 Packard Clipper was the first to be manufactured in South Bend. It challenged all of Dick Teague's considerable talents to take a Studebaker and add enough Packard trim to make it resemble a Packard. Detractors called the cars "Packabakers." Packard production at South Bend ended in 1958. (Courtesy of the *Packard Cormorant*)

MERCEDES-BENZ

The 190 SL: EXCELLENCE ON ROAD AND RALLY

The Mercedes-Benz 190 SL was designed fundamentally for driver and passenger pleasure. As a sports car, it is a high performance machine with particular emphasis placed on road characteristics. Four-wheel independent suspension utilizing a low pivot point, single-joint rear swing axle, large transverse cooling fins on the brake drums, and extremely precise recirculating ball steering with a pitman arm of tremendous strength, combine to endow the 190 SL with surprising potency on tortuous roads.

What else does the 190 SL offer? You will agree that you can virtually count the number of marques in the world, on your fingers, that provide workmanship of this calibre and, for a sports car, appointments of this degree of luxury. Taut leather, roll-up windows, a weather-proof top and faultless fittings are a pleasure in themselves. However, when you get them in a car that is both tractable, yet can be safely driven near the limit of adhesion, you have fun to the *nth* degree. And that's what the Mercedes-Benz 190 SL is for.

Mercedes-Benz motor cars are distributed exclusively in the U.S. by the Studebaker-Packard Corporation and sold and serviced through selected dealers franchised by Studebaker-Packard.

Studebaker-Packard
CORPORATION

The Mercedes was not a Packard, but Studebaker-Packard officials hoped it would replace the discontinued marque and give their dealers an expensive car to sell. The company advertised it as a quality, well-engineered, sporty automobile, evoking images of Packard's earlier advertisements. (James Pearsall's collection)

Packard's swan song. Only 588 of these Packard Hawks were manufactured in 1958. The super-charged Hawk produced 275 horsepower and sold for less than $4,000. (Ed Mark's collection, Packard Museum, Niles, Mich.)

Chapter 12

Model 1407 Convertible Victoria, 1936

The "Sitting Duck"

The parties responsible for the Studebaker-Packard merger gambled on the shaky proposition that they could take two companies losing a lot of money, fold them together, add a dollop of outside capital, and magically create a profitable combination. The premerger planning was so superficial, nobody knew just how this metamorphosis was to take place. Everyone assumed that administrative streamlining, interchangeability of parts, an enlarged dealer network, a positive public attitude, and a higher corporate credit rating would see S-P through its troubles.

S-P's officers knew, however, that success was going to be a complex, delicate, two-step process. Even if they made a profit, they still had to convince the nation's biggest bank and insurance companies to loan S-P about $100 million to retool its cars for 1957 and rebuild its dealer system. Nance had to jump-start his company with an infusion of outside capital. If the firm showed improving numbers in 1955, he stood a better chance of convincing the financial moguls to gamble on it. And if the completely redesigned 1957 Packards and Studebakers sold as well as anticipated, S-P would earn enough to use its internal resources to finance further restylings.

Nance's most important task was to improve on S-P's 1954 first three quarters' record loss of $25,919,000. The turnaround was not going to be easy–Nance predicted privately that the company would lose another $10 million in the fourth quarter. Those were hefty losses for a company with $250 million in assets and slightly more than $64 million in working capital. S-P also had $45 million in revolving credit from a 21-bank combine, and the Metropolitan and Prudential insurance companies had advanced a 20-year loan of $25 million to pay off Studebaker's $7.5 million debt and help finance Packard's modernization. The banks' revolving credit was available until December 31, 1956, but carried with it a stipulation that S-P keep $40 million in working capital or all funds advanced would immediately come due. Losses of $30 million per year plus the $50 million Packard revitalization program left Nance very little margin with which to work his magic. With the very best of luck, it would be a tight squeeze for S-P in its first two years.[1]

Initially, Nance appeared to have the company on track. Its fourth-quarter deficit was only one-fourth of that predicted, giving S-P a net loss of $26,178,315 for 1954. It was a lot of money, but at least Nance kept it below $30 million. The year-end news would have been even better, except Packard's erratic performance in December caused the division a $5 million drain, almost twice its forecast loss.[2]

Grant's estimate for the company's next-quarter loss was $2,600,000. This would have been the sort of good news Nance was anxious to spring on the press. Concentrating on getting Conner up to full production, debugging Packards, negotiating with Studebaker's union, and reorganizing his administration, Nance spent little time discussing financial figures with his board in the first couple of months, an indication he thought the company was pretty close to being on target. The only disappointing news Nance had for his directors early in the year was that he had to postpone a complete retooling for Studebaker in 1956 because he did not have the money. Nance hated Loewy's "European" styling, which Studebaker's own sales manager, William Keller, once called "the droopy penis look," and wanted to bring Studebaker into the mainstream of American auto fashions. Surprisingly, given that Nance thought the cars so ugly, demand for Studebakers rose sharply in 1955, and the Conner plant was clogged with Packard back orders by March.[3]

Early in April, the *Saturday Evening Post* broke the story that S-P had earned its first profit in March. Nance responded with a detailed press release on all the good things happening in South Bend and Detroit, including S-P's first-quarter sales, which were 71 percent ahead of those the previous year. He paid special attention to his pet pricing theory, something he called "dynamic pricing," whereby he set his prices based on the competition's, not his, manufacturing costs. Nance's notion was that competitive prices would stimulate sales and give the company the numbers on which it had predicated its budget. He had played with this idea at Packard, but it was doubtful that he ever gave it full application. Laudatory stories in the *New York Times*, the *New York Herald-Tribune*, and elsewhere recalled the halcyon days of early 1953 when he was making his name at East Grand.[4]

Privately, Nance was not quite so exuberant. He explained to his directors that the *Saturday Evening Post* had leaked the news before he was ready. Even in profitable March, S-P sales were 2,200 units under the forecast budget, an intimation that the profit was an accounting fluke. Nance told his directors that the first ten selling days in April had been "very good," but he was afraid that it was all an aberration and cut 2,000 cars from the schedules. He was bothered that S-P had improved its percentage of the domestic-car market every selling period except the first ten days in April. Packard was still a mess, and Nance predicted that the division would lose $21 million for the year—$7 million getting into production, another $5 million before it reached its targeted output, and the budgeted $9 million. As he flipped through the oversized charts for his directors, Nance may have thought back to 1954 when Grant estimated that Conner would save Packard $12 million, exactly the amount the company lost getting the plant into normal working order.[5]

April 1955 marked the apogee of Nance's and S-P's fortunes. Just when he thought he had a good chance to make it all work, everything seemed to collapse. And he brought some of his problems on himself. A *Herald-Tribune* reporter quoted him as saying that he would "settle for a substantial profit in 1955 and, for the time being, be content as No. 4 in the industry." His statement raised unrealistic expectations in the financial community and was impolitic, especially since he already knew the magnitude of S-P's first-quarter losses. Two weeks later, the *New York Times* headlined S-P's $5,694,000 deficit, only $1 million less than what the companies had leaked in 1954. Nance lost a great deal of personal credibility, and the public glare hurt S-P sales. More important, Mutual and Prudential insurance executives passed the word to Nance that he should be more careful. He took the hint and admitted that his comments "reflected very negatively on me personally as being irresponsible to the financial fraternity."[6]

Nance did not make that mistake again. Just before S-P was ready to release its disappointing second-quarter results, he took two days and "made the rounds" of New York and Chicago bankers. He reported to board member Russell Forgan, a Wall Street banker himself, that "we laid the cards on the table as to our results" and gave them "what was a reasonable expectancy for the balance of the year." Nance, who never felt comfortable among moneylenders, admitted to Forgan, "You never know, of course, whether the banks are with you when you really need them."[7]

By midsummer, S-P was showing slow, steady financial improvement. With losses of only $9,638,399 and Nance's public assurances that economies were being instituted in both plants, he created an expectation for a yearly deficit well under $20 million. It was not to be; the third quarter was a disaster. The Conner plant finally caught up with its back orders just as demand for its cars slumped badly. Packard's dealers waited for factory rebates and the new models to restart their selling efforts. The market was so competitive that by mid-August only GM and S-P were not yet giving such drawbacks. Studebaker was torn with labor strife throughout the quarter, and Nance complained that in July the factory was closed more than it was open and built only 3,000 cars.[8]

These difficulties dropped S-P's income during the traditionally less robust third quarter, but its overhead remained high and money flowed out of the corporate treasury. Worse, the company had to repay the government almost $8 million. Studebaker and Packard had signed "incentive" contracts with the Defense Department which stipulated that they could keep 20 percent of any excess profits earned if they beat targeted engine prices. They did so and "booked" their 20 percent, but they still owed the government the other 80 percent. S-P dragged out negotiations over exactly how much was owed, as Grant slyly observed, so "we can use this cash in our operations until such time as it is paid." Nance knew nothing of Studebaker's contractual problem; in March, he asked Grant, "What is the story on the money to be paid back to the Services that I hear mentioned?"[9]

He must have been astonished to discover the obligation, especially since he was pushing to bring more defense work into his factories. Grant, however, assured his boss that the sum "will affect neither our operations nor our working capital position" because it had been "completely accrued on the company books." It did seriously crimp S-P's cash position, however, and Nance appealed to Laughna, Churchill, and Brodie to conserve money. The payback came just as S-P was spending large sums in September on 1956 start-up costs and as Nance was trying to show financial progress.[10]

Nance's pleas to husband the firm's precious cash reserves had a desperate edge to them. He hated the thought of "going to the banks for loans while we are operating in a loss position," and it began to dawn on him what a shock the publication of S-P's third-quarter results would be. He postponed making them public until November 21. S-P lost a frightful $19,301,513 in the quarter, which meant that the company had in 1955 drained away almost $30 million of its assets. A few months later, Nance confessed to his directors what a blow the numbers had been. They did "considerable harm," drove away customers, and caused local bankers to restrict the credit lines they allowed S-P dealers.[11]

At the very time S-P was exposing its red ink publicly, Nance was forced to borrow $9.9 million from the company's revolving line of credit to keep his operation afloat. The $8 million defense payment, the $15 million spent to restyle the Studebaker, and the company's losses depleted his cash reserves. The loan came just three weeks before he was scheduled to make his appeal to the banks and insurance companies. Since September he had counted on the possibility of at least breaking even in the fourth quarter, and as late as Thanksgiving he thought he still had a "fighting chance." By December, however, he faced up to the reality that it was "not probable" and he grasped at the faint possibility of a profitable month. When Mendler tallied the figures—Grant had resigned October 31 to become the New York Central Railroad's treasurer—the results were not even close. S-P lost another $2 million.[12]

Nance immediately set out to control the damage. His initial impulse was to drop everything and make another pilgrimage to the New York and Chicago bankers. But it was new-model introduction time, and tradition dictated that he preside at dealer gatherings all over the country. Subconsciously, Nance probably did not want to face his creditors. Instead, he drafted a long letter, explaining that his need to borrow, S-P's horrible third-quarter results, and Grant's leaving "understandably could create some anxiety among the banks." He defended his company's performance on the grounds that it was substantially what he had predicted at the beginning of the year. He also reminded the moneymen that he had forecast S-P's drawing on its revolving credit by the end of 1955. If Nance was true to form, he had tempered his worst-case scenario with avowals to improve on it. It was his style to raise expectations even while giving a realistic appraisal of conditions. He even did it in his letter when, after he had told his board otherwise, he told the bankers that there was hope for "bringing the new company to a profit point by the end of 1955." It had been a "rugged year," he told them, but better times were ahead. Hoffman commented that this "will help to quiet their concern and keep them on the team."[13]

It was an austere time for the firm's shareholders as well. They received no dividends in 1955 and watched their shares decline from $15\frac{3}{8}$ to $10\frac{3}{8}$. S-P's market performance reflected the public's perception of Nance's policies and indicated the degree of confidence that investors had in the Independent's future. On a more practical level, Nance needed high share values to make his executive compensation package, which included stock options, attractive enough to entice talented managers from other companies. Moreover, he and his board were serious about diversification. With S-P's worrisome cash problems, they needed the stock to maintain its value so they could use it to pay for outside companies, thus conserving capital. Some market investors speculated in S-P shares because they could not believe that a company with $250 million in assets and reputations that extended back to the nineteenth century could fail. S-P by any standards was huge. It had more than 20,000 employees and ranked as the 75th-largest corporation in the nation.[14]

Ironically, Nance, to make his stock more attractive, was working overtime to shrink S-P. He struggled valiantly to cut his overhead and manufacturing costs so his break-even point would fall to some level that he could reasonably hope to meet. The man who made his reputation as the premier salesman of his age focused his energies on the company's internal problems rather than on sales. He was forced to think and act like a George Christopher. For the second time in the postwar era, Packard had the wrong type of executive as president.

Nevertheless, Nance proved he could ruthlessly slash costs and jobs. One difficulty was Hoffman's 100-day cost-reduction campaign at Studebaker in early 1954, which convinced many employees that expenses had already been cut to the bone. Nance admitted candidly, "From a standpoint of management, I am in a position of having to talk out of both sides of my mouth." He had to do something to "get our sales volume pumped up" while he pushed "some drastic cost drives." And after Hoffman's earlier budget slashing, he was afraid that "the workers" were no longer aware of the urgent need for internal cost reductions.[15]

Grant and Mendler worked out plans to consolidate departments and jobs to squeeze out the dollars they promised in their premerger estimates. That was all Nance initially intended, but losses in the first five months of the year forced him to push his timetable ahead and begin terminating excess managers. As usual, Nance moved deliberately. He hired McKinsey & Company to survey S-P's administrative costs and compare them with those in other companies. The report must have indicated that S-P was top heavy. Nance immediately organized a "crash program" to cut $15 million out of his "overhead" by the end of the year.[16]

Ever the man for catchy titles, Nance christened his plan "Operation 55" and by early May had it ready. It was cleverly calculated to put the distasteful decisions about who had to leave as far below his chief staff officers as possible. To head the program, Nance selected Jack Gordon from Packard's manufacturing division and made him accountable only to the president and the board. Nance then blurred the lines of responsibility when he set up two three-man committees, an evaluation group to determine priorities and "set targets," and a task force "to make studies in selected areas." The whole scheme, neatly designed to defuse anger and recriminations, was kept "confidential" because Nance was anxious that the project operate in such a way "that maintains the best possible morale."[17]

Operation 55 appeared to be aimed primarily at clearing out unneeded personnel at Packard. In early May, Gordon told central staff executives that Nance had planned to begin Packard cutbacks in the first quarter. Now that Conner had reached "full operating rate," he was "ready for the first shake-out." Six weeks into the first round of cuts, Grant warned Nance that to get Packard's break-even point down to the 64,000 autos promised at the merger, Operation 55 would have to cut another $1.2 million a month "in direct labor and overhead."[18]

In midsummer, Gordon asked Nance for permission to fire hourly workers, 1,940 men at South Bend and 1,593 at Conner, from October through December. Gordon promised that the reductions would save S-P $12,354,000 a year. Operation 55 gutted the company's payrolls. The tally at South Bend as of the end of August was 1,309 salaried workers fired and 272 more scheduled to leave. Departmental statistics indicated that the layoffs were not as well executed as Nance had hoped. Some departments were 33 percent above their targeted numbers while others, more protective or obdurate, were as much as 60 percent below their goals. Company-wide, the personnel cuts reduced the number of nonmanufacturing, salaried workers from 10,000 to 7,070. Their salaries and benefits still totaled $48 million. All Gordon managed to accomplish, however, was to trim the company's payroll back to its size on merger day, when Studebaker had about 15,000 workers and Packard about 9,000. As with everything else Nance tried to do in that fateful year of 1955, the harder he worked, the more elusive progress became.[19]

His efforts at diversification, for example, showed the same depressing trend. Since Nance had read Booz Allen's 1952 report he had dallied with such notions, some idiosyncratic, but he had never developed an overall strategy for diversification. After the merger, however, he wrote Grant that "several of the Directors are pushing me for such a program," and he outlined "the areas to be explored." A merger with AMC was conspicuous on his list, a strong indication that his directors were nudging him in that direction. He asked Grant to investigate either merging with or acquiring AMC, and he was also attracted by companies that would enable S-P "to become a prime contractor on defense." And he leaned toward buying a large parts-supplier because he thought that "the suppliers are bleeding."[20]

Nance, however, had already set the merger search in motion without benefit of guidelines. In late October, he asked Grant to study English auto companies because "down the road Studebaker must acquire an interest in an English owned Company to build cars in England and ship throughout the sterling area." Nance was thinking globally in the heady first days of S-P's existence. Hoge, the comptroller, said that British Motor Corporation Ltd. controlled about three-fourths of the British market, estimated at one million cars per year. That did not leave many companies available to Nance, but he settled on Rover as the best possibility. Unfortunately, Grant had a devilish time locating any information on the firm, and the possibility of S-P's purchase became academic as S-P's fortunes ebbed.[21]

S-P's highly centralized nature overburdened Nance, and he paid attention to acquisitions only when he had time to put his feet up on his desk and think. But he kept diversification possibilities tucked away in a corner of his mind and pursued them in scattershot fashion. In early April 1955, for example, he had Northrop Aircraft investigated. The report looked good. Northrop had an excellent engineering department, but the company had not won a design competition in two years and did a lot of subcontracting for McDonnell. Northrop was just what Nance was looking for, but he did nothing about it.[22]

April was Nance's month for a merger flurry. Just four days after the Northrop report crossed his desk, Johnson proposed that S-P buy Willys's Jeep business. Nance had looked at Willys when he was at Packard, but nothing came of it. That may have been because he was intrigued by Lear, Incorporated, and Hycon Manufacturing Company. These two, however, revealed just how difficult it was for S-P to purchase even the smallest companies. Lear grossed just $44 million in the first ten months of 1954, and with its 2,114,000 shares of stock selling at $12 a share, it would cost S-P an equal number of its own shares. That was "too large a part of our total capitalization to pay for one company earning about $2,500,000 a year," his investigator reported. Hycon designed and manufactured electronic and radio equipment, guided missile components, aerial photographic equipment, and rocket parts. Its slightly more than 2 million shares had a book value of only 86¢ per share but sold for more than $10, which worked out to about 40 times its annual earnings. E. E. Richards in S-P's finance department made no recommendation on Hycon but explained that S-P would have to pay far more for it than for Lear. That put it out of S-P's reach.[23]

Under continued prodding from his directors, Nance kept looking. For a time he was interested in Hallicrafters Company, which had made a reputation in the ham radio industry and also had a "line of small radios and . . . television sets." It was smaller than Lear and Hycon—annual sales in 1955 were expected to be $25 million with a profit of only $500,000. Nevertheless, Richards asked Grant's approval to look more closely at the prospect. At the same time, Grant complained that he was short-handed, and Richards suggested that a Studebaker accountant who "has dabbled in the stock market in a small way" and has "a fairly good sense of security values" be sent to look the company over. Nothing came from the effort except an inkling that S-P lacked the professional expertise to do the acquisitions job right.[24]

Nance's enthusiasm for buying auto supply companies and vertically integrating S-P along the lines of GM stumbled over the twin impediments of lack of capital and low production levels. At least, however, Nance had the accessories study done by professionals. His consultant recommended that if the company was serious about bringing suppliers in-house, it would have to merge with AMC to guarantee them enough volume, about 570,000 cars a year. Many "of the more desirable" parts firms would lose a "substantial portion of their automotive sales volume" if they became captive to S-P. Auto-Lite and Borg-Warner, the two "most desirable," would lose from half to three-quarters of their business if they cast their lot with S-P or an S-P/AMC combination. Most suppliers already had contracts with Ford and Chrysler and would gain nothing by joining S-P. By the third quarter of 1955, when S-P suffered a loss as large as most suppliers' yearly profits, Nance's drive for vertical integration stalled, but the consultant did reopen the debate about a merger with AMC.[25]

Nance's own directors prodded him to talk to Romney, yet he remained reluctant to approach his arch-rival. Nance, probably because he wanted to look as if he was doing something to satisfy his board, went to great pains early in 1955 to ferret out details of Romney's contract with AMC. He was undoubtedly pleased to see that Romney made less money than he did, but the skimpy information did not suggest how to approach an agreement.[26]

The *Wall Street Journal* did little to increase Nance's merger enthusiasm when it published a long article in April lauding AMC's first-year accomplishments and quoting Romney as saying that interchangeability of parts saved the company $15 million in 1955 tooling costs. Romney accurately predicted that AMC's first-quarter loss would be less than $1 million. The *Journal* pointed out that AMC had whittled its debt from $69.6 million down to $43.8 million and had $74 million in working capital, far more than S-P. None of this was new to Nance, but it strengthened his resolve not to open negotiations with AMC while his own company was faring so poorly.[27]

Relations between the two firms were strained. AMC continued to buy Packard V-8s, but early in 1955, when AMC asked to buy Studebaker V-8s to use in its cheaper Nashes and Hudsons, Nance said no. In April, Graves heard that AMC was tooling to manufacture its own V-8s, which meant that it would eventually cancel its order for Packard's motors. Grant suggested that Nance offer Studebaker V-8s to AMC because the loss of Packard's engine sales would cost S-P $3.3 million in 1957. Furthermore, Grant explained, S-P could make around a $2.8 million profit on the Studebaker V-8 business, which "would provide a margin of safety" for S-P. It "would also open the door to closer relations with AMC, but would not be irrevocable depending on which course might be followed in future." [28]

A week later, Nance reminded Grant that "I am not at all happy with getting these overall blanket statements that the company has to do this or that, without a presentation of assumptions on which these conclusions are predicated." Nevertheless, he gave Grant the go-ahead to work up the Studebaker V-8 proposal–after he discovered that his 6-cylinder Studebaker engine could not "take any more horsepower" and reasoned that he swap Romney the Rambler six for the smaller Studebaker V-8. Grant and Graves made their presentation to Romney on September 6. Just ten days later, in one of his kinder letters, he turned S-P down, explaining that he would not have the capacity if Rambler sales hit their expected mark in 1957. Romney also could not resist chiding Nance for not making the request personally. [29]

Romney could afford to be uncharacteristically pleasant. On September 26, he served notice to S-P that one year hence, AMC would no longer purchase Packard's V-8. This withdrawal meant that AMC did not have to pay the last third of its 30 percent contribution to Packard's V-8 tooling costs. The loss was a blow S-P could ill afford. Brodie reported that S-P would lose $1 million in tooling money, $1.05 million in profit, and $1.25 million in liquidation of fixed overhead. When Nance took this news to his board in November, at a meeting already overflowing with grim presentations, he fudged the magnitude of the pain. He told his directors only that S-P would lose $1 million in tooling funds and a 7 percent profit on each engine. He also blamed the loss on AMC, explaining that the real reason AMC dropped the contract was that it was getting out of the big car business. He neglected to mention his refusal to sell Romney the Studebaker engines. [30]

The severing of the last financial ties that bound the two Independents and S-P's worsening financial straits cooled what little merger ardor was left. By 1956, both Romney and Nance had staked their corporate reputations on creating the fourth-largest auto producer, and both publicly disdained any thoughts of merger. Their determined personalities, unlimited ambitions, and aggressive behavior toward each other sealed both men's fates.[31]

Nance's lot was cast with a woefully undercapitalized S-P; only Walter Chrysler back in 1927 had been able to create an auto business in modern times with so little capital. Nance had to borrow millions to get through 1957, and his friends in the financial community advised him to pull his revolving credit loans down quickly in 1955 so those institutions would be "frozen in" and would have to loan S-P more funds to protect their investments. Nance instead waited until he needed the money late in the year before making his first withdrawal. Afterward he remarked that he had been "perhaps naive." [32]

At the end of 1955, Nance judged that the time was right to approach the Metropolitan and Prudential insurance companies for a long-term loan. He was ready to introduce his 1956 models, the money people had digested S-P's huge third-quarter loss, and the fourth quarter looked as if it would show at least a much smaller loss. Most important, he was running out of time to "nail down," as he was wont to say, needed funds to retool his 1957 cars.

Nance softened up the moneylenders by stages. He had a good line of 1956 products to offer, with a heavily reworked Studebaker line and Packards that featured a new nonslip rear end, dubbed the "Twin-Traction Safety Differential," and a push-button transmission selector. He rented the Hotel Astoria's ballroom in New York City in December and ordered his product planning division to make a full-dress presentation of the company's planned 1957 offerings. When Stout, a member of Bremer's team, arrived at the Astoria, he was shocked to discover that there were only fourteen people in the audience, all insurance men. "It was an automobile salon in the old time sense," he remembered. Afterward, rumors spread through S-P offices that the "investors" were "with us," and orders were issued to speed up work on the 1957 models that would feature interchangeable body parts. Everything appeared to be on schedule, although news that the insurance companies wanted to see S-P's fourth-quarter results before making a final decision was a bit disquieting to some.[33]

Bremer and Nance also thought the formal presentation a success, and they were ready to move. Nance was confident, as he later wrote Father Theodore Hesburgh at Notre Dame, that S-P would "get new money into the company at the conclusion of our successful labor negotiations at South Bend." S-P, however, was staggered by a host of bad news at the start of the new year. It lost money in its last quarter, sales were down, and Packard was hit with another disaster when its engineers discovered in November that axle flanges supplied by Dana Corporation were prone to failure. The Packard division had to replace the defective parts on 5,200 cars, which tied up almost $20 million in inventory and increased the public's suspicion that the company no longer produced quality cars. Sales dropped even farther, and S-P feared a much larger loss in the first quarter of 1956.[34]

Nevertheless, the board's executive committee and Nance held a formal meeting with Metropolitan and Prudential representatives on January 15 to ask for a $50 million long-term loan, only half of what Nance had been saying he wanted. They needed $30 million to defray retooling costs and another $20 million to restructure their dealer organization. Nance presented a preview of the company's annual financial statement—a $29 million loss for 1955 and perhaps another $9 million the year after. He spoke in vague generalities. Five days later, he confessed to his board that he did not tell the insurance companies about S-P's exact credit requirements. But even at that late date, he remembered later, he still "assumed—Met. & Prud. would go along."[35]

Nance was stunned when the insurance companies sent word on January 27 that they would not advance S-P one red cent. As he later told Father Hesburgh, "You can appreciate our surprise and disappointment when it [the money] wasn't forthcoming." Instead of $95 million in credit, he was left with $45 million in his revolving credit line and about $50 million in working capital; if the latter dropped another $10 million, all S-P's debts would immediately come due. The company did not have enough money to bring out its 1957 models, and its 1956 losses were going to be a lot more than the $9 million Nance had put about publicly. He told his directors that the company could not lose $30 million again. Even if he pared tooling costs and used up all available credit, "the default on loan and credit agreements will occur probably between July and September and possibly earlier." He also confessed why he had been less than candid with the insurance companies about S-P's credit arrangements. The company's projected tooling costs were $8 million more than he was willing to admit to the financiers.[36]

For internal consumption, Nance told his staff that everything hinged on how well the firm did in the first quarter of 1956. Planning went on apace for the new models, although he sent orders to slash tooling costs to the "barebones." His last hope to salvage the only Independent "full line producer" was to try to borrow from the banks, and if that failed, to sell the company to a corporation with a fatter pocketbook. He had to do something quickly before news that S-P had no tooling money hit the press and killed its car sales. Nance hurried to pare costs everywhere while his board for the first time bestirred itself to solve its corporate woes. In the meantime, as Nance admitted to Notre Dame's president, "since early January, when our program had to be held in suspense, we have been the proverbial 'sitting duck.'" The vultures were circling.[37]

Chapter 13

Model 1807 Formal Sedan, 1940

Seeking a "Safe Harbor"

The insurance companies' refusal to grant S-P's loan sounded the company's death knell. Without fresh capital, it had no future, no new cars, and no coherent forward planning. The refusal shattered Nance's carefully laid plans to buy time to reestablish S-P's credibility in the auto markets. Now he knew that unless he radically changed the way S-P did business, it was headed inexorably for liquidation. His financial men figured that he had about 120 days to turn S-P around before the money ran out.

After buying 7.5 million cars in 1955, consumers were holding onto their money. The Federal Reserve Board tightened credit late in 1955, raising the discount rate charged to banks. New-car sales in the first quarter of the year dropped to an annual level of about 6.5 million, then to 6 million. Compounding all automobile companies' problems were the 750,000 unsold 1955 cars. A "normal" carryover was in the range of 300,000 to 400,000 cars. And the public was not taken with the new 1956 models. It was a face-lift year for the Big Three and S-P. Somehow Nance, without any product advantages, had to carve a larger niche out of a shrinking market. The hot pink and turquoise paint jobs on showroom models belied the deep gloom that settled over auto dealers and salesmen everywhere.[1]

Sales problems continued to plague Nance in 1956. For the first two months of the year, industry-wide sales fell 17 percent, but Studebaker's fell 23 percent and Packard's a thumping 67 percent. The latter's December sales collapse showed no signs of abating. Porta warned Nance on January 20 that although Packard and Studebaker plants had done a wondrous job of hitting their targeted 103 man-hours per car at South Bend and 107 at Conner, the company had to bolster its sales volume to "preserve our factory gains." His proof was that in January's first sixteen days, dealers had ordered only 400 new Packards and Clippers and fewer than 6,000 Studebakers. The company still had 36,000 passenger cars and 3,500 Studebaker trucks in dealer and factory stocks. The same day, Nance jumped on Laughna, ordering him to keep all expenses at Conner "peeled down to the absolute minimum," to hold tooling for 1957 Packards under $30 million, and to take a personal hand in "sales matters." He also counseled, "You must choose the whales and let the minnows go."[2]

In all his years of merchandising, Nance had never seen a sales collapse like Packard's. He blamed East Grand's woes on the company's third-quarter report, but he knew that that was too simple an explanation. He sent Shine out to talk to Packard dealers, who still groused about slow retail markets, their higher prices, lack of local advertising, poorly trained sales forces, low trade-in values, and poor quality. They did emphasize, however, that price was the "buying public's sole consideration" in the tight market. Shine told Nance that many Packard dealers, in order to survive, had taken on lines of appliances, farm implements, and outboard motors, so they did not always promote their autos full-time. Amazingly, he related, of all the dualed dealers he visited, not one had a Packard on display. Nance was shocked. He ordered O'Madigan to hire McKinsey & Company to survey dealers' problems in depth and report back. O'Madigan sent Nance a memo, explaining that a "lack of sufficient confidence" in the company was killing sales.[3]

Throughout 1955, S-P's sales declines had outpaced Nance's efforts to get his costs in line with his volume. But Nance had read his Packard history, and in the company's dying days he made one more attempt to pull off a bold stroke to increase his volume. Packard-Clipper's advertising agency, D'Arcy, recommended a new Packard for 1957, priced against the Buick Super and Roadmaster, the Olds 98, and the Chrysler Imperial, which were killing the Clipper. Nance brought to market, quickly and on the cheap, a Packard in the $3,000-to-$4,000 range that featured appointments superior to the Clipper's. The new offering, introduced on March 5, was a Clipper Custom, with a Packard front end and different side trim, sold as the Packard Executive, "for the young man on the way up." It was a nice-looking car and sold as fast as it rolled off the assembly line. Unfortunately Conner was only in production three more months and built a mere 2,815 copies.[4]

While S-P's directors debated the wisdom of default and liquidation, Nance made several desperate forays into the field to perk up Packard's sales. He spent money the company could ill afford and made torsion-bar suspension standard equipment on all East Grand autos. Soon after the *Wall Street Journal* broke the news on March 16 that S-P had been refused funds for tooling, he countered what he called a "distorted" and "scurrilous" story by setting up a nationwide closed-circuit TV broadcast to send all his dealers and salesmen an uplifting message calculated to "reassure them of our determination to continue with an aggressive program." He visited the largest Studebaker and Packard dealers and brought 100 of them to Detroit for management seminars to imbue them with Nance's "volume viewpoint." He also boosted local advertising in larger markets. The immediate result was that Studebaker's sales also fell as the public began to sense the severity of S-P's problems.[5]

Nance had promised the insurance companies in December that he would devote 1956 to solving his sales problem, a most difficult task in what *Business Week* called a "rolling recession," one in which the economy appeared to be booming everywhere except on the farms and in automobile showrooms. By the end of March, only 44 percent of Packard's dealers reported a profit as they flogged their wares in a worsening market. *Consumer Reports* noted on April Fool's Day that Studebaker and Packard had two of the lowest owner-loyalty rates in the industry, at 22 percent and 30 percent, respectively. Cadillac led the poll with a healthy 70 percent. Only Hudson, with a 16 percent rating, fell below Studebaker, and AMC was getting ready to stop making the car.[6]

To combat the slump, Nance resorted to his bag of tricks. Early in March, he announced that S-P would give each purchaser of a new Studebaker or Packard a $20,000 accidental death insurance policy, a response to AMC's promise of similar coverage. The programs were aimed at selling cars by touting their safety features. Lee Iacocca tried the same theme with his 1956 Fords and discovered very quickly that the public had no interest in automobile safety. But Nance had to try something.[7]

Nothing worked. S-P's accountants estimated in April that Packard would sell 47,950 cars by the end of the model run, far below the 60,000 budgeted, and would lose a staggering $47.5 million. Studebaker was projected to lose $27.5 million. And those figures were optimistic. Internal documents revealed that Packard had sold only 13,678 cars at the end of the first quarter—the estimate for the year was a bit over 40,000. Nance's dealers, with a much lower break-even rate than the factory's, sold at or just above their target levels. The company therefore needed more dealers to enable the factory to reach its own "bogie," somewhere near 80,000 units in 1956. The division's ad agency even told Nance that the number of dealers he had "would be inadequate to successfully introduce a new line for 1957." Almost gratuitously, his admen warned that if he did not do something immediately, the "company, as it is now conceived, will not long survive."[8]

If he could not increase sales, Nance's only recourse was to do what other auto companies had done—cut his output and expenses to lessen his losses. By early February, 28,000 autoworkers were laid off. Nance reluctantly closed down the entire Packard Clipper operation on February 2, laying off another 5,500 workers until the middle of the month. The announced reopening date came and went, but inventories were so high that the plants stayed shut. On February 22, Laughna talked to Nance about remaining closed through early March, but he warned that if there was a spring selling season, the plant would have to go on overtime at a penalty of $100 per car. Nance, ever the optimist, gambled on a sales resurgence and reopened the plant on March 5. The next day, layoffs began at South Bend to bring Studebaker inventories into balance. The Conner plant operated at less than half its capacity for exactly one month. Then it was closed from April 2 to April 10. Nance was converting his inventory into badly needed cash, but with a grand total of 229 Packards manufactured in all of February, he was mortgaging his future to do it. Laughna's statistics through April read like a tragedy: in the first four months, Conner built 9,155 cars, slightly more than a month's output back in the heady days of early 1953. Conner was scheduled to manufacture 34,551 in the model year, but Laughna figured that only 24,373 Packards and Clippers would be sold in 1956. Had Nance known that Laughna's figures were on the high side, he probably would have locked his office and retired to his Michigan farm.[9]

The interrupted production and faltering sales made it necessary for Nance to borrow from S-P's credit line for operating expenses. With Conner closed in February, he used another $9.9 million of his bank credit. On the theory that bad news should be disseminated all at once, he followed the devastating March 16 article in the *Wall Street Journal* by announcing on March 17 S-P's 1955 loss of $29,705,093. Nance had told the bankers of the deficit much earlier, but he had hinted that S-P would show a profit in the first quarter of 1956. He was wrong; on May 10, he revealed a $14,311,173 loss, double the company's deficit in 1955. Just three days earlier Romney announced that AMC had reduced its red ink for the first half of its fiscal year to less than $1 million dollars. Nance did not even put himself in GM's class–its quarterly report showed that the giant banked a $283 million profit on sales of over $3 billion.[10]

From January 27, the intent behind all Nance's efforts was to try to attract a merger partner. S-P's only hope for an infusion of fresh capital was to ally itself with another firm that could use S-P's huge tax write-offs to enhance its own financial position. Furthermore, Nance could offer a small but profitable defense business to sweeten the deal. His principal intangible assets were Studebaker's reputation for economy and durability and what remained of the grand old Packard name. He hoped to unite with one of the Big Three: if not, he was willing to effect a "working arrangement" with one, to slash his 1957 tooling costs. Nance thought of buying his body stampings from an outside source, Ford. He called Ernie Breech, Ford's chairman, and explained that he needed time to "get through the period immediately ahead" so S-P could "establish a permanent place for ourselves." Nance asked for body stampings and promised that S-P's redesigns would ensure that its cars "wouldn't detract or infringe on the appearance of your products." If Breech would sell him the stampings, Nance promised that he "could get enough money to see us thru."[11]

Breech encouraged Nance, who assigned Dick Stout and Richard Teague to adapt their 1957 styling plans to both Ford and GM body stampings. Stout remembered that he worked on "Project X" in a secret room, which was confirmed by the paperwork, all of which was stamped "Confidential" or even "Very Confidential." At the same time, Bremer compiled a dense report on the many problems involved in using Ford's shells. Bremer also showed that S-P could bring out cars substantially similar to its 1955 clay mock-ups, but using Ford components, for just under $28 million–a considerable savings. By February 3, Bremer had new drawings ready for Nance. The only telltale signs of the cars' Dearborn ancestry were their rooflines. Studebakers grew a few inches on Ford's chassis while Packard's interior got smaller in its Lincoln body. The 1957 Lincoln was the last year on that shell–in 1958, Packard would have to retool to accept the new Lincoln. But as Bremer philosophically put it, "This is not of immediate urgency."[12]

Work continued on the Ford project, and Nance's focus shifted toward the boardroom and how to save the company. The insurance companies' loan refusal created problems that transcended daily operations, and Nance needed the directors' outside financial contacts to rescue the company. At the board's January 20 meeting, Nance must have reported that he was not sanguine about getting the loan because the board created a finance committee composed of Russell Forgan, Homer Vilas, and Victor Manheim, the directors with the closest ties to Wall Street.[13]

The loan denial a week later enkindled the company's directors. They met informally, drew up survival plans, and played out scenarios. At their next formal gathering on February 27, they were all aware of their problems and options, but they were far from unanimous on what steps to take. Their most immediate problem was what to do about the 1957 tooling. Nance argued for face-lifting all three cars for $10.3 million, to carry the company until it could solve its financial problems. The board, however, was bolder and voted to restyle Packard for $27.8 million and make a "limited modification" on the Clipper for $1.5 million. It was willing to leave Studebaker unchanged until 1958, when engineers could achieve interchangeability of parts with the Clipper. The directors did agree that if the company could not raise new funds, they would fall back to Nance's plan for face-lifting the cars.[14]

The directors spent most of the daylong meeting discussing a half-dozen options for raising capital. These they intended to pursue "aggressively." S-P's creditor banks, to protect their interests, suggested that the board hire an outside financial consultant, D. C. Borden, a former vice president of First National City Bank of New York. Borden had done his homework. He waded right into the debate and thoroughly offended Nance's sensibilities before it was time for lunch. He suggested that Nance operate the company while the board handled its financial affairs, that funds not be appropriated for the original retooling program, and that inventory be converted with all possible speed into cash. He even asked Nance, point blank, whether Packard could ever be profitable. After lunch, Nance delivered a lengthy monologue in which he claimed that to be profitable, his dealers needed a cheaper Packard.[15]

The directors girded for the work ahead. They increased the finance committee by five, to include Nance and Hoffman, waived their board compensation, and decided to wait before releasing any financial figures to creditor banks. They approved $2 million for March tooling. Then, off record, the directors talked of selling S-P to Chrysler or to Kaiser Industries, selling Packard to Ford or to Chrysler, and merging with American Motors. They also considered selling S-P to International Harvester, General Dynamics, Curtiss-Wright, and Massey Harris. If none of these companies were interested, the board determined to raise capital from the insurance industry, a transaction Borden advised was probably illegal, from banks, from the government, or even from competitors. After an exhausting day, the directors finally ordered Nance to get $5 million in costs out of the Packard division.[16]

S-P's directors were not yet panicked or flustered. Their discussions were upbeat, rational, and infused with confidence that matters could be worked out. Afterward, however, their frenetic activities showed that they understood how close S-P was to the brink. They fanned out in every direction, petitioning corporations, banks, insurance companies, and the government for help. The directors apportioned their duties informally, and because most of their requests were made in private, Nance hired Heller & Associates to track their contacts. He wanted to be able to prove to S-P's stockholders and bankers that they were vigorously pursuing all their options. By the end of June, many directors had forgotten dates, names, and even the tenor of the conversations they had had. Their best recollections were that the finance committee met at least five times before the March board meeting and contacted six corporations, members of the Eisenhower administration, banks, and private investment houses. The board's workhorses were Maurice Moore, from Deport, Texas, who was a Studebaker holdover, a Columbia Law School graduate, and a partner in the law firm Cravath, Swain & Moore, and Russell Forgan, a former Packard director, a Princeton graduate, and a partner in Glore, Forgan & Company, a New York City investment house.[17]

On March 2, Moore contacted Nicholas Kelly, a trustee of the Chrysler estate and a member of that company's board, about a merger. Moore was armed with an internal report, "Study of Merger Possibilities," that investigated AMC, Chrysler, Ford, and International Harvester in detail. S-P's hope for a Chrysler deal hinged on rumors that Chrysler was going to make Plymouth a separate unit, which would leave Chrysler, Dodge, and DeSoto dealers without a low-priced car. Moore proposed to dual Studebaker with those dealers and suggested that Chrysler might want the Packard name "to give to a new car." Studebaker's trucks, he thought, would be a helpful addition to the Plymouth division, and Packard's new engine and transmission plant was an improvement over Chrysler's facilities. Most important, S-P's tax credits would enhance the third-largest carmaker's bottom line.[18]

"Tex" Colbert told Nance the next week that he was not interested, but the matter did not end there. In April, ZurSchmiede brought up Chrysler again, arguing "that this is the only solution w/i industry." Two days later, Nance dutifully went to see Colbert with a written proposal. The very next day Colbert called Nance's secretary and told her that there was no deal. Lest Nance miss the point, he followed with a "Dear Jim" letter.[19]

Chrysler was only one of the board's options. S-P's internal report predicted that an S-P/AMC merger was the only one in the industry that would guarantee the survival of the Studebaker and the Packard names. The combination would retain valuable tax credits, AMC would bring Kelvinator and S-P its defense business for diversification, the new company would have almost 6,000 dealerships, and AMC would gain S-P's new Utica plant. The disadvantages, however, were manifold. The two companies would have no more than 3.5 percent of the auto market, they would lack financial strength, their dealers would remain weak, and, as the report put it, they would have "excessive management personnel," especially at the top. So it was a measure of the directors' growing desperation that they approached AMC just before their March 23 board meeting. Heller could not find out who went to AMC, but it was a safe bet that Nance had not crossed Romney's threshold. It must have been a short meeting, for Heller noted that "no possibility was found to exist." AMC's rejection was so final that it was not even discussed at the next board gathering.[20]

AMC's refusal left only two possibilities in the auto industry. The idea of a merger with GM was so farfetched that S-P's planners did not even consider it. GM, however, had money, and S-P's creditors pushed Forgan to try to tap into it. On March 5, he "approached" George Whitney, chairman of J. P. Morgan & Company's board, for advice "on how to obtain [a] long-term loan" from the automotive giant. Whitney made an appointment for Forgan with GM's executive vice president, soon to be chairman of GM's board, Albert Bradley, who promised to consider Forgan's request. They met twice more, an indication that GM was at least willing to listen. When S-P's directors gathered on March 23, however, Forgan's comment that his talks with GM were "abortive" ended all hopes for the loan.[21]

While Forgan, Moore, and Nance waited for an appointment with Henry Ford II, they went hat in hand to International Harvester. S-P's report indicated the hope that the farm implement and truck manufacturer would bring the Independent financial strength, improved public acceptance, and a diversified product line. But IH dealers were located in rural areas, where they would not help S-P sales much, and Studebaker trucks did not complement IH's offerings. Forgan talked to executives at the implement company, and they were decidedly cold toward his proposal.[22]

International Harvester was not the only outside company approached by S-P directors during that hectic three-week period. Either Moore or Forgan went to see Hugh Knowlton, a partner at Kuhn, Loeb, to discuss a possible merger with Curtiss-Wright, a corporation heavily involved in defense work. Knowlton introduced Forgan to Curtiss-Wright's president, Roy T. Hurley, and they met again a week later.

Forgan told his fellow directors that Hurley showed "definite interest." Hurley said that if Forgan came back to him with a "program that is feasible financially," he would help S-P raise funds and get more defense work.[23]

In the midst of all this activity, Moore was unexpectedly approached by one of the new breed of postwar entrepreneurs, Royal Little, who had created the first corporate conglomerate. Starting in the depressed textile industry in the 1920's, Little bought and sold marginal companies and built up a giant, Textron, Inc. After the war, he branched out into other businesses, buying firms that had tax credits, cash, and salable assets. He sold off portions of the acquired companies, scaled them down, made them profitable, and with the cash from the sales began the process over again.[24]

Little was an engaging character. Almost 60 years old in 1956, he was a secretive man who operated out of an unpretentious Rhode Island office, had a passion for golf, and was well liked. He was no corporate raider; he liked to rebuild faltering companies and garnered a reputation for allowing their managers a free hand. All the publicity notwithstanding, his empire was not that large. Textron in 1956 had earnings of $6.5 million on sales of almost $250 million, which made it not much bigger than S-P. Little told Moore that he was primarily interested in S-P's tax carryover. Still optimistic they could work a deal with someone to keep S-P intact, the directors put Little off.[25]

S-P's directors did not talk to Little again until the end of April, when their options had narrowed to Curtiss-Wright and a federal bailout. In an "informal board meeting" on April 25, the directors authorized Moore "to reestablish negotiations which had previously been delayed." Moore met with Little five days later and found him still interested, but he wanted detailed information on S-P. The following week, he and several of his experts arrived in Detroit, to spend three days looking things over. Before the first day was out, he offered Moore merger terms—500 shares of Textron preferred and one-tenth of a share of common, worth about $27, for each S-P share. The price was good, but it was a takeover, not a merger, and the directors thought they could get a better deal from Hurley. The very next day Curtiss-Wright told S-P officials it did not want a merger, and S-P's interest in Little suddenly perked up again. Forgan met with him in mid-May for "further exploratory" discussions, but Forgan was wary because Little was famous for buying with stock and selling for cash. And Little shied away from promising to invest the $50 million S-P needed to have one more chance to crack the auto market.[26]

Stringing Little along for almost two months took a lot of courage. S-P's directors were under severe pressure to either solve their problems or liquidate the business. The bankers became more restive when S-P borrowed another $19.5 million in February to pay interest due on the loans it had already taken out and to use for operating expenses. When the directors came back less than a month later for another $9.9 million, all S-P's creditors grew skittish, especially since a merger deal seemed as far away as ever.[27]

The bankers were more a hindrance than a help with their ultimatums and contradictory advice. Some of them panicked; George Moore, executive vice president of First National City Bank, told Forgan in early March that S-P must file immediately for voluntary reorganization. Forgan convinced Moore that this was "inadvisable" but the exchange prompted a lengthy discussion at S-P's March 23 board meeting. Nance complained that the bankers did not understand how hard everyone was working to salvage the company. He and the board had enough problems, especially "with this thing collapsing."[28]

Forgan devoted a great deal of his time to calming officials at Chemical, Chase, and City banks, talks Forgan characterized as "rough." Henry MacTavish at Chase attacked Forgan because S-P's board did not meet more frequently. Forgan's counter that its finance committee met weekly did not mollify the angry banker. As Forgan explained to all S-P's creditors, the directors had taken a "calculated risk" and funded some tooling and asked for a month's grace to see what transpired. His discussions with insurance companies were no friendlier. Harry McConnell, second vice president at Metropolitan, also scored Forgan for an inactive board. Nettled, Forgan pointedly reminded McConnell that the insurance people had promised Nance that if he got his labor costs down, they would advance the necessary tooling funds. When they reneged, Forgan said, they put S-P in its present bind. Forgan also mentioned to McConnell that Moore at City wanted S-P to declare bankruptcy. McConnell replied, "Good God, you are not going to do that."[29]

In reality, the company's bankers were only saying what Nance and his board were thinking: liquidation was a real possibility. By March, Nance had already hired Ernst & Ernst's industrial division to make three quick studies of what would happen if no merger could be worked out. He wanted the figures on consolidating Packard and Studebaker production at South Bend, producing just Studebakers and trucks at South Bend, and liquidating the entire corporation. When Nance reported on Ernst & Ernst's contract, Hoffman angrily claimed that the board had already agreed on closing Packard immediately. ZurSchmiede cut Hoffman off and asked, "Why Packard?" Nobody answered. Nevertheless, the board authorized Nance to hire Heller & Associates to plan for the orderly disposal of S-P's assets.[30]

The directors were still not convinced that all was lost. They had been working hard since late February to convince Eisenhower's administration to step in with huge defense contracts that would bring millions of new dollars into S-P's treasury. The directors decided to try the Treasury Department. Hoffman went to Washington on February 29 and had lunch with Secretary George Humphrey, to explain S-P's problems. Five days later, Moore and Forgan "approached" Humphrey. They had specifics on S-P's plight and painted the worst possible financial and political scenarios if everything fell apart.[31]

Humphrey understood what the political fallout would be if S-P went bankrupt and left some 20,000 workers unemployed in two states vital to the Republican presidential effort. Moreover, Packard alone bought parts and services from some 30,000 suppliers who would be hurt if the division stopped producing cars. Humphrey sat down with Secretary of Commerce Sinclair Weeks, Attorney General Herbert Brownell, Postmaster General Arthur Summerfield, economic adviser Arthur Burns, and Ike's personal assistant, Gabriel Hauge, to discuss "autos." The group blamed the Federal Reserve Board's constriction of credit for the economic slowdown that threatened S-P, but offered the company nothing.[32]

S-P's directors kept up the pressure on the administration. Three days after the large meeting, Nance called on Humphrey. Then Hoffman, who made four transcontinental trips in March, stopped by six days later. At the March 23 directors' meeting, Forgan promised that "Washington has been covered from top to bottom." Cabinet members had assured company officials that if S-P could come up with a constructive plan, the administration would provide help, but Forgan warned that it would not be "all that we want."[33]

Board members suspended their political lobbying for the next two and one-half weeks, because a merger with Ford seemed possible. Nance, through Breech, finally arranged a Sunday meeting on March 25 with Henry II. Nance, Forgan, and Moore knew that Ford's "E" car was to come out in May 1958 and be sold through a new dealer network created from scratch. The trio offered a ready-made dealer system to handle the new offering, the infamous Edsel. They also suggested that Ford use the Packard name or make the new car a Lincoln and bring out Lincolns under the Packard name. Or, they continued, call the new car a Studebaker and then drop the Packard name or keep it for a prestige car that sold for more than a Lincoln.[34]

The initial meeting with Henry and his executives went well. Heller reported that "considerable interest was shown," and the S-P representatives promised to provide Ford with "complete operational information as soon as possible." S-P had the required documents ready in just five days. By then, however, Dearborn's ardor had cooled noticeably. Nance explained later that Henry was more interested in the merger than his "associates" were, and they convinced him to pull back. According to Heller, Ford told S-P officials that there could be no merger, but he expressed an interest in Packard's Utica plant and was amenable to participating in "an automobile industry loan to the Corporation." By April Fool's Day, all S-P's hopes about Ford, including being able to purchase Ford bodies, had been dashed.[35]

When the Ford talks ended, S-P was on the verge of collapse. Nance, who kept going to New York to meet with bankers, insurance men, and corporate officials, as well as talking with his finance committee and his board, while trying to run the company, was worn out and getting irritable. S-P was dissipating its working capital and assets at a frightening rate, and drastic steps had to be taken fast or there would not be anything left to merge or sell. He tried to give his directors a sense of just how critical affairs were when he explained at their March meeting that "orders had practically stopped." It was a waste of time to try to revive the firm's sales. The directors had to decide what parts of the company to kill off and what parts to try to salvage.[36]

Ernst & Ernst and Heller had drawn up elaborate outlines of the company's options. The bankers had advanced their own proposals for downsizing the company, and Curtiss-Wright wanted the board to make its plans before Hurley would talk seriously. Curtiss-Wright's president put forth his own thoughts to Forgan on what S-P should do. The directors faced a bewildering array of possibilities, which they discussed to death. What emerged from all the wranglings was that Packard's Detroit properties were going on the block. But the board disagreed on whether Packards should be built in South Bend. If S-P kept both lines, the directors faced critical tooling decisions, which begged the question of where the company was going to get funds. Packard's sale might destroy what was left of S-P's weakened dealer system. And behind it all, Nance kept insisting, was the intangible factor of public opinion. He pressed the board to do something big enough to catch the public's fancy and give it confidence in the company again.[37]

The implicit agreement to sell Packard was curiously ironic. Nance had built Packard's new plants to attract a merger partner. Afterward, however, the only things of value he had to sell were those very Packard facilities. Even if he could find a buyer for them, though, S-P would not be out of the woods. Nance guessed that S-P could get $30 million for Packard's Detroit assets but would take a $10 million loss in inventory and in tooling money already spent. That would swell S-P's working capital to $60 million, but it would cost $24 million to bring out a new Studebaker in 1957. That expense would put the company into default.[38]

The directors' only other viable option, discussed seriously for the first time in March, was to liquidate the whole company. Nance, who had given this distasteful choice a great deal of thought, said that it would have to be done swiftly to avoid public repercussions. He proposed to announce a minor face-lift for 1957, run out 1956 production as rapidly as possible to use up inventories, and shut down, without advance public notice. Over the next several months, S-P's directors avoided this drastic decision, leaving Nance to hold the operation together to buy time.[39]

Nance was forced to try to make the best of a bad situation, to press hard and badger everyone to cut costs and keep smiling. By mid-March, his bankers howled when S-P's market penetration fell to 2.5 percent after Nance had promised that he would raise it to 3.5 percent in 1956. They also did not like the fact that S-P had 102 "open points," areas without dealers.[40]

Nance struck hard at Packard. He ordered plant maintenance cut "to the bone," all advertising stopped after June, and "every bit of fat and frills" taken "out of our present organization." He explained that he took these crippling measures because his "primary objective is to conserve cash." And he cut deep. At an April 4 staff meeting, he suspended Packard tooling for at least two weeks and perhaps as long as two months. He emphasized that the news should not leak out, and Bremer later assured Nance that orders to suppliers had been "discreetly . . . held up." The cancellation of tooling and advertising sounded the death knell for Packard operations in Detroit. Moreover, by the third week in April, Nance ordered that all open Packard sales points be left unfilled "because of potential liability indicated by counsel in event of liquidation."[41]

It was clear from notes Nance made prior to his talks with the company's Chicago bankers on April 18 and 20 that he thought S-P had only three options—get a government or an industry loan guarantee, merge with an outside company, or liquidate. He told them that in addition, the Defense Department had to give S-P "immediate" contracts for truck and jet parts and another $100 million in contracts for jets and missile work in 1957. Automobile companies had to "purchase plants in Detroit" (a sure sign that Packard operations there were finished), sell S-P bodies, purchase S-P parts, and release some of their defense business. If, by some miracle, these things happened, Nance promised that he would "telescope" S-P, consolidate its manufacturing, and "try to reestablish confidence" in order to build sales. He predicted that S-P would run out of cash in May and would have to use more of its loan "to keep alive until [a] deal can be worked out." Nance warned the bankers that they should help keep S-P in business in order "to preserve [our] tax carry forward," which Nance estimated at $60 million, a figure that changed every time anyone mentioned it.[42]

Nance was talking to Chicago bankers as events in Washington were heating up. Just a week earlier he had had a long talk with Humphrey, and the following day, April 13, Humphrey wrote Weeks that "the Studebaker-Packard matter is becoming very pressing." The company's stockholders' meeting was to take place the next week, he said, "and nobody knows just how obstreperous that might be." The company had one "hot" negotiation pending, he added, but "if it fails, the problem will be very serious." Humphrey wanted to wait for the results of the "hot" discussion and then get together with Weeks to "see just what, if anything, further can be done."[43]

Weeks thought that it was all very simple. He dashed off a handwritten note to Humphrey the same day, asking, "Why cannot we do something on the engine business. Cordiner [of General Electric] said that's right on the table waiting to be served." A year earlier, Nance would have jumped at the prospect of a GE subcontract, but in April 1956, Weeks's suggestion fell far short of a realistic solution to S-P's problems. But the cabinet officers were paying attention and thinking in the right direction.[44]

President Eisenhower and his cabinet, at their April 20 meeting, listened as Burns argued that soft auto sales presaged a "minor recession this fall." Everyone around the table was angry at the Federal Reserve Board's actions to tighten credit. Ike chimed in that it "looks like the bankers wanted higher profit." Not all were sympathetic to the automakers' plight, however. Humphrey explained that the "industry was very foolish last year. And model changes for '57 will make sales in '56 very tough." Later, in a desultory discussion, Humphrey suggested that the only thing the administration could do "is begin to free up the money that can be done soon," which was exactly what Nance and his colleagues at S-P wanted.[45]

President Eisenhower spent almost all that afternoon discussing S-P. Hoffman came up to see him "about another matter," but the discussion, Ike remembered, soon turned to Studebaker's survival. Ike jotted in his diary that Hoffman "no longer has any executive authority whatever in the company," but that he "talked to me very pessimistically." Later, the president noted that "if one [auto] company would go under, it might practically dry up the market for a while and we would suffer accordingly." All the chief executive could do was "urge him to keep trying," but after Hoffman left, the president prodded his cabinet members to action. The last things he wanted in the autumn of an election year were tight money, a recession, and a major corporate disaster.[46]

Eisenhower asked Wilson to go to Detroit that weekend to see if auto executives had any defense contracts that "might be shifted to Packard-Studebaker [Ike habitually referred to S-P as Packard-Studebaker] (either prime or subcontract)," or whether "it might not be possible for one of the big companies to buy up one or two of the less efficient production units in the Packard-Studebaker combine." The president also urged Wilson to spend all the Defense Department's money before the end of the fiscal year "in paying bills that are current." Later that night, in his personal diary, he noted, "The Defense Department is now seeking to place a contract for some five thousand trucks; manifestly this would be of some help if it could be given to Studebaker, which has a good record in truck production."[47]

After the president talked to Wilson, Ike called Humphrey and told him categorically that S-P would get the order for 5,000 trucks. Wilson, however, had not put the contract out for bids, and Ike asked Humphrey to "find out if he can do it by negotiation right away, or under the law of depressed areas." The president also told his treasury secretary that "someone hinted to him that with the RFC [Reconstruction Finance Corporation] out of business, the Federal Reserve Board can make loans." The president thought that "within a week we ought to have something we can do" and reiterated that he was "anxious to have something on that contract down there."[48]

None of this was news to Humphrey, for that morning he had met with Weeks, Wilson, Summerfield, Burns, and Hauge in his office to thrash out S-P's problems. The treasury secretary was already considering two options that had originated either at bankers' meetings or with S-P's board. Plan A, as everyone called it, stipulated an auto industry guarantee of a $50 million loan to S-P, consolidation of all its manufacturing facilities in South Bend, and the sale of all its nondefense plants in Detroit. Under plan B, S-P would consolidate its facilities in South Bend, continue to build both cars, dual all its dealers, sell its Detroit plants, and buy its body shells from an outside supplier.[49]

By mid-April, Humphrey had told Nance, in no uncertain terms, that he did not like plan A but he would help S-P with the other. Humphrey did not want to see S-P liquidate. He told Nance to hold things together long enough to work out a deal on his own or to enable the government to help. Nance had real reservations about plan B. He thought that public reaction, even if the plan were successful, would not be favorable enough to boost sales. And contrary to what he told his bankers, he did not think he could "telescope and stay in business." S-P's directors saw no alternative to liquidation except merger and, under pressure from Humphrey, voted at the April 16 meeting to reopen talks with Chrysler and Curtiss-Wright.[50]

After the flurry of activity in Washington, Eisenhower and his cabinet decided to wait upon Wilson's talks in Detroit and the company's efforts to find a merger partner. But the administration was not going to get off the hook that easily. Colbert turned Nance down again. Wilson returned and told the president that no automaker was interested in buying Packard's Detroit operations or guaranteeing a loan for the struggling company. Nance reported to his board on May 2 that Ford had said he was willing to help if GM would, but GM refused. Nance concluded sadly, "We are not going to get any help." Curtiss-Wright would not make a deal with S-P because Hurley could not get the Defense Department to tell him what contracts he could expect if he helped S-P out. Everything was in a snarl.[51]

To compound the gloom in S-P's offices, Heller reported to an informal board meeting on April 24 that S-P's immediate liquidation would produce a $7 million equity deficit, which meant that shareholders would get nothing. Heller therefore recommended an "orderly" staged liquidation that would close Detroit operations at once and postpone until June the decision whether to close South Bend auto operations as well. The philosophy behind these moves was to protect what Nance called "the shell of the company," its defense contracts and tax credits. The plan called for joining production more closely to sales to keep dealers in business and for face-lifting the 1957 Studebaker in case the firm decided to keep South Bend open. In the meantime, the company had to win some large defense contracts to buoy public opinion. The best part, Nance thought, was that the plan forced the banks and the insurance companies to go along—otherwise, S-P could never repay them. The directors agreed that Heller's liquidation plan was S-P's "only acceptable alternative" and left the meeting determined to pursue it.[52]

When Heller presented his plan to the rest of the board in New York the following day, however, the members were not so pessimistic. They deferred action on such a drastic course "because of new activity in negotiations with Curtiss-Wright and the Federal Government." And they directed Moore to approach Textron to see if Little was still interested in a deal.[53]

Two days later, Forgan and Nance met in Washington with Humphrey, Hurley, "and others," where they heard that Wilson's weekend trip to Detroit had come to naught. For the remainder of the meeting Humphrey "put heat on Hurley" to make a deal, but Hurley wanted the administration to give him "extensive defense business commitments," which it was not prepared to do. On April 30, Forgan met with George Hill, Curtiss-Wright's vice president for finance, to review the financial situation, but in a company as highly centralized as Curtiss-Wright, Hill did not have authority to negotiate. By S-P's board meeting on May 2, Nance and his directors were almost certain that they would not get any deal "that makes sense" from Hurley. Moreover, Nance had checked into Hurley's personal wealth and found that he was "not worth much," maybe $3 million to $5 million. Nance was not impressed.[54]

With all other options seemingly closed, the directors returned to plans for "orderly" liquidation. Nance reminded them that according to Heller's estimates, S-P would take a $47.7 million loss when it liquidated its Detroit property, and "once you eliminate prod.—you are in liquidation—assets melt fast." Forgan argued for buying time. They should prepare a phase-out schedule and send Heller to the banks with it to argue for further borrowing. Forgan then took a phone call from Hurley. While he was out of the room, Hoffman proposed that the company start telescoping on Monday, five days away. When Forgan returned he reported that Hurley complained that folks in Washington talked a lot, "but didn't want to do anything." Hurley advised the board to "go ahead on [the] shrink back." Forgan phoned Hurley to tell him that Packard was going out of business on May 7. The disconsolate directors discussed the wisdom of declaring bankruptcy. Hurley waffled on what he thought S-P should do, finally advising, "Let your conscience be your guide." The directors had come to the end. No strategy aside from liquidation held much promise, and they were in tacit agreement to start dismantling Packard on Monday. The phone rang again; it was Hurley. The secretary abruptly stopped taking the minutes. There was still a faint hope.[55]

Chapter 14

Clipper, 1946

"Love Without Marriage"

The man on the phone talking to Forgan was a prototypical American success story. Roy T. Hurley was a man who, without much formal education, used his native talents to claw his way to the top of the business world. While he mingled with the nation's elite in half a dozen private clubs, he loved to proclaim himself a "jack knife" engineer whose standard refrain was "I took all the correspondence courses and read all the textbooks."[1]

Hurley's break came in 1935 when he became vice president of Bendix Aviation Corporation and was "discovered" there by Ernest Breech. Hurley gained valuable political experience during the war. He served as deputy chief of ordnance and as civilian adviser to the army ordnance chief. In 1948, when Breech left to help put Ford back on its feet, he took Hurley with him as director of manufacturing engineering. Hurley stayed less than two years before he was named president of venerable but moribund Curtiss-Wright.[2]

Curtiss-Wright was selling about $100 million worth of aircraft engines, propellers, and other items annually, and it drew its infrequent dividends from past earnings. Hurley changed all that. Like Nance, he was a stickler for planning and quickly gained a reputation as a man with a sharp eye for reducing expenses. He took a hands-on approach to management, hustled new contracts, slashed costs, and in 1953 paid out $6 million in dividends from current earnings. After six years at Curtiss-Wright's helm, he had increased its gross sales 500 percent.[3]

A big man, six feet tall, Hurley had a roundish face with closely set eyes and a small mouth, which lent him something of a devious air. That may have put Nance off from the start. But Hurley's commanding personality expressed itself in terse explosions of saying just what he thought. And he could be brutal. When an *Automotive News* reporter asked him why he took over the ailing automaker, Hurley answered, "When you find two drunks leaning together to hold each other up, separate them. If they find their way home, fine. If they fall down leave them lying in the gutter." He had a reputation as a workaholic. In 1953, he divorced his first wife, with whom he had had two daughters, and married his executive assistant, with whom he had two more children. He was right in the old Packard mold, however, for he also was an outdoorsman and loved to spend time "by the banks of quiet streams" catching his dinner.[4]

Hurley's personal proclivities did not lead him to S-P. A *New York Times* reporter explained his motivations perfectly when he suggested that Hurley was an executive "who can smell and capture a dollar, no matter how remote it may seem." Although he said publicly that he thought the automobile industry had a "damn good" future, he knew that there were not many dollars at S-P. He was drawn into the merger fray because S-P had defense contracts he could use to elicit further government work for Curtiss-Wright, unused facilities he needed, and tax advantages that could accrue to his company. Hurley had been negotiating with Daimler-Benz for rights to build its diesel engines and distribute its cars in the United States. S-P had established a dealers' service and parts organization that could put the German luxury cars on showroom floors quickly.[5]

To his credit, Hurley told Nance and Forgan from the first that he was interested in their "tax carry forward." But he wanted to see S-P's plans for survival. If he thought they were feasible, he promised that he would "help" S-P "get more defense work." In the meantime, Hurley visited Donald Quarles, air force secretary, seven times in the six weeks before April 20 to talk about F-103 and B-52 bomber contracts. He touched base with Humphrey on April 4, and all evidence indicates that Humphrey was the first to pressure Hurley to take over S-P in return for more defense work. It was not coincidental that in the midst of all the administration's meetings about S-P's troubles on April 20, Hurley came to talk to Quarles. Four days earlier, Nance had reported that Humphrey was in favor of a Curtiss-Wright "deal" and "was going to put heat on Hurley." He was also putting heat on S-P, telling Nance he had to exhaust the Curtiss-Wright possibility before the government would be willing to help.[6]

The gravest threat to the three-way negotiations was that S-P's working capital by the end of April was down to $41 million, just $1 million shy of default. So Humphrey pushed Hurley harder, but Nance proposed moving all his automobile production to South Bend and asked the government for $200 million in defense orders in 1957, a less than politic plea that must have irritated Hurley no end. Hurley wanted the government contracts. Moreover, Nance needed someone to make S-P a $20 million long-term loan to carry the company through its difficulties.

After GM turned down Wilson's request for a loan, Nance had scant hope of borrowing money anywhere else. Hurley told Nance and Forgan that he did not see how S-P could stay in the auto business. He wanted to use S-P's difficulties to leverage defense contracts for Curtiss-Wright, but he remained "unsold" on any merger plan, Nance reported, "because he can't get [the] deal he wants from G[overnment]." Hurley stepped up the pressure on the government by advising S-P's directors at their May 2 meeting to begin telescoping S-P's operations. He had talked to Wilson the day before, and he was certain that Wilson and Humphrey "had something in mind." Hurley was determined to find out what that "something" was worth, and he called Forgan again at that board meeting to ask for more time to work on a deal.[7]

A preliminary meeting took place on May 5, when Hurley presented a "firm proposal that stopped short of a formal merger." He did not want S-P; he wanted to use it as a front to pry defense orders from the Pentagon. To that end, he recommended that the banks loan S-P the last $15.3 million of its revolving credit, extend the maturity date of the whole $45 million debt by ten years, and waive the requirement of $40 million in working capital. The government would then give S-P, really Curtiss-Wright, a "substantial amount of additional defense business."[8]

S-P needed money immediately, but the $15.3 million drawdown was not enough. Hurley, however, did not want to invest any of his company's cash in S-P. Instead, he suggested that Daimler-Benz buy $5 million worth of unissued S-P stock at $5 per share and that the automaker issue three-year warrants to Curtiss-Wright for another 6.5 million shares at $5 per share. S-P stockholders would have to agree to reduce their stock's par value and to allow Daimler-Benz to sell its cars at the company's dealerships.[9]

It was not much of a deal. But Hurley promised S-P's board that if it acceded to the transaction, he would see Wilson the next day to ensure the government's contribution. If Wilson proved intractable, Hurley warned, the whole deal was off. S-P's directors balked, even after Forgan, its principal architect, announced that Metropolitan and Chase had agreed to the deal and Hurley had assured him that he had "another deal" with the government. Forgan admitted that the arrangement did not tie Hurley down and that it was risky to turn management over to someone who had nothing invested. But the option, he pointed out, was "to go down [the] drain." Irving S. Olds, a lawyer who had been U.S. Steel's chairman of the board until 1952 and the S-P board's special counsel in the negotiations, agreed. He also warned that stockholders might well sue the board for scheming to attract Curtiss-Wright by lowering the value of their stock. Forgan later admitted that Hurley asked him to release S-P's first-quarter statement immediately, to further depress the company's stock.[10]

The board recessed for lunch, during which Hurley said that he would consider a merger with S-P in six or seven months, but that he thought Curtiss-Wright should in the meantime take over S-P through some kind of management contract. By afternoon, S-P's other bankers were willing to go along, but by then Forgan was the one having second thoughts. He asked how the company could announce that Curtiss-Wright had taken over if no one from that firm came into S-P as president or director. Hurley merely said that he would give the issue consideration. At the end of the all-day session, the weary directors unanimously accepted the agreement. That left the problem of Nance, who would have to resign if Hurley took over. He was asked to leave the room while the board reviewed his employment agreement, which he had signed with Packard in 1952. The directors voted to allow him $75,000 in immediate severance pay and $77,000 in deferred compensation, and to transfer to him the cash value of a company-owned $600,000 life insurance policy. Always generous with their own, the directors also discussed Forgan's fee for negotiating the Curtiss-Wright agreement and decided that he would be compensated only if it went through. Nobody mentioned for the record whether the arrangement created a conflict of interest for Forgan.[11]

Forgan was going to have to wait for his money, however. Hurley was using him to pressure Wilson and had absolutely no intention of consummating the deal before he had gotten what he wanted from the Pentagon. Somebody, probably in Curtiss-Wright, tipped off the press that the S-P board members were meeting on May 8 to consider a merger. Hurley used the intentional leak to ratchet up the pressure on Wilson. He wrote the secretary of defense a long, presumptuous letter, explaining why he was calling the whole thing off. He cited a Michigan law that forbade the company to sell its stock for less than par value–in S-P's case, $10 a share. The rumors had dropped its value to $9, Hurley said, and when S-P published its quarterly loss of more than $14 million on

May 10, the stock fell even lower, just as Hurley had hoped. If the banks would advance the last $15.3 million in the revolving credit agreement, however, he promised that that money, with Daimler-Benz's infusion, would keep the company alive until the end of the year, long enough for Hurley and Wilson to work a deal.[12]

The only way out of the impasse, he said to Wilson, was a definite "schedule of production for defense products," which included more military trucks, the J-57 "engine parts contracts referred to in our past talks," and "substantial engine and facilities contracts" that would enable S-P to retain its "production capacity," thus ensuring "maintenance of the mobilization production base." Hurley hit the last theme hard, arguing that the company was essential to the national defense effort. He concluded with the bold statement that "we will be very happy to receive such a schedule," which he would "expect . . . to be in the form of a letter of intent which, if accepted by Curtiss-Wright, would be converted into firm contracts."[13]

To prod Wilson, Hurley released a blanket denial of merger to the press on May 11, stating that "there is no way we can see at this time that we can help them." The scribes were not distracted, however, and they continued to hammer at the S-P story. The *Times* reported that the deal would be consummated when Hurley won $400 million in defense contracts. Both companies told reporters that the deal was still on and that Curtiss-Wright was going to buy S-P's convertible debentures to tide the automaker over "while permitting a slow marriage of the two companies." Senator Capehart of Indiana waded into the fray with the premature announcement that he was working on a $20 million to $25 million contract for S-P to build military trucks. *Business Week* picked up the information that Nance and Hurley had met with Humphrey on May 4 to iron out the merger details. The magazine predicted that Curtiss-Wright would pump $6.5 million into S-P through the debenture scheme. That was the farthest thing from Hurley's mind. Until he had the defense contracts in hand, it was going to be the slowest marriage on record.[14]

After S-P's board agreed to the deal on May 8, its finance committee and Olds stayed in New York for another week, trailed by reporters who monitored their every movement. Rumors flew but nothing happened. On May 14, *Automotive News* reported that Wilson was making a "strenuous personal effort" to find a solution to S-P's problems. Capehart and Senator Charles Potter of Michigan announced that the Justice Department had no objections to the proposed merger. Nance put Shine to work to find out what kind of man Hurley was and who sat on his board, an indication of how little the desperate S-P managers knew about the prospective groom.[15]

Hurley had Wilson's attention. At a press conference on May 15, the defense secretary revealed that he was "taking a special look to see if defense contracts can be channeled to the financially pressed Studebaker-Packard Corporation." He even declared that "there are some things naturally headed that way" and covered himself with the observation that "defense contracts are awarded all the time." He bought Hurley's argument when he explained that "the defense department did not want to lose a good source of military supplies." He was careful, however, to assure other companies that he was not going to take any business from them, and he did "not want to waste money just to keep a company going." [16]

Hurley replied through the newspapers, acknowledging that Curtiss-Wright was "continuing to explore the possibilities of cooperating in extricating" S-P from its troubles. To succeed, Hurley said, S-P was going to have to win primary contracts for "products which would continue to be sold to the government for a long period." He was not going to be bought off with a paltry $100 million or so in defense orders. S-P was going to have to become a major player in defense production, or he was not going to touch the company. His disdain for S-P's tax write-offs made this clear. *Time*, in a May 21 article, supposed that Hurley wanted badly to acquire the automaker's tax breaks, which would net Curtiss-Wright $35 million. Hurley had set his sights much higher. He knew when he refused to merge that he was throwing away the tax benefits, but he also understood how quickly they would be dissipated to keep the auto company afloat. He promised Wilson on May 22 that if such a tax "advantage" ever did accrue to Curtiss-Wright "following a merger," he would "earmark" it for "the rehabilitation of Studebaker-Packard." [17]

The longer Hurley delayed, the weaker S-P became and the more the political season heated up. Two and one-half weeks after S-P's board approved his proposal, Hurley presented Wilson with his bill, "the minimum necessary for the successful rehabilitation" of S-P. His laundry list must have stunned the secretary. Hurley demanded $1,373,800,000 in government contracts over three years to rescue S-P and save 22,000 jobs. The defense contractor cautioned that there was not time to await "successive approvals" by the various military departments. His seventeen-page list, he said, constituted a "letter contract" and "should be signed" by Wilson and by the three secretaries of the military branches. Daimler-Benz, S-P, banks, and insurance companies, he promised, had already agreed. Hurley, however, had not met with S-P directors since May 8, and its board had not endorsed any of Hurley's specific proposals. [18]

The demands on Wilson were classic Hurley. The banks would have to waive their default clauses and loan the ailing automaker the last

$15.3 million of its revolving credit. Moreover, Humphrey and Wilson had cleared a $15 million loan from the Federal Reserve Board–Hurley had made that an integral part of his proposal. Curtiss-Wright promised to add $15 million to S-P's coffers, but Hurley made sure that none of it would come from his company's treasury. He planned to "advance" S-P the money "by way of progress payment against Curtiss-Wright subcontracts." In other words, it was government money. When all funds had been "advanced," Hurley would move his management experts into S-P "within twenty-four hours" to proceed "with the necessary changes in the organization, its operation, etc." [19]

Hurley's demands set off a flurry of meetings in Washington. Subsequent events revealed that he had overplayed his hand. He had misjudged how much the administration was willing to pay to contain the economic and political damage that might result from S-P's default. The government could purchase S-P outright for its book value of $250 million, less than 20 percent of what Hurley was asking. Moreover, the company's assets had steadily drained away and its actual value was closer to $100 million by mid-1956.

While the politicians were sorting his demands out, Hurley presented what he called his "joint program" to S-P's board for approval. The company's directors clearly thought that this was the final arrangement. That very morning, May 29, the banks and the insurance companies agreed to abide by their parts of the plan, and the directors applauded the additional $15 million that Curtiss-Wright offered. Forgan predicted that the "deal will be made in Washington," explaining that "CW has got so much business now–they will be embarrassed to back out. They are trying to get more." He assured them that "CW gets primary K [contract]–sub Ks." The only hitch was that the Germans, as the board always called Daimler-Benz, refused to buy into S-P for $5 million. They instead promised to finance their cars on the showroom floors for 30 days–a better bargain, the directors thought. The directors were bothered because they had nothing in writing from the Germans or from the Defense Department, and yet they were being asked to take a formal vote on the deal. They did not even know about their own futures. Royall Victor asked if the company would retain its directors, and the board's counsel admitted that he did not "know too much about this–present thinking [is] we ought to name some directors–but not a maj." Forgan had told the banks that Curtiss-Wright was going to run the company. The board then ratified the "principle" of the Curtiss-Wright proposal.[20]

Two days later, as S-P's directors were basking in their success, Hurley called a meeting to tell them that the deal was off. Washington had not come through. Wilson would promise only a $30 million contract on the

DART missile. Nance complained to Humphrey, and the treasury secretary suggested that he talk to Quarles. The morning of the June 2 board meeting, Nance and Forgan talked to the air force secretary about what contracts S-P could expect without Curtiss-Wright, but Quarles was not hopeful. He did tell them that Wilson could not give Hurley a production contract for the new J-65 when the engine had not even been tested. As an alternative, Wilson suggested that Hurley have S-P spin off its defense business into a subsidiary company that would draw up a management contract with Curtiss-Wright. Wilson promised that the subsidiary would get more defense business than he could give S-P because of the automaker's financial straits.[21]

The board was thrown into confusion. S-P's Federal Reserve Board loan was in doubt unless Curtiss-Wright took over S-P, but Olds recommended that they pursue the loan, request the remainder of their money from the banks, and investigate every option to avoid Chapter 10 bankruptcy. The directors' real fear was that Hurley would do what he threatened: issue his press release announcing that the deal was dead. They finally decided to invite Hurley to discuss Wilson's proposal, postpone any public announcement, and ask the banks to extend their loan deadlines.[22]

That very evening, the finance committee met with Curtiss-Wright officials and created a wholly S-P-owned subsidiary corporation composed of Packard's Utica and Studebaker's Chippewa plants. Victor noted that Hurley was enthusiastic about the new company "because it afforded the definite possibility of permitting them to participate . . . in an increased jet engine program." The board wrestled with how to finance its new creature, deciding first that it would take $5 million from its revolving credit and later that it would need $15 million, one-half of its available credit, including the Federal Reserve loan. Finally the board decided not to even mention the problem in its minutes.[23]

The new firm further confused Hurley's relationship with S-P. He would have a "management K" with the subsidiary, not its parent. The banks would scream, the board said, if they knew that Hurley was not at S-P's helm. Hurley admitted that he could not allow the parent to die if he had a contract with its subsidiary. He finally said that he would run S-P, but told the directors not to put that on paper. Forgan asked him to name three or four directors, but Hurley dissembled, promising more details within three days. McMillan reminded him that he had better hurry. The banks' extended deadlines expired on June 18.[24]

Meanwhile, the administration was working furiously to put together a defense package just big enough to tempt Hurley. Quarles, who handled the air force's contracts, met with Humphrey, Wilfred J. McNeil, the assistant secretary of defense and the department's comptroller, and Mansfield Sprague about specific S-P contracts. On June 6 the assistant secretary of the air force informed Humphrey about what the services were willing to do. S-P officials had not been informed, however. A *New York Times* reporter interviewed an unnamed S-P director, "leaving for a California vacation," that could only have been Hoffman, who said that everything is "up to Washington and it will probably take some time until everything jells." Little did he know just how much time.[25]

Officials on all three sides hoped that by Thursday, June 7, the whole deal could be wrapped up. When Hurley, Olds, and Forgan met at two o'clock, it was clear that even though no defense contracts had been put in writing, Hurley was ready to go. Hurley thought that everything would be in order within a week and told Forgan that "defense Ks are being prepared." Wilson and Quarles had severely trimmed Hurley's original demands to between $200 million and $250 million in new defense contracts. Apparently that was enough for Hurley. He asked the board to allow Curtiss-Wright's managers to come into S-P's departments before formal arrangements were signed. Forgan was in favor of it, telling his fellow directors that "this would indicate that he intends to go thru with [the] deal." It also meant, as Forgan was blunt enough to add, that "JJN would go."[26]

Forgan then asked Nance for his comments. Nance, whose job since January had been all but impossible, started amiably enough, observing that he had attempted "to be helpful in getting this into a parking place," but his manner quickly turned mean. He admitted that his relations with Hurley "have not been pleasant." Nance recalled that at the meeting with Hurley in Washington, he "took a terrific beating" but "turned the other cheek." Nance said that Hurley had told the bankers, in Nance's presence, that there was "nothing wrong with the auto business if you know how to run it." "Worse," Nance continued, Hurley "had ignored me. Gone around [the] end with people in [the] organization–been out there [in Detroit] without calling me." "I am not going to be humiliated in this manner," Nance said. "I have my own position to think of from [the] public relations standpoint." Wanting to leave S-P with some grace and dignity, he argued that a "meeting should be called" with Hurley and that "I should be there to make a statement." Therefore, he concluded, "I am not going to resign at this time."[27]

Hurley had no doubt pressured Forgan to move Nance out of the way quickly. To work through Nance would compromise Curtiss-Wright's assumed authority. Manheim plumbed the depths of the accountability problem when he asked Forgan, "Are we going to be directors of a Co. which H is running?" Forgan answered, "Yes." After a rather aimless

discussion, ZurSchmiede finally admitted that "we have no alternative—
we are in bankruptcy. . . . It gets us into defense business which might be
our savior." With no other options, the board agreed to allow Hurley's
executives into the company but passed a face-saving motion for Nance,
giving him the authority to designate S-P officials who would work with
Curtiss-Wright and who would "make recommendations to and function through the president." By June 7, Hurley and Nance were running S-P.[28]

With everything set to go, but no papers signed, a curious calm settled over negotiations for three weeks. On June 11, a *Newsweek* article
called "Report on a Romance" predicted that "a June wedding" looked
more and more remote. A Curtiss-Wright executive was reported to have
"sighed" and told the magazine that "when this is over, I'm going to
write a book on how to say 'no comment' one thousand different ways."
The *Wall Street Journal* reported a "lag" in the negotiations. The *Times*
was more hopeful, predicting that Curtiss-Wright would make a firm offer during the week of June 17. Behind the scenes, however, work continued apace to combine the two firms. Brodie met with Hurley and his men
on June 8 and 9. He later wrote Nance a long, gossipy memo, claiming
that Curtiss-Wright wanted to take over S-P's defense work to "put them
in a better position to present it as a combined program." In effect,
Brodie was on his way out, and Hurley did not have many firm commitments from the Defense Department.[29]

Curtiss-Wright's boss had also given some thought to Packard's fate.
Brodie told Nance that the "Packard group" spent the evening of June 8
"resolving a proposed program" for 1957 that recommended dropping
the Clipper entirely and moving production of the Executive and Packard to South Bend. The cars, Brodie heard, would use the Studebaker
289-cubic-inch V-8 with a supercharger. Everyone understood that the
Packard-Clipper division's days in Detroit were numbered. Its sales
tumbled in the first two weeks of May, and Heller, at Nance's request,
drew up a program "for immediate termination" of production on May
22. Because of the shortage of time and the pending agreement with
Curtiss-Wright, however, the actual closing was postponed. Instead,
production was "stretched out," to await Hurley's decision after he took
over. Nance also understood that if he precipitously closed Packard,
public reaction would immediately hurt Studebaker's sales, which were
holding up much better.[30]

Local no. 190 at East Grand organized a write-in to President Eisenhower pleading for defense contracts so they could keep their jobs.
The White House was flooded with letters in mid-May from frightened

Packard workers, many of whom had spent their lives with the company and were apprehensive about being thrown into the street at the end of their careers. The letters also showed how much the company's work force had changed. One of the oldest employees, Harold Hannan, who had invested 49 years at Packard, represented the days when most of the workers were Irish, men from Ferry's generation. In the 1920's the work force contained many Central Europeans, reflecting the ethnic makeup of the city, and most of the workers who pleaded with Ike bore names such as Skierkowski, Markoirch, Hojnacki, Panepucci, Podzorski, and Waseil.[31]

The decision to save Packard was not in Ike's hands, however. His goal was to prevent S-P's corporate collapse with or without Packard. Every Curtiss-Wright proposal left for future resolution the question of a separate Packard division. As Packard's sales performance worsened, however, the old carmaker became expendable. And when S-P chartered its subsidiary defense corporation on June 4, Packard no longer had an engine and transmission plant. That finally sealed the fate of Conner and East Grand. S-P's board members knew they had killed Packard, but nobody mentioned it, at least not for the record. In all of May, the Packard division sold only 2,500 cars retail and 1,700 to its dealers. At those rates, East Grand was selling about 60,000 cars less than it needed to break even.[32]

The stage was set by the end of the first week in June to shut Packard down. Nance and his directors awaited only the final agreement with Hurley to make the fatal move. Nance considered taking the step himself, but he and his board talked to Hurley first. He assented but asked the company to keep its Packard engineering force and styling section intact in case S-P later decided to build Packards in South Bend. If the company instead decided to manufacture just Studebakers, which were losing only $2 million a month, Nance could fire 406 Packard and Studebaker engineers and stylists and save $2.5 million a year.[33]

Nance wanted to close Packard without executing S-P. His original plan was to order manufacturing suspended on June 15, citing high inventories, and promise that production would resume as soon as possible. But the Curtiss-Wright deal was hanging fire, and his next ploy was to announce a five-day shutdown for the week of June 18 to take inventory. That date, too, passed without action. Finally, on the verge of running out of money, Nance ordered the production of 1956 Packards halted on June 25, leaving open the question of when the new models would appear. At the start of 1956, Packard had 9,200 employees in Detroit; at the plant's closing, there were only 5,000 left. The abrupt shutdown put 2,700 of them immediately out on the street. Another 1,800 engaged in defense work kept their jobs, and 500 stayed on temporarily for maintenance and janitorial duties.[34]

The closure came with so little warning that few preparations had been made. Weeks later, a Studebaker engineer was sent to Detroit to help with the clean-up. This veteran of the bloody fighting in the Pacific opened up a floor-to-ceiling freezer in the employees' dining room kitchen and instantly vomited. It had been full of frozen turkeys and had been unplugged, the birds left to rot. Dick Teague, still working at empty East Grand, called it "the last days in the bunker." They worked on the marque's 1957 offerings and had built a full-sized prototype of the new car they hoped to show Curtiss-Wright to get tooling permission. The car, Black Bess, looked like a "mule," according to Teague. It boasted a new torsion-bar suspension design, an improved Ultramatic, and a 400-cubic-inch V-8, but it was so crudely assembled that Teague claimed, "If we had shown it to Curtiss-Wright we'd have had to show it to them blind-folded because . . . they wouldn't have loaned us a dime." "You knew goddam well the end was close," Teague wistfully remembered, "but you kept hoping for a life raft." Misch finally ordered Teague to cut Bess up. He called in Red Lux, a welder who had been with Packard since Macauley's early days, and gave him the job. The humor around the deserted plant was as black as Bess. Teague recounted that there were two black cars in the studio when he told Lux to cut up "the black one." Lux dismantled the right car, but Teague came back and said, "My God, Red, what have you done? Not this one, man, the one over in the corner!" The old welder was horrified until Teague laughed and let him in on the joke.[35]

While the engineers and the stylists awaited word of their fate, maintenance workers systematically went through the plant and removed filing cabinets from offices, emptied them and saved them to be auctioned. The company's history was taken across the boulevard and burned in the powerhouse. Some employees sneaked in each night and stole papers that were to be burned. Teague even smuggled documents out of the plant under the hood of his car. All told, some 70 tons of Packard's history were saved. Eventually they ended up at the Studebaker National Museum in South Bend.[36]

Nance knew nothing about the document burning. He had enough problems, trying to bring what was left of S-P into a "parking space." With little prospect of getting better terms from Wilson, Hurley concluded that he would minimize his connection with S-P. He even began to dislike the idea of a defense subsidiary because it had already involved him in S-P's management and pulled him closer to a merger he did not want. At the end of June, Hurley decided to reject the subsidiary, especially since it carried with it no lucrative contracts. He would make a straight deal with S-P for some badly needed factory space and for Aerophysics, which was definitely going to receive the DART missile contract.[37]

Hurley concocted a "new joint program" the day before S-P's scheduled June 27 board meeting. He did not like the Federal Reserve Board's terms for its $15 million loan, according to which the money would go to the subsidiary, not S-P, but the automaker would have to pledge its "real" assets as security. Moreover, Hurley had not received permission from the IRS to assume S-P's tax write-offs, nor had he won any firm contracts from Wilson. Therefore, he proposed that Curtiss-Wright lease the company's Utica and Chippewa plants for $25 million in advance, assume S-P's military contracts, pay $2 million for Aerophysics, continue the management contract (the one nobody understood), and try to bring Daimler-Benz into the deal. The Germans had become problematical because one Max Hoffman already had a contract to distribute Daimler-Benz products in Los Angeles and New York City. It was unclear whether that gave him the right to sell the cars nationwide.[38]

For once, S-P's directors refused to toady to Hurley. Throughout the negotiations, they had grasped at every option he tossed them, but this time he offered too little. Chief among the directors' objections was that Hurley was going to buy the only part of their business that offered any hope. In return, as Hoffman cryptically noted, this "leaves us with 27 mil for auto bus.," not enough to survive. Manheim warned that Hurley had not cleared this plan with Wilson, nor did he have any new defense contracts. Further, the proposal made S-P's deal with its own banks iffy.[39]

Only Forgan, who pushed hard for every Hurley deal, liked this one. Hoffman, who was in business with his son, Lathrop, in a large but financially troubled Studebaker dealership in Los Angeles, spoke to the preservation of Studebaker's dealer force as he always did. After hours of discussion, board members returned to the possibility of S-P staying independent. Manheim, Hoffman, ZurSchmiede, Blair, Victor, and perhaps Nance appeared willing to gamble on liquidating S-P and hope something would be left over for stockholders. Forgan suggested that they explore the possibility of going it alone, look into the legal requirements for stockholder approval, and continue talking to Hurley. Nance ended the meeting on a petulant note–he agreed with Manheim's earlier suggestion to sell off the auto business and use the funds to buy new companies.[40]

Hurley was shocked that S-P's directors had pulled back from his offer. The following morning, he rushed back to New York City from Washington, D.C., to exert his powers of persuasion on S-P's directors. He,

William Hanaway, and Lloyd V. Almirall, of Abbott & Morgan, counsel for Curtiss-Wright, met Victor and Olds for lunch on June 28. They worked overtime to convince the two men that Hurley's "new" deal was of great benefit to S-P. But Olds was not convinced. He later told his fellow directors that S-P's defense "business [was] substantial and you made money." He warned them, "If we lease plant to CW for 12 years and turn over def K—we cannot carry on the type of defense we have carried on before." Forgan, who still liked the deal, rejoined, "You haven't got defense Ks. Also this does not mean you are out of defense business if you have cash you can buy defense facilities and maybe Ks." Victor, who was willing to compromise with Hurley if he would sweeten his proposal, offered to sell only part of S-P's defense business to Curtiss-Wright. Both ideas died a quick death because everyone understood that Hurley would never agree.[41]

Olds then put the board's dilemma succinctly: "I think you have a real problem. . . . If you want to make a deal because it is better than Ch. X [Chapter 10 bankruptcy], that is a business decision for you to make." But, he warned that "you must take whatever risk there is." The consultant then earned his fee, saying, "If you want a straight legal opinion you're going to get a negative answer, Co. can't last 2 weeks." He advised supporting Nance's earlier proposal, to "lease important part of business. Give us some cash—with which to liquidate business." The directors, as usual, remained undecided and finally authorized their finance committee to continue negotiating with Hurley, "having in mind views of members of Bd and opinion of counsel."[42]

With the negotiations stalled, S-P rapidly disintegrated. Its second-quarter loss was $21,154,283, bringing its half-year deficit to a crushing $35,465,456. Technically, under the provisions of its original contracts, the corporation was bankrupt. At the last June board meeting, Nance reported that S-P was down to $18 million in cash and $30 million in working capital, $10 million below the agreed-upon minimum. And the losses were growing—$270,000 of its working capital was melting away each day. The figures increased the pressure on S-P's directors to make a deal, any deal, to salvage whatever was left.[43]

In early July, the action shifted to Washington, where Eisenhower's men made yet another try to bring Hurley and S-P together. Humphrey and Quarles were the point men who embarked on a round of conferences with Defense Department people and corporate suppliers. Humphrey talked to Max Golden, deputy to the assistant secretary of the air force for material, and then met with Ernest Breech about enlarging his company's jet-engine contract and passing part of the additional business on to S-P. Quarles called in Ralph Cordiner, president of

General Electric, to discuss the "second CW proposal," which involved a repair contract for the J-47 turbojet engines. He also talked to Wilfred J. McNeil, Defense's comptroller and assistant secretary, about shunting some propeller work to Curtiss-Wright. By July 13, Quarles had lined up what he could promise Hurley and scheduled a conference with Sprague, Hurley, and Golden.[44]

It was clear that a final arrangement, agreeable to all sides, had been put together. On July 23, Nance sent Francis Elmendorf of Heller & Associates a cryptic telegram: "Wednesday now agreed upon by both parties." And when S-P's board convened in New York City on July 25, the very brevity and formality of its minutes signaled that everything was done. The only bump in the road was a truncated board meeting held July 10 in Detroit attended by only Ferry, McMillan, and ZurSchmiede, all old Packard hands. The three proposed "certain suggestions as to the Corporation's affairs," almost certainly a plan for S-P to go it alone, given the opinions they had voiced in the full board meetings. They later "believed these suggestions were unnecessary." The meeting was stricken from the formal board minutes but survived in their handwritten version.[45]

On July 25, the outline of the final pact was evident, even if many of its details were still vague. S-P's defense subsidiary became a wholly owned Curtiss-Wright corporation, Utica Bend, to which S-P leased its two defense plants and turned over its military contracts. And with the sale of Aerophysics to Curtiss-Wright, S-P took itself completely out of the defense business. In return, Curtiss-Wright paid $25 million in advance to lease the Utica and Chippewa plants, slightly under $2 million for Aerophysics, and $10 million for the S-P defense contracts. The question of Curtiss-Wright's relationship with S-P remained a sticky one. Under intense pressure from Wilson and Humphrey, Hurley finally agreed to a formal management contract, the terms of which carefully minimized Curtiss-Wright's liabilities. S-P's board did get a clause that committed Hurley, now S-P's real boss, to keep the company in the automobile business. The contract did not mention Packard, and Hurley still had no agreement with the Germans.[46]

Problems remained, however. The banks demanded that half of the money Curtiss-Wright paid to S-P be used to repay bank loans. Hurley refused. The insurance companies wanted to put new restrictions on S-P's working capital. Hurley again refused. The banks and insurance companies agreed to drop their demands. Informally, Hurley told S-P to concentrate its auto business in South Bend, which it had already done, but he left open the question of whether there would be a 1957 Packard. Hoffman made a last-ditch effort to bail out his son's Los Angeles distributorship, offering shares in it to the directors. They postponed discussion on it. Having expressed agreement with the general outline of the Curtiss-Wright plan, they adjourned until the next day.[47]

The July 26 meeting was a mere formality. The long, difficult negotiations were over, and S-P got much less than it had hoped. It desperately wanted a merger with Curtiss-Wright to gain some long-term financial stability. To the very end, Hurley refused, even bargaining away many of his desired defense contracts to retain his corporate independence. Forgan explained to the directors why it was impossible to merge. He said that although the agreement was unsatisfactory, it was the best S-P could hope for; the only other option was to declare bankruptcy. The directors unanimously voted "to go ahead with the Curtiss-Wright program."[48]

The only unfinished business was the replacement of redundant personnel. Albert Behnke was fired, and Brodie tendered his resignation. Nance was out of a job the moment the agreement was initialed. He had retained a law firm to negotiate his financial settlement. The board authorized paying him $286,000—five months' salary—and the cash value of his company insurance policy, but it was less than happy with the settlement and asked company counsel "to evaluate, *if possible*." Nance and Hoffman resigned; Churchill and Porta were elected to take their places. It was almost over.[49]

But not quite. The contracts were not signed at the meeting on July 27, as everyone present assumed. That very afternoon, Nance granted an extensive interview to William Harris of *Fortune* magazine to tell his side of the story. The article, which read as though Nance had written it, angered old Studebaker hands such as Hoffman and Porta and probably Curtiss-Wright people as well. On July 30, he received a telegram at his lonely East Grand office, telling him that the final signing had been postponed because "Curtiss-Wright has not as yet obtained certain commitments with respect to defense contracts which it requires to go ahead with the program." That same day, *Time* ran an article revealing that Hurley had received $500 million in defense orders for saving S-P.[50]

In truth, however, Hurley was still not sure what to expect. He complained to Wilson that the Pentagon was dragging its feet, and he refused to sign the joint program documents until Wilson handed him a list of military commitments. The snafu prompted another flurry of meetings inside the Pentagon among Quarles, Humphrey, Wilson, and Courtney Johnson. Finally, on August 4, Wilson announced, "That portion of the negotiation which concerned the Department of Defense has been finalized." S-P's board met the following Monday, August 6, signed the contract, and simultaneously stipulated that the board was still legally responsible for the company and that all corporate plans should come through its members.[51]

With the hard bargaining finally over, everyone involved in the negotiations fudged the truth, starting with Eisenhower. At his press conference briefing, it was decided that Ike would assert that "no contracts [were] taken away from anyone else." He was further instructed to say that his administration participated in the discussions because it did not want to see the loss of skilled technicians "that might be needed in [the] national interest." He could admit to ordering Wilson to "see what he could do to keep Studebaker-Packard alive," but was advised to emphasize that it "was done on the basis of national interest."[52]

Wilson was even less forthcoming. He told the *Wall Street Journal* that his department's role in the talks was "a little complicated." He admitted that "it amounted to letting Curtiss-Wright know what defense work could be expected," and he repeated that his department did not take work away from any other company. Hurley just plain lied, telling reporters, "The agreement was not contingent upon any promise by the Department of Defense of additional defense contracts." That very day, he wrote to Quarles, thanking him "for the vast amount of time and consideration" he had given S-P's "problems insofar as they affect the Department of Defense, the Air Force" and for the efforts of Wilson, Humphrey, and Manny Sprague.[53]

Never had so few vied for the plaudits for saving 10,000 jobs; everyone connected with the deal was wary in an election year. And it did not take long for the joint program to become a political issue. Democratic Senator Estes Kefauver, running for vice president, charged in October that Wilson had withheld defense contracts from S-P, forcing the company to merge with Curtiss-Wright. It remained a partisan issue even after the elections. In the summer of 1957, Congressman F. Edward Hébert, chairman of the Armed Services Subcommittee, charged that Wilson took away from GE a $3 million repair contract for the J-47 engine and gave it to Curtiss-Wright as part of the S-P bailout deal. Worse, Hébert said, the $3 million ballooned by $25 million because the government had to equip the Utica plant to do the work. He disclosed that the funds for the contract were personally handled by Manny Sprague, then the department's general counsel and later an assistant defense secretary. Hurley conceded in testimony that the contract was awarded after he had agreed to help S-P out, but he refused to comment on the dollar amounts. He did admit that he thought his deal with Wilson had "bailed out" the government politically.[54]

The government's cost of saving S-P was never disclosed. Public reports put the figure at $500 million. Hurley gave this number some credence when he announced that Curtiss-Wright would place $100 million in orders annually for three years at each of the two former S-P plants, for a total of $600 million. Confusing the issue, he then admitted that those sums included contracts S-P already had or was promised. Immediately after S-P's directors signed the papers, Wilson released $52 million in contracts to Curtiss-Wright, $36,077,000 for 2½-ton trucks and the expected $15,565,000 for the DART missile. In August 1957, Curtiss-Wright received another $25 million truck contract. Eight months later came the last of the deal, $40,807,226 for 5,000 more vehicles, bringing the total to $117,749,226. Curtiss-Wright also picked up navy contracts totaling $5,926,723. The Utica Bend Corporation won an additional $1 million for its J-57 production facilities and the disputed $3 million to repair the older J-47 jets. If Hébert was correct, Utica Bend also foisted off on the government the $25 million costs of readying the Utica plant for the work. Over the three years of the agreement, about $136,000,000 in defense contracts were publicly reported to have gone to Utica Bend. Other monies, funneled directly through Curtiss-Wright, were probably also part of the package to bail S-P out. Clearly, Hurley won far less than he originally expected, and at the end he agreed to the deal only halfheartedly.[55]

The last hurdle was a stockholders' meeting to approve the contract and vote to lower their stock's par value from $10 to $1 a share. A minority of shareholders rallied around a Detroit attorney, Sol Dann, who had vociferously opposed the Studebaker-Packard merger in the first place and who declared that Curtiss-Wright was trying to take S-P over at "bankrupt prices." He proposed selling S-P off and distributing $15 a share to the stockholders (S-P shares on that date sold for $6.87 each). The shareholders gathered in Detroit on October 31, brushed aside Dann's complaints, voted to ratify the agreement, lowered their par values, and allowed Curtiss-Wright its stock option.[56]

The gestation period for the Curtiss-Wright takeover was just over nine months, during which S-P's managers and directors focused their energies on salvaging something, anything, from the corporate wreck. The constant public attention on the carmaker's financial plight devastated its car sales, and throughout 1956, Nance watched his monthly deficits swell. What baffled him to the day he turned in his keys was why the bottom fell out of Packard's sales when the division offered a fairly competitive product. The old arch-salesman never appreciated how devastating were the quality control problems in 1955 and 1956, the steady barrage of bad financial news from S-P, and the "orphan" stigma. And Packards, even at the very end in Detroit, were expensive orphans. Whatever the reasons, however, its sales debacle made it expendable.

Even though former Packard men ran S-P, most of them were newcomers and did not have the corporate loyalty of those who had invested their careers in East Grand. Undoubtedly, that made it easier for Nance to close Packard. And Hurley's constant delays hurt any chance for a "real" merger that might have carried Packard through the year. Teague had an appealing design readied for 1957 that might have saved the marque for a few more years. But in all the hullabaloo that surrounded the efforts to resuscitate S-P, Packard slipped away, almost unnoticed except by those who labored in its factories. On August 6, as Hurley and S-P's directors signed the documents sealing the agreement, the unspoken question was whether there would ever be another Packard. Nobody knew the answer.

Chapter 15

Mayfair hardtop, 1952

"Ask the
Man Who
Owned One"

The odds appeared long that Packard would survive in the "new" Studebaker-Packard Corporation. Hurley evinced little interest in South Bend's automotive efforts, content to make his profits from the defense contracts he had gotten from the Pentagon. Churchill, the company's new president, was a technician in the mold of Christopher, rather than a showman in Nance's style, and from the first favored emulating AMC. He and Hurley agreed that S-P would have to seek profitable niches and exploit them. He believed there was a mass market for a cheap, stripped-down automobile that he could sell for less than the Big Three charged for their basic models.

Churchill first had to buy time to reposition S-P in the market. He had to hold his dealer organization together until he could give it an attractive, low-priced car. In August 1956, many of his dealers were still Packard outlets, and he needed a mid-priced auto to tide them over until he could, in Nance's favorite phrase, "turn the thing around." Churchill learned that he could build a new Packard at South Bend for only $1 million by using as many off-the-shelf Studebaker items as possible and hanging just enough Packard ornamentation on the cars to make them distinctive. The decision to bring out the 1957 models was an expedient. Packard was not vital to the firm's future.

The decision to produce a 1957 Packard was made piecemeal and without much soul-searching. The car was of necessity a flawed product, introduced without enthusiasm, and peripheral to the company's main business. Moreover, its future depended upon factors totally extraneous to its qualities. If Churchill brought the 1957 Packard out close to new-car introduction time, late fall or early winter, it would have a fighting chance to sell enough copies to become a corporate asset.

That "if" became problematical after most of the old Packard hands bailed out of the company. Their hasty exits had left Nance with a shrinking executive corps throughout early 1956, when he could not afford new hires. Graves and Powers resigned at the end of April, and Bremer and Mendler left in May. Most stayed until the end, but with the signing of the documents in August, the old "key men" fled in droves. Monaghan, Brodie, Behnke, Scribner, Laughna, Frederick Raeder, and Nance decamped. Even some former Packard board members left. Blair and ZurSchmiede, who had been so active, resigned at the end of the year. Earle Anthony, long a fixture *in absentia* and a power behind the throne, gave up his seat in February 1957.[1]

At the end of August, Nance was reported to be "resting" at his Michigan farm, where he was quoted as saying, "For the first time since I left college, I'm unemployed." He did not stay that way long. In October, Ford's board of directors elected him vice president of marketing. At 55 years of age, Nance filled a gap at Ford. Its highest executives were thinking of retirement while the oldest of its division chiefs was only 48. For the first time in his career, Nance was in a staff position, but *Business Week* predicted that he would work in close conjunction with Henry Ford II and his friend, chairman Ernest Breech.[2]

Ford was on the verge of bringing out the Edsel, and on January 15, 1958, Nance was appointed vice president of the Mercury, Edsel, Lincoln Division. Rumors were that Robert McNamara feared Nance as a rival for the company's top spot and schemed with his network of "whiz kids" to undermine Nance's standing with the autocratic Henry Ford II. Nance had vaulted over two of the "kids" to take divisional control, and there were bitter feelings from the first. When the Edsel flopped in the 1958 recession, Henry made Nance the scapegoat for the debacle. Nance resigned on September 4, 1958, with yet another auto failure added to his legend. He accepted the presidency of the Central National Bank in Cleveland, Ohio, on April 18, 1960, rising to become its chairman and chief executive officer. Later he explained that he was attracted to banking because he had learned at Packard and S-P that those who had the money had the power. Nance remained active until the very end—at age

83, he still went to work every day. On Sunday, July 22, 1984, he drove up to his camp at Bellaire, Michigan, on Torch Lake, for some relaxation. He was found dead there several days later.[3]

According to many observers back in August 1956, Hurley's takeover announcement gave scant hope to Packard supporters. He proclaimed the abandonment of the "fourth full-line auto builder" philosophy and promised that S-P would "operate in selected, diversified areas of the automotive field." A "Packard division official," however, told the *Wall Street Journal* that Packard had a "semi-face" lifted car ready to go for 1957 and had an all-new 1957 automobile based on the Predictor on "the shelf."[4]

Three days later, the *New York Times* profiled S-P's new president. Churchill hewed to the Curtiss-Wright line, saying no decision had been made on Packard. On August 11, *Business Week* opined that Hurley "seemed to be thinking" that he ought to "dump the Packard," give his dealers Mercedes to sell instead, and then "perhaps" bring back a restyled big Packard for the 1958 season. The *Detroit Times* did not think there was time to rejuvenate the grand old name at South Bend and editorialized that Packard's famous slogan would have to be altered to read "Ask the Man Who Owned One."[5]

The speculation was fueled by the fact that nobody inside S-P knew whether the company was going to produce Packards either. At the August 6 board meeting, Churchill warned that Packard was one of the most "serious problems" facing the company and that the decision had to be made within the month. In other words, Hurley had not made up his mind. On August 20, when the directors sat again, the factory reported 1,409 Packards still in stock; dealers and distributors had another 5,008, enough to keep them in business until the new cars appeared. The board approved Packard's continuance as "an interim model through 1957" and elected to build the car on a Studebaker Classic chassis and put in a Golden Hawk engine. The body would be standard Studebaker issue adorned with "features of Packard and Clipper styling" on the front and rear. The new Packard Executive would sell for $150 less than its bigger 1956 cousin, and for $450 more than the Studebaker Classic. Accountants projected that the new Packards could be brought into production for only $1.1 million, which would be amortized over expected sales of 4,000 to 6,900. Hurley concluded the discussion with the observation, "This looks good."[6]

It took some time for S-P to make the news public. In fact, it took some time for the company to make anything public, because its South Bend offices were in complete chaos. When an *Automotive News* reporter called South Bend to hear what the board had decided about Packard, the operator told him that Nance was "on vacation" and connected him with someone named Dykstra, at Curtiss-Wright's headquarters, whose first name she did not know. Dykstra transferred the reporter to a lawyer named Mullin, "who just flew in" and who did not know what was going on either. The reporter gave up. Stockholders were told of the Packard decision in an August 27 letter in which Churchill announced that their company had lost more than $35 million in six months and had taken a $28 million write-down on closing out its Detroit facilities. The total deficit was $63,465,456, more than one-third of S-P's gross sales for the period.[7]

The shutdown and sale of Packard's Detroit assets proved an ongoing headache. Chrysler refused to accept the Conner plant, and S-P could not find another company willing to sublet it, so the automaker was stuck making quarterly lease payments. After much haggling, S-P's directors struck a deal with Chrysler in April to buy their way out of the lease for $935,968 and save $1,340,871 over the remaining contractual period. They had much less luck divesting themselves of Packard's other assets. Nance's spanking-new, all-automated engine line, on which he had spent $27 million, proved unsalable. S-P brought the head-manufacturing machinery to South Bend, where it was stored. Utica Bend had to have the Utica plant empty by November 1, 1957, so the board authorized $200,000 to move all the rest of the equipment into East Grand. Nobody wanted that facility either, and S-P turned it over to a commercial real estate company to unload. Hurley, a man without much sentiment, expressed the view that the whole Packard complex on the Boulevard was a slum. He tried to have the city tear it down to save the estimated $5 million it would cost to raze a property valued at only $1 million. By autumn, the directors became more anxious to dispose of all Packard's properties because S-P stood to gain tax benefits if they were sold in calendar 1957. Finally, in a fire sale at the end of the year, S-P practically gave its assets away at auction: the engine machinery for a paltry $200,000, property on Woodward Avenue for $100,000, and the whole East Grand complex to a rug merchant for $750,000.[8]

Churchill desperately needed whatever money he could raise from surplus properties. S-P finished 1956 with a net loss of $43,318,257, but with a break-even point of only 150,000 units, everyone anticipated a better 1957. Consumers, however, were still wary. New-car prices in 1957 were higher and payments larger, and many potential buyers decided to drive their old cars one more year. As industry sales slumped, Churchill resorted to cutting costs, and he had about as much success as Nance. In April 1957, his break-even point was down to 104,000 cars, and he was pushing hard to get it to 80,000, a number once within Packard's reach.[9]

The company had actually made an $895,000 profit in the last two months of 1956, and with Hurley's takeover, expectations were raised. Moreover, S-P began to exploit market niches. It announced a stripped-down Champion called the Scotsman, the cheapest new car on the market, which dealers could sell for a patriotic $1,776 and still make a profit. At the other end of the spectrum, where Packard used to hold sway, S-P finally signed a contract with Daimler-Benz to market Mercedes starting May 20, 1957, when Max Hoffman's contract expired. The luxury imports were tagged to sell at between $3,500 and $13,000.[10]

The profits did not flow very long. S-P registered a first-quarter loss of $2,498,357 on sales of more than $58 million. To soften the news, Churchill mentioned that March had shown a slight profit and the company might be operating at a "profitable rate" by year's end. The president explained that his severe internal economies had reduced administrative costs from $1,125,000 in 1955 to only $350,000 in 1957. Even Churchill took a salary cut, from $64,000 in 1956 to $60,000 in 1957. S-P officials were encouraged, demand for the Scotsman was high, and with Mercedes trickling into showrooms, Porta was forecasting only a $4.14 million loss for the year, a minor miracle. In the summer, however, everything turned sour. Sales fell, June and July losses were larger than expected, and almost 50 percent of the Mercedes were damaged in shipment. Hurley thought he had the answer to the company's sales woes, however. He wanted S-P to sell a German automobile, the Goggomobil, a small, squarish, almost Jeep-like car, that would retail for between $1,000 and $1,400. He was obviously watching Volkswagen's amazing success and wanted to emulate it. The board reluctantly agreed to look into the idea and sent Churchill to Germany in September. He found that the factory's output was much lower than Hurley had been told, and the car required a great deal of handwork. In January 1958, the board voted to discontinue negotiations with the German carmaker.[11]

By then, S-P was in deep financial trouble, having lost more than $11 million in 1957. It was selling only half the expected number of Mercedes, sales of all its other cars were down, and its 1957 production totals, 67,394 Studebakers and 5,495 Packards, were far below its break-even point. The good news was that sales across the industry had slumped 26 percent, and S-P's were down only 15 percent. By February, conditions were bleaker. S-P's January losses were $2,333,000, and it had a 79-day inventory of cars. J. Cheever Cowdin, a new director, suggested that the company pare its offerings to only two low-priced cars, one to sell at $1,500 and the other at $2,000, and end Packard production. Churchill demurred, saying that his dealers were not equipped to handle volume selling. Instead, he countered with a brand-new car, a Rambler-sized automobile, that S-P could tool for less than $8 million. The board authorized $400,000 to begin work on what would become the Studebaker Lark.[12]

When the directors gathered on April 24, 1958, to hear their first-quarter results, they were a somber lot. Porta said that the company had lost another $6,249,480 on sales of 11,257 cars, down from the 22,372 vehicles they had sold in the first quarter of 1957. A sense of desperation began to seep into South Bend's executive offices. S-P dealers were averaging only 2.1 sales per month, and their number had shrunk to just about 2,000. The company desperately needed more cash and working capital, and if the funds were not forthcoming, Porta predicted, it would only have about $9 million in cash by Christmas. Churchill fired another 759 salaried personnel and delayed contributing the $27 million to Packard's pension fund that S-P owed. By early August, the situation appeared hopeless. S-P lost $7,019,685 in the second quarter and in six months had manufactured only 19,556 units. Nobody saw much hope for the immediate future.[13]

In the midst of the financial crisis, Packard was all but forgotten. There was no longer a distinct Packard "division." That had disappeared in 1957 when Packard styling and engineering were folded in with their Studebaker counterparts. The Packard Clipper (there was no Executive in 1957) was obviously a Studebaker in disguise. Dubbed the "Packabaker," the new Packard featured an automatic transmission and a supercharged Studebaker V-8 as standard equipment. Consumers could choose between a station wagon for $3,093 or a four-door sedan for $2,933. The Packabaker was unabashedly a medium-priced car, and, bearing the "orphan" stigma, it outpaced the segment's decline.[14]

The rumors there would be no 1957 Packard did not help the Packabaker's sales any, and its late introduction hurt it more. Production was scheduled to begin on December 17, 1956, months after competitors had begun their production runs. Not enough were available for sale until January 24, 1957. Packard missed the important fall selling season, as it had in 1955.[15] Packard's faltering sales, coupled with the company's delicate financial position, led the directors to ignore it. The single exception to their silence was after Hurley returned from Europe. He ordered S-P's chief stylist, Duncan McRae, to adapt the Ferrari styling to a Hawk. McRae modified a Studebaker Hawk, added a 275-horsepower, supercharged V-8 to provide it with muscle, and called it a Packard Hawk. To McRae's surprise, Hurley ordered it put into production. Packard Hawks hit the showroom floors with the face-lifted 1958 Studebakers on

254
══
"Ask the Man Who Owned One"

October 15, but the rest of the Packards did not appear until January 11, 1958. The company previewed them, however, in a special *New York Times* eight-page supplement on Sunday, December 8. S-P offered a Packard sedan, station wagon, and hardtop. Although it touted the new Packards as the "most original cars on the road," they still revealed their Studebaker heritage. More damaging, the company pushed its Packard prices into the $3,600-to-$4,200 range, which did little to enhance the cars' marketability.[16]

Packard's days were clearly numbered, however, even before the new models reached the display floors. The company was in horrible financial shape. In November 1957, Hurley warned his directors that if they did not do something it would run out of cash by January. In October, they built 11,500 of the 1958s when they only had orders for 7,000. Nobody, Hurley continued, could figure out where the cash was going to come from. Mercedes sales were so poor that Churchill asked Daimler-Benz to stop shipping new cars. In the midst of Hurley's dismal recitation, Hugh Ferry proposed that "the Corporation should give serious consideration to discontinuing the Packard line in 1959 if sales of that particular line are not improved." No vote was taken, but the irony of Packard's former president making the suggestion could not have been lost on the assemblage. Ferry understood that Packard was finished, and perhaps he was saddened by what the car had become, a pale reflection of its past glories, lacking the dignity it had once enjoyed.[17]

The directors decided to wait before they made a final decision on Packard. Five days before Christmas, 1957, S-P's sales manager told the board that it was too early to tell whether the new Packards would sell, but Packard's penetration of the national market that month was exactly zero. Churchill proposed in January to narrow the company's range of models, but he mentioned that he was "flexible . . . as to the continuation of the Packard line." When the new Packards did not catch the public's fancy, he told his directors on February 24 that he wanted to drop Packard to save the $1 million he could use to tool the Lark. The directors never voted to kill Packard; they just nodded in assent. When Churchill presented his 1959 program for approval at a special May 8 board meeting, he omitted any mention of Packard. The decision to put Packard out of its misery was made easier by its abysmal sales – of only 1,745 cars in 1958. When the sales manager reported to the board in July, he gave the figures for each Studebaker model and ended, "Plus a few Packard sales." He did not even dignify them with a number.[18]

The news of Packard's demise was announced on July 13, but nobody at S-P took responsibility for it. The *New York Times* and the *Wall Street Journal* ran retrospective pieces, emphasizing Packard's past, and

256
=====

"Ask the
Man Who
Owned
One"

explained its death by saying that S-P's "destiny is tied to smaller cars." The *Times* pointed out that with Packard's demise, only 16 remained of the 2,700 nameplates that had appeared since 1893. *Business Week* headlined its story "Ask the Man Who Owned One" and compared the fall of Nash, Hudson, Packard, Willys, Kaiser, Crosley, and Frazer to the disappearance of automobile companies in the depression.[19]

Packard was dead, but Studebaker still lived—barely. Churchill had a two-pronged policy in mind when he buried Packard: bring out the Lark and commence acquisitions so the company could take advantage of its tax carryovers, which were due to start running out in 1959. A month after he announced that there would not be another Packard, he reported that Abraham Sonnabend, the man *Time* called "the marrying Sam of the corporate merger business," would join S-P's board. Hurley took that opportunity to cut all his ties with S-P. The automaker renegotiated its debts, and its Lark became an instant success. Production at South Bend reached 84 cars an hour, a plant record. The company returned a net profit of more than $28 million in 1959, a company record. S-P failed to follow up on the Lark's success, however. In 1961, Sherwood Egbert, of the McCulloch Chain Saw company, became S-P's president. The flamboyant Egbert went after acquisitions, redesigned the Lark, and brought out a new fiberglass automobile, the Avanti. The stockholders dropped the Packard name from S-P on April 26, 1962. Studebaker struggled along with small losses each year. The Avanti was not the success Egbert had hoped, and the company could not raise tooling money to bring out an all-new car in 1964. In 1963, Byers Burlingame, who had overseen Packard's close-out in Detroit, became Studebaker's president. It was his lot to order the South Bend factory closed in December. Production was continued for three more years at the company's Hamilton, Ontario, plant. Small profits on its operation and the unavailability of money for a new 1967 model led to its being closed in March 1966. A year later, Studebaker merged with Worthington of Canada, and in 1979, the McGraw-Edison Company absorbed Studebaker-Worthington. The Studebaker name disappeared from the corporate landscape.[20]

Packard exited the car world with a whimper in 1958, its glory years long behind it. The Packabakers were not bad cars; they just were not honored additions to the venerable Packard legend. But not all the cars that the Packard Motor Car Company had built were classics. Some, such as the bathtubs and the early 1955 models, did not do the company's reputation proud either. Even the 1956 Packard, with its defective axle flanges, served notice that Packard quality had slipped to industry norms. Moreover, by the 1950's, automobiles had become more technologically sophisticated. Even medium-priced cars offered amenities such as push-button radios, power seats and windows, air-conditioning, automatic transmissions, power steering and brakes, power antennas, and the like, features formerly found only on the most expensive luxury editions. Packard did not so much fall from great heights as see other automakers climb up to them and offer the consumer the same comforts, in a larger range of models, for a few hundred dollars less. Packards became less distinctive, and that progressively cost them what was left of their reputation.

The generation of car buyers who grew up after the last Packard rolled off the South Bend assembly line had the final word on Packard. The "classic," senior Packards of the late 1920's and the depression have sold for more than $1 million to collectors, but the 1957s and 1958s have commanded much more modest prices and have held their value about as well as the bathtubs and the prewar 6-cylinder sedans. The Packard Hawk, which soared only one year and was limited to a run of 588 copies, has retained its value, on account of its rarity more than anything else.

In Packard's 59 years, Warren, Detroit, and South Bend factories manufactured more than 1.6 million automobiles. But Packard's longevity and reputation were not enough to save her. The grande dame of the business lost control of her own destiny and for her final four years was captive to an orphan automaker. Like the dowager who outlived her generation, Packard had nobody on the inside left at the end to speak for her, to proclaim her glories. Only the press and the few devout Packard families and fans mourned her passing.[21]

The Autopsy

The reasons for Packard's demise have long been debated. The most common assertion is that the Independent did not have a chance in the 1950's against the combined resources of the Big Three. GM, Ford, and Chrysler achieved economies of scale that enabled them to engineer, style, manufacture, advertise, and sell their automobiles for less than Packard, Nash, Hudson, Studebaker, Willys, and Kaiser. They also set standards for styling, quality, price, and performance that the Independents had to follow. They dominated radio, newspapers, magazines, and eventually television with their slick advertisements and promotions. They upped the competitive intensity in the industry by radically changing their body styles at least every three years. It was impossible for Independents such as Packard to keep pace; from 1941 through 1956, it offered only two basic body shells.

Yet the other major Independent did not succumb to such pressures. Nash and Hudson were not much stronger financially than Studebaker and Packard in 1954. Indeed, Hudson was virtually moribund at the moment of the merger. George Mason and George Romney, however, steered a course for the little automaker that enabled it to keep its independence until Chrysler bought it in 1987. AMC did have the advantage of its profitable Kelvinator appliance line, but that did not make the critical difference in its survival. Packard did not die because it was small and not very cost-efficient. Those disabilities only eroded the firm's profit margins. They hurt, but they were not fatal.

Bad management did not kill Packard, either. In fact, in its 59 years, it was blessed with uncommonly good executive officers. From James Ward Packard and Alvan Macauley through James J. Nance and Harold Churchill, the company attracted an unbroken series of driven, talented, and even imaginative men to its helm. All of them were demanding chief executives who knew what they were about. The automobiles they built reflected the Packard tradition and their quest for an edge that set their products above the rest. They did not always achieve it in the postwar years. Once Packard, under Christopher's ministrations, adopted mass-production techniques, it was foregone that the Packard "plus" would be diluted. Macauley made the decision in the late 1920's, though, and nobody ever accused him of pandering to the masses.

More specifically, Nance did not kill Packard. He has been charged with every sin from ignorance to stupidity. As Packard's last president, he had to bear the ignominy of emptying East Grand's halls. The appliance man had no background in the industry and was innocent of many of the intricacies of building cars, but he was a fast learner and brought to the company many talents that it badly needed. He also gave the firm a sense of direction. His dream of restoring Packard to its leadership in the prestige market was possible–with luck. Nance aped Macauley's strategy: build an expensive, elegant automobile to continue the firm's reputation and a medium-priced offering, distinctively Packard, that brought in needed volume. It had worked for decades at East Grand, and Nance was certain that he could continue the tradition. He fired hundreds of old Packard employees. His detractors charged that he replaced them with Hotpoint cronies who knew nothing about the industry. His new hires, however, also brought skills that would help Packard, especially in purchasing, budgeting, and accounting. Packard was full of deadwood by 1952–with no retirement plan, employees hung around forever. In retiring them, Nance made room for new blood and ideas. He drove everyone, including himself, at a terrific pace to catch up. He achieved his short-range objectives to modernize Packard while losing his fight to keep it in business, but that does not make him guilty of Packard's death. Henry Ford II and Ernest Breech at Ford did not think so, either. They brought him into the highest councils of their company with the implied promise that he would be the leading candidate for the Ford presidency. Had there been no recession in 1958, Nance might well have won Ford's number-one slot. The man was, by any yardstick, a success in the auto business, despite the salient fact that he buried two automobile nameplates.

Nance's policies, especially his move into the Conner plant and his modernization plan that cost Packard $50 million it did not have, did not kill the firm. Influenced by the Booz Allen report, Nance was convinced that Packard should bring its body manufacturing back under its own roof, but he never planned to do it in 1954. Nance agreed to cram the body and assembly operations into Conner only because he believed that the disrupted market in 1954 was temporary and that he would have the resources to enlarge Conner before he moved in. Events overtook planning, however, and he had to make do with what he could afford, a smaller Conner factory. He and Ray Powers put the best face on it, announcing that a single-story plant was more modern, and went ahead with production. Nance's detractors argued that the flawed 1955s were the result, and to some extent, they were right. The 1955 Packards, however, were the company's most radically redesigned offerings since the 120s. Powers and his manufacturing men had to build a car with a new engine, a redesigned transmission, an untried suspension system, and a heavily face-lifted body. They had to work in a brand-new plant, and the time constraints were severe. After a rough six-month shakedown period, they rolled cars out of Conner that were as good as any of the company's postwar offerings. And the cramped factory was capable of manufacturing enough cars to exceed the firm's break-even point, around 80,000 units per year. It was not the men inside Conner who were responsible for the failure to sell enough Packards to make a profit.

In making his modernization plans, Nance thought in large terms, and the price tag on the Utica motor and transmission works, Conner, and a strengthened dealer network was higher than anything East Grand veterans had seen. Nance understood that Packard had long plowed its earnings into dividends rather than capital improvements. Its manufacturing facilities in bad shape, it lost its reputation for clever engineering, and it even trailed the low-priced three in some innovations. Packard followed rather than led. Nance was willing to assume debt to modernize the company. He hoped to strengthen Packard so the company could survive the difficult competitive period expected once war restrictions were lifted and then be positioned for an advantageous merger.

The merger with Studebaker was not fatal, either. It was not a union that Nance particularly wanted—since 1951 he had leaned toward joining Nash. The merger was precipitous, as he admitted later. Had he known the extent of South Bend's weaknesses, he would have had second thoughts. On paper, however, the union looked propitious, for it gave Packard the cheaper car that Booz Allen had insisted it needed to survive. Studebaker's long history and its good reputation for engineering and economy strengthened Packard's reputation for engineering and luxury. Its styling was a bit quirky, though, and it would take several years to work out interchangeability of parts to achieve promised economies. Ironically, interchangeability was eventually achieved by making the Packard a Studebaker. Studebaker's losses were greater than anticipated and were a drag on S-P. But it was Packard's decline in 1956, coupled with the Eisenhower administration's political determination to save S-P at minimum cost to the taxpayers, that forced the company into Roy Hurley's grasping hands.

Each of the setbacks hurt Packard, but none was severe enough by itself to fell the East Grand automaker. Like Gulliver entrapped by a host of Lilliputians, Packard was weakened by a complex, intricately interwoven set of circumstances and events. And percolating through them all was the crushing weight of Packard's past. For two decades, Packard traded on its earlier reputation for elegance. In the postwar period, however, the gap between that reputation and reality widened. Even Nance could not escape the dead hand of history; he and his managers found it impossible to renew or discard the firm's past to turn a new face to the buying public. The burden of Packard's history was already heavy when Nance took over the company. The roots of its demise spread more deeply.

Nance identified as Packard's first serious misstep Macauley's decision to call his 120 a Packard instead of following Cadillac's example with its cheaper LaSalle. That error, he thought, was compounded when Macauley brought out his 6-cylinder cars, which bore all the familiar Packard styling trademarks and the company's revered name. Nance understood that the 120 and its smaller siblings were not a fatal error. The cars were absolutely necessary for the company's survival in the depression. But they blurred the public's conception of the marque. Without a doubt, they undermined Packard's tradition of making cars for discerning motorists who wanted the very best and could afford to pay handsomely. Public confusion deepened in the late 1930's as Packard cheapened its more expensive cars. Macauley paid the price of catering to middlebrow tastes and pocketbooks when he brought men such as Christopher, Gilman, and Packer into East Grand. They changed the company's whole tone. They bet their careers on Packard's success in the middle-priced field while still touting the company's reputation for building the world's finest automobile. That contradiction became apparent in the immediate postwar period. Despite the few seven-passenger Clippers and limousines that the company manufactured, Packard essentially competed with Buick and Oldsmobile rather than Cadillac. Nance was right–Packard had given the luxury market to Cadillac "on a silver platter." Packard chose the more practical, short-term strategy of going for volume and a lower profit per vehicle and saved the company. Cadillac, by contrast, gambled and settled for lower production while its image makers adroitly created a postwar market for its cars.

Packard's leaders, no matter how talented, failed to understand the huge demographic changes the war wrought in the United States. Like most thoughtful men, they feared that the country would revert to hard times. If that happened, Packard was well positioned with its Clipper to prosper. Surprisingly, however, the nation boomed in the late 1940's, men made fortunes from the war, the Marshall Plan increased exports, the Cold War kept defense spending at unnaturally high levels, and personal incomes rose, all of which enlarged the luxury-car market. But its mainstay was no longer the old families who hid at the end of long, curving driveways. The newly rich wanted to flaunt their wealth. The product of rapid change, they looked for newness and innovation in the cars they drove. They liked acceleration and tail fins and toothy grilles, which proclaimed they were on the cutting edge, and Cadillac courted them. Packard, by contrast, retained the best of its traditional styling and its tried-and-true engineering. Its cars were as good as those in the 1930's, but they appealed to the more conservative, the financially more timid buyers. Packard could have rectified its marketing mistake without mortal pain in 1948. Instead, it manufactured the bathtubs.

Packard was far from unique in losing its way in the nation's car markets. Even Cadillac, which had so smartly avoided the shoals of changing tastes and demographics, miscalculated after the gas crisis hit the United States in 1973. Caught flatfooted with a stable of huge automotive offerings, GM officials instituted a crash program to "downsize" their cars. One result was the Cadillac Cimarron. This four-person car, no bigger than a small Chevrolet, lacked the amenities of a large, comfortable luxury car. It looked cheap, cheaper than the 120 had appeared next to the 12-cylinder models. Cadillac saw its mistake and discontinued the Cimarron but then restyled its larger cars to resemble GM's other medium-sized offerings. GM's luxury division blurred its image and paid the price. In the 1980's, its share of the growing luxury market fell ten points. Lincoln, luckily, did not have enough money to retool a smaller car after Ford spent billions to develop the Taurus and the Sable. The Lincoln remained a very large car and, by 1990, trailed Cadillac sales by only two percentage points.[1]

Cadillac's fall from grace handed other car manufacturers, especially the Japanese and the German automakers, the opportunity to enter the field with a vengeance. Mercedes, BMW, Lexus, and Infiniti all increased their sales. The cars, no bigger than the unloved, medium-sized Cadillacs, were touted for their superior quality and technological innovations—exactly the advantages Packard had used to dominate that market. By the mid-1980's, the U.S. luxury market was almost 10 percent of all car sales, what it had been at the end of the 1920's. Cadillac lost its marketing edge, like Packard had in the late 1940's, just as wealthy Americans were increasing their share of the national income and prospects at the apex of the auto market looked the brightest.

In the postwar period, Packard had a reputation as an old folks' car, the kiss of death. Everyone had a grandfather or a favorite uncle who owned a Packard as big as a house. According to Nance's surveys, Packard buyers were older, more affluent, and loyal to the marque. Older people buy fewer cars, drive them less, and keep them longer. They impart an image to a car that makes it difficult to sell, even to the elderly. Lincoln and Cadillac were gaining that reputation in the 1990's. The average age of a Lincoln Towncar purchaser was 62; only its Continental Mark VII attracted a younger following of positively supple 45-year-olds. The average age of those who bought Cadillac's top-of-the-line Brougham was 66. The other twenty companies competing in the top price brackets wooed younger, more affluent buyers to their showrooms with advanced styling, comfort, and sporty offerings. It was Cadillac's tail fins against the bathtubs all over again, except that in the 1990's the competition was international. The goals remained the same, however: position a luxury model as the smart conveyance for those on their way up, build cars that exuded a youthful quality, and sell the consumer dependability, service, and value. That was exactly what Packard had done in its heyday, when it was as successful as Cadillac, Mercedes, and the Japanese competitors were later.[2]

Inside the East Grand offices, Packard executives aged with their customers. Jesse Vincent, Alvan Macauley, and Hugh Ferry retained their talents as they grew older, but they became more resistant to change, less willing to take risks, and more complacent about what they were doing. The *idée fixe* was that Packard was still the finest automobile on the market at any price, and that the public would therefore continue to purchase it because of its distinguished heritage. Packard's managers wallowed in that self-delusion. They built a $2,700 automobile that was overpriced in its class and seemed genuinely surprised when consumers did not buy it. An excellent example of their obtuseness was their continuance of the model series designation, a system that perplexed even the most avid Packard devotee, until Nance changed it in 1955. It had the ring of exclusiveness, but it obscured the truth that Packard could no longer afford to change its cars whenever it wanted. To prosper, the company had to bring out retooled or face-lifted cars every year at the same time as the competition.

Packard was a much-weakened company by midcentury, but it was far from moribund and still boasted the potential of competing with the Big Three. What killed Packard was the one-two-three punch of circumstances outside the company's control that, when combined with its other difficulties, made it impossible for Nance and his "key men" to keep the firm in business. After the knockout punches, Packard's only hope for survival lay with the federal government's willingness to provide a massive infusion of funds as it did for Chrysler 24 years later. Given the prevailing political ideology of the mid-1950's, however, it was a false hope.

Packard was staggered by the outbreak of the Korean War. Just as the company finally mustered the internal cohesion to set its managerial house in order and make forward plans in the late 1940's and brought out its handsome 1951 body, the government allocated raw materials to automakers based on their earlier production figures. Worse, the war cut into every company's car sales. Packard's prospects before the conflict were exceedingly bright, and its auto sales might well have given the company the necessary profits to rejuvenate its facilities and dealer system. Its auto sales would have also enabled the firm to retool from internal revenues a much-needed new body three or four years later.

President Ferry counterpunched with what appeared to be a wise short-term strategy, that of actively seeking government war contracts that would give his company the millions of dollars it needed to rebuild its auto business. It was the company's form of diversification, as Nance was later fond of saying. For two years Ferry's decision was successful as Packard's gross income from the defense business exceeded that from its auto sales. But the war was far too short to save the company, for just after Nance committed millions of dollars to upgrade the firm's auto-manufacturing facilities, dollars he expected to earn from his defense contracts, the federal government abruptly canceled its orders.

That blow could not have landed at a worse time: Henry Ford II had decided to challenge Chevrolet for first place in sales, and both companies squeezed every car possible from their factories. Packard faced the feared buyer's market with a three-year-old car and no money to retool. Henry Ford II, by contrast, had invested more than $1 billion in a new plant, and he and GM had the will and resources to carry on the fight as long as necessary. All the Independents, not just Packard, lacked resources and staying power, and quickly lost market share. By the spring of 1953, just as Packard was enjoying its best selling spree in years, the company was doomed.

Nance was caught off guard. He assumed that 1955 would be Packard's critical year because by then, the buyer's market would have returned. In addition, the country was due for a recession, which would cut into sales. Had Nance been right, Packard would have been stronger, for the new facilities would have been in place—barely. Instead, the race began two years early, long before he could expect any returns from his new plant. Packard could not keep up financially, although its 1955 cars indicated just how clever its engineers and stylists could be with slim budgets. Packard became, if not technologically obsolescent, more old-fashioned-looking, thereby exacerbating its difficulties in appealing to younger consumers and first-time Packard buyers.

The 1953 selling spree fundamentally rearranged automakers' traditional markets. The medium-priced market had been Packard's milieu since 1935 and after Mercury joined the fray in 1938 had been something of an exclusive club with more or less assured percentages for all. It was a more profitable niche than the lower levels, but it was a small foothold for an Independent to sustain itself. Back in 1952, Packard's consultants warned that the company would have to expand the percentage of the market in which it competed. Nance, however, never had the resources to bring out a lower-priced Packard and failed to become a major player in the upper reaches of the car market. The Big Three improved their cheaper cars, cutting sales out of the medium-price range, where Packard's Clipper was fighting for its life.

The Big Three's sales managers brought intense pressure to bear on their dealers in 1953 to absorb their factories' excess production. The new-car glut strained Packard's weakest point, its dealers. Packard did not have its own finance company, so its dealers used their local banks to pay for their cars and loan their customers money. When all the Independents reported large losses in 1954, bankers everywhere became wary of loaning their dealers money and charged premium rates when they did. Moreover, in the heated car market of late 1953 and after, Packard suffered from owner loyalty. As Packard resale values continued to drop, many Packard owners bought new Packards because the local dealers would allow more on their trade-ins. Lots overflowed with used Packards, many of them bathtubs, that the dealers could not unload and could ill afford to carry. Nance could only offer his traditional end-of-the-model-year discounts. But those reductions hurt. Packard dealers, groused Nance, began to wait for them and eased up on their selling efforts during the summer. They took their profits in the fall at the factory's expense. It was a common cycle in the business, but it became poisonous in the hard-sell days of 1953.

Some of Packard's wounds were self-inflicted. No decision that emanated from Detroit or South Bend was more destructive than S-P's attempt to become a fourth full-line automobile producer. Even the company's bankers warned Nance that the country did not need and would not support such a company. The decision, however, appeared to have been almost an afterthought, the outgrowth of historical forces that shaped the Independents. Rumors of their merger had drifted through Detroit's watering holes for decades, and the men who advocated such unions predicated their plans on the "best fit" among companies. They sought mergers between firms that complemented each other rather than competed, to expand their market coverage without making huge capital expenditures. The logical outcome of such a strategy was to try to create a "Big Fourth."

The Studebaker-Packard merger fit neatly into this philosophy. Grant's list of merger benefits emphasized the complementary aspects of the union and predicted that all the expected good things would happen. The Nash-Hudson combine, however, did not enjoy the "fit" that S-P did. It was well established in the cheaper end of the market and in the middle range; it had nothing to offer against Packard, Cadillac, Lincoln, and Chrysler. Romney initially tried to fight in those markets and even bought Packard V-8s to jazz up his medium-priced cars. He quickly saw the error of his ways and repositioned AMC to capture the cheapest markets, which the Big Three had abandoned when their lower-priced cars grew bigger and more expensive. AMC's Rambler proved a huge success. By 1960, AMC accounted for 7.5 percent of industry sales and enjoyed a $48 million profit. After Romney left the company's presidency in 1962, his successors tried to make AMC a full-line producer again and even contended in the luxury market with the Ambassador. The strategy was a disaster: AMC lost $100 million between 1966 and 1971. The company survived only after returning to Romney's earlier tactics. It brought out the Gremlin and the Pacer, both designed by Teague. In a brilliant stroke in 1971, it bought Kaiser Jeep, a profitable operation, and later joined with Renault. The two deals kept the firm alive until 1987.[3]

S-P spanned a broader spectrum of the market, which made repositioning more difficult for Nance. Instead, the market did it for him. It drove Packard and Clipper out of business and reduced Studebaker to the Lark and the Hawk. Some critics argued that Nance should have shrunk Packard until its break-even point approximated its sales. His $50 million modernization program raised Packard's break-even point to about 80,000 units a year, a sales level the company had achieved only five times in its history. In 1956, with sales of 13,432, Nance would have had to close down his engine and Ultramatic plant and purchase that equipment outside. S-P would have been saddled with additional millions of square feet of unused floor space. Nance could have followed Rolls Royce and manufactured a few thousand hand-built cars for those who demand something different. Recent experience, however, indicates that this transformation would not have solved Packard's problems. The venerable English manufacturer faced the same difficulties that Packard struggled with. Its "cheaper" model, the Bentley, outsold its more expensive stablemate. To stem the erosion of the Rolls Royce's prestige, the company needed to tool separate bodies for its cars.[4]

Overall, however, Packard was a success. It was one of the few companies that survived its infancy, it ruled the roads for decades, and its 59-year life span far exceeded the norm for automakers. It was one of the last of the 2,700 American automobile companies to disappear. Unlike most of them, it was fondly remembered by many. A surprisingly large number of its cars are still on the road, parked lovingly in garages around the world, or gracing the halls of museums. The vacant offices and factory floors at East Grand stand as mute testimony to the Irish and Central European workmen who took pride in their craftsmanship, and to James Ward Packard, Jesse Vincent, Henry Joy, Alvan Macauley, and the rest who masterminded the classic examples of the automakers' art that flowed through its gates. Because Packard was enveloped in a "mystique," perhaps novelists should have the final word. Michael Dorris and Louise Erdrich, in their *Crown of Columbus*, summed up the importance of the automobile in the American psyche: "A vehicle is an extension of one's self, the four-wheeled face one presents to the world. . . . A car announces its occupants."[5] For decades, Packard did just that.

Reference
Matter

Notes

Articles and books mentioned only once in the Notes are cited in full when they occur, as are all newspaper and magazine articles; for all other references, full citations can be found in the Bibliography. Abbreviations of locations of collections of personal papers and corporate reports are as follows: AHC, Automotive History Collection; DC, Dartmouth College Library; DDEL, Dwight D. Eisenhower Presidential Library; HST, Harry S. Truman Presidental Library; SNMA, Studebaker National Museum Archives; and WRHS, Western Reserve Historical Society. For further details, see the Primary Sources section of the Bibliography.

Citations for the Studebaker National Museum Archives are based on the organization of the Packard records when I used them. The material had originally been sent to Syracuse University, where archivists began to bring some order out of the chaos. Before they could finish, however, Syracuse gave the papers to the SNMA. When I used them they still retained the Syracuse system, but many of the documents had not been organized in any way. After I finished my research in South Bend, the SNMA began a systematic reorganization of all its papers, and thus my citations for many documents may no longer reflect their current locations. For example, I understand that what I cite as the A. J. Porta papers may be recataloged as the Paul Shine papers.

CHAPTER 1. *Ascent of the Marque*

1. David L. Lewis, "Ford Country," *Cars & Parts* (Apr. 1989), p. 64.
2. Griffith Borgeson, "Marmon's Masterpieces," *Automobile Quarterly* (second quarter, 1989), pp. 122–23.
3. Kimes, p. 16.
4. Ibid., p. 35.
5. *Horseless Age*, May 16, 1900.
6. Adams, p. 278.

7. *Horseless Age*, Sept. 26, 1900; Seltzer, pp. 250–51.

8. John Lauritz Larson, "James Frederick Joy," in Frey, pp. 208–12.

9. Glasscock, p. 107.

10. Kimes, p. 62.

11. Ibid., p. 64.

12. Ibid., p. 94.

13. Flink, p. 59; Adams, p. 2.

14. Paul G. Hoffman Papers, box 151, in HST.

15. Doolittle, p. 371; Nevins and Hill, *Ford: The Times, the Man, the Company*, p. 255; Kimes, p. 777; Scott, p. 17.

16. Kimes, pp. 110, 127.

17. *Time*, July 22, 1929, p. 41.

18. Kimes, p. 101.

19. *Time*, Nov. 4, 1935, p. 68; Jaffe, p. 58.

20. *Detroit Free-Press*, Sept. 15, 1950; *Detroit News*, Dec. 9, 1954; Kimes, pp. 154–55.

21. Jesse Vincent Correspondence, AHC.

22. Hendry, p. 70; Kimes, pp. 131–35.

23. Kimes, pp. 155 (quotation), 157 (quotation); Scott, p. 26.

24. Kimes, pp. 778–80.

25. Davis, pp. xi, 10, 13.

26. Kimes, p. 228.

27. Seltzer, p. 249.

28. Kimes, pp. 780–81.

29. Ibid., pp. 236–40; Scott, pp. 36–37.

30. Kimes, pp. 803, 272, 282; Seltzer, p. 250; Adams, p. 284; Brierly, p. 22.

31. Adams, p. 284.

32. Georgano, pp. 165–66, 310–11, 655–56, 519–20, 255–56, 185–87, 555.

33. Sloan, p. 155; Hendry, p. 134.

34. Kimes, pp. 281, 294; Hendry, p. 134.

35. U.S. Department of Commerce, pp. 462, 94.

36. Kimes, p. 296.

37. Georgano, pp. 261–62, 455–56, 110–11, 310–11, 208, 540, 550–51.

38. Ibid., pp. 433, 189.

39. Ebert, pp. 5–6; Fine, *Automobile Under the Blue Eagle*, pp. 140–41.

40. Kimes, p. 302.

41. Hendry, app. 8; Kimes, pp. 400–410.

42. Kimes, pp. 340–41.

43. Ebert, p. 8.

CHAPTER 2. *Episcopalian Cars for Methodists*

1. "Packard," *Fortune* (Jan. 1937), p. 55; Packard 1933 *Annual Report*, in SNMA (quotation).

2. "Product Flow Chart," in Richard Stout Collection, Delray Beach, Fla.

3. Packard 1933, 1943 *Annual Reports*; Hokanson, p. 11; *Dictionary of American Biography*, Supp. III, 1941–45 (New York, 1973), pp. 549–51; *Time*, Nov. 4, 1935.

4. Kimes, p. 451; "Packard," *Fortune* (Jan. 1937), p. 55; Galbraith, p. 146; *New York Times*, Oct. 23, 1929; *Time*, Nov. 4, 1935; Scott, p. 102.

5. "This Date in Packard History," *Cormorant News-Bulletin* (July 1989), p. 2; "Packard," *Fortune* (Jan. 1937), p. 110; *New York Times*, Mar. 3, 1965; Margery Gilman, interview by author, Dec. 2, 1987.

6. "Packard," *Fortune* (Jan. 1937), p. 110; Gilman, interview, Dec. 2, 1987.

7. *Motor News* (Mar. 1947), pp. 12, 25; *National Cyclopaedia of American Biography*, 44:194–95.

8. Lyman Slack, letter to author, Nov. 28, 1987; Scott, p. 129; "Packard," *Fortune* (Jan. 1937), p. 116; clipping attached to *Motor News* (Mar. 1947), p. 25, in George T. Christopher file, AHC.

9. Kimes, p. 454; "Packard," *Fortune* (Jan. 1937), p. 118.

10. Kimes, pp. 177, 303, 686–87, 695 (quotations); Michael Kollins, interview by author, June 21, 1988.

11. "Packard," *Fortune* (Jan. 1937), p. 114 (quotation); Kollins, interview, June 21, 1988 (quotation).

12. Kimes, pp. 457, 458, 463; "Packard," *Fortune* (Jan. 1937), p. 118.

13. "Packard," *Fortune* (Jan. 1937), p. 114; Kimes, p. 454.

14. Kimes, pp. 454–59.

15. "Packard," *Fortune* (Jan. 1937), p. 114.

16. U.S. Department of Commerce, p. 462; Packard 1935 *Annual Report*; Kimes, pp. 349, 807.

17. Packard, 1934, 1936, 1937 *Annual Reports*; Kimes, p. 807.

18. Kimes, pp. 470, 790–91; Packard 1937 *Annual Report*.

19. Scott, p. 111.

20. Kimes, pp. 364, 481, 786–87.

21. Ibid., pp. 807–8.

22. Einstein, pp. 223–24, 241, 230–31, 228 (quotation).

23. Packard 1940 *Annual Report*.

24. Sloan, pp. 238–40; Kimes, p. 490 (quotation).

25. Gilbert Zimmerman, "Reinhart in Retrospect," *Packards International Magazine* (summer 1986), p. 9; Kimes, p. 491; Richard Stout, interview by author, Apr. 29, 1987.

26. Kimes, pp. 492–97, 492–93 (quotation); Joel Prescott, "Who Really Designed the Clipper? Packard Designer William Reithard Recalls the Origins of a Classic," *Packard Cormorant* (spring 1992), pp. 4–9.

27. Kimes, pp. 497–99.

28. Kollins, interview, June 21, 1988.

29. Hendry, p. 242; Goodrich, "The Packard I Knew," p. 14A; Bonsall, p. 312.

30. Hendry, app. 7, p. 247.

31. Kimes, pp. 364–65, 367; "Packard," *Fortune* (Jan. 1937), p. 55 (quotation).

32. Richard Stout, interview by author, Apr. 29, 1987.

33. George Packard Lott, "Why We Lost Packard–An Opinion," *Packard Cormorant* (fall 1973), pp. 38, 40 (quotation).

34. Richard M. Langworth and George L. Hamlin, eds., "James J. Nance Talks Packard," *Packard Cormorant* (autumn 1976), p. 5.

35. Eleanor Paton, "Remembering Packard with Owen Goodrich, Part I: From Golden Age to Golden Anniversary," *Packard Cormorant* (autumn 1979), p. 5.

36. Goodrich, "The Rise and Fall of Packard as I Saw It," p. 14; Goodrich to Menno Duerksen, Oct. 17, 1977, in Duerksen's collection, Memphis, Tenn.

37. William B. Harris, "Last Stand of the Auto Independents?" *Fortune* (Dec. 1954), p. 115.

38. Slack to author, Nov. 28, 1987 (quotation), Dec. 11, 1987 (quotation).

39. Kimes, pp. 485–87. Quotation on p. 487.

40. Einstein, pp. 204–5, 206, 211, 212–215. Quotations on pp. 206, 211.

41. Ebert, pp. 8–11.

42. Menno Duerksen, "Of Packard Cars: Part II," *Packards International Magazine* (spring 1986), p. 26; Turnquist, p. 160.

CHAPTER 3. *The Dogs of War*

1. Kimes, pp. 504–7.

2. Packard 1941 *Annual Report*, p. 5; Kimes, p. 507 (quotation).

3. Kimes, pp. 508, 510.

4. Packard 1942 *Annual Report*, p. 5; Packard 1941 *Annual Report*, p. 5; Packard 1943 *Annual Report*, p. 9; Kimes, p. 507.

5. Packard 1945 *Annual Report*, pp. 3, 4; Packard 1942 *Annual Report*, pp. 3, 6; Packard 1941 *Annual Report*, p. 4.

6. *Detroit Free-Press*, Jan. 23, 1942.

7. Packard Board Minutes, Mar. 13, 1942, in SNMA; Margery Gilman, interview by author, Dec. 2, 1987; Packard Board Minutes, Mar. 25, 1942 (quotation).

8. *Detroit Free-Press*, Apr. 23, 1942 (quotation); Packard Board Minutes, Apr. 22, 1942; *New York Times*, Mar. 3, 1965.

9. Packard 1942 *Annual Report*, p. 7 (quotation); Packard 1943 *Annual Report*, pp. 11, 21.

10. Packard 1944 *Annual Report*, pp. 22, 11, 13; Packard Board Minutes, Nov. 10, 1943, June 14, 1944, Oct. 25, 1944, computed from appropriations through May 9, 1945.

11. Kimes, pp. 519, 520; Packard 1941 *Annual Report*, p. 3; Richard Stout, interview by author, Apr. 29, 1987; Stuart Blond, "Russian 'Packard' at Hershey," *Cormorant News-Bulletin* (Dec. 1988), pp. 4–5.

12. Packard 1945 *Annual Report*, pp. 4–7; Kimes, pp. 516–18.

13. Packard 1946 *Annual Report*, p. 6; Packard 1945 *Annual Report*, p. 7 (quotation); *New York Times*, Aug. 5, 1945 (quotation), Aug. 19, 1945 (quotation).

14. Packard 1945 *Annual Report*, p. 6 (quotation); *New York Times*, Nov. 6, 1945.

15. Packard 1946 *Annual Report*, p. 9; *New York Times*, Aug. 13, 1946, Sept. 18, 19, 22, 1946.

16. Kimes, p. 518.

17. Packard 1946 *Annual Report*, p. 9; *New York Times*, Sept. 18, 1946 (quotation); Kimes, p. 518.

18. Packard 1946 *Annual Report*, p. 4; *New York Times*, Nov. 14, 1946 (quotation).

19. Kimes, pp. 792–93, 808.

20. Packard Board Minutes, Feb. 12, 1946, May 8, 1946, Jan. 22, 1947; Packard 1946 *Annual Report*, cover; Kimes, p. 793.

21. Kimes, pp. 528 (quotation), 530 (quotation).

22. Richard M. Langworth, "Of Tail Fins and V-8's," *Automobile Quarterly* (third quarter, 1975), pp. 311, 312 (quotation).

23. Ibid., p. 310.

24. *Business Week*, Jan. 31, 1948, pp. 33–34; Langworth, "Of Tail Fins," p. 315.

25. Langworth, "Of Tail Fins," pp. 320, 312.

26. Hendry, app. 8; Kimes, pp. 808–9; Packard 1947–50 *Annual Reports*.

CHAPTER 4. *A Troubled Packard*

1. Lyman Slack, letter to author, Nov. 28, 1987.

2. Packard Board Minutes, June 25, 1947, Aug. 15, 1947, Jan. 6, 28, 1948; Slack to author, Nov. 19, 1987; *New York Times*, Apr. 20, 1948.

3. Packard Board Minutes, Nov. 25, 8, 1950, Aug. 22, 1951, Oct. 24, 1951.

4. *New York Times*, May 14, 1947, Aug. 6, 1947; Packard Board Minutes, May 12, 1948, Aug. 30, 1948, Oct. 13, 1948.

5. Packard 1949 *Annual Report*, p. 3; Packard Board Minutes, July 13, 1949; Richard Stout, interview by author, Apr. 29, 1987.

6. "Adventures of Henry and Joe in Autoland," *Fortune* (Mar. 1946), pp. 98, 97, 98–103, 229–34; Langworth, p. 266; Packard Board Minutes, July 21, 1947.

7. Slack to author, Nov. 28, 1987 (quotation); Packard Board Minutes, July 21, 1947 (quotation); Langworth, pp. 266, 221, 172.

8. *New York Times*, Oct. 8, 1954; Mahoney, pp. 134–35, 151–52; *Motor News* (May 1947), pp. 13, 25.

9. Packard Board Minutes, Feb. 3, 1948; *Business Week*, Dec. 27, 1947, p. 59 (quotation).

10. Mahoney, pp. 132, 135; Slack to author, Nov. 28, 14, 1987; Packard Board Minutes, Feb. 3, 1948 (quotation).

11. Packard Board Minutes, Mar. 10, 1948, Apr. 16, 1948.

12. Mahoney, pp. 108, 132, 169 (quotation).

13. Packard Board Minutes, Apr. 19, 1948, July 26, 1948; *New York Times*, June 17, 18, 30, 1948, Sept. 24, 1948; Packard 1948 *Annual Report*, p. 3.

14. Packard 1948 *Annual Report*, pp. 3, 4; *U.S. News & World Report*, Nov. 19, 1948, p. 16 (quotation).

15. *Business Week*, Jan. 3, 1948, pp. 33 (quotation), 34 (quotation).

16. *Newsweek*, Aug. 2, 1948, p. 62.

17. *Newsweek*, May 9, 1949, p. 72, Jan. 24, 1949, p. 55; Richard Langworth, "Styling Postwar (3): The Evolution of 'High Pockets,'" *Packard Cormorant* (spring 1990), p. 6.

18. Packard 1948 *Annual Report*, p. 4; Packard Board Minutes, July 26, 1948, Jan. 2, 1950, Oct. 13, 1948, Oct. 12, 1947; Kimes, p. 535.

19. *New York Times*, May 3, 10, 1949, July 19, 1949; Packard Board Minutes, Mar. 23, 1949, May 25, 1949.

20. Packard Board Minutes, May 23, 1949; Kimes, pp. 542–43.

21. Kimes, p. 542; Packard Board Minutes, Sept. 14, 1949 (quotation).

22. Kimes, p. 535 (quotation); Packard Board Minutes, Nov. 23, 1949 (quotation).

23. Packard Board Minutes, Sept. 28, 1949.

24. Packard Board Minutes, Oct. 5, 1949.

25. Ibid. (quotation); Slack to author, Nov. 14, 1987; Kimes, p. 543 (quotation).

26. Packard Board Minutes, Oct. 5 (quotation), Oct. 26, 1949.

27. Packard Board Minutes, Oct. 26, 1949, Feb. 23, 1949, Jan. 17, 1950; *The National Cyclopaedia of American Biography*, 44:195.

28. Packard 1949 *Annual Report*, p. 4.

CHAPTER 5. *The Ferry Years*

1. Packard News Service, n.d., Clipping File, AHC; *Detroit News*, Jan. 4, 1950; Packard News Service, n.d.; *Detroit News*, Nov. 8, 1954; Packard News Service, n.d.; W. H. Ferry, letter to author, Sept. 17, 1991.

2. "Hugh J. Ferry," Clipping File, AHC.

3. Lyman Slack, letter to author, Nov. 28, 1987.

4. Ferry to author, Oct. 28, 1991.

5. Slack to author, Nov. 28, 1987.

6. *Time*, Aug. 28, 1950, p. 70; Ferry to author, Oct. 28, 1991.

7. Minutes of the Operating Committee, Dec. 7, 1950, in Supporting Materials for the Board of Directors box, SNMA.

8. A. J. Porta Papers, ser. 1, box 2, SNMA.

9. *Consumer Reports* (Dec. 1951), pp. 314–28.

10. Michael Kollins, interview by author, June 21, 1988; *Business Week*, Oct. 28, 1950, p. 21; *New York Times*, Apr. 19, 1952.

11. *Consumer Reports* (Dec. 1951), pp. 314–28.

12. *New York Times*, Aug. 27, 1950, Sept. 8, 1951, Nov. 4, 1951, Dec. 26, 1951.

13. *New York Times*, Aug. 27, 1950, Aug. 15, 1950; Packard 1951 *Annual Report*, p. 5.

14. *New York Times*, Aug. 27, 15, 1950; *U.S. News & World Report*, Nov. 3, 1950, p. 16; *Business Week*, Oct. 28, 1950, p. 23.

15. *Business Week*, Dec. 29, 1951, p. 27; Ebert, p. 22.

16. Einstein, pp. 255–56 (quotation).

17. Ibid., p. 256 (quotation); Packard Board Minutes, June 27, 1951.

18. Ebert, p. 47.

19. Maxon, 1951 Packard Buyer Survey, in James J. Nance Papers, ser. 2, box 18, SNMA; "Packard," *Fortune* (Jan. 1937), p. 118.

20. Maxon, 1951 Packard Buyer Survey.

21. Ibid.

22. Maxon, 1952 Public Survey, in Nance Papers, ser. 2, box 18. Minutes of the Operating Committee, Nov. 28, 1951, Jan. 7, 1952, in Supporting Materials for the Board of Directors box, SNMA.

23. Kimes, p. 556; *New York Times*, Feb. 18, 1951.

24. Packard Board Minutes, Dec. 15, 1951; Kimes, pp. 553–54.

25. Kimes, p. 555.

26. Ibid., p. 556.

27. Packard 1950 *Annual Report*, p. 4; Packard Board Minutes, Nov. 21, 1950.

28. Packard 1950 *Annual Report*, p. 5; Packard Board Minutes, Aug. 22, 1951, Apr. 21, 1952; Packard 1952 *Annual Report*, p. 6; Packard 1951 *Annual Report*, pp. 5–6.

29. Packard 1947 *Annual Report*, n.p.; Packard 1950 *Annual Report*, p. 3; Packard 1952 *Annual Report*, p. 6.

30. Packard Board Minutes, Feb. 9, 1950; *Who's Who in America, 1960–61*, pp. 2, 267, 983; *New York Times*, Feb. 11, 1950, Apr. 17, 1951; Packard Board Minutes, Feb. 13, 1951.

31. Packard Board Minutes, June 29, 1950 (quotation), Dec. 27, 1950, Sept. 13, 1950; Frederick Rush, "The Nance Papers, Part V; The Merger Battle. Why I Broke with Jim Nance," *Packard Cormorant* (spring 1986), p. 3 (quotation).

32. E. R. Taylor to Nance, Apr. 16, 1951, in Porta Papers, ser. 1, box 2.

33. Ebert, p. 252; Richard Langworth and George L. Hamlin, eds., "James J. Nance Talks Packard," *Packard Cormorant* (autumn 1976), p. 4 (quotation).

34. Rush, "Why I Broke with Nance," p. 3; Packard Board Minutes, May 1, 1952; Kimes, p. 557; "Agreement Between the Packard Motor Car Company and James J. Nance," May 1, 1952, in Studebaker-Curtiss-Wright Transactions box, Nance Settlement file, SNMA.

35. *New York Times*, July 30, 1952; Packard Board Minutes, Sept. 13, 1950.

36. Booz Allen & Hamilton, "General Survey of the Packard Motor Car Company," in Porta Papers, ser. 2, boxes 5–9.

37. Booz Allen & Hamilton, "General Survey of Packard Motor Car Company, Volume I, Future Business Course," p. 19, in Porta Papers, ser. 2, box 5 (hereinafter Booz Allen I); Booz Allen & Hamilton, "General Survey of Packard Motor Car Company, Volume II, Summary Report and Top Organization," p. 1, Porta Papers, ser. 2, box 9 (hereinafter Booz Allen II).

38. Booz Allen II, p. 2 (quotation); Booz Allen I, pp. 6 (quotation), 29.

39. Booz Allen I, p. 23.

40. Booz Allen II, p. 32.

41. Ibid., p. 3. Quotations on pp. 32–33.

42. Ibid., pp. 34–36. Quotation on p. 34.

CHAPTER 6. *"Hail to the Chief"*

1. Goodrich, "The Rise and Fall of Packard as I Saw It," p. 8; Stout interview, Apr. 29, 1987; *Detroit Free-Press*, May 13, 1952; *Time*, May 19, 1952, p. 102; Lyman Slack, interview by author, Dec. 11, 1987; Michael Kollins, interview by author, June 21, 1988; Margery Warren, interview by John B. Wolford, Aug. 28, 1984, for the Indiana University Oral History Research Center, Bloomington.

2. *Fortune* (June 1950), p. 160.

3. *Detroit News*, June 24, 1952; *Detroit Free-Press*, Aug. 22, 1954.

4. *Detroit News*, June 24, 1952; *Who's Who in America, 1956–57*, p. 1874.

5. *Time*, Nov. 11, 1951, pp. 98, 99.

6. *Fortune* (June 1950), pp. 160, 162; *Newsweek*, May 26, 1952, p. 82.

7. *Time*, Nov. 26, 1951, p. 99.

8. *Cleveland Plain Dealer*, Feb. 19, 1978.

9. *Fortune* (June 1950), p. 162.

10. *Business Week*, May 17, 1952, p. 29.

11. Nance to H. W. Hitchcock, Oct. 7, 1952, in Nance Papers, ser. 1, box 19; *Detroit News*, June 24, 1952; *Newsweek*, Nov. 3, 1952, p. 78.

12. Richard Stout, interview by author, Apr. 29, 1987; "Official Program, Camp Packard II, Sept. 17–19, 1954," in Richard Stout Collection, Delray Beach, Fla.

13. Stout, interview, Apr. 29, 1987.

14. Ibid.; Goodrich, "The Packard I Knew," n.p.; Michael Kollins, interview by author, June 21, 1988.

15. Stout, interview, Apr. 29, 1987; interview with Clara Brown, conducted by John B. Wolford, Aug. 27, 1984, p. 34, for the Indiana University Oral History Research Center, Bloomington.

16. Nance's speech to Packard Motor Car Club, Los Angeles, Sept. 14, 1980.

17. Author's survey of Packard papers, SNMA.

18. Ibid.

19. Ibid.; Warren, interview, Aug. 28, 1984, p. 13.

20. Warren, interview, Aug. 28, 1984, pp. 15 (quotation), 16.

21. Ibid., pp. 14–15.

22. *Newsweek*, Nov. 3, 1952, p. 78 (quotation); Packard Board Minutes, May 19, 1952; Milton Tibbetts to Nance, June 3, 1952, in Nance Papers, ser. 1, box 19; Packard Board Minutes, June 25, 1952.

23. *New York Times*, July 30, 1952; Packard Public Relations release, July 29, 1952, in Nance Papers, ser. 1, box 19; Packard Board Minutes, July 23, 1952, Sept. 24, 1952, July 8, 1953, Oct. 6, 1953; Van Ark to Nance, Dec. 10, 1952, in Nance Papers, ser. 1, box 20; Kimes, p. 561.

24. *New York Times*, July 24, 1952; *Business Week*, July 26, 1952, p. 24; Packard Public Relations release, July 29, 1952, in Nance Papers, ser. 1, box 19; *New York Times*, Aug. 22, 1952; Behnke to Nance, Nov. 7, 1952, in Nance Papers, ser. 1, box 18; Packard Executive Committee Minutes, Nov. 24, 1952, in Nance Papers, ser. 1, box 15; *New York Times*, Dec. 13, 1952.

25. Nance to Grant, Sept. 5, 1952, in Nance Papers, ser. 1, box 19 (quotation); Nance to Grant, Dec. 29, 1952, ibid. (quotation); Nance to Graves, Dec. 24, 1952, ibid. (quotation).

26. Graves to J. R. Ferguson, Oct. 30, 1952, in Nance Papers, ser. 1, box 19; Nance to Stout, Sept. 22, 1980, in Stout Collection, Delray Beach (quotation).

27. Nance, "A Tide in the Affairs of Men," *Packard Cormorant* (spring 1976), p. 10 (quotation); *New York Times*, July 30, 1952 (quotation); *Newsweek*, Sept. 22, 1952, p. 83 (quotation); Nance to Grant, Sept. 5, 1952, in Nance Papers, ser. 1, box 19.

28. Nance to Fred Adams, Dec. 5, 1952, in Nance Papers, ser. 1, box 20 (quotation); Nance to L. R. Maxon, Dec. 29, 1952, in Nance Papers, ser. 1, box 18 (quotation).

29. Nance to Monaghan and R. W. Straughn, Oct. 6, 1952, in Nance Papers, ser. 1, box 19 (quotation); *Newsweek*, Nov. 3, 1952, p. 78.

30. Clipper Program Planning Committee, Oct. 3, 1952, in Nance Papers, ser. 1, box 19.

31. Nance to C. E. Briggs, Nov. 3, 1952, in Nance Papers, ser. 1, box 18 (quotation); Lee Copp to Maxon, Oct. 20, 1952, ibid.

32. Nance speech to "key man" group, Aug. 1952, in Nance Papers, ser. 1, box 19.

33. Ibid.

34. Monaghan to Nance, Aug. 1952, ibid.; Packard Executive Committee Minutes, Dec. 1952, ibid.

35. Packard Executive Committee Minutes, Sept. 5, 29, 1952, in Nance Papers, ser. 1, box 15; Nance to Walters, Oct. 16, 1952, in Nance Papers, ser. 1, box 20 (quotation); *Who's Who in America, 1974–75*, p. 1303.

36. Packard Dealers' Survey Results, Dec. 1952, n.p., in Nance Papers, ser. 1, box 19.

37. *New York Times*, Nov. 20, 1952.

38. Grant to Nance, June 26, 1952, in Nance Papers, ser. 1, box 19.

39. Packard Public Relations release, July 29, 1952, ibid.; Grant to Nance, Aug. 5, 1952, ibid.

40. Grant to Nance, Oct. 2, 1952, ibid.

41. Nance to George Reifel, July 22, 1952, ibid.

42. Packard Board Minutes, Jan. 28, 1953.

43. Nance to Brodie, June 6, 1952, in Nance Papers, ser. 1, box 18.

44. Nance to Reifel, June 27, 1952, in Nance Papers, ser. 1, box 19.

45. Packard Board Minutes, Oct. 29, 1952; Nance to Grant, Nov. 14, 1952, in Nance Papers, ser. 1, box 19; "Long Range Planning: Body Manufacturing," Nov. 21, 1952, ibid. (quotation).

46. Packard Board Minutes, Dec. 20, 1952, Jan. 28, 1953, Feb. 17, 1953, Mar. 26, 1953.

47. *Business Week*, May 17, 1952, p. 29; C. W. Brownell to Nance, June 6, 1952, in Nance Papers, ser. 1, box 19 (quotation); Special Meeting of Packard Executive Committee, minutes, Sept. 5, 1952, in Nance Papers, ser. 1, box 15 (quotation); Packard Board Minutes, Dec. 20, 1952 (quotation).

48. Special Meeting of Packard Executive Committee, minutes, Sept. 5, 1952, in Nance Papers, ser. 1, box 15.

49. Packard Board Minutes, Jan. 28, 1953; Nance to C. E. Briggs, July 30, 1952, in Nance Papers, ser. 1, box 19; Nance to Reifel, Aug. 28, 1952, ibid. (quotation).

50. Special meeting of Product Planning Committee, minutes, Nov. 13, 1952, in Nance Papers, ser. 1, box 15.

51. Nance to Grant, Dec. 23, 1952, in Nance Papers, ser. 1, box 5; Grant to Nance, Dec. 30, 1952, ibid. (quotation); Nance to C. E. Briggs, Dec. 24, 1952, in Nance Papers, ser. 1, box 18 (quotation); Grant to Nance, Aug. 20, 1952, in Nance Papers, ser. 1, box 19.

CHAPTER 7. *"God Save the King—and Packard!"*

1. Nance's goals, Jan. 1953, in Nance Papers, ser. 1, box 16 (quotation); *New York Times*, Jan. 4, 1953.

2. Walters to Nance, Feb. 17, 1953, in Nance Papers, ser. 1, box 11.

3. Nance to Grant, Mar. 17, 1953, in Nance Papers, ser. 1, box 5; Nance to David Austin, Feb. 11, 1953, in Nance Papers, ser. 1, box 4 (quotation); Avery Adams to Nance, Feb. 4, 1953, ibid.

4. Packard Board Minutes, Feb. 17, 1953, Mar. 26, 1953, Apr. 29, 1953, May 27, 1953.

5. Packard Board Minutes, Mar. 26, 1953; Nance to Grant, Mar. 3, 1953, in Nance Papers, ser. 1, box 5.

6. *Time*, May 14, 1953, pp. 96 (quotation), 98.

7. Packard Board Minutes, Apr. 20, 1953, May 27, 1953, July 18, 1953, Aug. 26, 1953.

8. Nance to Grant, Apr. 13, 1953, in Nance Papers, ser. 1, box 5 (quotation); Packard Board Minutes, May 27, 1953 (quotation).

9. *Business Week*, Oct. 31, 1953, p. 32; C. F. McCandless to Nance, Dec. 15, 1953, in Nance Papers, ser. 1, box 14.

10. *U.S. News & World Report*, July 17, 1953, p. 73.

11. Ibid.; *New York Times*, July 20, 1953.

12. Editors of *Automobile Quarterly*, pp. 142–43; McCandless to Nance, Dec. 15, 1953, in Nance Papers, ser. 1, box 14.

13. McCandless to Nance, Dec. 15, 1953, in Nance Papers, ser. 1, box 14; *U.S. News & World Report*, Aug. 2, 1953, p. 27.

14. Walters to Nance, Apr. 23, 1953, in Nance Papers, ser. 1, box 11; Nance to C. E. Briggs, Mar. 6, 1953, in Nance Papers, ser. 1, box 5 (quotation).

15. Ross Schroeder to Nance, Apr. 28, 1953, in Nance Papers, ser. 1, box 18; *New York Times*, Apr. 29, 1953 (quotation).

16. Paul Shine to Nance, Mar. 3, 1953, in Nance Papers, ser. 1, box 11; Packard Board Minutes, May 27, 1953.

17. John Briggs to Nance, Mar. 18, 1953, in Nance Papers, ser. 1, box 18; Nance to Shine, June 23, 1953, in Nance Papers, ser. 1, box 11.

18. Nance to Monaghan, June 11, 1953, in Nance Papers, ser. 1, box 6 (quotation); Nance to C. E. Briggs, Sept. 9, 1953, in Nance Papers, ser. 1, box 5.

19. George Brodie to Nance, Apr. 30, 1953, in Nance Papers, ser. 1, box 13; Robert Blythin to Nance, May 13, 1953, ibid.; Walters to Nance, May 27, 1953, ibid.; Wilmer Hoge to Nance, Apr. 4, 1953, ibid.; Nance to C. E. Briggs, Sept. 9, 1953, in Nance Papers, ser. 1, box 5 (quotation).

20. Nance to C. E. Briggs and Walters, June 19, 1953, in Nance Papers, ser. 1, box 16; Nance to Walters, June 29, 1953, ibid. (quotation); Nance to Van Ark, Sept. 9, 1953, in Nance Papers, ser. 1, box 11; H. H. Johnson to Nance, Sept. 16, 1953, ibid.

21. Nance to Walters and O. F. Frost, July 8, 1953, in Nance Papers, ser. 1, box 11 (quotation); Nance to Grant, Sept. 1, 1953, in Nance Papers, ser. 1, box 5 (quotation).

22. Packard Board Minutes, Nov. 18, 1953; Nance to B. Burlingame, Oct. 28, 1953, in Nance Papers, ser. 1, box 5.

23. Nance to "Key Men," Nov. 13, 1953, in Nance Papers, ser. 1, box 16.

24. Burlingame to Grant, Dec. 1, 1953, in Nance Papers, ser. 1, box 5.

25. Packard Board Minutes, July 8, 1953, Aug. 26, 1953, Oct. 6, 1953, Nov. 18, 1953, Dec. 21, 1953.

26. Packard Board Minutes, Dec. 21, 1953; Grant to Nance, Nov. 11, 1953, in Nance Papers, ser. 1, box 13.

27. Grant to Nance, Dec. 17, 1953, in Nance Papers, ser. 1, box 15.

28. Packard Board Minutes, Jan. 19, 1953.

29. Nance, "A Tide in the Affairs of Men," *Packard Cormorant* (spring 1976), p. 11.

30. Goldman, pp. 248 (quotation), 249.

31. Quotations in Diggins, pp. 130, 136, and Kimes, p. 579.

32. Drew Pearson's Merry-Go-Round, undated, unidentified newspaper clipping, in Hoffman Papers, box 150, HST.

33. Packard Board Minutes, Mar. 2, 1953, July 8, 1953; Brodie to Nance, June 29, 1953, in Nance Papers, ser. 1, box 5.

34. Nance to Roger Kyes, Aug. 26, 1953, in Nance Papers, ser. 1, box 3.

35. Nance to Grant, Sept. 17, 1953, in Nance Papers, ser. 1, box 5.

36. W. H. Klenke to Nance, Sept. 30, 1953, in Nance Papers, ser. 1, box 18; Packard Board Minutes, Aug. 26, 1953.

37. Brodie to Nance, June 19, 1953, in Nance Papers, ser. 1, box 5; Brodie to Nance, Jan. 1, 1954, in Nance Papers, ser. 1, box 12; Packard Board Minutes, Oct. 6, 1953.

38. Packard Board Minutes, Dec. 21, 1953, Oct. 6, 1953; Brodie to Nance, Oct. 30, 1953, in Nance Papers, ser. 1, box 5; Brodie to Nance, Jan. 1, 1954, in Nance Papers, ser. 1, box 12.

39. *Detroit Free-Press*, May 27, 1954.

40. Nance to Grant, Feb. 3, 1953, in Nance Papers, ser. 1, box 5.

41. *New York Times*, Oct. 24, 1953; Nance's memo of conversation with C. F. Fisher, Nov. 13, 1953, in Nance Papers, ser. 1, box 15 (quotation).

42. Packard Board Minutes, Nov. 18, 1953.

43. Nance's summary of discussion with Tex Colbert, Dec. 31, 1953, in Nance Papers, ser. 1, box 14 (quotation); Packard Board Minutes, Dec. 21, 1953.

44. Nance's summary of discussion with Colbert, Dec. 31, 1953, in Nance Papers, ser. 1, box 14.

45. *New York Times*, Dec. 29, 1953; Grant to Nance, Jan. 5, 1954, in Nance Papers, ser. 1, box 14 (quotation).

46. R. E. Bremer to Nance, Jan. 7, 1954, in Nance Papers, ser. 1, box 14; Nance to Grant, Jan. 8, 1954, ser. 1, box 13.

47. Grant to Nance, Mar. 24, 1954, in Nance Papers, ser. 1, box 13; Packard Facilities Planning document, Feb. 1, 1954, pp. 12 (quotation), 14 (quotation), 16, 17, ibid.

48. Packard Board Minutes, Feb. 17, 1954, May 13, 1954; Nance to Colbert, May 18, 1954, in Nance Papers, ser. 1, box 7.

49. Packard Board Minutes, May 13, 1954; Nance to Colbert, May 18, 1954, in Nance Papers, ser. 1, box 7.

50. Packard Board Minutes, June 17, 1954; *Detroit Free-Press*, May 27, 28, 1954.

51. Nance to Product Planning Committee, Apr. 2, 1953, in Nance Papers, ser. 1, box 18.

52. Packard 1953 *Annual Report*, p. 13 (quotation); Kimes, p. 570.

53. *Collectible Automobile* (Oct. 1986), pp. 10–12, 15 (quotation); Kimes, pp. 580–81.

54. *Collectible Automobile* (Oct. 1986), p. 16; *Detroit Free-Press*, Feb. 8, 18 (quotation), 1954.

55. Packard Board Minutes, Feb. 17, 1954, Mar. 26, 1954; Grant to Nance, Jan. 13, 1953, in Nance Papers, ser. 1, box 6.

56. Nance to Graves, Oct. 14, 1953, in Nance Papers, ser. 1, box 6 (quotation); Vincent to C. E. Briggs, Jan. 11, 1954, in Nance Papers, ser. 1, box 4; Briggs to Nance, Jan. 21, 1954, ibid. (quotation).

57. Graves to Nance, June 30, 1954, in Nance Papers, ser. 1, box 13.

58. Vincent to Nance, May 27, 1953, in Nance Papers, ser. 1, box 18.

59. Graves to Nance, June 25, 1953, in Nance Papers, ser. 1, box 6.

60. Packard Board Minutes, July 8, 1953; Bremer to Graves, June 18, 1954, in Nance Papers, ser. 1, box 12; Nance to Graves, Oct. 1, 1954, in Nance Papers, ser. 1, box 4; W. E. Schwieder to Graves, Oct. 25, 1954, ibid.

61. Bremer to Nance, Jan. 7, 1954, in Nance Papers, ser. 1, box 14; Kimes, pp. 588–89; A. E. Wilson to Grant, June 5, 1953, in Nance Papers, ser. 1, box 18.

62. Nance to Graves, Feb. 18, 1953, in Nance Papers, ser. 1, box 6; Graves to Nance, Feb. 19, 1954, ibid. (quotation); Robin Jones, "My Years with Packard Styling (2): The Packard Challenge," *Packard Cormorant* (winter 1993–94), p. 16.

63. *New York Times*, Mar. 11, 1953 (quotation), Apr. 29, 1953.

64. Grant to Nance, Feb. 4, 17 (quotation), 1953, in Nance papers, ser. 1, box 5; Nance to Grant, Feb. 4, 1954, ibid.

65. Nance to Walters, Aug. 31, 1953, in Nance Papers, ser. 1, box 11.

CHAPTER 8. *"Rapidly Approaching Bankruptcy"*

1. Editors of *Automobile Quarterly*, p. 143.

2. Nance to Grant, Sept. 17, 1953, in Nance Papers, ser. 1, box 5 (quotation); "Major Objectives for 1954," n.d., in Nance Papers, ser. 1, box 12.

3. "Major Objectives for 1954," in Nance Papers, ser. 1, box 12.

4. Packard sales department, "A Brief Summary of the Current Position," n.d. [ca. mid-1953], in Nance Papers, ser. 1, box 16; Editors of *Automobile Quarterly*, p. 143; Bremer to Nance, Jan. 6, 1954, in Nance Papers, ser. 1, box 12.

5. Packard Board Minutes, Dec. 21, 1953, Feb. 17, 1954, Apr. 19, 1954, May 13, 1954.

6. Packard Board Minutes, Oct. 6, 1953.

7. Packard Board Minutes, Nov. 18, 1953, Feb. 17, 1954, Apr. 19, 1954, May 13, 1954.

8. *Automotive News*, June 14, 1954.

9. Packard 1953 *Annual Report*, p. 14; Packard Board Minutes, July 28, 1954.

10. "Packard Dealer Survey," with R. W. Russell to Nance, Apr. 23, 1954, in Nance Papers, ser. 1, box 14.

11. "Continuing Owner Survey, February–March 1954," with Russell to Nance, May 22, 1954, ibid.; U.S. Department of Commerce, p. 95.

12. Packard Board Minutes, Nov. 18, 1953, Dec. 21, 1953, Feb. 17, 1954.

13. Packard Board Minutes, Jan. 19, 1954, Feb. 17, 1954; *Detroit Free-Press*, Feb. 9, 1954.

14. Burlingame to Nance, Mar. 5, 1954, in Nance Papers, ser. 1, box 13.

15. *New York Times*, May 4, 1954; Packard Board Minutes, Apr. 19, 1954, May 13, 1954.

16. Packard Board Minutes, Dec. 21, 1953, Jan. 19, 1954, Feb. 17, 1954, Apr. 19, 1954, July 28, 1954.

17. Grant to Nance, Mar. 1, 1954, in Porta Papers, ser. 1, box 2.

18. Ibid.

19. Ibid.

20. Nance to C. E. Briggs, May 12, 1954, in Nance Papers, ser. 1, box 12.

1. Nance to Brodie, Feb. 6, 1953, in Nance Papers, ser. 1, box 5 (quotation); Henry Alexander to Nance, Mar. 2, 1953, in Nance Papers, ser. 1, box 1; Harold Vance to Hoffman, Feb. 6, 1953, in Hoffman Papers, box 150, HST; Alexander to Nance, Mar. 23, 1953, in Nance Papers, ser. 1, box 1 (quotation).

2. Nance to Brodie, Mar. 17, 1953, in Nance Papers, ser. 1, box 5; Brodie to Nance, Mar. 23, 1953, ibid. (quotation).

3. Alexander to Nance, Apr. 4, 1953, in Nance Papers, ser. 1, box 1.

4. Quotations in Alexander to Nance, Mar. 30, 1953, Apr. 10, 1953, in Nance Papers, ser. 1, box 1.

5. Nance to Grant, June 11, 1953, in Nance Papers, ser. 1, box 5.

6. Ibid.; Grant to Nance, July 15, 1953, in Nance Papers, ser. 1, box 5.

7. Nance to Grant, Aug. 10, 1953, ibid.

8. *New York Times*, Oct. 7, 1953; Packard Board Minutes, Aug. 26, 1953.

9. "Consumer Attitude Toward Independent Automobile Companies," Oct. 24, 1953, in Nance Papers, ser. 1, box 5.

10. *New York Times*, Oct. 24, 1953; Edwin Blair to Nance, Oct. 27, 1953, in Nance Papers, ser. 1, box 1 (quotation).

11. *New York Times*, Nov. 4, 1953; *Newsweek*, Nov. 11, 1953.

12. Packard Board Minutes, Nov. 18, 1953.

13. *New York Times*, Nov. 27, 1953; Nance to William Gellert, Dec. 1, 1953, in Nance Papers, ser. 1, box 2; Graves to Nance, Dec. 3, 1953, in Nance Papers, ser. 1, box 13 (quotation).

14. Studebaker Board Minutes, Apr. 28, 1953, p. 1460; May 22, 1953, p. 1465; June 26, 1953, pp. 1471, 1472; July 24, 1953, p. 1487; Sept. 25, 1953, p. 1492.

15. Studebaker Board Minutes, Sept. 25, 1953, pp. 1496 (quotation), 1497.

16. Studebaker Board Minutes, Oct. 23, 1953, p. 1500, Nov. 2, 1953, pp. 1507-8.

17. Studebaker Board Minutes, Dec. 18, 1953, pp. 1513-14, 1515, 1516-17.

18. Studebaker Board Minutes, Jan. 22, 1954, pp. 1518-20 (quotation), 1522, Feb. 23, 1954, p. 1525.

19. "Conference with Borden Notes," Feb. 1, 1956, in Porta Papers, ser. 1, box 4 (quotation); Nance to Grant, Jan. 8, 1954, in Nance Papers, ser. 1, box 13; Bremer to Nance, Jan. 11, 1954, in Nance Papers, ser. 1, box 12; Nance to C. E. Briggs, Jan. 18, 1954, ibid.

20. *New York Times*, Jan. 15, 1954 (quotation); Packard Board Minutes, Jan. 19, 1954 (quotation), Feb. 17, 1954; John McQuigg to Nance, Jan. 29, 1954, in Nance Papers, ser. 1, box 8 (quotation).

21. Packard Board Minutes, Feb. 17, 1954; Nance to William Harding, Feb. 2, 1954, in Nance Papers, ser. 1, box 10 (quotation).

22. Packard Board Minutes, Feb. 17, 1954.

23. *New York Times*, Mar. 6, 1954.

24. W. H. Ferry to author, Oct. 28, 1991; Packard Board Minutes, Aug. 17, 1954; Ferry to Nance, Mar. 17, 1954, in Nance Papers, ser. 1, box 14 (quotation).

25. Packard Board Minutes, Apr. 19, 1954.

26. Studebaker Board Minutes, Apr. 28, 1954, p. 1548, Mar. 26, 1954, p. 1535, Apr. 28, 1954, pp. 1550-54 (quotation on p. 1554).

27. Packard Board Minutes, Apr. 19, 1954, May 13, 1954.

28. Hoffman's 1954 appointment schedule, in Hoffman Papers, box 95, HST (quotation); Nance to Brodie, Apr. 21, 1954, in Nance Papers, ser. 1, box 12.

29. Grant and E. C. Mendler, "Benefits of Merger of Studebaker and Packard," May 1, 1954, pp. 1 (quotation), 2; Lehman Brothers, "Studebaker and Packard, Part II: Suggested Basis of Consolidation," May 4, 1954, both in Packard Board of Directors, Supporting Documents, May 12, 1954, meeting, SNMA.

30. Grant and Mendler, "Benefits of Merger," pp. 4, 7, 16–18, 27 (quotation).

31. Lehman Brothers, "Studebaker and Packard, Part II," May 4, 1954, pp. 1, 2, in Packard Board of Directors, Supporting Documents, misfiled under Annual Reports, 1936–38.

32. Ibid., pp. 6–8, 5 (quotation), 9–10. The numbers do not quite add up because of fractional shares.

33. Packard Board Minutes, May 13, 1954.

34. "Purchase Agreement between the Studebaker Corporation and the Packard Motor Car Company," June 22, 1954, in Studebaker Board Meetings, Supplementary Documents, SNMA.

35. Studebaker Board Minutes, May 28, 1954, pp. 1558–60; Packard Board Minutes, June 17, 1954; Nance to George Martin, July 20, 1954, in Nance Papers, ser. 1, box 9.

36. Studebaker Board of Directors, Supplementary Documents, June 10, 28, 1954.

37. Packard Board Minutes, July 18, 1954; Studebaker Board Minutes, Aug. 16, 1954, p. 1575, July 6, 1954 (rough draft, n.p.), July 23, 1954, pp. 1573–74.

38. Packard Board Minutes, July 28, 1954 (quotation); Grant to Nance, July 26, 1954, in Nance Papers, ser. 1, box 13.

39. Robert Ebert, "An Economic Analysis of the Decline of the Packard Motor Car Company," *Packards International Magazine* (July–Aug. 1968), p. 19; Richard M. Langworth and George L. Hamlin, eds., "James J. Nance Talks Packard," *Packard Cormorant* (autumn 1976), p. 5 (quotation).

40. *Business Week*, June 26, 1954, p. 28 (quotation); *Time*, June 28, 1954, p. 84; Nance to Grant, July 21, 1954, in Nance Papers, ser. 1, box 13 (quotation).

41. Grant to Nance, Aug. 10, 1954, in Nance Papers, ser. 1, box 13.

42. Ibid.

43. Ibid.

44. George Romney to Nance, June 24, 1954, in Nance Papers, ser. 1, box 6 (quotation); McQuigg to Nance, June 28, 1954, in Nance Papers, ser. 1, box 8 (quotation); Nance to Romney, June 28, 1954, in Nance Papers, ser. 1, box 6.

45. Shareholders' letters quoted in Frederick Rush, "The Nance Papers, Part V; The Merger Battle. Why I Broke with Jim Nance," *Packard Cormorant* (summer 1986), pp. 7–13.

46. *Studebaker Spotlight* (Aug.–Sept. 1954), p. 2.

47. Packard Board Minutes, Nov. 11, 1954; Dawes, pp. 123–24.

48. Packard Board Minutes, July 28, 1954.

CHAPTER 10. *Slow Off the Line*

1. Ewing Reilley to Nance, June 28, 1954, in Nance Papers, ser. 1, box 21.

2. Nance notes, n.d. [ca. June 1954], ibid. (quotation); Reilley to Nance, June 28, 1954, ibid. (quotation).

3. Grant and E. C. Mendler, "Benefits of Merger of Studebaker and Packard," May 1, 1954, in Packard Board of Directors, Supporting Documents, May 12, 1954, meeting, SNMA; Reilley to Nance, June 28, 1954, in Nance Papers, ser. 1, box 21 (quotation).

4. Nance to Bremer, July 6, 1954, in Nance Papers, ser. 1, box 12; Nance to Bremer, Sept. 29, 1954, in Nance Papers, ser. 1, box 13 (quotation).

5. Nance to Grant, Sept. 7, 1954, in Nance Papers, ser. 1, box 13 (quotation); Nance to Churchill and Graves, Sept. 7, 1954, in Nance Papers, ser. 1, box 10.

6. Studebaker-Packard Corporation, Board of Directors Minutes, Oct. 4, 1954, in SNMA.

7. Reilley to Nance, Sept. 24, 1954, in Nance Papers, ser. 1, box 21; Nance to Reilley, Oct. 4, 1954, in Nance Papers, ser. 1, box 9 (quotation); Mendler to Hoffman, Nov. 13, 1956, in Hoffman Papers, box 47, HST (quotation).

8. Reilley to Nance, Oct. 1, 1954, p. vi, in Nance Papers, ser. 1, box 21.

9. Ibid., p. iv.

10. Ibid., p. vii.

11. *New York Times*, Nov. 29, 1954; *Studebaker Spotlight* (Dec. 1954), p. 2; Nance to administration and executive management, Dec. 15, 30, 1954, both in Nance Papers, ser. 1, box 14; *Studebaker Spotlight* (Jan. 1955), p. 2; S-P Board Minutes, Jan. 21, 1955.

12. S-P Press Release, Aug. 24, 1955, in Nance Papers, ser. 2, box 2; R. P. Laughna vita, ca. Jan. 1, 1955, in Nance Papers, ser. 2, box 3.

13. Nance to administrative and executive group, Jan. 24, 1955, in Nance Papers, ser. 2, box 4; Nance to administrative and executive group, Jan. 25, 1955, ibid.; Nance to administrative and executive group, Jan. 28, 1955, ibid.; *New York Times*, Aug. 25, 1955.

14. List of Officers as of Feb. 1, 1955, in Nance Papers, ser. 2, box 2.

15. Mendler to Hoffman, Nov. 13, 1956, in Hoffman Papers, box 47, HST.

16. Nance to Members of Operating Committee, Packard Division, Jan. 18, 1955, in Nance Papers, ser. 2, box 2.

17. Nance's notes for Sept. 9, 1955, meeting, ibid.

18. V. L. Casson to Nance, Mar. 29, 1956, in Porta Papers, ser. 2, box 3.

19. Nance to Members of the Administration Committee, Apr. 19, 1956, in Nance Papers, ser. 2, box 12.

20. Nance's notes for conference with Borden, Feb. 1, 1956, in Porta Papers, ser. 1, box 4 (quotation); Outline of talk given to Chicago bankers, Apr. 18, 20, 1956, ibid.

21. Grant to Nance, June 22, 1955, in Nance Papers, ser. 2, box 2; Mendler to Hoffman, Nov. 13, 1956, in Hoffman Papers, box 47, HST.

22. Grant to Nance, June 22, 1955, in Nance Papers, ser. 2, box 2; Nance to Grant, Nov. 3, 1954, in Nance Papers, ser. 1, box 13.

23. Grant to Nance, June 22, 1955, in Nance Papers, ser. 2, box 2.

24. Ibid.

25. S-P Board Minutes, Nov. 19, 1954; Hoffman to Hugo Morrison, Mar. 2, 1956, in Hoffman Papers, box 15, HST; *U.S. News & World Report*, Aug. 20, 1954, p. 102.

26. *U.S. News & World Report*, Aug. 20, 1954, p. 98.

27. Hoffman to Louis Horvath, July 29, 1954, in Porta Papers, ser. 1, box 4; *New York Times*, Aug. 6, 13, 1954; *Newsweek*, Aug. 20, 1954, p. 101; *Business Week*, July 16, 1955, p. 133.

28. S-P Board Minutes, Oct. 4, 1954, Nov. 19, 1954, Dec. 17, 1954.

29. Nance's notes on talk with Walter Reuther, n.d., in Porta Papers, ser. 1, box 4.

30. S-P Board Minutes, Jan. 21, 1955 (quotation); *New York Times*, Jan. 20, 22, 1955; C. D. Scribner to Nance, Jan. 20, 1955, in Nance Papers, ser. 2, box 6 (quotation).

31. Hoffman to Paul Clark, Feb. 1, 1955, in Hoffman Papers, box 46, HST (quotation); "Memorandum of Understanding Between Studebaker-Packard and Local #5," Feb. 3, 1955, in Porta Papers, ser. 1, box 4.

32. S-P Board Minutes, Mar. 18, 1955 (quotation); S-P handwritten board minutes, June 17, 1955 (quotation).

33. *New York Times*, July 7, 10 (quotation), 15, 1955; S-P Board Minutes, July 15, 1955; *Business Week*, July 16, 1955, p. 132.

34. *New York Times*, July 21, 1955; *Wall Street Journal*, July 21, 1955.

35. *Business Week*, July 16, 1955, p. 134 (quotation), July 23, 1955, p. 118; *Des Moines Sunday Register*, July 24, 1955.

36. *Business Week*, July 23, 1955, p. 118.

37. *New York Times*, Aug. 2, 1955; *Wall Street Journal*, Aug. 3, 17, 1955; *South Bend Tribune*, Aug. 14, 1955.

38. *New York Times*, Sept. 2, 11, 1955; Scribner to Nance, Jan. 20, 1955, in Nance Papers, ser. 2, box 6; *Business Week*, Oct. 22, 1955, Nov. 10, 1955; *Wall Street Journal*, Nov. 10, 1955.

39. Nance to S-P Directors, Nov. 9, 1955, in Hoffman Papers, box 46, HST (quotation); S-P handwritten board minutes, Aug. 19, 1955.

40. *New York Times*, Jan. 8, 1956; *Wall Street Journal*, Jan. 9, 1956; Nance to Hoffman, Jan. 9, 1956, in Hoffman Papers, box 13, HST (quotation).

41. *Newsweek*, Jan. 16, 1956 (quotation); *Wall Street Journal*, Jan. 9, 1956; S-P handwritten board minutes, Nov. 18, 1955; Nance to Laughna and Churchill, Jan. 11, 1956, in Nance Papers, ser. 2, box 12 (quotation).

42. Editors of *Automobile Quarterly*, p. 143; "S-P Volume Projection, 1946–1957," n.d., in Nance Papers, ser. 2, box 1.

43. Editors of *Automobile Quarterly*, p. 143; S-P Board Minutes, Dec. 17, 1954.

44. Kimes, p. 595; Dawes, p. 124; S-P Board Minutes, Nov. 19, 1954; N. C. DeSantis to Nance, Nov. 29, 1954, in Nance Papers, ser. 1, box 13; Nance to Graves, note on DeSantis letter, Nov. 29, 1954, in Nance Papers, ser. 1, box 13 (quotation); S-P Board Minutes, Dec. 17, 1954 (quotation); Nance to Powers, Jan. 20, 1955, in Nance Papers, ser. 2, box 5 (quotation).

45. Grant to Nance, Jan. 13, 1955, in Porta Papers, ser. 1, box 1; S-P Board Minutes, Mar. 18, 1955; S-P handwritten board minutes, Mar. 18, 1955 (quotation).

46. Casson to Nance, Apr. 13, 1955, in Nance Papers, ser. 2, box 2; Nance to Powers, Apr. 22, 1955, in Nance Papers, ser. 2, box 5 (quotation).

47. Kimes, p. 596 (quotation); Gordon Van Ark to Nance, Feb. 23, 1955, in Nance Papers, ser. 2, box 1 (quotation).

48. "Presidents Report, Customer Relations Department, March, 1955," in Nance Papers, ser. 2, box 3; S-P handwritten board minutes, Mar. 18, 1955; Nance to Powers, Mar. 7, 1955, in Kimes, p. 596 (quotation); Nance to Powers, Mar. 17, 1955, ibid. (quotation).

49. Kimes, p. 597.

50. D. S. McNally to Mendler, Sept. 16, 1955, in Porta Papers, ser. 2, box 3.

51. Kimes, p. 597; S-P Board Minutes, Jan. 21, 1955.

52. S-P Board Minutes, Apr. 18, 1955; Nance to Laughna, June 13, 1955, in Nance Papers, ser. 2, box 3 (quotation); Nance's note on Shine to Nance, July 6, 1955, in Nance Papers, ser. 2, box 6 (quotation).

53. Nance to H. L. Misch, Aug. 31, 1955, in Nance Papers, ser. 2, box 4; Kimes, p. 588.

54. *Wall Street Journal*, May 10, 1955; *New York Times*, May 20, 1955; Grant to Nance, June 3, 1955, in Nance Papers, ser. 2, box 2.

55. S-P Board Minutes, Aug. 19, 1955; S-P handwritten board minutes, Aug. 19, 1955 (quotation), Sept. 16, 1955.

56. Administrative committee minutes, Oct. 31, 1955, in Nance Papers, ser. 2, box 12; S-P handwritten board minutes, Nov. 18, 1955 (quotation).

57. David Bird II, "Automotive Renaissance Man: Dick Teague," *Automobile Quarterly* (winter 1992), pp. 6–9.

58. Kimes, pp. 584, 586; Bird, "Teague," p. 10 (quotation).

59. Kimes, pp. 588, 589–91.

60. Ibid., pp. 592–94.

61. *New York Times*, Apr. 13, 1955 (quotation), July 1, 1955 (quotation); Richard Stout, interview by author, Apr. 29, 1987.

62. Bird, "Teague," p. 13 (quotation); Kimes, p. 587.

63. Bird, "Teague," p. 13; Kimes, p. 587.

64. Bird, "Teague," p. 13.

65. Kimes, pp. 608, 614–15, 625–26; Stout, interview by author, Apr. 29, 1987.

CHAPTER 11. *"Life or Death for Packard in 1955"*

1. *New York Times*, Oct. 5, 6, 1954.

2. Clare Briggs to Nance, Aug. 23, 1954, in Nance Papers, ser. 1, box 12.

3. Nance to W. E. Macke, Sept. 13, 1954, in Nance Papers, ser. 1, box 14; H. A. Wichert to Nance, Sept. 24, 1954, ibid. (quotation).

4. Nance to Clare Briggs and Dan O'Madigan, Sept. 13, 1954, in Nance Papers, ser. 1, box 12 (quotation); "General Proposal for Merchandising the Packard Line in 1955," n.d., ibid.

5. Nance to Clare Briggs, Oct. 18, 1954, ibid.

6. *New York Times*, Jan. 4, 1955; Clare Briggs to Nance, Jan. 25, 1955, in Nance Papers, ser. 2, box 2 (quotation); Nance to Clare Briggs and O'Madigan, Dec. 3, 1954, in Nance Papers, ser. 1, box 13.

7. Nance to O'Madigan and William Keller, Feb. 17, 1955, in Nance Papers, ser. 2, box 5.

8. Nance to O'Madigan, Mar. 7, 1955, in Nance Papers, separate unmarked folder.

9. Ibid.; Nance to O'Madigan, Sept. 25, 1955, in Nance Papers, ser. 2, box 5.

10. Edwards, p. 219.

11. S-P Board Minutes, Nov. 19, 1954; *Business Week*, Aug. 21, 1954, p. 59.

12. Nance to O'Madigan, Mar. 7, 1955, in Nance Papers, separate unmarked folder.

13. William Keller to District Sales Managers, Nov. 11, 1955, in Nance Papers, ser. 2, box 3.

14. Nance to Laughna, Dec. 27, 1955, ibid.; Nance to Churchill, Dec. 2, 1955, in Nance Papers, ser. 2, box 2 (quotation).

15. S-P Board Minutes, Aug. 19, 1955, Sept. 16, 1955, Dec. 16, 1955 (quotation); S-P handwritten board minutes, Aug. 19, 1955, Sept. 16, 1955.

16. *Business Week*, Dec. 17, 1955, p. 67; S-P Board Minutes, Jan. 20, 1956 (quotation).

17. *New York Times*, Jan. 3, 1956.

18. Nance to O'Madigan and Keller, Apr. 4, 1955, in Nance Papers, ser. 2, box 5.

19. Nance to Earle Anthony, Apr. 11, 1955, in Nance Papers, ser. 2, box 10.

20. *Wall Street Journal*, Dec. 12, 1955.

21. *New York Times*, Sept. 27, 1954 (quotation); *Chicago Tribune*, Sept. 27, 1954.

22. *Chicago Tribune*, Sept. 28, 1954.

23. Grant to Nance, Nov. 8, 1954, in Nance Papers, ser. 1, box 13.

24. Courtney Johnson to Nance, Mar. 22, 1955, in Nance Papers, ser. 2, box 3.

25. S-P Board Minutes, Nov. 19, 1954; Grant to Nance, Nov. 26, 1954, in Nance Papers, ser. 1, box 13; Grant to Nance, Jan. 6, 1955, in Nance Papers, ser. 2, box 2; W. Bollay to Brodie, Sept. 14, 1955, ibid.; Brodie to Nance, Jan. 18, 1956, in Nance Papers, ser. 2, box 12.

26. Johnson to Nance, Mar. 31, 1955, in Nance Papers, ser. 2, box 3; Johnson to Nance, Apr. 12, 1955, in Nance Papers, ser. 2, box 12.

27. Brodie to Nance, Apr. 22, 1955, in Nance Papers, ser. 2, box 2.

28. Johnson to Frank Higgins, June 17, 1955, in Hoffman Papers, box 46, HST.

29. Johnson to Brodie, June 23, 1955, ibid.

30. Johnson to Hoffman, June 29, 1955, ibid. (quotation); Johnson to Brodie, June 20, 1955, ibid. (quotation).

31. Nance to Hoffman, n.d. [ca. June 24, 1955], ibid. (quotation); Brodie to Nance, Feb. 10, 1955, in Nance Papers, ser. 2, box 2 (quotation).

32. Homer Capehart to Nance, July 12, 1955, in Nance Papers, ser. 2, box 9; Johnson to Nance, July 11, 1955, in Nance Papers, ser. 2, box 3; Nance to Edwin Blair, July 18, 1955, in Nance Papers, ser. 2, box 9; Harold Talbott to Capehart, July 26, 1955, ibid. (quotation).

33. S-P handwritten board minutes, July 15, 1955 (quotation), Nov. 18, 1955 (quotation), Jan. 20, 1956; S-P Board Minutes, Sept. 16, Nov. 18, 1955.

34. U.S. Atomic Energy Commission to Nance, Jan. 17, 1955, in Nance Papers, ser. 2, box 2 (quotation); Nance to Brodie, Jan. 19, 1955, ibid. (quotation).

35. Vance to Hoffman, Nov. 7, 1955, in Hoffman Papers, box 46, HST; E. E. Richards to Nance, May 18, 1955, in Nance Papers, ser. 2, box 6; Hoffman to Vance, Nov. 23, 1955, in Hoffman Papers, box 46, HST (quotation); Hoffman to Vance, Dec. 7, 1955, ibid. (quotation).

36. Brodie to Nance, Dec. 21, 1955, in Nance Papers, ser. 2, box 12.

37. Brodie to Nance, Feb. 1, 2, 1956, Apr. 18, 1956, all in Nance Papers, ser. 2, box 12.

38. Brodie to Nance, Apr. 18, 1956, ibid.

CHAPTER 12. *The "Sitting Duck"*

1. S-P 1954 *Annual Report*, p. 6; Grant to Nance, Aug. 30, 1954, in Nance Papers, ser. 1, box 13; Edwards, p. 79; S-P Board Minutes, Aug. 16, 1954; Packard Board Minutes, Sept. 22, 1954.

2. S-P 1954 *Annual Report*, p. 6; Nance to Powers, Jan. 20, 1955, in Nance Papers, ser. 2, box 5.

3. S-P Board Minutes, Dec. 17, 1954, Jan. 21, 1955 (quotation); Loren Pennington, "Prelude to Chrysler: The Eisenhower Administration Bails Out Studebaker-Packard," p. 22, n. 20, manuscript in Pennington's possession.

4. S-P Press Release, n.d. [ca. Apr. 7, 1955], in Nance Papers, ser. 2, box 4 (quotation); *New York Times*, Mar. 19, 1955; *New York Herald-Tribune*, Apr. 25, 1955.

5. S-P Board Minutes, Apr. 18, 1955; S-P handwritten board minutes, Apr. 18, 1955 (quotation).

6. *New York Herald-Tribune*, Apr. 25, 1955 (quotation); *New York Times*, May 7, 1955; Nance to Patrick A. Monaghan, May 16, 1955, in Nance Papers, ser. 2, box 4 (quotation).

7. Nance to Russell Forgan, July 26, 1955, in Nance Papers, ser. 2, box 11.

8. S-P handwritten board minutes, Aug. 19, 1955.

9. Grant to Nance, Mar. 10, 1955, in Nance Papers, ser. 2, box 2; Nance to Grant, Mar. 10, 1955, ibid. (quotation).

10. Grant to Nance, Mar. 10, 1955, in Nance Papers, ser. 2, box 2; Nance to Brodie, Sept. 22, 1955, ibid.; Nance to Laughna and Churchill, Sept. 22, 1955, ibid.

11. Nance to Laughna and Churchill, Sept. 22, 1955, ibid. (quotation); *Wall Street Journal*, Nov. 21, 1955; S-P Board Minutes, Jan. 20, 1955 (quotation).

12. S-P Board Minutes, Jan. 20, 1956.

13. Quotations in Nance to Forgan, Dec. 2, 1955, in Nance Papers, ser. 2, box 11; Nance to John McDonaugh, Dec. 2, 1955, in Hoffman Papers, box 46, HST; Hoffman to Nance, Dec. 8, 1955, ibid.

14. *Bank and Quotation Records* (New York, 1956).

15. Nance to Grant and Mendler, Oct. 25, 1954, in Nance Papers, ser. 1, box 13.

16. Nance to Grant and Porta, May 2, 1955, in Nance Papers, ser. 2, box 2.

17. Nance to Administration Committee, May 3, 1955, in Porta Papers, ser. 1, box 3.

18. Ibid.; John Gordon to Administration Committee, May 1955, in Porta Papers, ser. 1, box 3 (quotation); Grant to Nance, June 22, 1955, in Nance Papers, ser. 2, box 2 (quotation).

19. Gordon to Nance, July 14, 1955, in Nance Papers, ser. 1, box 3; Casson to Nance, Mar. 29, 1956, in Porta Papers, ser. 2, box 3; Edwards, p. 43; *New York Times*, Nov. 10, 1955, Dec. 22, 1955.

20. S-P Board Minutes, Oct. 4, 1955; Nance to Grant, Nov. 1, 1954, in Nance Papers, ser. 1, box 13 (quotation).

21. Nance to Grant, Oct. 26, 1954, in Porta Papers, ser. 1, box 2 (quotation); Hoge to Grant, Oct. 29, 1954, ibid.; Grant to Nance, Nov. 1, 1954, ibid.

22. O. E. Rogers to Brodie, Apr. 8, 1955, in Nance Papers, ser. 2, box 6.

23. Johnson to Nance, Apr. 12, 1955, in Nance Papers, ser. 2, box 12; E. E. Richards to Nance, Apr. 20, 1955, in Nance Papers, ser. 2, box 6 (quotation).

24. Richards to Grant, June 7, 1955, in Nance Papers, ser. 2, box 15.

25. Richards to Nance, June 14, 1955, in Porta Papers, ser. 1, box 2.

26. Nance to Blythin, Feb. 28, 1955, in Nance Papers, ser. 2, box 2; Blythin to Nance, Apr. 12, 1955, in Nance Papers, ser. 2, box 12.

27. *Wall Street Journal*, Apr. 18, 1955.

28. Grant to Nance, Apr. 13, 1955, in Nance Papers, ser. 2, box 2.

29. Nance to Grant, Apr. 20, 1955, ibid. (quotation); Romney to Nance, Sept. 16, 1955, in Nance Papers, ser. 2, box 10.

30. Brodie to Nance, Sept. 26, 1955, Oct. 5, 1955, both in Nance Papers, ser. 2, box 2; Grant to Nance, Apr. 13, 1955, ibid.; S-P Board Minutes, Nov. 18, 1955.

31. Nance to John Sloan, Mar. 2, 1956, June 7, 1956, both in Nance Papers, ser. 2, box 16; *New York Times*, Apr. 17, 1956; *Wall Street Journal*, Apr. 17, 1955; William Harris, "The Breakdown of Studebaker-Packard," *Fortune* (Oct. 1956), p. 228. Nance had talked to Harris on July 13, 1956.

32. Nance's notes for conference with Borden, Feb. 1, 1956, in Porta Papers, ser. 1, box 4.

33. Richard Stout, interview by author, Apr. 29, 1987 (quotation); Richard Stout, "On Introducing the Fifty-Sixth Series," *Packard Cormorant* (autumn 1978), p. 11 (quotation).

34. Nance to Fr. Theodore Hesburgh, Mar. 27, 1956, in Nance Papers, ser. 2, box 13; Kimes, p. 609.

35. S-P Board Minutes, Jan. 20, 1956; Harris, "Breakdown of S-P," p. 229; Nance's notes for conference with Borden, Feb. 1, 1956, in Porta Papers, ser. 1, box 4, SNMA (quotation).

36. S-P Board Minutes, Feb. 27, 1956 (quotation); Nance to Hesburgh, Mar. 27, 1956, in Nance Papers, ser. 2, box 13 (quotation).

37. Nance to Hesburgh, Mar. 27, 1956, in Nance Papers, ser. 2, box 13 (quotation); S-P Board Minutes, Feb. 27, 1956 (quotation).

CHAPTER 13. *Seeking a "Safe Harbor"*

1. Porta to Nance, Apr. 20, 1956, in Nance Papers, ser. 2, box 15; *New York Times*, Mar. 18, 1956.

2. *Wall Street Journal*, Mar. 16, 1956; Porta to Nance, Jan. 20, 1956, in Nance Papers, ser. 2, box 15 (quotation); Nance to Laughna, Jan. 20, 1956, in Nance Papers, ser. 2, box 14 (quotation).

3. Shine to Nance, Jan. 26, 1956, in Nance Papers, ser. 2, box 16 (quotation); O'Madigan to Nance, Feb. 13, 1956, in Nance Papers, ser. 2, box 15 (quotation).

4. D'Arcy, "Marketing Factors, Pro and Con; New Product Development, 1957," in Nance Papers, ser. 2, box 10; Kimes, p. 612 (quotation).

5. Kimes, p. 612; *Wall Street Journal*, Mar. 16, 1956; Nance to C. G. Heisler, Mar. 22, 1956, in Nance Papers, ser. 2, box 9 (quotation); S-P Board Minutes, Mar. 23, 1956 (quotation), Feb. 27, 1956; Blythin to O'Madigan, Mar. 16, 1956, in Nance Papers, ser. 2, box 12.

6. *Business Week*, May 12, 1956 (quotation); Robinson to Laughna, Mar. 30, 1956, in Nance Papers, ser. 2, box 19; *U.S. News & World Report*, Mar. 30, 1956, p. 45; *Consumer Reports* (Apr. 1956), p. 160; Monaghan to Nance, May 4, 1956, in Nance Papers, ser. 2, box 14.

7. *Wall Street Journal*, Mar. 7, 1956; *Automotive News*, Apr. 2, 15, 1956.

8. "Projected Sales and Profit or Loss," n.d. [ca. Apr. 1, 1956], in Harold Churchill Papers, ser. 1, box 6, SNMA; Packard Division, "Regional Performance, Year to Date," Apr. 20, 1956, in Nance Papers, ser. 2, box 12; "Studebaker-Packard Comparative Economic Unit Analysis," Jan. 4, 1956, in Nance Papers, ser. 2,

box 15; "Proposal for Key Market Development, Studebaker-Packard Corporation, April 1956," in Nance Papers, ser. 2, box 10 (quotation).

9. *New York Times*, Feb. 3, 1956; Laughna to Nance, Feb. 22, 1956, in Nance Papers, ser. 2, box 15; *New York Times*, Mar. 5, 6 (quotation), 1956; *Automotive News*, Apr. 9, 1956; Gordon to Nance, Feb. 27, 1956, in Nance Papers, ser. 2, box 12; Laughna to Nance, Apr. 24, 1956, in Nance Papers, ser. 2, box 14.

10. *New York Times*, Mar. 17, 1956, May 10, 1956; Porta to Nance, Mar. 27, 1956, in Nance Papers, ser. 2, box 15; *Automotive News*, Apr. 23, 1956, May 7, 1956.

11. *Time*, Apr. 30, 1956; Bremer to Nance, Feb. 3, 1956, in Porta Papers, ser. 1, box 1; Nance's notes, n.d., ibid. (quotation).

12. Richard Stout, interview by author, May 6, 1987; Richard Stout, "On Introducing the Fifty-Sixth Series," *Packard Cormorant* (autumn 1978), p. 7 (quotation); Bremer to Nance, Feb. 3, 1956, in Porta Papers, ser. 1, box 1 (quotation).

13. S-P Board Minutes, Jan. 20, 1956.

14. S-P handwritten board minutes, Feb. 27, 1956.

15. Ibid.

16. Ibid.

17. *Who's Who in America, 1960–61*, pp. 2050, 980–81.

18. Heller & Associates, "Record of Efforts Directed at Preserving the Corporation, January–June, 1956," Supplemental Board Papers, SNMA (hereinafter Heller); "Study of Merger Possibilities," n.d., in Porta Papers, ser. 1, box 2 (quotation).

19. Heller, p. 3; S-P Board Minutes, Mar. 23, 1956, Apr. 16, 1956 (quotation); L. L. Colbert to Nance, Apr. 20, 1956, in Nance Papers, ser. 2, box 10.

20. "Study of Merger Possibilities," in Porta Papers, ser. 1, box 2 (quotation); Heller, p. 3 (quotation); *Wall Street Journal*, Apr. 17, 1956; *New York Times*, Apr. 17, 1956.

21. Heller, pp. 5–6 (quotation); S-P handwritten board minutes, Mar. 23, 1956 (quotation).

22. "Study of Merger Possibilities," in Porta Papers, ser. 1, box 2; Heller, p. 3; S-P Board Minutes, Mar. 23, 1956; Brodie to Nance, Mar. 21, 1956, in Nance Papers, ser. 1, box 12.

23. S-P handwritten board minutes, Mar. 23, 1956.

24. Sobel, pp. 350–72.

25. Ibid., p. 369; S-P handwritten board minutes, Mar. 23, 1956.

26. Heller, pp. 6 (quotation), 7; S-P handwritten board minutes, May 2, 1956.

27. S-P Board Minutes, Feb. 27, 1956, Mar. 23, 1956.

28. *Who's Who in America, 1960–61*, p. 2046; Heller, p. 3 (quotation); S-P handwritten board minutes, Mar. 23, 1956 (quotation).

29. S-P handwritten board minutes, Mar. 23, 1956 (quotation), Apr. 16, 1956.

30. S-P handwritten board minutes, Mar. 23, 1956.

31. George Humphrey's 1956 appointment book, in George M. Humphrey Papers, folder 79, WRHS; Heller, p. 2.

32. Humphrey appointment book, in Humphrey Papers, folder 79, WRHS.

33. Hoffman's 1956 schedule book, in Hoffman papers, box 96, HST; S-P handwritten board minutes, Mar. 23, 1956 (quotation).

34. Nance's notes, n.d., in Porta Papers, ser. 1, box 1; "Study of Merger Possibilities," in Porta Papers, ser. 1, box 2.

35. Heller, p. 4 (quotation); S-P handwritten board minutes, Apr. 16, 1956 (quotation).

36. S-P handwritten board minutes, Mar. 23, 1956.

37. Ibid.

38. Ibid.

39. Ibid.

40. Nance to Churchill and Laughna, Mar. 14, 1956, in Nance Papers, ser. 2, box 12.

41. Nance to Administration Committee, Mar. 27, 1956, in Nance Papers, ser. 2, box 12; Nance to Joe Moreau, Apr. 4, 1956, in Nance Papers, ser. 2, box 14 (quotation); Nance to Churchill, Laughna, and Brodie, Apr. 9, 1956, in Nance Papers, ser. 2, box 12; Bremer to Nance, Apr. 18, 1956, in Nance Papers, ser. 2, box 9 (quotation); Heller, p. 5 (quotation).

42. Nance, Outline of talk given to Chicago bankers, Apr. 18, 20, 1956, in Porta Papers, ser. 1, box 4.

43. Humphrey appointment book, in Humphrey Papers, folder 79, WRHS; Humphrey to Sinclair Weeks, Apr. 13, 1956, in Sinclair Weeks Papers, box 37, DC.

44. Weeks to Humphrey, Apr. 13, 1956, in Weeks Papers, box 37, DC.

45. Cabinet Notes, Ann Whitman File, box 4, Cabinet Series, DDEL.

46. Dwight D. Eisenhower Diary, Apr. 20, 1956, in Ann Whitman File, box 15, DDEL.

47. Ann Whitman Diary, Apr. 20, 1956, in Ann Whitman File, box 8, DDEL; DDE Diary, Apr. 20, 1956, in Ann Whitman File, box 15, DDEL (quotation).

48. DDE Diary, Apr. 20, 1956, in Ann Whitman File, box 15, DDEL.

49. Humphrey appointment book, in Humphrey Papers, folder 79, WRHS; S-P handwritten board minutes, Apr. 16, 1956.

50. S-P handwritten board minutes, Apr. 16, 1956.

51. S-P handwritten board minutes, May 21, 1956.

52. Heller, p. 6 (quotation); S-P handwritten board minutes, May 2, 1956 (quotation).

53. Heller, p. 6.

54. Ibid. (quotation); S-P handwritten board minutes, May 2, 1956 (quotation).

55. S-P handwritten board minutes, May 2, 1956.

CHAPTER 14. *"Love Without Marriage"*

1. *Who's Who in America, 1960–61*, p. 1431; *Automotive News*, Aug. 13, 1956 (quotation); *New York Times*, Aug. 5, 1956 (quotation).

2. *Automotive News*, Aug. 13, 1956.

3. *New York Times*, Aug. 5, 1956.

4. *Automotive News*, Aug. 13, 1956 (quotation); *Who's Who in America, 1960–61*, p. 1431; *New York Times*, Aug. 5, 1956 (quotation).

5. *New York Times*, Aug. 5, 1956 (quotation); S-P handwritten board minutes, Apr. 16, 1956.

6. S-P handwritten board minutes, Mar. 23, 1956 (quotation); Daily Air Force Secretary's Diary for 1956, in Quarles Papers, 1952–59, box 1, DDEL; Humphrey appointment book, in Humphrey Papers, folder 79, WRHS; S-P handwritten board minutes, Apr. 16, 1956 (quotation).

7. S-P handwritten board minutes, May 2, 1956.

8. Heller, p. 7 (quotation); S-P handwritten board minutes, May 8, 1956 (quotation).

9. S-P handwritten board minutes, May 8, 1956.

10. Ibid.

11. Ibid.

12. *Wall Street Journal*, May 9, 1956; Roy Hurley to Charles Wilson, May 9, 1956, in Humphrey Papers, folder 79, WRHS.

13. Hurley to Wilson, May 9, 1956, in Humphrey Papers, folder 79, WRHS.

14. *Wall Street Journal*, May 11, 1956 (quotation); *New York Times*, May 11, 1956; *Business Week*, May 12, 1956.

15. *New York Times*, May 15, 1956; *Automotive News*, May 14, 1956 (quotation); Ernest Rushmer to Shine, May 16, 1956, in Porta Papers, ser. 2, box 2.

16. *Wall Street Journal*, May 16, 1956 (quotation); *New York Times*, May 16, 1956 (quotation).

17. *Wall Street Journal*, May 17, 1956 (quotation); *Time*, May 21, 1956, p. 96; Hurley to Wilson, May 22, 1956, in Humphrey Papers, folder 79, WRHS (quotation).

18. Hurley to Wilson, May 26, 1956, in Humphrey Papers, folder 79, WRHS.

19. Ibid.

20. Daily Air Force Secretary's Diary for 1956, in Quarles Papers, 1952–59, box 1, DDEL; Humphrey appointment book, in Humphrey Papers, folder 79, WRHS; Ann Whitman Diary, May 30, 1956, in Ann Whitman File, box 8, DDEL; S-P handwritten board minutes, May 29, 1956 (quotation).

21. S-P handwritten board minutes, June 2, 1956.

22. Ibid.

23. Ibid., June 4, 1956.

24. Ibid.

25. Daily Air Force Secretary's Diary for 1956, in Quarles Papers, 1952–59, box 1, DDEL; *New York Times*, June 5, 1956 (quotation); Hoffman's 1956 schedule book, in Hoffman Papers, box 96, HST.

26. S-P handwritten board minutes, June 7, 1956.

27. Ibid.

28. Ibid.

29. *Newsweek*, June 11, 1956, 82–88 (quotation on p. 88); *Wall Street Journal*, June 14, 1956 (quotation); *New York Times*, June 17, 1956; Brodie to Nance, June 11, 1956, in Nance Papers, ser. 2, box 12.

30. Brodie to Nance, June 11, 1956, in Nance Papers, ser. 2, box 12; Roy White, Jr., "Memorandum on Important Policy Questions Requiring an Early Decision," June 6, 1956, in Nance Papers, ser. 2, box 13 (quotation).

31. General File, box 1012, Studebaker-Packard folder, Central Files, DDEL.

32. S-P Board Minutes, June 4, 1956.

33. Scribner to Nance, June 6, 1956, in Nance Papers, ser. 2, box 15; Casson to Nance, June 6, 1956, in Nance Papers, ser. 2, box 12.

34. *Wall Street Journal*, June 27, 1956; *New York Times*, June 27, 1956.

35. Unidentified former Studebaker engineer, conversation with author, June 1987; Kimes, p. 619 (quotation); David Bird II, "Automotive Renaissance Man: Dick Teague," *Automobile Quarterly* (winter 1992), p. 13 (quotation); Kimes, quotations in pp. 621, 619.

36. Tom Brubaker, Director of the Studebaker National Museum, conversation with author, July 1986.

37. S-P handwritten board minutes, June 27, 1956.

38. Ibid.

39. Ibid.

40. Ibid.

41. Humphrey appointment book, in Humphrey Papers, folder 79, WRHS; Daily Air Force Secretary's Diary for 1956, in Quarles Papers, 1952–59, box 1, DDEL; S-P handwritten board minutes, June 28, 1956 (quotation).

42. S-P handwritten board minutes, June 28, 1956.

43. Ibid.

44. *New York Times*, June 30, 1956; Daily Air Force Secretary's Diary for 1956, in Quarles Papers, 1952–59, box 1, DDEL.

45. Nance to Paul Clark, July 12, 1956, in Nance Papers, ser. 2, box 12; Telegram, Nance to Frank Elmendorf, July 23, 1956, in Nance Papers, ser. 2, box 13 (quotation); meeting, July 10, 1956, mentioned in S-P Board Minutes, July 26, 1956 (quotation).

46. S-P Board Minutes, July 25, 1956; "Advisory Management Agreement, Curtiss-Wright & Studebaker-Packard," Aug. 1956, pp. 1–5, in Churchill Papers, ser. 1, box 6.

47. S-P handwritten board minutes, July 25, 1956.

48. S-P handwritten board minutes, July 26, 1956.

49. Ibid.

50. Bert Gross to William Harris, July 27, 1956, in Nance Papers, ser. 2, box 11; telegram, Clark to Nance, July 30, 1956, in Nance Papers, ser. 2, box 12 (quotation); *Time*, July 30, 1956, pp. 64–65.

51. Humphrey appointment book, in Humphrey Papers, folder 79, WRHS; Daily Air Force Secretary's Diary for 1956, in Quarles Papers, 1952–59, box 1, DDEL; Staff Notes, Aug. 4, 1956, 1–15 file, Staff Research Group, in White House Office Papers, box 24, DDEL (quotation).

52. S-P handwritten board minutes, Aug. 6, 1956 (quotation); Press Conference Series, Briefings, Aug. 8, 1956, in DDE Papers, Ann Whitman File, box 5, DDEL (quotation).

53. *Wall Street Journal*, Aug. 8 (quotation), 9, 1956 (quotation); Hurley to Quarles, Aug. 9, 1956, in Quarles Papers, box 7, DDEL.

54. *Wall Street Journal*, July 19, 1957 (quotation), Oct. 25, 1956.

55. *Wall Street Journal*, Aug. 6, 7, 1956, Aug. 28, 1957, Apr. 21, 1958, July 22, 1957; *Detroit Times*, Aug. 9, 1956; *Detroit Free-Press*, Aug. 9, 1956; William Harris, "The Breakdown of Studebaker-Packard," *Fortune* (Oct. 1956), p. 232.

56. *Wall Street Journal*, Aug. 15, 1956 (quotation); *New York Times*, Aug. 15, 1956, Sept. 27, 1956; S-P Board Minutes, Oct. 31, 1956.

CHAPTER 15. *"Ask the Man Who Owned One"*

1. S-P Board Minutes, May 2, 1956.

2. Nance to Ernie Breech, Aug. 3, 1956, in Nance Papers, ser. 2, box 9; *Business Week*, Aug. 25, 1956, p. 34; *Automotive News*, Oct. 1, 1956; *Wall Street Journal*, Oct. 4, 1956; *New York Times*, Oct. 11, 1956; *Business Week*, Oct. 13, 1956, p. 31.

3. *Detroit Free-Press*, Feb. 16, 1958, Apr. 19, 1960; *New York Times*, Sept. 6, 1958; *Automotive News*, Feb. 24, 1964; Richard Stout, interview with author,

Apr. 29, 1987; Richard Langworth, "James J. Nance," *Packard Cormorant* (autumn 1984), p. 3.

4. *Wall Street Journal*, Aug. 6, 1956.

5. *New York Times*, Aug. 9, 1956; *Business Week*, Aug. 11, 1956, p. 27 (quotation); *Detroit Times*, Aug. 19, 1956.

6. S-P Board Minutes, Aug. 6, 20, 1956 (both quotations).

7. *Automotive News*, Aug. 20 (quotation), 27, 1956; Churchill to Stockholders, Aug. 27, 1956, in Col. J. G. Vincent Correspondence, AHC.

8. *Automotive News*, Oct. 4, 1956, Apr. 25, 1957, Mar. 29, 1957, June 20, 1957, July 25, 1957, Sept. 15, 1957, Dec. 29, 1957, June 18, 1958; *Wall Street Journal*, Dec. 23, 1957.

9. S-P 1956 *Annual Report*, p. 5; *New York Times*, Dec. 1, 1957; *Business Week*, Apr. 20, 1957; S-P Board Minutes, Feb. 28, 1957.

10. *Business Week*, Apr. 20, 1957.

11. S-P Board Minutes, June 20, 1957, July 25, 1957, Sept. 15, 1957, Jan. 30, 1958.

12. S-P Board Minutes, Sept. 15, 1957, Oct. 3, 1957, Nov. 15, 1957, Jan. 30, Feb. 24, 1958; Editors of *Automobile Quarterly*, p. 142.

13. S-P Board Minutes, Mar. 14, 27, 1958, Jan. 30, 1958, Apr. 24, 1958; *New York Times*, May 10, 1958, Aug. 2, 1958, Apr. 25, 1958; S-P Board Minutes, May 8, 1958, June 18, 1958, July 24, 1958.

14. *New York Times*, Dec. 7, 1956; *Wall Street Journal*, Jan. 15, 1957; *Business Week*, Nov. 9, 1957, p. 81.

15. *New York Times*, Dec. 1, 16, 1956; S-P Board Minutes, Jan. 29, 1957, Feb. 28, 1957; Kimes, p. 809.

16. Kimes, pp. 630–31; S-P Board Minutes, Sept. 15, 1957; *New York Times*, Oct. 10, 1957, Dec. 8, 1957 (Advertising Supplement), Jan. 19, 1958.

17. S-P Board Minutes, Nov. 15, 1957.

18. S-P Board Minutes, Dec. 20, 1957, Jan. 30, 1958 (quotation), Feb. 24, 1958, May 8, 1958, July 24, 1958 (quotation).

19. *New York Times*, July 13, 1958 (quotation); *Wall Street Journal*, July 14, 1958; *Business Week*, June 19, 1958, p. 29 (quotation).

20. *Time*, Aug. 18, 1958, p. 78 (quotation); Kimes, p. 633; Beatty, Furlong, and Pennington, pp. 36–60.

21. *New York Times*, Feb. 8, 1958.

EPILOGUE: *The Autopsy*

1. *New York Times*, Apr. 14, 1991.

2. Ibid.; *New York Times*, Sept. 8, 1991.

3. *New York Times*, Mar. 15, 1987.

4. *Sunday Times* (London), Dec. 15, 1991.

5. Dorris and Erdrich, p. 215.

Bibliography

Primary Sources

Dartmouth College Library, Hanover, N.H.: Sinclair Weeks Papers.

Detroit Public Library. Automotive History Collection.

Dwight D. Eisenhower Presidential Library, Abilene, Kans. Papers of: Sherman Adams, Herbert Brownell, Arthur Burns, Cabinet, Dwight D. Eisenhower, Gabriel Hauge, Paul G. Hoffman, George M. Humphrey, Arthur Minnich, Donald Quarles, Sinclair Weeks, Ann Whitman, and Press Conferences.

Studebaker National Museum Archives, South Bend, Ind. Papers of: Harold Churchill, James J. Nance, A. J. Porta; Packard *Annual Reports*, Packard Motor Car Company Board of Directors Minutes, Studebaker *Annual Reports*, Studebaker Corporation Board of Directors Minutes, and Studebaker-Packard Corporation Board of Directors Minutes.

Harry S. Truman Presidential Library, Independence, Mo. Papers of Paul G. Hoffman.

Western Reserve Historical Society, Cleveland, Ohio. Papers of George M. Humphrey.

Indiana University Oral History Research Center, Bloomington. Interviews with Clara Brown, Harold Churchill, John Harrington, Clifford MacMillan, John Piechowiak, and Margery Warren.

Interviews by author with W. H. Ferry, Margery Gilman, Michael Kollins, Loren Pennington, Lyman Slack, and Richard Stout.

Automotive News, a trade publication; *Automobile Quarterly*, the leading auto history periodical; the *Cormorant News-Bulletin*, the bimonthly publication of the Packard Automobile Club; the *Detroit Free-Press*; the *Detroit News*; *Horseless Age*, a very early newspaper concerned solely with the new auto industry; the *Packard Cormorant*, the quarterly publication of the Packard Automobile Club; *Packards International Magazine*, the quarterly publication of Packards International Motor Car Club; and *Ward's Automotive Reports*, the journal of the automobile industry.

Secondary Sources

Adams, Walter, ed. *The Structure of American Industry: Some Case Studies*. New York, 1954.

Association of Licensed Automobile Manufacturers. *Handbook of Gasoline Automobiles*. New York, 1904.

Bain, Joe. *Barriers to New Competition*. Cambridge, Mass., 1956.

Banner, Paul. "Competition in the Automobile Industry." Ph.D. dissertation, Harvard University, 1954.

Beatty, Michael, Patrick Furlong, and Loren Pennington. *Studebaker: Less Than They Promised*. South Bend, Ind., 1984.

Blond, Stuart R. "The Duke of Earle: Earle C. Anthony." *Packard Cormorant* (summer 1985).

Bonsall, Thomas. *The Lincoln Motorcar: Sixty Years of Excellence*. Baltimore, Md., 1981.

Brierley, Brooks T. *There Is No Mistaking a Pierce Arrow*. Coconut Grove, Fla., 1986.

Brooks, John. *Fate of the Edsel and Other Business Adventures*. New York, 1963.

Cannon, William A., and Fred K. Fox. *Studebaker: The Complete Story*. Blue Ridge, Pa., 1981.

Chamberlin, Edward. *The Theory of Monopolistic Competition*. Cambridge, Mass., 1956.

Chandler, Alfred. *Giant Enterprise: Ford, General Motors, and the Automobile Industry*. New York, 1964.

Chonoy, Eli. *Automobile Workers and the American Dream*. Garden City, N.Y., 1955.

Chow, Gregory C. *Demand for Automobiles in the United States: A Study in Consumer Durables*. Amsterdam, 1957.

Chrysler, Walter C., and Boyden Spakes. *Life of an American Workman*. New York, 1937.

Clymer, Floyd. *Treasury of Early American Automobiles*. New York, 1950.

Davis, Donald Finlay. *Conspicuous Production: Automobiles and Elites in Detroit, 1899–1933*. Philadelphia, 1988.

Dawes, Nathaniel. *The Packard, 1942–62*. New York, 1975.

Denison, Merrill. *The Power to Go*. Garden City, N.Y., 1956.

Dickey, Philip S., III. *The Liberty Engine*. Washington, D.C., 1968.

Diggins, John Patrick. *The Proud Decades: America in War and Peace, 1941–1960*. New York, 1988.

Donovan, Frank. *Wheels for a Nation*. New York, 1965.

Doolittle, James Rood. *The Romance of the Automobile Industry*. New York, 1916.

Dorris, Michael, and Louise Erdrich. *The Crown of Columbus*. New York, 1991.

Duerksen, Menno. "Free Wheeling Packard, Part III." *Packards International Magazine* (summer 1986).

Durant, Margery. *My Father*. New York, 1929.

Ebert, Robert. "An Economic Analysis of the Decline of the Packard Motor Car Company." M.A. thesis, Western Reserve University, 1967.

Editors of *Automobile Quarterly. The American Car Since 1775.* New York, 1971.

Edwards, Charles E. *Dynamics of the United States Automobile Industry.* Columbia, S.C., 1965.

Einstein, Arthur. "The Advertising of the Packard Motor Car Company, 1899–1956." M.A. thesis, Michigan State University, 1959.

Epstein, Ralph C. *The Automobile Industry: Its Economic and Commercial Development.* New York, 1928.

Fine, Sidney. *The Automobile Under the Blue Eagle: Labor, Management and the Automobile Manufacturing Code.* Ann Arbor, Mich., 1962.

———. *Sit Down: The General Motors Strike of 1936–1937.* Ann Arbor, Mich., 1969.

Fisher, Franklin, Zvi Griliches, and Carl Kaysen. "The Costs of the Automobile Model Changes Since 1949." *Journal of Political Economy* 70 (Oct. 1962).

Flink, James J. *America Adopts the Automobile, 1895–1910.* Cambridge, Mass., 1970.

Frey, Robert L., ed. *Encyclopedia of American Business History and Biography: Railroads in the Nineteenth Century.* New York, 1988.

Galbraith, John Kenneth. *The Great Crash: 1929.* Boston, 1961.

Georgano, G. N., ed. *The Complete Encyclopedia of Motorcars: 1885 to the Present.* New York, 1973.

Glasscock, C. B. *The Gasoline Age: The Story of the Men Who Made It.* Indianapolis, 1937.

Godshall, Jeffrey I. "Dodge: And Then There Were Three." *Automobile Quarterly* (second quarter, 1986).

Goldman, Eric. *The Crucial Decade and After: America, 1945–1960.* New York, 1961.

Goodrich, Owen. "The Packard I Knew." Unfinished manuscript in Menno Duerksen's collection, Memphis, Tenn.

———. "The Rise and Fall of Packard as I Saw It." Unfinished manuscript in Menno Duerksen's collection, Memphis, Tenn.

Greenleaf, William. *Monopoly on Wheels: Henry Ford and the Selden Automobile Patent.* Detroit, 1961.

Harrah-Conforth, Jeanne. "And I Thank God for the Union Every Day: An Account of Women's Experiences Working in the Indiana Auto Industry." *Indiana Folklore and Oral History* 14, no. 2 (July–Dec. 1985): 113–35.

Hendry, Maurice. *Cadillac: The Standard of the World.* Princeton, N.J., 1979.

Hewitt, Charles M. *Automobile Franchise Agreements.* Homewood, Ill., 1956.

Hokanson, Drake. *The Lincoln Highway.* Iowa City, 1988.

Huttman, John. "The Automobile in the 1920s: The Critical Decade." In *Essays in Economic and Business History: Selected Papers from the Economic and Business Historical Society.* East Lansing, Mich., 1988.

Jaffe, Morton H. *Alvan Macauley: Automotive Leader and Pioneer.* N.p., n.d.

Keats, John. *Insolent Chariots.* Philadelphia, 1958.

Kennedy, Edward. *The Automobile Industry.* New York, 1941.

Kimes, Beverly R., and Richard Langworth, eds. *Packard: A History of the Motor Car and the Company.* Princeton, N.J., 1978.

Lacey, Robert. *Ford: The Men and the Machine.* New York, 1986.

Langworth, Richard M. *Kaiser-Frazer: The Last Onslaught on Detroit.* Princeton, N.J., 1975.

Laux, James M. *The Automobile Revolution: The Impact of an Industry.* Chapel Hill, N.C., 1982.

Leland, Mrs. Wilfred C., and Minnie Dubbs Millbrook. *Master of Precision: Henry M. Leland*. Detroit, 1966.

Longstreet, Stephen. *A Century on Wheels: The Story of Studebaker*. New York, 1952.

MacDonald, Robert. *Collective Bargaining in the Automobile Industry*. New Haven, Conn., 1963.

MacManus, Theodore F., and Norman Beasley. *Men, Money and Motors: The Drama of the Automobile*. New York, 1929.

Mahoney, Thomas. *The Story of George Romney: Builder, Salesman, Crusader*. New York, 1960.

May, George S. *R. E. Olds: Auto Industry Pioneer*. Grand Rapids, Mich., 1977.

Moore, Donald. "The Automobile Industry." In *The Structure of American Industry*, edited by Walter Adams. New York, 1954.

Morris, Lloyd. *Not So Long Ago*. New York, 1949.

Nevins, Allan, and Frank E. Hill. *Ford: Expansion and Challenge, 1915–1932*. New York, 1957.

———. *Ford: The Times, the Man, the Company*. New York, 1954.

Niemeyer, Glenn A. *The Automotive Career of Ransom E. Olds*. East Lansing, Mich., 1963.

Packard Motor Car Company. *Twice Across the Great Silence*. Detroit, ca. 1913.

Pound, Arthur. *The Turning Wheel: The Story of General Motors Through Twenty-Five Years, 1908–1933*. Garden City, N.Y., 1934.

Rae, John B. *The American Automobile*. Chicago, 1965.

———. *American Automobile Manufacturers: The First Forty Years*. Philadelphia, 1959.

———. "The Engineer-Entrepreneur in the American Automobile Industry." *Explorations in Entrepreneurial History* (Oct. 1955).

———. *The Road and the Car in American Life*. Cambridge, Mass., 1970.

Ralston, Marc. *Pierce Arrow*. New York, 1980.

Raucher, Alan R. *Paul G. Hoffman: Architect of Foreign Aid*. Lexington, Ky., 1985.

Roe, Fred. *Duesenberg: The Pursuit of Perfection*. London, 1982.

Rothschild, Emma. *Paradise Lost: The Decline of the Auto-Industrial Elite*. New York, 1973.

Scott, Michael G. H. *Packard: The Complete Story*. Blue Ridge Summit, Pa., 1985.

Seltzer, Lawrence H. *A Financial History of the American Automobile Industry: A Study of the Ways in Which the Leading American Producers of Automobiles Have Met Their Capital Requirements*. Boston, 1928.

Sloan, Alfred P., Jr. *My Years with General Motors*. Garden City, N.Y., 1964.

Sobel, Robert. *The Entrepreneurs*. New York, 1974.

Stout, Richard H. *Make 'Em Shout Hooray!* New York, 1988.

Suits, Daniel. "The Demand for New Automobiles in the United States, 1929–1956." *Review of Economics and Statistics* (Nov. 1958).

Turnquist, Robert E. *The Packard Story*. New York, 1965.

U.S. Congress. House of Representatives. Committee on Interstate and Foreign Commerce. *Automobile Dealer Franchises*. Hearings, 84th Cong., 2d sess., 1956.

———. *Automobile Marketing Practices*. Hearings, 84th Cong., 2d sess., 1956.

———. House of Representatives. Committee on the Judiciary, Subcommittee on Antitrust and Monopoly. *A Study of Antitrust Laws*. Hearings, 84th Cong., 1st sess., 1955.

————. Joint Committee on the Economic Report, Subcommittee on Economic Stabilization. *Automation and Technological Change*. Hearings, 84th Cong., 1st sess., 1955.

U.S. Department of Commerce. *Historical Statistics of the United States: Colonial Times to 1957*. Washington, D.C., 1961.

————. Senate. Committee on the Judiciary, Subcommittee on Anti-Trust and Monopoly. *A Study of Anti-Trust Laws*. Hearings, 84th Cong., 1st sess., 1955.

U.S. Federal Trade Commission. *Report on Mergers and Acquisitions*. H. Doc. 169. 84th Cong., 1st sess., 1955.

————. *Report on the Motor Vehicle Industry*. H. Doc. 468. 84th Cong., 1st sess., 1939.

Vatter, Harold. *Small Enterprise and Oligopoly: A Study of the Butter, Flour, Automobile, and Glass Container Industries*. Corvallis, Ore., 1955.

White, Lawrence J. *The Automobile Industry Since 1945*. Cambridge, Mass., 1971.

Wik, Reynold. *Henry Ford and Grass Roots America*. Ann Arbor, Mich., 1972.

Williamson, Samuel T. *My Forty Years with Ford*. New York, 1962.

Wolford, John B. "Memories, Dreams, Recollections: A Sampler from Studebaker Oral Histories." *Indiana Folklore and Oral History* 14, no. 2 (July–Dec. 1985). 87–111.

Index

In this index an "f" after a number indicates a separate reference on the next page, and an "ff" indicates separate references on the next two pages. A continuous discussion over two or more pages is indicated by a span of page numbers, e.g., "57–59." *Passim* is used for a cluster of references in close but not consecutive sequence.

Abbott & Morgan, 242
Adams, Ruth, 45f
Aerophysics Development
    Corporation, 190, 243
Air Material Command, 118
Alexander, Henry, 142f
Alger, Fred, 12
Alger, Horatio, 2
Alger, Russell A., 12
Allison, William, 178
Almirall, Lloyd V., 242
AMC automobiles and company, 5f, 68, 78, 124, 145, 153ff, 171f, 186, 188ff, 213, 215, 267; and merger, 148–49, 203, 205f, 216–18
AMC models: Gremlin, 267; Pacer, 267
American Arithmometer Company, 15
Anna M. Rosenberg Associates, 147, 150
Anthony, Earle, 54, 58, 63, 79, 150, 184, 188, 250
Arbib, Richard, 75
Asterita, George, 143
Atlas missile, 190
Auburn automobile, 2, 20

Austin automobile and company, 102
Austin model: Bantam, 102
Auto-Lite Corporation, 148, 205
Automotive Council for War
    Production, 48

B-52 bombers, 192, 230
Bantam automobile, 102
Barit, Robert, 145
Behnke, Albert, 92, 138, 165, 244
Bendix Aviation Corporation, 229
Bentley automobile, 268
Black Bess automobile, 180, 240
Blair, Edwin, 76, 145, 192, 241, 250
Blythin, Robert, 92, 186
BMW automobile, 264
Bodman, Henry, 57f, 76
Bogle, Henry, 58, 63, 73, 77
Bollay, Dr. W., 191
Booz Allen & Hamilton, 79–86 *passim*, 92–97 *passim*, 101, 158, 203, 261f
Borden, D. C., 167, 216
Borg-Warner Corporation, 146, 148, 205
Boyer, Joseph H., 12, 15f

Bradley, Albert, 218

Breech, Ernest, 215, 221, 229, 242, 250, 260

Bremer, Roger, 92, 121f, 126f, 132, 148, 162, 165f, 207, 215, 223, 250

Briggs, Clare E., 95, 97, 101f, 111ff, 125-26, 134, 138, 165, 184f

Briggs, Walter O., 120

Briggs Body Company, 5, 48, 62f, 92, 99f, 108, 116, 119

British Motor Corporation Ltd., 204

Brodie, George, 62, 100, 118f, 142, 165, 191ff, 200, 238, 244, 250

Brown, Clara, 89

Brown, Neil, 175

Brownell, C. Wayne, 92

Brownell, Herbert, 101, 192, 221

Brucker, Wilber, 193

Brunn Company, 33

Buehrig, Gordon, 20

Buick automobile and corporate division, 13, 19, 21, 30, 36, 60, 65, 111, 177, 263

Buick models: Marquette, 40; Roadmaster, 212; Super, 212

Burlingame, Byers, 115, 134, 256

Burns, Arthur, 221, 224f

Burroughs Corporation, 15f

Cadillac automobile and corporate division, 10, 13, 18f, 21, 35-41 *passim*, 50-51, 54, 60, 70f, 74, 80, 92, 94f, 126, 213, 263-64, 267

Cadillac models: Brougham, 264; Cimarron, 263; Coupe de Ville, 51; LaSalle, 19ff, 35, 262

Capehart, Homer, 192, 233

Chase National Bank, 220, 232

Chemical National Bank, 120

Chevrolet automobile and corporate division, 4, 19, 37, 60, 97, 110ff, 125, 132

Christopher, George Thurman, 28-39 *passim*, 43-71 *passim*, 76f, 127, 202, 262

Chrysler, Walter, 18, 20, 207

Chrysler automobile and company, 18f, 35, 47f, 51, 60, 65, 71f, 108, 111, 117, 119f, 143, 171, 190, 205, 216f, 259, 265, 267; and Conner, 120-24, 252

Chrysler models: Airflow, 21, 34; Cordoba, 18; Imperial, 212

Churchill, Harold, 146, 163, 165, 173, 187, 200, 249, 251f, 253f, 260

Clark, Paul, 165

Colbert, Lester Lum ("Tex"), 4, 120ff, 123, 217, 226

Collins, Richard, 175

Conner plant, 120-24, 173-75, 198, 200, 212ff, 239, 252, 261

Cord, Erret Lobban, 20

Cordiner, Ralph J., 86, 224, 242

Cowdin, J. Cheever, 253

Creative Industries, 125

Curtiss-Wright, 147, 216-22 *passim*, 226f, 231-37 *passim*, 243, 245-46

Daimler-Benz company, 230-35 *passim*, 241, 253, 255

Dana Corporation, 205

Dann, Sol, 246

D'Arcy Advertising Agency, 212

Darrin, Howard ("Dutch"), 33f, 125

DART missile, 190, 236, 241, 246

DeLorean, John Z., 127

DeSoto automobile, 11, 217

Detrola Corporation, 54

Dietrich, Inc., 33

Dillon, Reed & Company, 148

Dodge automobile and company, 18f, 31, 217

Draper, Dorothy, 75

Duerksen, Menno, 40

Duesenberg, Frederick, 18

Duesenberg automobile and company, 2, 20

Duff, Anderson, & Clark, 143

Dulles, John Foster, 117

Earl, Harley J., 19, 50

Ebert, Robert, 40

Edison General Appliance Company, 85

Edsel automobile, 221, 250

Egbert, Sherwood, 256

Einstein, Arthur, 40

Eisenhower, Dwight D., 6, 108, 116f, 189f, 226, 245, 262

Elliott, Kenneth, 146-47

Elliott, Robert, 142-43

Elmendorf, Francis, 243

Erdrich, Dorris, 268

Erdrich, Louise, 268

Ernst & Ernst, 220, 222

F-103, 230

Federal Reserve Board, 188, 211, 221, 224f, 235f, 241

Feldmann, Charles, 75

Ferry, Hugh, 43, 53, 58f, 63-79 *passim*, 83, 86, 91, 149f, 158, 243, 255, 264f

Ferry, Robert, 69, 72

Ferry, W. H. ("Ping"), 69

First National City Bank, 167, 216, 220

Ford, Edsel, 20

Ford, Henry, 3, 9, 18

Ford, Henry II, 3, 110, 149, 221-22, 250, 260, 265

Ford automobile and company, 4, 13, 19, 60, 65, 72, 112, 117, 132, 139, 167, 171, 185, 190, 192, 205, 250, 259, 265-66; help for S-P, 215f; race with Chevrolet, 110-11

Ford models: Edsel, 221, 250; Model T, 9; Mustang, 18; Taurus, 263

Forgan, Russell, 199-200, 216-22 *passim*, 226-27, 230ff, 237, 241, 244

Franklin automobile, 2, 13, 19

Frazer, Joseph, 55

Frazer automobile and company, 129, 256

Frigidaire, 84f

General Dynamics, 216

General Electric, 85, 109, 190, 224, 245

General Motors, 3, 5, 10, 25f, 28, 34f, 39, 55, 64, 81, 84-85, 98, 112, 143, 145, 162, 167, 171f, 177, 189, 200, 205, 218, 231, 259; ad costs and sales, 186, 189, 215; and defense business, 117, 189-90, 191-92; help for S-P, 215, 226; 1945 strike, 47

Gilman, Max, 27ff, 34ff, 41-46 *passim*, 56, 64, 68, 262

Glore, Forgan & Company, 149, 217

Goggomobil automobile, 253

Golden, Max, 242

Goodrich, Owen, 3, 39, 83, 88

Cordon, Jack, 202f

Graham-Paige automobile, 55

Grant, Richard, 84

Grant, Walter, 91f, 98-99, 100ff, 110, 114ff, 118, 126, 128, 136-37, 161-66 *passim*, 186, 189f, 198-208 *passim*; and break-even problems, 167-68, 174, 203; and Conner plant, 120-24,

177; merger plans, 138, 143, 150-51, 155-56

Graves, William, 48, 55, 62, 77, 115, 138, 145f, 151, 163, 165f, 174, 250; and V-8, 125-27, 176, 206

Greiner, Karl, 62

Hallicrafters Company, 204

Hamlin, George, 38

Hanaway, William, 242

Handy, James, 97

Harding, William, 148

Harris, William B., 39, 244

Harris Trust Bank of Chicago, 28

Hauge, Gabriel, 221, 225

Hebert, F. Edward, 245f

Heller and Associates, 217-22 *passim*, 226, 243

Henney company, 75

Henry J automobile, 127, 129

Hershey, Franklin, 50

Hesburgh, Father Theodore, 207ff

Higgins, Frank, 190ff

Hill, George, 227

Hill & Knowlton, 188

Hitchcock, H. W., 87

Hoelzle, Eugene, 62

Hoffman, Max, 241, 253

Hoffman, Paul, 118, 139-53 *passim*, 158, 168ff, 187-93 *passim*, 201f, 216-27 *passim*, 237, 241, 243f

Hoge, Wilmer B., 92

Horvath, Louis, 169, 189

Hotpoint, 4, 77f, 84ff, 91f, 108, 260

Hudson automobile and company, 4f, 16-21 *passim*, 30, 60, 71, 78, 111, 119, 124, 133, 141, 143ff, 188, 206, 213, 256, 259; and merger, 144, 148

Hudson model: Jet, 129

Humphrey, George, 221-26 *passim*, 230f, 236f, 242f, 244f

Hupmobile automobile, 2

Hurley, Roy T., 218-19, 222, 227-37 *passim*, 241-45, 250-56 *passim*, 262

Hutchinson, R. A., 164

Hycon Manufacturing Company, 204f

Iacocca, Lee, 4, 18, 213

Independents, 18, 21, 55, 111ff, 128, 144, 158, 171, 186ff, 218, 267; image of, 95f, 112f

Industry advisory committee, War Production Board, 85
Infiniti automobile, 264
International Harvester Company, 216ff

J-47 turbojet, 76, 116, 243, 245, 264
J-57 jet engine, 192, 194, 233, 246
J-65 jet engine, 236
Jackson, Henry, 189
JATO rockets, 190
Jeep, 102, 190f, 204
John Hancock company, 123
Johnson, Courtney V., 165, 190ff, 244
Joy, Henry Bourne, 11-14, 26, 268
J. P. Morgan & Company, 218

Kahn, Albert, 12
Kaiser, Edgar, 191
Kaiser, Henry, 49, 55f
Kaiser-Frazer automobile and company, 51, 55-56, 125
Kaiser Industries, 216, 256, 259
Kaiser-Willys Company, 142-43, 158, 189
Kefauver, Estes, 245
Keller, William W., 184f, 188, 198
Kelly, Nicholas, 217
Kelvinator, 155, 218, 259
Kimes, Beverly Rae, 1
Knights of Labor, 172
Kollins, Michael, 34, 79, 83, 88
Knowlton, Hugh, 218
Knudsen, William S., 94
Korean War, 4f, 54, 71, 75, 81, 85, 108, 116f, 265
Kuhn, Loeb and Company, 149, 218
Kyes, Roger, 118

Langworth, Richard, 38, 50
LaSalle automobile, 19f, 35, 262
Laughna, R. P., 165, 173f, 176, 200, 214, 250
LCM-8 transport, 190
Lear, Incorporated, 204f
LeBaron coachwork company, 33
Lehman Brothers, 143, 148ff, 151-53
Leland, Henry, 18
Lennen & Newell, 148
Lewis, Roger, 192f
Lexus automobile, 264
Lincoln automobile and company, 18, 81, 215, 263, 267

Lincoln-Mercury division, 92, 113
Lincoln models: Continental Mark II, 18; Continental Mark VII, 264; Model K, 20, 35; Towncar, 264; Zephyr, 34f
Little, Royal, 219
Locomobile automobile, 2
Loewy, Raymond, 162, 198
Lott, George Packard, 38
Lux, Red, 240

MacArthur, Douglas, 10
Macauley, Edward, 34, 177
Macauley, James Alvan, 14-22 *passim*, 26-41 *passim*, 48, 68, 70, 78, 84, 91, 103, 177, 260, 262, 264, 268; fires Gilman, 45-46; and Nash merger, 57-59; resigns as president and becomes chairman, 32f
McCahill, Tom, 50
McConnell, Harry, 220
McDonnell Corporation, 204
McGraw-Edison Company, 256
Macke, William, 185
McKinsey & Company, 162, 164, 202, 212
McMillan, James, 56f, 77, 236, 243
McMillan, Phillip, 12
McNamara, Robert, 250
McNeil, Wilfred J., 236, 243
McQuigg, John L., 148, 156
McRae, Duncan, 254
MacTavish, Henry, 220
Manheim, Victor, 216, 237, 241
Mannheim, Frank, 143, 149, 176
Marmon automobile and company, 2, 20, 40
Mason, George, 56ff, 78, 80, 128, 157f, 259; and mergers, 141, 145-50 *passim*, 155
Massachusetts Mutual company, 123
Massey-Harris, 216
Maxon, Inc., 72f, 94, 113, 132, 184
Maxwell automobile, 13
Medaris, John, 191
Mendler, E. C., 150f, 154, 161-67 *passim*, 201f, 250
Mercedes-Benz automobile, 125, 251, 253, 264
Mercury automobile and corporate division, 37, 115, 126, 132, 177, 266
Mercury models: Cougar, 18; Sable, 263

Mergers, 80, 119, 123, 127ff, 137-53
  passim
Merlin aircraft engine, 44f
Merrill Lynch, 143
Metropolitan Insurance Company, 198,
  208, 220, 232
Misch, H. L., 165, 240
Mitchell-Bentley, 125
Monaghan, Patrick, 77, 91-96 *passim*,
  112, 250
Moore, George, 220
Moore, Maurice, 217ff
Morgenthau, Henry, Jr., 44
Mortrude, Don, 61
Murray Body, 148
Murray Corporation, 127
Mutual Benefit Life, 123, 153

Nance, James Battelle, 88
Nance, James J., 4, 38, 67f, 73, 75ff,
  125, 176; biographical, 83-91,
  250-51; and company finances, 98,
  154-55, 158-59, 166, 167-68,
  197-200, 201, 208, 214, 218, 223;
  and Conner, 119-24; and Curtiss-
  Wright, 218, 237f, 243; and defense
  matters, 109, 118, 189f, 192ff; first
  year at Packard, 91-98 *passim*,
  115-16; goals of, 107, 131-32; and labor, 168-73; and mergers, 78, 101,
  129, 138-39, 141-57 *passim*, 188,
  205f, 218f, 221-22; and organization, 79, 161-67, 202, 204-5, 239;
  personal, 78, 103, 107, 109, 153, 232,
  244, 250; and politics, 221, 224-25,
  230-31; and production, 114, 176,
  183; and product planning, 79,
  99-100, 102, 127-28, 178ff, 212-13,
  215; and sales, 111-12, 133-34,
  180-81, 184-85, 212, 260
Nance, Laura Battelle, 88
Nance, Marcia Lou, 88
Nash, Charles, 56f
Nash automobile and company, 4f, 18,
  21, 69, 101f, 110, 119, 129, 133, 188,
  256, 259; and merger, 101, 142-48
  passim
Nash-Kelvinator Corporation, 56f
Nash models: Ambassador, 128, 188;
  Rambler, 4, 102, 129
National Cash Register Company, 14,
  84
National Production Authority, 72, 92

Naylor, Richard, 40
Newberry, John, 12
Newberry, Truman, 11f
"New Packard Program," 94, 107
Nixon, Richard M., 190
Northrop Aircraft, 204

Oerlikon Tool and Arms Company, 193
Office of Price Administration, 47
Office of Price Stabilization, 71
Ogden, William, 169, 171
Ohio Automobile Company, 11
Olds, Irvin S., 232f, 236f, 242
Oldsmobile automobile and corporate
  division, 19, 30, 71, 91, 126, 134, 177,
  263
Oldsmobile models: "98," 212; Viking,
  40
O'Madigan, Daniel, 176-77, 184ff, 188,
  212

P-38 Lightning, 50
Packabaker, 254, 256
Packard, James Ward, 1, 10-15 *passim*,
  84, 260, 268
Packard, William Doud, 10, 12
Packard models: Model A, 10; Model B,
  11; Model 30, 13, 16; Model 48, 16;
  "100," 101; "110," 31, 37, 103;
  "115C," 31, 33, 101; "116," 17;
  "120," 25-32 *passim*, 36f, 38f, 80,
  103, 262; "160," 32; "180," 32;
  "200," 70f; "300," 70; "400," 70f;
  "400" hardtop, 184; 1957 models,
  250ff; Balboa, 124, 179; bathtubs,
  49f, 61-62, 70, 256, 263, 266; Caribbean, 67, 75, 93, 114, 124, 126, 129,
  176, 178; Clipper, 34, 38, 41, 47, 94f,
  98, 101, 111f, 113f, 119, 124f, 128,
  132, 145-46, 179, 184, 188, 212, 216,
  238, 263, 266f; Clipper Custom,
  212; Clipper Special, 134; Executive,
  213, 251; Gray Wolf II, 124; Hawk,
  254-55, 257; Light Eight, 21f; Mayfair, 74-75; "Packette," 127-28;
  Panama, 134; Pan American, 67, 75,
  124; Panther, 124f; Predictor, 180,
  251; Request, 179
Packard Motor Car Company, 12, 35,
  63-64, 70, 79, 262, 268; Board of
  Directors, 53f, 62, 99, 152-53, 255;
  and Cadillac, 51, 94, 263; consumer
  surveys, 73-74, 135; costs, profits,

and losses, 14–22 *passim*, 30f, 45,
49, 116, 131, 135f, 153, 155, 163, 168,
197f, 201, 207, 214, 220–25 *passim*,
231, 236; dealers, 29f, 37, 46, 54, 61,
77, 92, 96–97, 109, 112, 114, 133–38
passim, 175, 177, 184, 186f, 212ff,
218, 222f, 251, 254, 257, 266; defense
business, 75–76, 80–81, 99, 109,
116, 118–19, 181–83, 190, 241, 243;
demise of, 238, 239–40, 247, 256;
engineering department, 115, 176;
image and reputation, 9–10, 17, 32f,
35, 73, 75, 263f, 266; markets, 44,
60, 70, 266; and mergers, 55–59,
151–53; motors, 16f, 17f, 22, 25, 31ff,
37, 40, 98, 101f, 115, 125–27; parts
department, 175–76; production,
product, and quality, 11, 27, 36,
48–49, 54, 59, 72, 109, 121, 173–80
passim, 215; sales, 32, 211f, 239,
246–47; sales department, 95, 134,
138, 166, 179–87 *passim*; shares and
shareholders, 26, 157–58; tooling
costs, 60, 63, 114, 198, 200, 208,
216; workers, 30, 48, 59, 63, 68, 91;
working capital, 54, 98, 115, 136f;
and World War II, 41, 44–45, 51–53
Packards, used, 110–11
Packard-Studebaker, 153
Packer, Bill, 29–30, 267
Parker, Robert, 57
Pearson, Drew, 117
Peerless automobile, 2, 16, 20
Phillips, Richard K., 39
Pierce Arrow automobile, 2, 16, 20
Pierce Arrow model: Silver Arrow, 20
Pittsburgh Steel Company, 54, 108
Plymouth automobile and corporate
division, 4, 18f, 110f
Pontiac automobile and corporate divi-
sion, 28, 30f, 37, 65, 177, 185
Porta, A. J., 165, 167, 170, 212, 244, 253f
Potter, Charles, 233
Powers, Ray, 92, 112, 137, 164, 169f,
174–78 *passim*, 250, 261
Pratt and Whitney, 86, 192f
Prudential Insurance Company, 198f,
207–8

Quarles, Donald, 193, 230, 236f, 242f,
244f

Raeder, Frederick, 250
Rambler automobile company, 13

Rauthrauff & Ryan, 184f
Reconstruction Finance Corporation,
225
Refrigerator Discount Corporation, 155
Reifel, George, 62, 92, 99, 100f, 102f
Reilley, Ewing, 162ff
Reinhart, John, 33, 49–50, 62f
Renault automobile and company, 267
Reo automobile and truck company,
13, 40, 117, 191
Reuther, Walter, 169–70
Richards, E. E., 204f
Rolls Royce automobile and company,
268
Rollston coachwork company, 33
Romney, George, 6, 47, 58, 128, 149,
156–57, 191, 205; and AMC, 206,
215, 218, 259, 267
Roosevelt, Elliott, 37
Roosevelt, Franklin D., 10, 37f, 46, 88
Roosevelt, Theodore, 10
Rosebrook, John, 72f
Rover automobile and company, 204
Rush, Frederick, 77, 157
Russell, Robert, 135, 144

Schmidt, William, 177, 179
Shine, Paul, 112, 176, 212, 233
Slack, Lyman, 29, 39, 53–54, 56, 63,
69, 83
Sloan, Alfred, 3, 33
Smith, Barney & Company, 141, 148
Sonnabend, Abraham, 256
*Specialty Equipment & Machinery
Company v. Zell and Packard*, 127
Spencer, Leroy, 71, 77, 79, 92
Sprague, Mansfield, 237, 243, 245
Stevenson, Adlai, 117
Stout, Richard, 38, 55, 83, 88f, 93, 117,
179, 207, 215
Straugh, Robert, 92
Studebaker automobile and company,
3, 5, 18f, 21, 31, 78, 91f, 96, 98f,
117–23 *passim*, 129–57 *passim*,
167–71, 190
Studebaker models: Avanti, 256; Clas-
sic (1957), 251; Erskine, 40; Golden
Hawk, 251; Hawk, 267; Lark, 254ff,
267; Scotsman, 253; Starlight
Coupe, 162
Studebaker-Packard Corporation, 4, 6,
173, 187, 259; break-even points, 171,
173f, 201, 252; and Curtiss-Wright,
229–32, 245f; defense contracts,

190, 194, 200, 223f, 225f, 231, 245–46; diversification, 202, 256; labor problems, 168–72, 200, 202f; mergers, 155, 203, 215, 261–62; and 1957 Packard, 254; profit and loss, 155, 173f, 183, 187, 195–200 *passim*, 206ff, 213f, 232, 235, 242, 246, 252–56; sales, 212f, 223, 238, 253; stock, 201–2, 232–33, 246; on verge of collapse, 222f, 225–27, 234, 238, 242; working capital, 222f, 242, 254f
Studebaker-Worthington, 256
Summerfield, Arthur, 221, 225

Taft, Robert, 117
Taft, William Howard, 10
Talbott, Harold, 189, 192f
Taylor, Ed, 185
Teague, Richard, 124f, 177–78, 179f, 240, 247, 267
Textron, Inc., 219, 226
Tibbetts, Milton, 62, 69
Torsion-bar suspension, 75, 178–79, 240
Truman, Harry S., 10
Turnquist, Robert E., 40

UAW-CIO no. 190, 238–39
Ultramatic, 15, 54, 81, 97, 101, 109, 115, 127, 135, 176, 178, 240, 268
Union Bag and Paper Corporation, 76
United Auto Workers, 171
United Motors, 153
U.S. Steel, 108, 232
Utica-Bend, 239, 243, 246, 252
Utica Proving Ground, 29, 47

Van Ark, Gordon, 92, 175
Vance, Harold, 78, 117, 139, 142, 146–53 *passim*, 158, 169, 190, 193

Vandeburg, Clyde, 125
Victor, Royall, 235f, 241f
Vilas, Homer, 76, 216
Vincent, Charles Helm, 29
Vincent, Jesse G., 17, 21, 27, 29, 40, 44, 54, 58, 62–64, 125, 137, 177, 264, 268; biographical sketch, 15–16; leaves Packard, 77; and V-12, 126–27
Volkswagen automobile, 253

Walters, Frederick, 91, 97, 108, 110f, 129
War Assets Administration, 54
War Production Board, 85
Warren, Margery, 83, 90f
Weeks, Sinclair, 221, 224f
Whitney, George, 218
Wichert, H. A., 184
Wilhelmina, Queen, 78
Willys automobile and company, 256, 259
Willys-Overland company, 18, 102
Wilson, Charles E. ("Electric Charlie"), 95
Wilson, Charles E. ("Engine Charlie"), 4, 117f, 189, 191, 225f, 231–35 *passim*, 240–46 *passim*
Wolf, K. B., 193
Wright, Frank Lloyd, 120

Yeager, Howard, 34
Young & Rubicam, 32f, 71–72

Zenith company, 85
ZIS automobile, 46–47
ZurSchmiede, W. Thomas, 58, 63, 78, 220, 238, 241, 243, 250

Library of Congress Cataloging-in-Publication Data

Ward, James Arthur.
  The Fall of the Packard Motor Car Company / James A. Ward.
    p.   cm.
  Includes bibliographical references and index.
  ISBN 0-8047-2457-1 (cl.) : ISBN 0-8047-3165-9 (pbk.)
    1. Packard Motor Car Company–History.   2. Automobile
industry and trade–United States–History.   I. Title.
HD9710.U54P39   1995
338.7´6292222–dc20

                                                94-39283
                                                CIP

⊗ This book is printed on acid-free, recycled paper.

Original printing 1995
Last figure below indicates year of this printing:

04   03   02   01   00   99